Jaguar XJ6 Automotive Repair Manual

by Mike Stubblefield and John H Haynes

Member of the Guild of Motoring Writers

Models covered:
All Jaguar XJ6 models
1988 through 1994

(49011 - 8Q6)

ABCDEF

Haynes Publishing Group
Sparkford Nr Yeovil
Somerset BA22 7JJ England

Haynes North America, Inc
861 Lawrence Drive
Newbury Park
California 91320 USA

Acknowledgements

Wiring diagrams provided exclusively for Haynes North America, Inc. by Valley Forge Technical Information Services. Thanks are due to Jean Preis, Rich Wilson and Ray Marcuse of Silver Star Jaguar (Thousand Oaks, CA), Rick Calaci of Conejo Imports (Newbury Park, CA) and Jim Strohmeier and Jonathan Lund of British Motor Cars (Thousand Oaks, CA), for providing valuable technical information. Technical writers who contributed to this project include Jeff Kibler, Robert Maddox and Jay Storer.

A book in the Haynes Automotive Repair Manual Series

Printed in the U.S.A.

ISBN 1 56392 237 1

Library of Congress Catalog Card Number 97-70289

Contents

Haynes mechanic, author and photographer with 1989 Jaguar XJ6

About this manual

Its purpose

The purpose of this manual is to help you get the best value from your vehicle. It can do so in several ways. It can help you decide what work must be done, even if you choose to have it done by a dealer service department or a repair shop; it provides information and procedures for routine maintenance and servicing; and it offers diagnostic and repair procedures to follow when trouble occurs.

We hope you use the manual to tackle the work yourself. For many simpler jobs, doing it yourself may be quicker than arranging an appointment to get the vehicle into a shop and making the trips to leave it and pick it up. More importantly, a lot of money can be saved by avoiding the expense the shop must pass on to you to cover its labor and overhead costs. An added benefit is the sense of satisfaction and accomplishment that you feel after doing the job yourself.

Using the manual

The manual is divided into Chapters. Each Chapter is divided into numbered Sections, which are headed in bold type between horizontal lines. Each Section consists of consecutively numbered paragraphs.

At the beginning of each numbered Section you will be referred to any illustrations which apply to the procedures in that Section. The reference numbers used in illustration captions pinpoint the pertinent Section and the Step within that Section. That is, illustration 3.2 means the illustration refers to Section 3 and Step (or paragraph) 2 within that Section.

Procedures, once described in the text, are not normally repeated. When it's necessary to refer to another Chapter, the reference will be given as Chapter and Section number. Cross references given without use of the word "Chapter" apply to Sections and/or paragraphs in the same Chapter. For example, "see Section 8" means in the same Chapter.

References to the left or right side of the vehicle assume you are sitting in the driver's seat, facing forward.

Even though we have prepared this manual with extreme care, neither the publisher nor the author can accept responsibility for any errors in, or omissions from, the information given.

NOTE

A **Note** provides information necessary to properly complete a procedure or information which will make the procedure easier to understand.

CAUTION

A **Caution** provides a special procedure or special steps which must be taken while completing the procedure where the Caution is found. Not heeding a Caution can result in damage to the assembly being worked on.

WARNING

A **Warning** provides a special procedure or special steps which must be taken while completing the procedure where the Warning is found. Not heeding a Warning can result in personal injury.

Introduction

These models are equipped with dual overhead cam inline six-cylinder engines. The engines feature a computer-controlled ignition system and electronic fuel injection. Transmissions are a four-speed automatic equipped with a lock-up torque converter. The transmission is mounted to the back of the engine, and power is transmitted to the fully independent rear axle through a two-piece driveshaft. The differential is bolted solidly to a frame crossmember and drives the wheels through driveaxles equipped with inner and outer U-joints.

The front suspension is fitted with upper and lower control arms, coil springs and shock absorbers. The rear suspension is an independent type suspension which also has coil spring/shock absorber assemblies and a lower control arm. The rear driveaxle acts as the upper control arm.

Power-assisted Anti-lock Brake Systems (ABS) with four-wheel disc brakes are standard equipment on all models covered in this manual. Power rack-and-pinion steering is also standard equipment.

Vehicle identification numbers

Vehicle Identification Number

The Vehicle Identification Number (VIN) is located on the right inner fender panel of the engine compartment and on a plate on top of the dash, just inside the windshield **(see illustrations)**. It contains valuable information such as where and when the vehicle was manufactured, the model year and the body style. This number can be used to cross-check the registration and license.

Engine serial number

The engine serial number is located on the engine block, just behind the distributor **(see illustration)**.

Transmission identification number

The automatic transmission identification number is stamped on a plate that is riveted to the left side of the transmission housing just above the transmission oil pan **(see illustration)**.

Vehicle Emissions Control Information (VECI) label

The emissions control information label is found on the underside of the hood or on the inner fenderwell. This label contains information on the emissions control equipment installed on the vehicle **(see illustration)**.

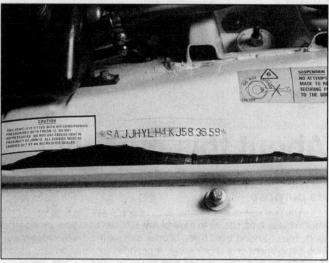

The VIN is stamped on the right inner fender panel of the engine compartment

The VIN is also present on the left side of the dashboard

The engine identification number is stamped on the right side of the engine block just behind the distributor

The transmission identification number is located on the left side of the transmission housing just above the oil pan

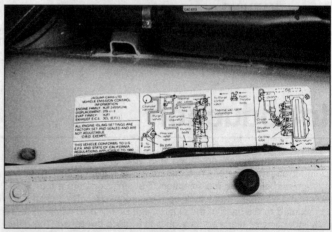

The Vehicle Emissions Control Information label is affixed to the left side inner fenderwell

Anti-theft audio system

General information

1   Some models are equipped with an audio system which includes an anti-theft feature that will render the stereo inoperative if stolen. If the power source to the stereo is cut, the stereo won't work even if the power source is immediately re-connected. If your vehicle is equipped with this anti-theft system, do not disconnect the battery or remove the stereo unless you have the individual code number for the stereo.

2   Refer to your vehicle's owner's manual for more complete information on this audio system and its anti-theft feature.

Buying parts

Replacement parts are available from many sources, which generally fall into one of two categories - authorized dealer parts departments and independent retail auto parts stores. Our advice concerning these parts is as follows:

Retail auto parts stores: Good auto parts stores will stock frequently needed components which wear out relatively fast, such as clutch components, exhaust systems, brake parts, tune-up parts, etc. These stores often supply new or reconditioned parts on an exchange basis, which can save a considerable amount of money. Discount auto parts stores are often very good places to buy materials and parts needed for general vehicle maintenance such as oil, grease, filters, spark plugs, belts, touch-up paint, bulbs, etc. They also usually sell tools and general accessories, have convenient hours, charge lower prices and can often be found not far from home.

Authorized dealer parts department: This is the best source for parts which are unique to the vehicle and not generally available elsewhere (such as major engine parts, transmission parts, trim pieces, etc.).

Warranty information: If the vehicle is still covered under warranty, be sure that any replacement parts purchased - regardless of the source - do not invalidate the warranty!

To be sure of obtaining the correct parts, have engine and chassis numbers available and, if possible, take the old parts along for positive identification.

Maintenance techniques, tools and working facilities

Maintenance techniques

There are a number of techniques involved in maintenance and repair that will be referred to throughout this manual. Application of these techniques will enable the home mechanic to be more efficient, better organized and capable of performing the various tasks properly, which will ensure that the repair job is thorough and complete.

Fasteners

Fasteners are nuts, bolts, studs and screws used to hold two or more parts together. There are a few things to keep in mind when working with fasteners. Almost all of them use a locking device of some type, either a lockwasher, locknut, locking tab or thread adhesive. All threaded fasteners should be clean and straight, with undamaged threads and undamaged corners on the hex head where the wrench fits. Develop the habit of replacing all damaged nuts and bolts with new ones. Special locknuts with nylon or fiber inserts can only be used once. If they are removed, they lose their locking ability and must be replaced with new ones.

Rusted nuts and bolts should be treated with a penetrating fluid to ease removal and prevent breakage. Some mechanics use turpentine in a spout-type oil can, which works quite well. After applying the rust penetrant, let it work for a few minutes before trying to loosen the nut or bolt. Badly rusted fasteners may have to be chiseled or sawed off or removed with a special nut breaker, available at tool stores.

If a bolt or stud breaks off in an assembly, it can be drilled and removed with a special tool commonly available for this purpose. Most automotive machine shops can perform this task, as well as other repair procedures, such as the repair of threaded holes that have been stripped out.

Flat washers and lockwashers, when removed from an assembly, should always be replaced exactly as removed. Replace any damaged washers with new ones. Never use a lockwasher on any soft metal surface (such as aluminum), thin sheet metal or plastic.

Fastener sizes

For a number of reasons, automobile manufacturers are making wider and wider use of metric fasteners. Therefore, it is important to be able to tell the difference between standard (sometimes called U.S. or SAE) and metric hardware, since they cannot be interchanged.

All bolts, whether standard or metric, are sized according to diameter, thread pitch and length. For example, a standard 1/2 - 13 x 1 bolt is 1/2 inch in diameter, has 13 threads per inch and is 1 inch long. An M12 - 1.75 x 25 metric bolt is 12 mm in diameter, has a thread pitch of 1.75 mm (the distance between threads) and is 25 mm long. The two bolts are nearly identical, and easily confused, but they are not interchangeable.

In addition to the differences in diameter, thread pitch and length, metric and standard bolts can also be distinguished by examining the bolt heads. To begin with, the distance across the flats on a standard bolt head is measured in inches, while the same dimension on a metric bolt is sized in millimeters (the same is true for nuts). As a result, a standard wrench should not be used on a metric bolt and a metric

wrench should not be used on a standard bolt. Also, most standard bolts have slashes radiating out from the center of the head to denote the grade or strength of the bolt, which is an indication of the amount of torque that can be applied to it. The greater the number of slashes, the greater the strength of the bolt. Grades 0 through 5 are commonly used on automobiles. Metric bolts have a property class (grade) number, rather than a slash, molded into their heads to indicate bolt strength. In this case, the higher the number, the stronger the bolt. Property class numbers 8.8, 9.8 and 10.9 are commonly used on automobiles.

Strength markings can also be used to distinguish standard hex nuts from metric hex nuts. Many standard nuts have dots stamped into one side, while metric nuts are marked with a number. The greater the number of dots, or the higher the number, the greater the strength of the nut.

Metric studs are also marked on their ends according to property class (grade). Larger studs are numbered (the same as metric bolts), while smaller studs carry a geometric code to denote grade.

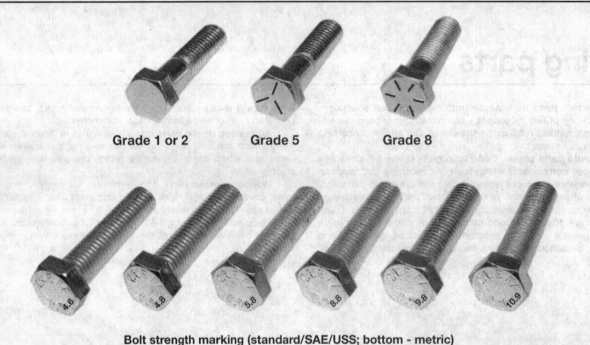

Bolt strength marking (standard/SAE/USS; bottom - metric)

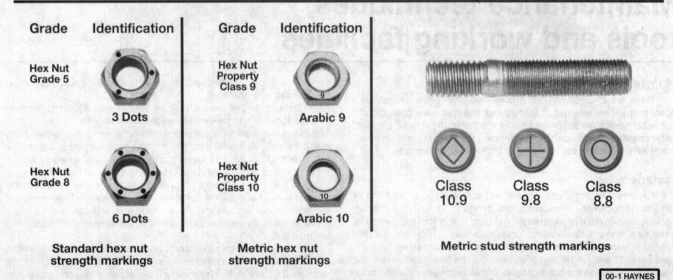

Grade	Identification
Hex Nut Grade 5	3 Dots
Hex Nut Grade 8	6 Dots

Standard hex nut strength markings

Grade	Identification
Hex Nut Property Class 9	Arabic 9
Hex Nut Property Class 10	Arabic 10

Metric hex nut strength markings

Class 10.9   Class 9.8   Class 8.8

Metric stud strength markings

It should be noted that many fasteners, especially Grades 0 through 2, have no distinguishing marks on them. When such is the case, the only way to determine whether it is standard or metric is to measure the thread pitch or compare it to a known fastener of the same size.

Standard fasteners are often referred to as SAE, as opposed to metric. However, it should be noted that SAE technically refers to a non-metric fine thread fastener only. Coarse thread non-metric fasteners are referred to as USS sizes.

Since fasteners of the same size (both standard and metric) may have different strength ratings, be sure to reinstall any bolts, studs or nuts removed from your vehicle in their original locations. Also, when replacing a fastener with a new one, make sure that the new one has a strength rating equal to or greater than the original.

Tightening sequences and procedures

Most threaded fasteners should be tightened to a specific torque value (torque is the twisting force applied to a threaded component such as a nut or bolt). Overtightening the fastener can weaken it and cause it to break, while undertightening can cause it to eventually come loose. Bolts, screws and studs, depending on the material they are made of and their thread diameters, have specific torque values, many of which are noted in the Specifications at the beginning of each Chapter. Be sure to follow the torque recommendations closely. For fasteners not assigned a specific torque, a general torque value chart is presented here as a guide. These torque values are for dry (unlubricated) fasteners threaded into steel or cast iron (not aluminum). As was previously mentioned, the size and grade of a fastener determine the amount of torque that can safely be applied to it. The figures listed

Metric thread sizes	Ft-lbs	Nm
M-6	6 to 9	9 to 12
M-8	14 to 21	19 to 28
M-10	28 to 40	38 to 54
M-12	50 to 71	68 to 96
M-14	80 to 140	109 to 154

Pipe thread sizes		
1/8	5 to 8	7 to 10
1/4	12 to 18	17 to 24
3/8	22 to 33	30 to 44
1/2	25 to 35	34 to 47

U.S. thread sizes		
1/4 - 20	6 to 9	9 to 12
5/16 - 18	12 to 18	17 to 24
5/16 - 24	14 to 20	19 to 27
3/8 - 16	22 to 32	30 to 43
3/8 - 24	27 to 38	37 to 51
7/16 - 14	40 to 55	55 to 74
7/16 - 20	40 to 60	55 to 81
1/2 - 13	55 to 80	75 to 108

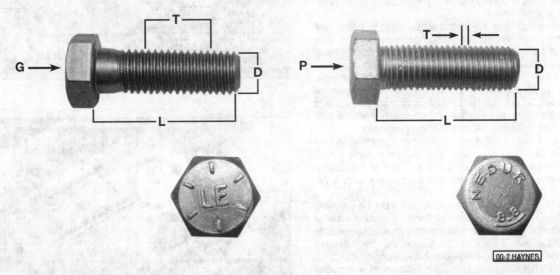

Standard (SAE and USS) bolt dimensions/grade marks

G   Grade marks (bolt strength)
L   Length (in inches)
T   Thread pitch (number of threads per inch)
D   Nominal diameter (in inches)

Metric bolt dimensions/grade marks

P   Property class (bolt strength)
L   Length (in millimeters)
T   Thread pitch (distance between threads in millimeters)
D   Diameter

here are approximate for Grade 2 and Grade 3 fasteners. Higher grades can tolerate higher torque values.

Fasteners laid out in a pattern, such as cylinder head bolts, oil pan bolts, differential cover bolts, etc., must be loosened or tightened in sequence to avoid warping the component. This sequence will normally be shown in the appropriate Chapter. If a specific pattern is not given, the following procedures can be used to prevent warping.

Initially, the bolts or nuts should be assembled finger-tight only. Next, they should be tightened one full turn each, in a criss-cross or diagonal pattern. After each one has been tightened one full turn, return to the first one and tighten them all one-half turn, following the same pattern. Finally, tighten each of them one-quarter turn at a time until each fastener has been tightened to the proper torque. To loosen and remove the fasteners, the procedure would be reversed.

Component disassembly

Component disassembly should be done with care and purpose to help ensure that the parts go back together properly. Always keep track of the sequence in which parts are removed. Make note of special characteristics or marks on parts that can be installed more than one way, such as a grooved thrust washer on a shaft. It is a good idea to lay the disassembled parts out on a clean surface in the order that they were removed. It may also be helpful to make sketches or take instant photos of components before removal.

When removing fasteners from a component, keep track of their locations. Sometimes threading a bolt back in a part, or putting the washers and nut back on a stud, can prevent mix-ups later. If nuts and bolts cannot be returned to their original locations, they should be kept in a compartmented box or a series of small boxes. A cupcake or muffin tin is ideal for this purpose, since each cavity can hold the bolts and nuts from a particular area (i.e. oil pan bolts, valve cover bolts, engine mount bolts, etc.). A pan of this type is especially helpful when working on assemblies with very small parts, such as the carburetor, alternator, valve train or interior dash and trim pieces. The cavities can be marked with paint or tape to identify the contents.

Whenever wiring looms, harnesses or connectors are separated, it is a good idea to identify the two halves with numbered pieces of masking tape so they can be easily reconnected.

Gasket sealing surfaces

Throughout any vehicle, gaskets are used to seal the mating surfaces between two parts and keep lubricants, fluids, vacuum or pressure contained in an assembly.

Many times these gaskets are coated with a liquid or paste-type gasket sealing compound before assembly. Age, heat and pressure can sometimes cause the two parts to stick together so tightly that they are very difficult to separate. Often, the assembly can be loosened by striking it with a soft-face hammer near the mating surfaces. A regular hammer can be used if a block of wood is placed between the hammer and the part. Do not hammer on cast parts or parts that could be easily damaged. With any particularly stubborn part, always recheck to make sure that every fastener has been removed.

Avoid using a screwdriver or bar to pry apart an assembly, as they can easily mar the gasket sealing surfaces of the parts, which must remain smooth. If prying is absolutely necessary, use an old broom handle, but keep in mind that extra clean up will be necessary if the wood splinters.

After the parts are separated, the old gasket must be carefully scraped off and the gasket surfaces cleaned. Stubborn gasket material can be soaked with rust penetrant or treated with a special chemical to soften it so it can be easily scraped off. A scraper can be fashioned from a piece of copper tubing by flattening and sharpening one end. Copper is recommended because it is usually softer than the surfaces to be scraped, which reduces the chance of gouging the part. Some gaskets can be removed with a wire brush, but regardless of the method used, the mating surfaces must be left clean and smooth. If for some reason the gasket surface is gouged, then a gasket sealer thick enough to fill scratches will have to be used during reassembly of the components. For most applications, a non-drying (or semi-drying) gasket sealer should be used.

Hose removal tips

Warning: *If the vehicle is equipped with air conditioning, do not disconnect any of the A/C hoses without first having the system depressurized by a dealer service department or a service station.*

Hose removal precautions closely parallel gasket removal precautions. Avoid scratching or gouging the surface that the hose mates against or the connection may leak. This is especially true for radiator hoses. Because of various chemical reactions, the rubber in hoses can bond itself to the metal spigot that the hose fits over. To remove a hose, first loosen the hose clamps that secure it to the spigot. Then, with slip-joint pliers, grab the hose at the clamp and rotate it around the spigot. Work it back and forth until it is completely free, then pull it off. Silicone or other lubricants will ease removal if they can be applied between the hose and the outside of the spigot. Apply the same lubricant to the inside of the hose and the outside of the spigot to simplify installation.

As a last resort (and if the hose is to be replaced with a new one anyway), the rubber can be slit with a knife and the hose peeled from the spigot. If this must be done, be careful that the metal connection is not damaged.

If a hose clamp is broken or damaged, do not reuse it. Wire-type clamps usually weaken with age, so it is a good idea to replace them with screw-type clamps whenever a hose is removed.

Tools

A selection of good tools is a basic requirement for anyone who plans to maintain and repair his or her own vehicle. For the owner who has few tools, the initial investment might seem high, but when compared to the spiraling costs of professional auto maintenance and repair, it is a wise one.

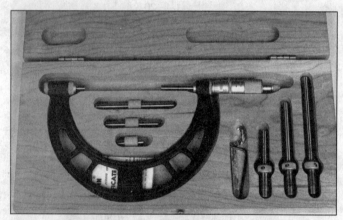

Micrometer set

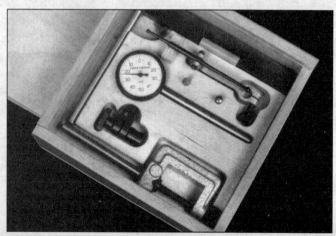

Dial indicator set

Dial caliper

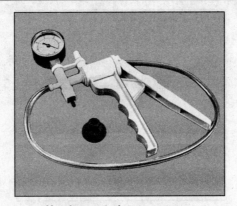

Hand-operated vacuum pump

Timing light

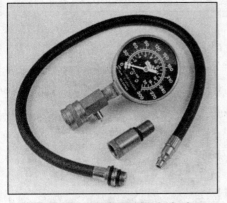

Compression gauge with spark plug hole adapter

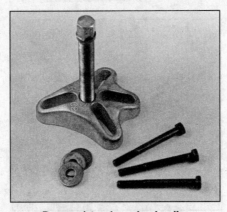

Damper/steering wheel puller

General purpose puller

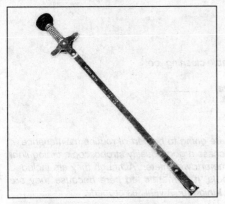

Hydraulic lifter removal tool

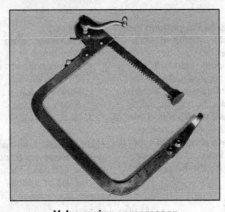

Valve spring compressor

Valve spring compressor

Ridge reamer

Piston ring groove cleaning tool

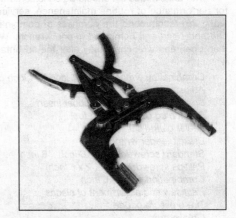

Ring removal/installation tool

Ring compressor

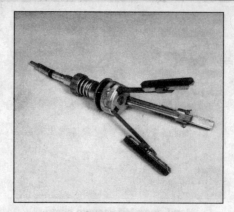
Cylinder hone

Brake hold-down spring tool

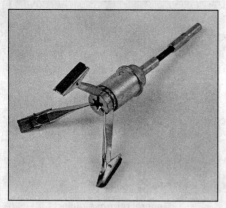
Brake cylinder hone

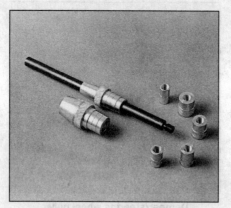
Clutch plate alignment tool

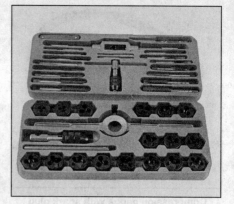
Tap and die set

To help the owner decide which tools are needed to perform the tasks detailed in this manual, the following tool lists are offered: *Maintenance and minor repair, Repair/overhaul* and *Special*.

The newcomer to practical mechanics should start off with the *maintenance and minor repair* tool kit, which is adequate for the simpler jobs performed on a vehicle. Then, as confidence and experience grow, the owner can tackle more difficult tasks, buying additional tools as they are needed. Eventually the basic kit will be expanded into the *repair and overhaul* tool set. Over a period of time, the experienced do-it-yourselfer will assemble a tool set complete enough for most repair and overhaul procedures and will add tools from the special category when it is felt that the expense is justified by the frequency of use.

Maintenance and minor repair tool kit

The tools in this list should be considered the minimum required for performance of routine maintenance, servicing and minor repair work. We recommend the purchase of combination wrenches (box-end and open-end combined in one wrench). While more expensive than open end wrenches, they offer the advantages of both types of wrench.

Combination wrench set (1/4-inch to 1 inch or 6 mm to 19 mm)
Adjustable wrench, 8 inch
Spark plug wrench with rubber insert
Spark plug gap adjusting tool
Feeler gauge set
Brake bleeder wrench
Standard screwdriver (5/16-inch x 6 inch)
Phillips screwdriver (No. 2 x 6 inch)
Combination pliers - 6 inch
Hacksaw and assortment of blades
Tire pressure gauge
Grease gun

Oil can
Fine emery cloth
Wire brush
Battery post and cable cleaning tool
Oil filter wrench
Funnel (medium size)
Safety goggles
Jackstands (2)
Drain pan

Note: *If basic tune-ups are going to be part of routine maintenance, it will be necessary to purchase a good quality stroboscopic timing light and combination tachometer/dwell meter. Although they are included in the list of special tools, it is mentioned here because they are absolutely necessary for tuning most vehicles properly.*

Repair and overhaul tool set

These tools are essential for anyone who plans to perform major repairs and are in addition to those in the maintenance and minor repair tool kit. Included is a comprehensive set of sockets which, though expensive, are invaluable because of their versatility, especially when various extensions and drives are available. We recommend the 1/2-inch drive over the 3/8-inch drive. Although the larger drive is bulky and more expensive, it has the capacity of accepting a very wide range of large sockets. Ideally, however, the mechanic should have a 3/8-inch drive set and a 1/2-inch drive set.

Socket set(s)
Reversible ratchet
Extension - 10 inch
Universal joint
Torque wrench (same size drive as sockets)
Ball peen hammer - 8 ounce
Soft-face hammer (plastic/rubber)
Standard screwdriver (1/4-inch x 6 inch)

Standard screwdriver (stubby - 5/16-inch)
Phillips screwdriver (No. 3 x 8 inch)
Phillips screwdriver (stubby - No. 2)
Pliers - vise grip
Pliers - lineman's
Pliers - needle nose
Pliers - snap-ring (internal and external)
Cold chisel - 1/2-inch
Scribe
Scraper (made from flattened copper tubing)
Centerpunch
Pin punches (1/16, 1/8, 3/16-inch)
Steel rule/straightedge - 12 inch
Allen wrench set (1/8 to 3/8-inch or 4 mm to 10 mm)
A selection of files
Wire brush (large)
Jackstands (second set)
Jack (scissor or hydraulic type)

Note: *Another tool which is often useful is an electric drill with a chuck capacity of 3/8-inch and a set of good quality drill bits.*

Special tools

The tools in this list include those which are not used regularly, are expensive to buy, or which need to be used in accordance with their manufacturer's instructions. Unless these tools will be used frequently, it is not very economical to purchase many of them. A consideration would be to split the cost and use between yourself and a friend or friends. In addition, most of these tools can be obtained from a tool rental shop on a temporary basis.

This list primarily contains only those tools and instruments widely available to the public, and not those special tools produced by the vehicle manufacturer for distribution to dealer service departments. Occasionally, references to the manufacturer's special tools are included in the text of this manual. Generally, an alternative method of doing the job without the special tool is offered. However, sometimes there is no alternative to their use. Where this is the case, and the tool cannot be purchased or borrowed, the work should be turned over to the dealer service department or an automotive repair shop.

Valve spring compressor
Piston ring groove cleaning tool
Piston ring compressor
Piston ring installation tool
Cylinder compression gauge
Cylinder ridge reamer
Cylinder surfacing hone
Cylinder bore gauge
Micrometers and/or dial calipers
Hydraulic lifter removal tool
Balljoint separator
Universal-type puller
Impact screwdriver
Dial indicator set
Stroboscopic timing light (inductive pick-up)
Hand operated vacuum/pressure pump
Tachometer/dwell meter
Universal electrical multimeter
Cable hoist
Brake spring removal and installation tools
Floor jack

Buying tools

For the do-it-yourselfer who is just starting to get involved in vehicle maintenance and repair, there are a number of options available when purchasing tools. If maintenance and minor repair is the extent of the work to be done, the purchase of individual tools is satisfactory. If, on the other hand, extensive work is planned, it would be a good idea to purchase a modest tool set from one of the large retail chain stores. A set can usually be bought at a substantial savings over the individual tool prices, and they often come with a tool box. As additional tools are

needed, add-on sets, individual tools and a larger tool box can be purchased to expand the tool selection. Building a tool set gradually allows the cost of the tools to be spread over a longer period of time and gives the mechanic the freedom to choose only those tools that will actually be used.

Tool stores will often be the only source of some of the special tools that are needed, but regardless of where tools are bought, try to avoid cheap ones, especially when buying screwdrivers and sockets, because they won't last very long. The expense involved in replacing cheap tools will eventually be greater than the initial cost of quality tools.

Care and maintenance of tools

Good tools are expensive, so it makes sense to treat them with respect. Keep them clean and in usable condition and store them properly when not in use. Always wipe off any dirt, grease or metal chips before putting them away. Never leave tools lying around in the work area. Upon completion of a job, always check closely under the hood for tools that may have been left there so they won't get lost during a test drive.

Some tools, such as screwdrivers, pliers, wrenches and sockets, can be hung on a panel mounted on the garage or workshop wall, while others should be kept in a tool box or tray. Measuring instruments, gauges, meters, etc. must be carefully stored where they cannot be damaged by weather or impact from other tools.

When tools are used with care and stored properly, they will last a very long time. Even with the best of care, though, tools will wear out if used frequently. When a tool is damaged or worn out, replace it. Subsequent jobs will be safer and more enjoyable if you do.

How to repair damaged threads

Sometimes, the internal threads of a nut or bolt hole can become stripped, usually from overtightening. Stripping threads is an all-too-common occurrence, especially when working with aluminum parts, because aluminum is so soft that it easily strips out.

Usually, external or internal threads are only partially stripped. After they've been cleaned up with a tap or die, they'll still work. Sometimes, however, threads are badly damaged. When this happens, you've got three choices:

1) *Drill and tap the hole to the next suitable oversize and install a larger diameter bolt, screw or stud.*
2) *Drill and tap the hole to accept a threaded plug, then drill and tap the plug to the original screw size. You can also buy a plug already threaded to the original size. Then you simply drill a hole to the specified size, then run the threaded plug into the hole with a bolt and jam nut. Once the plug is fully seated, remove the jam nut and bolt.*
3) *The third method uses a patented thread repair kit like Heli-Coil or Slimsert. These easy-to-use kits are designed to repair damaged threads in straight-through holes and blind holes. Both are available as kits which can handle a variety of sizes and thread patterns. Drill the hole, then tap it with the special included tap. Install the Heli-Coil and the hole is back to its original diameter and thread pitch.*

Regardless of which method you use, be sure to proceed calmly and carefully. A little impatience or carelessness during one of these relatively simple procedures can ruin your whole day's work and cost you a bundle if you wreck an expensive part.

Working facilities

Not to be overlooked when discussing tools is the workshop. If anything more than routine maintenance is to be carried out, some sort of suitable work area is essential.

It is understood, and appreciated, that many home mechanics do not have a good workshop or garage available, and end up removing an engine or doing major repairs outside. It is recommended, however, that the overhaul or repair be completed under the cover of a roof.

A clean, flat workbench or table of comfortable working height is an absolute necessity. The workbench should be equipped with a vise that has a jaw opening of at least four inches.

As mentioned previously, some clean, dry storage space is also required for tools, as well as the lubricants, fluids, cleaning solvents, etc. which soon become necessary.

Sometimes waste oil and fluids, drained from the engine or cooling system during normal maintenance or repairs, present a disposal problem. To avoid pouring them on the ground or into a sewage system, pour the used fluids into large containers, seal them with caps and take them to an authorized disposal site or recycling center. Plastic jugs, such as old antifreeze containers, are ideal for this purpose.

Always keep a supply of old newspapers and clean rags available. Old towels are excellent for mopping up spills. Many mechanics use rolls of paper towels for most work because they are readily available and disposable. To help keep the area under the vehicle clean, a large cardboard box can be cut open and flattened to protect the garage or shop floor.

Whenever working over a painted surface, such as when leaning over a fender to service something under the hood, always cover it with an old blanket or bedspread to protect the finish. Vinyl covered pads, made especially for this purpose, are available at auto parts stores.

Booster battery (jump) starting

Observe these precautions when using a booster battery to start a vehicle:

a) *Before connecting the booster battery, make sure the ignition switch is in the Off position.*
b) *Turn off the lights, heater and other electrical loads.*
c) *Your eyes should be shielded. Safety goggles are a good idea.*
d) *Make sure the booster battery is the same voltage as the dead one in the vehicle.*
e) *The two vehicles MUST NOT TOUCH each other!*
f) *Make sure the transaxle is in Neutral (manual) or Park (automatic).*
g) *If the booster battery is not a maintenance-free type, remove the vent caps and lay a cloth over the vent holes.*

Connect the red jumper cable to the positive (+) terminals of each battery **(see illustration)**.

Connect one end of the black jumper cable to the negative (-) terminal of the booster battery. The other end of this cable should be connected to a good ground on the vehicle to be started, such as a bolt or bracket on the body.

Start the engine using the booster battery, then, with the engine running at idle speed, disconnect the jumper cables in the reverse order of connection.

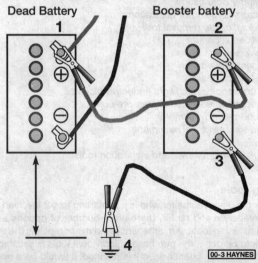

Make the booster battery cable connections in the numerical order shown (note that the negative cable of the booster battery is NOT attached to the negative terminal of the dead battery)

Jacking and towing

Jacking

Warning: *The jack supplied with the vehicle should only be used for changing a tire or placing jackstands under the frame. Never work under the vehicle or start the engine while this jack is being used as the only means of support.*

The vehicle should be on level ground. Place the shift lever in Park, if you have an automatic, or Reverse if you have a manual transaxle. Block the wheel diagonally opposite the wheel being changed. Set the parking brake.

Remove the spare tire and jack from stowage. Remove the wheel cover and trim ring (if so equipped) with the tapered end of the lug nut wrench by inserting and twisting the handle and then prying against the back of the wheel cover. Loosen the wheel lug nuts about 1/4-to-1/2 turn each.

Remove the trim cap from the jacking point **(see illustration)**. Engage the scissors-type jack with the channel in the frame rail nearest the wheel to be changed. There is a front and rear jacking point on each side of the vehicle **(see illustration)**.

Turn the jack handle clockwise until the tire clears the ground. Remove the lug nuts and pull the wheel off. Replace it with the spare.

Install the lug nuts with the beveled edges facing in. Tighten them snugly. Don't attempt to tighten them completely until the vehicle is lowered or it could slip off the jack. Turn the jack handle counterclockwise to lower the vehicle. Remove the jack and tighten the lug nuts in a diagonal pattern.

Install the cover (and trim ring, if used) and be sure it's snapped into place all the way around.

Stow the tire, jack and wrench. Unblock the wheels.

Towing

The best way to tow these vehicles is on a flat-bed tow truck. However, the vehicle can be towed with the front wheels off the ground if the driveshaft is disconnected at the differential and suspended out of the way, or, provided that the towing distance is no farther than 30 miles, an extra 1.8 quarts (1.7 liters) of automatic transmission fluid is added to the transmission (this extra fluid must be drained before driving the vehicle). It can also be towed with the rear wheels suspended. In either case, a cradle-type towing device, not a sling type, must be used.

The vehicle can be towed for *very short distances* with all four wheels on the ground. The tow strap should be attached to the towing loops, if equipped, or around the rear arm of the lower control arm, inboard of the coil spring. The shift lever must be in the N position and the ignition key must be turned to position II to unlock the steering column.

Remove the plastic trim cap from the frame rail

Insert the jack into the frame rail (there are two jacking points on each side of the vehicle)

Automotive chemicals and lubricants

A number of automotive chemicals and lubricants are available for use during vehicle maintenance and repair. They include a wide variety of products ranging from cleaning solvents and degreasers to lubricants and protective sprays for rubber, plastic and vinyl.

Cleaners

Carburetor cleaner and choke cleaner is a strong solvent for gum, varnish and carbon. Most carburetor cleaners leave a dry-type lubricant film which will not harden or gum up. Because of this film it is not recommended for use on electrical components.

Brake system cleaner is used to remove grease and brake fluid from the brake system, where clean surfaces are absolutely necessary. It leaves no residue and often eliminates brake squeal caused by contaminants.

Electrical cleaner removes oxidation, corrosion and carbon deposits from electrical contacts, restoring full current flow. It can also be used to clean spark plugs, carburetor jets, voltage regulators and other parts where an oil-free surface is desired.

Demoisturants remove water and moisture from electrical components such as alternators, voltage regulators, electrical connectors and fuse blocks. They are non-conductive, non-corrosive and non-flammable.

Degreasers are heavy-duty solvents used to remove grease from the outside of the engine and from chassis components. They can be sprayed or brushed on and, depending on the type, are rinsed off either with water or solvent.

Lubricants

Motor oil is the lubricant formulated for use in engines. It normally contains a wide variety of additives to prevent corrosion and reduce foaming and wear. Motor oil comes in various weights (viscosity ratings) from 5 to 80. The recommended weight of the oil depends on the season, temperature and the demands on the engine. Light oil is used in cold climates and under light load conditions. Heavy oil is used in hot climates and where high loads are encountered. Multi-viscosity oils are designed to have characteristics of both light and heavy oils and are available in a number of weights from 5W-20 to 20W-50.

Gear oil is designed to be used in differentials, manual transmissions and other areas where high-temperature lubrication is required.

Chassis and wheel bearing grease is a heavy grease used where increased loads and friction are encountered, such as for wheel bearings, balljoints, tie-rod ends and universal joints.

High-temperature wheel bearing grease is designed to withstand the extreme temperatures encountered by wheel bearings in disc brake equipped vehicles. It usually contains molybdenum disulfide (moly), which is a dry-type lubricant.

White grease is a heavy grease for metal-to-metal applications where water is a problem. White grease stays soft under both low and high temperatures (usually from -100 to +190-degrees F), and will not wash off or dilute in the presence of water.

Assembly lube is a special extreme pressure lubricant, usually containing moly, used to lubricate high-load parts (such as main and rod bearings and cam lobes) for initial start-up of a new engine. The assembly lube lubricates the parts without being squeezed out or washed away until the engine oiling system begins to function.

Silicone lubricants are used to protect rubber, plastic, vinyl and nylon parts.

Graphite lubricants are used where oils cannot be used due to contamination problems, such as in locks. The dry graphite will lubricate metal parts while remaining uncontaminated by dirt, water, oil or acids. It is electrically conductive and will not foul electrical contacts in locks such as the ignition switch.

Moly penetrants loosen and lubricate frozen, rusted and corroded fasteners and prevent future rusting or freezing.

Heat-sink grease is a special electrically non-conductive grease that is used for mounting electronic ignition modules where it is essential that heat is transferred away from the module.

Sealants

RTV sealant is one of the most widely used gasket compounds. Made from silicone, RTV is air curing, it seals, bonds, waterproofs, fills surface irregularities, remains flexible, doesn't shrink, is relatively easy to remove, and is used as a supplementary sealer with almost all low and medium temperature gaskets.

Anaerobic sealant is much like RTV in that it can be used either to seal gaskets or to form gaskets by itself. It remains flexible, is solvent resistant and fills surface imperfections. The difference between an anaerobic sealant and an RTV-type sealant is in the curing. RTV cures when exposed to air, while an anaerobic sealant cures only in the absence of air. This means that an anaerobic sealant cures only after the assembly of parts, sealing them together.

Thread and pipe sealant is used for sealing hydraulic and pneumatic fittings and vacuum lines. It is usually made from a Teflon compound, and comes in a spray, a paint-on liquid and as a wrap-around tape.

Chemicals

Anti-seize compound prevents seizing, galling, cold welding, rust and corrosion in fasteners. High-temperature ant-seize, usually made with copper and graphite lubricants, is used for exhaust system and exhaust manifold bolts.

Anaerobic locking compounds are used to keep fasteners from vibrating or working loose and cure only after installation, in the absence of air. Medium strength locking compound is used for small nuts, bolts and screws that may be removed later. High-strength locking compound is for large nuts, bolts and studs which aren't removed on a regular basis.

Oil additives range from viscosity index improvers to chemical treatments that claim to reduce internal engine friction. It should be noted that most oil manufacturers caution against using additives with their oils.

Gas additives perform several functions, depending on their chemical makeup. They usually contain solvents that help dissolve gum and varnish that build up on carburetor, fuel injection and intake parts. They also serve to break down carbon deposits that form on the inside surfaces of the combustion chambers. Some additives contain upper cylinder lubricants for valves and piston rings, and others contain chemicals to remove condensation from the gas tank.

Miscellaneous

Brake fluid is specially formulated hydraulic fluid that can withstand the heat and pressure encountered in brake systems. Care must be taken so this fluid does not come in contact with painted surfaces or plastics. An opened container should always be resealed to prevent contamination by water or dirt.

Weatherstrip adhesive is used to bond weatherstripping around doors, windows and trunk lids. It is sometimes used to attach trim pieces.

Undercoating is a petroleum-based, tar-like substance that is designed to protect metal surfaces on the underside of the vehicle from corrosion. It also acts as a sound-deadening agent by insulating the bottom of the vehicle.

Waxes and polishes are used to help protect painted and plated surfaces from the weather. Different types of paint may require the use of different types of wax and polish. Some polishes utilize a chemical or abrasive cleaner to help remove the top layer of oxidized (dull) paint on older vehicles. In recent years many non-wax polishes that contain a wide variety of chemicals such as polymers and silicones have been introduced. These non-wax polishes are usually easier to apply and last longer than conventional waxes and polishes.

Conversion factors

Length (distance)

Inches (in)	X	25.4	= Millimetres (mm)	X 0.0394	= Inches (in)
Feet (ft)	X	0.305	= Metres (m)	X 3.281	= Feet (ft)
Miles	X	1.609	= Kilometres (km)	X 0.621	= Miles

Volume (capacity)

Cubic inches (cu in; in³)	X	16.387	= Cubic centimetres (cc; cm³)	X 0.061	= Cubic inches (cu in; in³)
Imperial pints (Imp pt)	X	0.568	= Litres (l)	X 1.76	= Imperial pints (Imp pt)
Imperial quarts (Imp qt)	X	1.137	= Litres (l)	X 0.88	= Imperial quarts (Imp qt)
Imperial quarts (Imp qt)	X	1.201	= US quarts (US qt)	X 0.833	= Imperial quarts (Imp qt)
US quarts (US qt)	X	0.946	= Litres (l)	X 1.057	= US quarts (US qt)
Imperial gallons (Imp gal)	X	4.546	= Litres (l)	X 0.22	= Imperial gallons (Imp gal)
Imperial gallons (Imp gal)	X	1.201	= US gallons (US gal)	X 0.833	= Imperial gallons (Imp gal)
US gallons (US gal)	X	3.785	= Litres (l)	X 0.264	= US gallons (US gal)

Mass (weight)

Ounces (oz)	X	28.35	= Grams (g)	X 0.035	Ounces (oz)
Pounds (lb)	X	0.454	= Kilograms (kg)	X 2.205	= Pounds (lb)

Force

Ounces-force (ozf; oz)	X	0.278	= Newtons (N)	X 3.6	= Ounces-force (ozf; oz)
Pounds-force (lbf; lb)	X	4.448	= Newtons (N)	X 0.225	= Pounds-force (lbf; lb)
Newtons (N)	X	0.1	= Kilograms-force (kgf; kg)	X 9.81	= Newtons (N)

Pressure

Pounds-force per square inch (psi; lbf/in²; lb/in²)	X	0.070	= Kilograms-force per square centimetre (kgf/cm²; kg/cm²)	X 14.223	= Pounds-force per square inch (psi; lbf/in²; lb/in²)
Pounds-force per square inch (psi; lbf/in²; lb/in²)	X	0.068	= Atmospheres (atm)	X 14.696	= Pounds-force per square inch (psi; lbf/in²; lb/in²)
Pounds-force per square inch (psi; lbf/in²; lb/in²)	X	0.069	= Bars	X 14.5	= Pounds-force per square inch (psi; lbf/in²; lb/in²)
Pounds-force per square inch (psi; lbf/in²; lb/in²)	X	6.895	= Kilopascals (kPa)	X 0.145	= Pounds-force per square inch (psi; lbf/in²; lb/in²)
Kilopascals (kPa)	X	0.01	= Kilograms-force per square centimetre (kgf/cm²; kg/cm²)	X 98.1	= Kilopascals (kPa)

Torque (moment of force)

Pounds-force inches (lbf in; lb in)	X	1.152	= Kilograms-force centimetre (kgf cm; kg cm)	X 0.868	= Pounds-force inches (lbf in; lb in)
Pounds-force inches (lbf in; lb in)	X	0.113	= Newton metres (Nm)	X 8.85	= Pounds-force inches (lbf in; lb in)
Pounds-force inches (lbf in; lb in)	X	0.083	= Pounds-force feet (lbf ft; lb ft)	X 12	= Pounds-force inches (lbf in; lb in)
Pounds-force feet (lbf ft; lb ft)	X	0.138	= Kilograms-force metres (kgf m; kg m)	X 7.233	= Pounds-force feet (lbf ft; lb ft)
Pounds-force feet (lbf ft; lb ft)	X	1.356	= Newton metres (Nm)	X 0.738	= Pounds-force feet (lbf ft; lb ft)
Newton metres (Nm)	X	0.102	= Kilograms-force metres (kgf m; kg m)	X 9.804	= Newton metres (Nm)

Power

Horsepower (hp)	X	745.7	= Watts (W)	X 0.0013	= Horsepower (hp)

Velocity (speed)

Miles per hour (miles/hr; mph)	X	1.609	= Kilometres per hour (km/hr; kph)	X 0.621	= Miles per hour (miles/hr; mph)

Fuel consumption*

Miles per gallon, Imperial (mpg)	X	0.354	= Kilometres per litre (km/l)	X 2.825	= Miles per gallon, Imperial (mpg)
Miles per gallon, US (mpg)	X	0.425	= Kilometres per litre (km/l)	X 2.352	= Miles per gallon, US (mpg)

Temperature

Degrees Fahrenheit = (°C x 1.8) + 32

Degrees Celsius (Degrees Centigrade; °C) = (°F - 32) x 0.56

*It is common practice to convert from miles per gallon (mpg) to litres/100 kilometres (l/100km), where mpg (Imperial) x l/100 km = 282 and mpg (US) x l/100 km = 235

Safety first!

Regardless of how enthusiastic you may be about getting on with the job at hand, take the time to ensure that your safety is not jeopardized. A moment's lack of attention can result in an accident, as can failure to observe certain simple safety precautions. The possibility of an accident will always exist, and the following points should not be considered a comprehensive list of all dangers. Rather, they are intended to make you aware of the risks and to encourage a safety conscious approach to all work you carry out on your vehicle.

Essential DOs and DON'Ts

DON'T rely on a jack when working under the vehicle. Always use approved jackstands to support the weight of the vehicle and place them under the recommended lift or support points.

DON'T attempt to loosen extremely tight fasteners (i.e. wheel lug nuts) while the vehicle is on a jack - it may fall.

DON'T start the engine without first making sure that the transmission is in Neutral (or Park where applicable) and the parking brake is set.

DON'T remove the radiator cap from a hot cooling system - let it cool or cover it with a cloth and release the pressure gradually.

DON'T attempt to drain the engine oil until you are sure it has cooled to the point that it will not burn you.

DON'T touch any part of the engine or exhaust system until it has cooled sufficiently to avoid burns.

DON'T siphon toxic liquids such as gasoline, antifreeze and brake fluid by mouth, or allow them to remain on your skin.

DON'T inhale brake lining dust - it is potentially hazardous (see *Asbestos* below).

DON'T allow spilled oil or grease to remain on the floor - wipe it up before someone slips on it.

DON'T use loose fitting wrenches or other tools which may slip and cause injury.

DON'T push on wrenches when loosening or tightening nuts or bolts. Always try to pull the wrench toward you. If the situation calls for pushing the wrench away, push with an open hand to avoid scraped knuckles if the wrench should slip.

DON'T attempt to lift a heavy component alone - get someone to help you.

DON'T rush or take unsafe shortcuts to finish a job.

DON'T allow children or animals in or around the vehicle while you are working on it.

DO wear eye protection when using power tools such as a drill, sander, bench grinder, etc. and when working under a vehicle.

DO keep loose clothing and long hair well out of the way of moving parts.

DO make sure that any hoist used has a safe working load rating adequate for the job.

DO get someone to check on you periodically when working alone on a vehicle.

DO carry out work in a logical sequence and make sure that everything is correctly assembled and tightened.

DO keep chemicals and fluids tightly capped and out of the reach of children and pets.

DO remember that your vehicle's safety affects that of yourself and others. If in doubt on any point, get professional advice.

Asbestos

Certain friction, insulating, sealing, and other products - such as brake linings, brake bands, clutch linings, torque converters, gaskets, etc. - may contain asbestos. Extreme care must be taken to avoid inhalation of dust from such products, since it is hazardous to health. If in doubt, assume that they do contain asbestos.

Fire

Remember at all times that gasoline is highly flammable. Never smoke or have any kind of open flame around when working on a vehicle. But the risk does not end there. A spark caused by an electrical short circuit, by two metal surfaces contacting each other, or even by static electricity built up in your body under certain conditions, can ignite gasoline vapors, which in a confined space are highly explosive. Do not, under any circumstances, use gasoline for cleaning parts. Use an approved safety solvent.

Always disconnect the battery ground (-) cable at the battery before working on any part of the fuel system or electrical system. Never risk spilling fuel on a hot engine or exhaust component. It is strongly recommended that a fire extinguisher suitable for use on fuel and electrical fires be kept handy in the garage or workshop at all times. Never try to extinguish a fuel or electrical fire with water.

Fumes

Certain fumes are highly toxic and can quickly cause unconsciousness and even death if inhaled to any extent. Gasoline vapor falls into this category, as do the vapors from some cleaning solvents. Any draining or pouring of such volatile fluids should be done in a well ventilated area.

When using cleaning fluids and solvents, read the instructions on the container carefully. Never use materials from unmarked containers.

Never run the engine in an enclosed space, such as a garage. Exhaust fumes contain carbon monoxide, which is extremely poisonous. If you need to run the engine, always do so in the open air, or at least have the rear of the vehicle outside the work area.

If you are fortunate enough to have the use of an inspection pit, never drain or pour gasoline and never run the engine while the vehicle is over the pit. The fumes, being heavier than air, will concentrate in the pit with possibly lethal results.

The battery

Never create a spark or allow a bare light bulb near a battery. They normally give off a certain amount of hydrogen gas, which is highly explosive.

Always disconnect the battery ground (-) cable at the battery before working on the fuel or electrical systems.

If possible, loosen the filler caps or cover when charging the battery from an external source (this does not apply to sealed or maintenance-free batteries). Do not charge at an excessive rate or the battery may burst.

Take care when adding water to a non maintenance-free battery and when carrying a battery. The electrolyte, even when diluted, is very corrosive and should not be allowed to contact clothing or skin.

Always wear eye protection when cleaning the battery to prevent the caustic deposits from entering your eyes.

Household current

When using an electric power tool, inspection light, etc., which operates on household current, always make sure that the tool is correctly connected to its plug and that, where necessary, it is properly grounded. Do not use such items in damp conditions and, again, do not create a spark or apply excessive heat in the vicinity of fuel or fuel vapor.

Secondary ignition system voltage

A severe electric shock can result from touching certain parts of the ignition system (such as the spark plug wires) when the engine is running or being cranked, particularly if components are damp or the insulation is defective. In the case of an electronic ignition system, the secondary system voltage is much higher and could prove fatal.

Troubleshooting

Contents

This Section provides an easy reference guide to the more common problems which may occur during the operation of your vehicle. These problems and their possible causes are grouped under headings denoting various components or systems, such as Engine, Cooling system, etc. They also refer you to the Chapter and/or Section which deals with the problem.

Remember that successful troubleshooting is not a mysterious "black art" practiced only by professional mechanics. It is simply the result of the right knowledge combined with an intelligent, systematic approach to the problem. Always work by a process of elimination, starting with the simplest solution and working through to the most complex - and never overlook the obvious. Anyone can run the gas tank dry or leave the lights on overnight, so don't assume that you are exempt from such oversights.

Finally, always establish a clear idea of why a problem has occurred and take steps to ensure that it doesn't happen again. If the electrical system fails because of a poor connection, check all other connections in the system to make sure that they don't fail as well. If a particular fuse continues to blow, find out why - don't just replace one fuse after another. Remember, failure of a small component can often be indicative of potential failure or incorrect functioning of a more important component or system.

Engine

1   Engine will not rotate when attempting to start

1   Battery terminal connections loose or corroded (Chapter 1).
2   Battery discharged or faulty (Chapter 1).
3   Damaged left rear window harness shorting against glass rail inside door, causing battery to drain (Chapter 12).
4   Automatic transmission not completely engaged in Park (Chapter 7).
5   Broken, loose or disconnected wiring in the starting circuit (Chapters 5 and 12).
6   Starter motor pinion jammed in flywheel ring gear (Chapter 5).
7   Starter solenoid faulty (Chapter 5).
8   Starter motor faulty (Chapter 5).
9   Ignition switch faulty (Chapter 12).
10   Starter pinion or flywheel teeth worn or broken (Chapter 5).
11   Internal engine problem (Chapter 2B).
12   Inertia switch activated (Chapter 12).
13   Starter relay defective (Chapter 5).
14   Engine ground strap loose or missing.

2   Engine rotates but will not start

1   Fuel tank empty.
2   Battery discharged (engine rotates slowly) (Chapter 5).
3   Battery terminal connections loose or corroded (Chapter 1).
4   Leaking fuel injector(s), faulty fuel pump, pressure regulator, etc. (Chapter 4).
5   Fuel not reaching fuel injection system (Chapter 4).
6   Ignition components damp or damaged (Chapter 5).
7   Fuel injector stuck open (Chapter 4).
8   Worn, faulty or incorrectly gapped spark plugs (Chapter 1).
9   Broken, loose or disconnected wiring in the starting circuit (Chapter 5).
10   Loose distributor is changing ignition timing (Chapter 1).
11   Broken, loose or disconnected wires at the ignition coil or faulty coil (Chapter 5).
12   1988 and 1989 models may have electrical connector damage between the fuel pump relay and the fuel pump (see Chapter 12).
13   Coolant temperature sensor shorting on hood liner (see Chapter 11).
14   Defective Mass Airflow (MAF) sensor (Chapter 6).

3   Engine hard to start when cold

1   Battery discharged or low (Chapter 1).
2   Fuel system malfunctioning (Chapter 4).
3   Injector(s) leaking (Chapter 4).
4   Distributor rotor carbon tracked (Chapter 5).
5   Water enters the air cleaner housing near the left front wheel arch (Chapter 4).

4   Engine hard to start when hot

1   Air filter clogged (Chapter 1).
2   Fuel not reaching the fuel injection system (Chapter 4).
3   Corroded battery connections, especially ground (Chapter 1).
4   Fuel vaporizes at fuel pump inlet. Install dual fuel pumps (Chapter 4).
5   Fuel vapors from charcoal canister enter intake during idle and cause idling, stalling and starting problems (Chapter 6).

5   Starter motor noisy or excessively rough in engagement

1   Pinion or flywheel gear teeth worn or broken (Chapter 5).
2   Starter motor mounting bolts loose or missing (Chapter 5).

6   Engine starts but stops immediately

1   Loose or faulty electrical connections at distributor, coil or alternator (Chapter 5).
2   Insufficient fuel reaching the fuel injector(s) (Chapters 1 and 4).
3   Damaged fuel injection system speed sensors (Chapter 5).
4   Faulty fuel injection relays (Chapter 5).
5   Leaking threaded adapter on the EGR valve (Chapter 6)

7   Oil puddle under engine

1   Oil pan gasket and/or oil pan drain bolt seal leaking (Chapter 2).
2   Oil pressure sending unit leaking (Chapter 2).
3   Valve cover gaskets leaking (Chapter 2).
4   Engine oil seals leaking (Chapter 2).
5   Cylinder head rear plate gasket leaking (Chapter 2).
6   Alternator mounting bolt threads leaking oil (Chapter 5).
7   Oil cooler or oil cooler lines leaking (Chapter 3).

8   Engine lopes while idling or idles erratically

1   Vacuum leakage (Chapter 2).
2   Air filter clogged (Chapter 1).
3   Fuel pump not delivering sufficient fuel to the fuel injection system (Chapter 4).
4   Leaking head gasket (Chapter 2).
5   Timing belt/chain and/or sprockets worn (Chapter 2).
6   Camshaft lobes worn (Chapter 2).
7   EGR valve stuck open (Chapter 6).

9   Engine misses at idle speed

1   Spark plugs worn or not gapped properly (Chapter 1).
2   Faulty spark plug wires (Chapter 1).
3   Vacuum leaks (Chapter 1).
4   Incorrect ignition timing (Chapter 5).
5   Uneven or low compression (Chapter 2).
6   Restricted EGR vacuum hose (Chapter 6).

10   Engine misses throughout driving speed range

1   Fuel filter clogged and/or impurities in the fuel system (Chapter 1).
2   Low fuel output at the injectors (Chapter 4).
3   Faulty or incorrectly gapped spark plugs (Chapter 1).
4   Incorrect ignition timing (Chapter 5).
5   Cracked distributor cap, disconnected distributor wires or damaged distributor components (Chapter 1).
6   Leaking spark plug wires (Chapter 1).
7   Faulty emission system components (Chapter 6).
8   Low or uneven cylinder compression pressures (Chapter 2).
9   Weak or faulty ignition system (Chapter 5).
10   Vacuum leak in fuel injection system, intake manifold or vacuum hoses (Chapter 4).
11   Crankshaft sensor teeth damaged or missing (see Chapter 12).
12   Distributor installed incorrectly (see Chapter 5).

11 Engine stumbles on acceleration

1 Spark plugs fouled (Chapter 1).
2 Fuel injection system malfunctioning (Chapter 4).
3 Fuel filter clogged (Chapters 1 and 4).
4 Incorrect ignition timing (Chapter 5).
5 Intake manifold air leak (Chapter 4).
6 Collapsed or damaged fuel tank caused by plugged EVAP system (see Chapter 6).

12 Engine surges while holding accelerator steady

1 Intake air leak (Chapter 4).
2 Fuel pump faulty (Chapter 4).
3 Loose fuel injector harness connections (Chapters 4 and 6).
4 Defective ECU (Chapter 6).

13 Engine stalls

1 Idle speed incorrect (Chapter 1).
2 Fuel filter clogged and/or water and impurities in the fuel system (Chapter 1).
3 Distributor components damp or damaged (Chapter 5).
4 Faulty emissions system components (Chapter 6).
5 Faulty or incorrectly gapped spark plugs (Chapter 1).
6 Faulty spark plug wires (Chapter 1).
7 Vacuum leak in the fuel injection system, intake manifold or vacuum hoses (Chapter 4).

14 Engine lacks power

1 Incorrect ignition timing (Chapter 5).
2 Excessive play in distributor shaft (Chapter 5).
3 Worn rotor, distributor cap or wires (Chapters 1 and 5).
4 Faulty or incorrectly gapped spark plugs (Chapter 1).
5 Fuel injection system malfunctioning (Chapter 4).
6 Faulty coil (Chapter 5).
7 Brakes binding (Chapter 1).
8 Automatic transmission fluid level incorrect (Chapter 1).
9 Clutch slipping (Chapter 8).
10 Fuel filter clogged and/or impurities in the fuel system (Chapter 1).
11 Emission control system not functioning properly (Chapter 6).
12 Low or uneven cylinder compression pressures (Chapter 2).

15 Engine backfires

1 Emissions system not functioning properly (Chapter 6).
2 Ignition timing incorrect (Chapter 1).
3 Faulty secondary ignition system (cracked spark plug insulator, faulty plug wires, distributor cap and/or rotor) (Chapters 1 and 5).
4 Fuel injection system malfunctioning (Chapter 4).
5 Vacuum leak at fuel injector(s), intake manifold or vacuum hoses (Chapter 4).

16 Pinging or knocking engine sounds during acceleration or uphill

1 Incorrect grade of fuel.
2 Distributor installed incorrectly (Chapter 5).
3 Fuel injection system malfunction (Chapter 4).
4 Improper or damaged spark plugs or wires (Chapter 1).
5 Worn or damaged distributor components (Chapter 5).
6 Faulty emission system (Chapter 6).
7 Vacuum leak (Chapter 4).

8 Fuel rail feed (inlet) hose has hardened, resulting in knocking noise near dash (see Chapter 4).

17 Engine runs with oil pressure light on

1 Low oil level (Chapter 1).
2 Idle rpm too low (Chapter 1).
3 Short in wiring circuit (Chapter 12).
4 Faulty oil pressure sending unit (Chapter 2).
5 Worn engine bearings and/or oil pump (Chapter 2).

18 Engine diesels (continues to run) after switching off

1 Idle speed too high (Chapter 4).
2 Excessive engine operating temperature (Chapter 3).
3 Incorrect fuel octane grade.

19 Engine rattles at startup

1 Failure of upper timing chain tensioner (Chapter 2).

Engine electrical system

20 Battery will not hold a charge

1 Alternator drivebelt defective or not adjusted properly (Chapter 1).
2 Electrolyte level low (Chapter 1).
3 Battery terminals loose or corroded (Chapter 1).
4 Alternator not charging properly (Chapter 5).
5 Loose, broken or faulty wiring in the charging circuit (Chapter 5).
6 Short in vehicle wiring (Chapters 5 and 12).
7 Internally defective battery (Chapters 1 and 5).
8 Damaged left rear window harness shorting against glass rail inside door, causing battery to drain (Chapter 12).

21 Discharge warning light fails to go out

1 Faulty alternator or charging circuit (Chapter 5).
2 Alternator drivebelt defective or out of adjustment (Chapter 1).
3 Alternator voltage regulator inoperative (Chapter 5).

22 Discharge warning light fails to come on when key is turned on

1 **Warning** light bulb defective (Chapter 12).
2 Fault in the printed circuit, dash wiring or bulb holder (Chapter 12).

Fuel system

23 Excessive fuel consumption

1 Dirty or clogged air filter element (Chapter 1).
2 Incorrectly set ignition timing (Chapter 5).
3 Emissions system not functioning properly (Chapter 6).
4 Fuel injection internal parts excessively worn or damaged (Chapter 4).
5 Low tire pressure or incorrect tire size (Chapter 1).

24 Fuel leakage and/or fuel odor

1   Leak in a fuel feed or vent line (Chapter 4).
2   Tank overfilled.
3   Fuel injector internal parts excessively worn (Chapter 4).

Cooling system

25 Overheating

1   Insufficient coolant in system (Chapter 1).
2   Water pump drivebelt defective or out of adjustment (Chapter 1).
3   Radiator core blocked or grille restricted (Chapter 3).
4   Thermostat faulty (Chapter 3).
5   Radiator cap not maintaining proper pressure (Chapter 3).
6   Ignition timing incorrect (Chapter 5).

26 Overcooling

1   Faulty thermostat (Chapter 3).

27 External coolant leakage

1   Deteriorated/damaged hoses; loose clamps (Chapters 1 and 3).
2   Water pump seal defective (Chapters 1 and 3).
3   Leakage from radiator core or header tank (Chapter 3).
4   Engine drain or water jacket core plugs leaking (Chapter 2).
5   Hoses behind water pump leaking (Chapter 3).

28 Internal coolant leakage

1   Leaking cylinder head gasket (Chapter 2).
2   Cracked cylinder bore or cylinder head (Chapter 2).

29 Coolant loss

1   Too much coolant in system (Chapter 1).
2   Coolant boiling away because of overheating (Chapter 3).
3   Internal or external leakage (Chapter 3).
4   Faulty radiator cap (Chapter 3).

30 Poor coolant circulation

1   Inoperative water pump (Chapter 3).
2   Restriction in cooling system (Chapters 1 and 3).
3   Water pump drivebelt defective/out of adjustment (Chapter 1).
4   Thermostat sticking (Chapter 3).

Automatic transmission

Note: *Due to the complexity of the automatic transmission, it is difficult for the home mechanic to properly diagnose and service this component. For problems other than the following, the vehicle should be taken to a dealer or transmission shop.*

31 Fluid leakage

1   Automatic transmission fluid is a deep red color. Fluid leaks should not be confused with engine oil, which can easily be blown by air flow to the transmission.
2   To pinpoint a leak, first remove all built-up dirt and grime from the transmission housing with degreasing agents and/or steam cleaning. Then drive the vehicle at low speeds so air flow will not blow the leak far from its source. Raise the vehicle and determine where the leak is coming from. Common areas of leakage are:
   a) *Pan (Chapters 1 and 7)*
   b) *Dipstick/filler tube (see below)*
   c) *Transmission fluid cooler lines (Chapter 7)*
   d) *Speedometer sensor (Chapter 7)*
3   Make sure the dipstick is a tight fit inside the filler tube. If the seal at the top of the dipstick is worn or damaged, replace the seal or the dipstick. If fluid continues to leak from the top of the dipstick tube, inspect the breather, which is a plastic cap secured by a clip to the top of the extension housing. This breather can be plugged by the noise-deadening foam installed in the transmission tunnel, causing transmission fluid to leak from the top of the dipstick tube.

32 Transmission fluid brown or has a burned smell

Transmission fluid burned (Chapter 1).

33 Shift cable problems

1   Chapter 7 deals with adjusting the shift cable. Common problems which may be attributed to a poorly adjusted shift cable are:
   a) *Engine starting in gears other than Park or Neutral.*
   b) *Indicator on shift lever pointing to a gear other than the one actually being used.*
   c) *Vehicle moves when in Park.*
2   Refer to Chapter 7 for the shift cable adjustment procedure.

34 Transmission will not downshift with accelerator pedal pressed to the floor

Kickdown cable out of adjustment (Chapter 7).

35 Engine will start in gears other than Park or Neutral

1   Neutral start/back-up light switch malfunctioning (Chapter 7).
2   Shift cable out of adjustment (Chapter 7).

36 Transmission slips, shifts roughly, is noisy or has no drive in forward or reverse gears

There are many probable causes for the above problems, but the home mechanic should be concerned with only one possibility - fluid level. Before taking the vehicle to a dealer service department or transmission repair shop, check the level and condition of the fluid as described in Chapter 1. Correct the fluid level as necessary or change the fluid if needed. If the problem persists, have a professional diagnose the probable cause.

Brakes

Note: *Before assuming that a brake problem exists, make sure that:*
   a) *The tires are in good condition and properly inflated (Chapter 1).*
   b) *The front end alignment is correct (Chapter 10).*
   c) *The vehicle is not loaded with weight in an unequal manner.*

37 Vehicle pulls to one side during braking

1   Incorrect tire pressures (Chapter 1).
2   Front end out of line (have the front end aligned).
3   Unmatched tires on same axle.
4   Restricted brake lines or hoses (Chapter 9).
5   Malfunctioning caliper assembly (Chapter 9).
6   Loose suspension parts (Chapter 10).
7   Loose calipers (Chapter 9).
8   Brake pads contaminated with oil or grease (Chapter 9).

38 Noise (high-pitched squeal when the brakes are applied)

Front and/or rear disc brake pads worn out. The noise comes from the wear sensor rubbing against the disc. Replace pads with new ones immediately (Chapter 9).

39 Brake roughness or chatter (pedal pulsates)

1   Excessive lateral disc runout (Chapter 9).
2   Parallelism not within specifications (Chapter 9).
3   Uneven pad wear caused by caliper not sliding due to improper clearance or dirt (Chapter 9).
4   Defective disc (Chapter 9).

40 Excessive pedal effort required to stop vehicle

1   Malfunctioning power brake booster (Chapter 9).
2   Partial system failure (Chapter 9).
3   Excessively worn pads (Chapter 9).
4   Piston in caliper stuck or sluggish (Chapter 9).
5   Brake pads contaminated with oil or grease (Chapter 9).
6   New pads installed and not yet seated. It will take a while for the new material to seat against the disc.
7   Accumulator in power hydraulic system defective (see a Jaguar dealer).

41 Excessive brake pedal travel

1   Partial brake system failure (Chapter 9).
2   Insufficient fluid in master cylinder (Chapters 1 and 9).
3   Air trapped in system (Chapters 1 and 9).

42 Dragging brakes

1   Master cylinder pistons not returning correctly (Chapter 9).
2   Restricted brakes lines or hoses (Chapters 1 and 9).
3   Incorrect parking brake adjustment (Chapter 9).

43 Grabbing or uneven braking action

1   Malfunction of power brake booster unit (Chapter 9).
2   Binding brake pedal mechanism (Chapter 9).
3   Brake pads contaminated with oil or grease (Chapter 9).

44 Brake pedal feels spongy when depressed

1   Air in hydraulic lines (Chapter 9).

2   Master cylinder mounting bolts loose (Chapter 9).
3   Master cylinder defective (Chapter 9).

45 Brake pedal travels to the floor with little resistance

Little or no fluid in the master cylinder reservoir caused by leaking caliper piston(s), loose, damaged or disconnected brake lines (Chapter 9).

46 Parking brake does not hold

1   Parking brake cable or parking brake shoes improperly adjusted (Chapter 9).
2   Parking brake shoes need replacement (Chapter 9).

Suspension and steering systems

Note: *Before attempting to diagnose the suspension and steering systems, perform the following preliminary checks:*

a) Tires for wrong pressure and uneven wear.
b) Steering universal joints from the column to the steering gear for loose connectors or wear.
c) Front and rear suspension and the rack and pinion assembly for loose or damaged parts.
d) Out-of-round or out-of-balance tires, bent rims and loose and/or rough wheel bearings.

47 Vehicle pulls to one side

1   Mismatched or uneven tires (Chapter 10).
2   Broken or sagging springs (Chapter 10).
3   Wheel alignment out of specifications (Chapter 10).
4   Front brakes dragging (Chapter 9).

48 Abnormal or excessive tire wear

1   Wheel alignment out of specifications (Chapter 10).
2   Sagging or broken springs (Chapter 10).
3   Tire out-of-balance (Chapter 10).
4   Worn shock absorber (Chapter 10).
5   Overloaded vehicle.
6   Tires not rotated regularly.

49 Wheel makes a "thumping" noise

1   Blister or bump on tire (Chapter 10).
2   Improper shock absorber action (Chapter 10).

50 Shimmy, shake or vibration

1   Tire or wheel out-of-balance or out-of-round (Chapter 10).
2   Loose, worn or out-of-adjustment wheel bearings (Chapter 1).
3   Worn tie-rod ends (Chapter 10).
4   Worn balljoints (Chapter 10).
5   Excessive wheel runout (Chapter 10).
6   Blister or bump on tire (Chapter 10).

51 Hard steering

1   Lack of lubrication at balljoints, tie-rod ends and rack-and-pinion assembly (Chapter 1).
2   Front wheel alignment (Chapter 10).
3   Low tire pressure(s) (Chapter 1).

52 Poor returnability of steering to center

1   Lack of lubrication at balljoints and tie-rod ends (Chapter 1).
2   Binding in balljoints (Chapter 10).
3   Binding in steering column (Chapter 10).
4   Lack of lubricant in rack-and-pinion assembly (Chapter 10).
5   Front wheel alignment (Chapter 10).

53 Abnormal noise at the front end

1   Lack of lubrication at balljoints and tie-rod ends (Chapter 1).
2   Damaged shock absorber mounting (Chapter 10).
3   Worn control arm bushings or tie-rod ends (Chapter 10).
4   Loose stabilizer bar (Chapter 10).
5   Loose wheel nuts (Chapter).
6   Loose suspension bolts (Chapter 10).

54 Wander or poor steering stability

1   Mismatched or uneven tires (Chapter 10).
2   Lack of lubrication at balljoints and tie-rod ends (Chapter 1).
3   Worn shock absorbers (Chapter 10).
4   Loose stabilizer bar (Chapter 10).
5   Broken or sagging springs (Chapter 10).
6   Front or rear wheel alignment (Chapter 10).

55 Erratic steering when braking

1   Wheel bearings worn (Chapter 1).
2   Broken or sagging springs (Chapter 10).
3   Leaking wheel cylinder or caliper (Chapter 9).
4   Warped discs (Chapter 9).

56 Excessive pitching and/or rolling around corners or during braking

1   Loose stabilizer bar (Chapter 10).
2   Worn shock absorbers or mounts (Chapter 10).
3   Broken or sagging springs (Chapter 10).
4   Overloaded vehicle.

57 Suspension bottoms

1   Overloaded vehicle.
2   Worn shock absorbers (Chapter 10).
3   Incorrect, broken or sagging springs (Chapter 10).
4   Defective power hydraulic system or leaking rear shock absorbers (Chapter 10).

58 Cupped tires

1   Front wheel or rear wheel alignment (Chapter 10).
2   Worn shock absorbers (Chapter 10).
3   Wheel bearings worn (Chapter 10).
4   Excessive tire or wheel runout (Chapter 10).
5   Worn balljoints (Chapter 10).

59 Excessive tire wear on outside edge

1   Inflation pressures incorrect (Chapter 1).
2   Excessive speed in turns.
3   Front end alignment incorrect (excessive toe-in). Have professionally aligned.
4   Suspension arm bent or twisted (Chapter 10).

60 Excessive tire wear on inside edge

1   Inflation pressures incorrect (Chapter 1).
2   Front end alignment incorrect (toe-out). Have professionally aligned.
3   Loose or damaged steering components (Chapter 10).

61 Tire tread worn in one place

1   Tires out-of-balance.
2   Damaged or buckled wheel. Inspect and replace if necessary.
3   Defective tire (Chapter 1).

62 Excessive play or looseness in steering system

1   Wheel bearing(s) worn (Chapter 10.
2   Tie-rod end loose or worn (Chapter 10).
3   Steering gear loose or worn (Chapter 10).

63 Rattling or clicking noise in rack-and-pinion

1   Insufficient or improper power steering fluid in steering system (Chapter 10).
2   Steering gear mounts loose (Chapter 10).

Chapter 1
Tune-up and routine maintenance

Contents

Specifications

Recommended lubricants and fluids

Note: *Listed here are manufacturer recommendations at the time this manual was written. Manufacturers occasionally upgrade their fluid and lubricant specifications, so check with your local auto parts store for current recommendations.*

Engine oil

Type.. API certified SE or SF energy conserving oil

Viscosity .... See accompanying chart

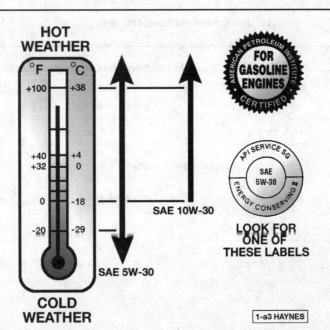

HOT WEATHER

SAE 10W-30

SAE 5W-30

COLD WEATHER

FOR GASOLINE ENGINES

AMERICAN PETROLEUM INSTITUTE CERTIFIED

API SERVICE SG
SAE 5W-30
ENERGY CONSERVING II

LOOK FOR ONE OF THESE LABELS

Recommended engine oil viscosity

1-a3 HAYNES

Recommended lubricants and fluids (continued)

Fuel	Unleaded gasoline, 87 octane or higher
Automatic transmission fluid	DEXRON IID
Engine coolant	Jaguar #110 Phosphate free antifreeze or equivalent
Brake fluid	DOT 4 only
Power steering system (1988, 1989, 1993 and 1994)	DEXRON IID or Type F automatic transmission fluid
Power hydraulic system (1990, 1991 and 1992)	Castrol 5966 hydraulic system mineral oil only
Differential fluid	
Standard differential	A.P.I. GL5 80W-90
Powr lok differential	A.P.I. GL5 90 gear oil
Wheel bearings and chassis	Multi-purpose lithium-base grease

Capacities*

Engine oil (with filter change)	8.5 quarts
Cooling system	13.5 quarts
Automatic transmission (fluid and filter change)	3.2 quarts
Differential	2.2 quarts

*All capacities approximate. Add as necessary to bring up to appropriate level.

Ignition system

Spark plug type and gap	
Type	RC9YC Champion or equivalent
Gap	0.025 inch
Spark plug wire resistance	10,000 to 25,000 ohms
Engine firing order	1-5-3-6-2-4
Distributor rotation	Clockwise
Ignition timing	Not adjustable

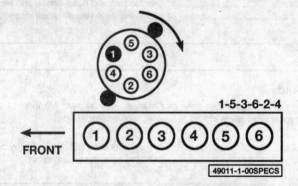

Cylinder location and distributor rotation

Idle speed adjustment	No adjustments necessary (see Chapter 4)

Brakes

Disc brake pad minimum thickness	
Front	5/32 inch
Rear	1/8 inch
Parking brake shoe minimum thickness	1/16 inch
Parking brake adjustment	3 to 5 clicks

Torque specifications

	Ft-lbs (unless otherwise indicated)
Automatic transmission pan bolts	72 in-lbs
Automatic transmission dipstick tube nut	15
Spark plugs	17 to 21
Wheel lug nuts	75

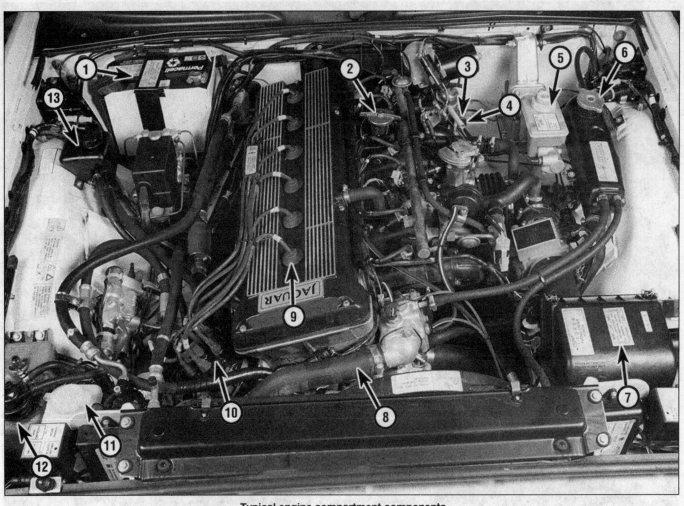

Typical engine compartment components

1	Battery	8	Upper radiator hose
2	Oil filler cap	9	Spark plugs
3	Engine oil dipstick (not visible)	10	Distributor
4	Automatic transmission dipstick (not visible)	11	Windshield washer fluid reservoir
5	Brake fluid reservoir	12	Power hydraulic system fluid reservoir
6	Coolant reservoir (expansion tank)	13	Power steering fluid reservoir
7	Air cleaner housing		

Typical engine compartment underside components

1	Air conditioning compressor	7	Steering gear boot
2	Stabilizer bar	8	Steering gear
3	Drivebelts	9	Engine oil pan drain plug (two locations)
4	Alternator	10	Catalytic converter
5	Lower radiator hose	11	Tie-rod end
6	Lower control arm		

Typical rear underside components

1	Rear suspension control arms	5	Rear driveaxle
2	Differential drain plug	6	Mufflers
3	Differential filler plug (not visible)	7	Parking brake cable
4	Exhaust pipe	8	Fuel filter

1 Maintenance schedule

The maintenance intervals in this manual are provided with the assumption that you, not the dealer, will be doing the work. These are the minimum maintenance intervals recommended by the factory for vehicles that are driven daily. If you wish to keep your vehicle in peak condition at all times, you may wish to perform some of these procedures even more often. Because frequent maintenance enhances the efficiency, performance and resale value of your car, we encourage you to do so. If you drive in dusty areas, tow a trailer, idle or drive at low speeds for extended periods or drive for short distances (less than four miles) in below freezing temperatures, shorter intervals are also recommended.

When your vehicle is new, it should be serviced by a factory authorized dealer service department to protect the factory warranty. In many cases, the initial maintenance check is done at no cost to the owner.

Every 250 miles or weekly, whichever comes first

Check the engine oil level (Section 4)
Check the engine coolant level (Section 4)
Check the windshield washer fluid level (Section 4)
Check the battery electrolyte (Section 4)
Check the tires and tire pressures (Section 5)

Every 3000 miles or 3 months, whichever comes first

All items listed above plus:
Check the automatic transmission fluid level (Section 6)
Check the power steering fluid level (Section 7)
Check the power hydraulics fluid level (Section 8)
Change the engine oil and oil filter (Section 9)

Every 6000 miles or 6 months, whichever comes first

All items listed above plus:
Check and service the battery (Section 10)
Check the cooling system (Section 11)
Inspect and replace if necessary all
    underhood hoses (Section 12)
Inspect and replace if necessary the windshield
    wiper blades (Section 13)
Rotate the tires (Section 14)
Inspect the brake system (Section 15)*
Inspect the fuel system (Section 16)
Check the differential lubricant level (Section 17)

Every 12,000 miles or 12 months, whichever comes first

Inspect the suspension and steering
    components (Section 18)
Lubricate the chassis (Section 19)
Replace the air filter (Section 20)

Check, repack and adjust the front wheel bearings
    (Section 21)
Inspect the seat belts (Section 22)

Every 24,000 miles or 24 months, whichever comes first

All items listed above plus:
Inspect the evaporative emissions control system
    (Section 23)
Replace the fuel filter (Section 24)
Replace the spark plugs (Section 25)
Inspect and replace if necessary the spark plug wires,
    distributor cap and rotor (Section 26)
Check and adjust if necessary the engine drivebelts
    (Section 27)
Service the cooling system (drain, flush and refill)
    (Section 28)
Change the brake fluid (Section 29)
Change the automatic transmission fluid and filter
    (Section 30)**
Change the differential lubricant (Section 31)**

Every 48,000 miles or 48 months, whichever comes first

Inspect the exhaust system (Section 32)

Every 52,500 miles

Replace the oxygen sensor (Chapter 6)
Replace the catalytic converter (Chapter 6)
Replace the evaporative emissions control canister
    (Chapter 6)

* *This item is affected by "severe" operating conditions as described below. If your vehicle is operated under "severe" conditions, perform all maintenance indicated with an asterisk (*) at 3000 mile/3 month intervals. Severe conditions are indicated if you mainly operate your vehicle under one or more of the following conditions:*

Operating in dusty areas
Towing a trailer
Idling for extended periods and/or low speed operation
Operating when outside temperatures remain below
    freezing and when most trips are less than 4 miles

** *If operated under one or more of the following conditions, change the automatic transmission fluid and differential lubricant every 12,000 miles:*

In heavy city traffic where the outside temperature
    regularly reaches 90-degrees F (32-degrees C)
    or higher
In hilly or mountainous terrain
Frequent trailer pulling

2   Introduction

This Chapter is designed to help the home mechanic maintain the vehicle for peak performance, economy, safety and long life.

On the following pages is a master maintenance schedule, followed by sections dealing specifically with each item on the schedule. Visual checks, adjustments, component replacement and other helpful items are included. Refer to the **accompanying illustrations** of the engine compartment and the underside of the vehicle for the location of various components.

Servicing your vehicle in accordance with the mileage/time maintenance schedule and the following Sections will provide it with a planned maintenance program that should result in a long and reliable service life. This is a comprehensive plan, so maintaining some items but not others at the specified service intervals will not produce the same results.

As you service your vehicle, you will discover that many of the procedures can - and should - be grouped together because of the nature of the particular procedure you're performing or because of the close proximity of two otherwise unrelated components to one another.

For example, if the vehicle is raised for any reason, you should inspect the exhaust, suspension, steering and fuel systems while you're under the vehicle. When you're rotating the tires, it makes good sense to check the brakes and wheel bearings since the wheels are already removed.

Finally, let's suppose you have to borrow or rent a torque wrench. Even if you only need to tighten the spark plugs, you might as well check the torque of as many critical fasteners as time allows.

The first step of this maintenance program is to prepare yourself before the actual work begins. Read through all sections pertinent to the procedures you're planning to do, then make a list of and gather together all the parts and tools you will need to do the job. If it looks as if you might run into problems during a particular segment of some procedure, seek advice from your local parts man or dealer service department.

3   Tune-up general information

The term tune-up is used in this manual to represent a combination of individual operations rather than one specific procedure.

If, from the time the vehicle is new, the routine maintenance schedule is followed closely and frequent checks are made of fluid levels and high wear items, as suggested throughout this manual, the engine will be kept in relatively good running condition and the need for additional work will be minimized.

More likely than not, however, there will be times when the engine is running poorly due to lack of regular maintenance. This is even more likely if a used vehicle, which has not received regular and frequent maintenance checks, is purchased. In such cases, an engine tune-up will be needed outside of the regular routine maintenance intervals.

The first step in any tune-up or engine diagnosis to help correct a poor running engine would be a cylinder compression check. A check of the engine compression (Chapter 2 Part B) will give valuable information regarding the overall performance of many internal components and should be used as a basis for tune-up and repair procedures. If, for instance, a compression check indicates serious internal engine wear, a conventional tune-up will not help the running condition of the engine and would be a waste of time and money.

The following series of operations are those most often needed to bring a generally poor running engine back into a proper state of tune.

Minor tune-up

Check all engine related fluids (Section 4)
Clean, inspect and test the battery (Section 10)
Check the cooling system (Section 11)
Check all underhood hoses (Section 12)

Check the fuel system (Section 16)
Check the air filter (Section 20)
Replace the spark plugs (Section 25)
Inspect the distributor cap and rotor (Section 26)
Inspect the spark plug and coil wires (Section 26)
Check and adjust the drivebelts (Section 27)

Major tune-up

All items listed under Minor tune-up, plus . . .
Replace the air filter (Section 20)
Replace the fuel filter (Section 24)
Replace the spark plug wires (Section 26)
Replace the distributor cap and rotor (Section 26)
Check the charging system (Chapter 5)
Check the ignition system (Chapter 5)

4   Fluid level checks
(every 250 miles or weekly)

Note: *The following are fluid level checks to be done on a 250 mile or weekly basis. Additional fluid level checks can be found in specific maintenance procedures which follow. Regardless of intervals, be alert to fluid leaks under the vehicle which would indicate a problem to be corrected immediately.*

1   Fluids are an essential part of the lubrication for the cooling, brake, windshield wiper and other systems. Because these fluids gradually become depleted and/or contaminated during normal operation of the vehicle, they must be periodically replenished. See *Recommended lubricants and fluids* and *capacities* at the beginning of this Chapter before adding fluid to any of the following components. **Note:** *The vehicle must be on level ground before fluid levels can be checked.*

Engine oil

Refer to illustrations 4.2, 4.4 and 4.6

2   The engine oil level is checked with a dipstick that is located on the left side of the engine **(see illustration)**. The dipstick extends through a metal tube from which it protrudes down into the engine oil pan.

3   The oil level should be checked before the vehicle has been driven, or about 15 minutes after the engine has been shut off. If the oil is checked immediately after driving the vehicle, some of the oil will remain in the upper engine components, producing an inaccurate reading on the dipstick.

4   Pull the dipstick from the tube and wipe all the oil from the end

4.2 The engine oil dipstick (arrow) is located on the left side of the engine

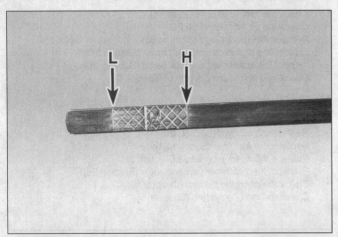

4.4 The oil level should be at or near the H mark - if it isn't, add enough oil to bring the level to near the H mark (it takes one full quart to raise the level from the L to the H mark)

4.6 The oil filler cap (arrow) is located on the left side of the engine - always make sure the area around the opening is clean before unscrewing the cap to prevent dirt from contaminating the engine

4.8 The coolant reservoir is located on the left inner fender panel - add coolant to bring the level to the base of the filler neck on the reservoir

with a clean rag or paper towel. Insert the clean dipstick all the way back into its metal tube and pull it out again. Observe the oil at the end of the dipstick. At its highest point, the level should be between the L and H marks **(see illustration)**.

5   It takes one quart of oil to raise the level from the L mark to the H mark on the dipstick. Do not allow the level to drop below the L mark or oil starvation may cause engine damage. Conversely, overfilling the engine (adding oil above the H mark) may cause oil fouled spark plugs, oil leaks or oil seal failures.

6   Oil is added to the engine after removing the oil filler cap located to the left of the valve cover **(see illustration)**. Use a funnel to prevent spills. After adding the oil, reinstall the dipstick and check the oil level again to make sure the oil is at the proper level. Then install the filler cap hand tight.

7   Checking the oil level is an important preventive maintenance step. A continually dropping oil level indicates oil leakage through damaged seals, defective gaskets, or past worn rings or valve guides. If the oil looks milky in color or has water droplets in it, a cylinder head gasket may be blown or the head or block may be cracked and the engine should be checked immediately. The condition of the oil should also be checked. Each time you check the oil level, slide your thumb and index finger up the dipstick before wiping off the oil. If you see small dirt or metal particles clinging to the dipstick, the oil should be changed (see Section 9).

Engine coolant

Refer to illustration 4.8

Warning: *Do not allow antifreeze to come in contact with your skin or painted surfaces of the vehicle. Flush contaminated areas immediately with plenty of water. Don't store new coolant or leave old coolant lying around where it's accessible to children or pets! They're attracted by its sweet smell and may drink it. Ingestion of even a small amount of coolant can be fatal! Wipe up garage floor and drip pan spills immediately. Keep antifreeze containers covered and repair cooling system leaks as soon as they're noticed.*

8   All vehicles covered by this manual are equipped with a pressurized coolant recovery system. A coolant expansion tank is located on the left inner fenderwell of the engine compartment **(see illustration)**. On 1988 and 1989 models, if the coolant gets too hot during engine operation, coolant can escape through the pressurized cap on the expansion tank, then through a connecting hose into the secondary reservoir located behind the left front wheel opening. As the engine cools, the coolant is automatically drawn back into the cooling system to maintain the correct level.

9   The coolant level should be checked regularly. The level will vary with the temperature of the engine. **Warning:** *Never remove the radia-*

tor cap or the coolant recovery reservoir cap when the engine is running or has just been shut down, because the cooling system is hot. Escaping steam and scalding liquid could cause serious injury. When the engine is cold, the coolant level should be at the base of the filler neck on the expansion tank. If it isn't, remove the cap from the expansion tank and add coolant to bring the level up to the base of the filler neck on the tank. Use only PHOSPHATE FREE type coolant with a mixture ratio of 55/45 anti-freeze and water. Do not use supplemental inhibitor additives. If only a small amount of coolant is required to bring the system up to the proper level, water can be used. However, repeated additions of water will dilute the recommended antifreeze and water solution. In order to maintain the proper ratio of antifreeze and water, it is advisable to top up the coolant level with the correct mixture.

10   If the coolant level drops within a short time after replenishment, there may be a leak in the system. Inspect the radiator, hoses, engine coolant filler cap, drain plugs and water pump. If no leak is evident, have the expansion tank pressure cap pressure tested by your dealer or a qualified repair shop.

11   If it is necessary to open the expansion tank pressure cap, wait until the system has cooled completely, then wrap a thick cloth around the cap and turn it to the first stop. If any steam escapes, wait until the system has cooled further, then remove the cap.

4.14 The windshield washer fluid reservoir is located in the right front corner of the engine compartment

4.15 Remove the cell caps to check the water level in the battery - if the level is low, add distilled water only

12   When checking the coolant level, always note its condition. It should be relatively clear. If it is brown or rust colored, the system should be drained, flushed and refilled. Even if the coolant appears to be normal, the corrosion inhibitors wear out with use, so it must be replaced at the specified intervals.

13   Do not allow antifreeze to come in contact with your skin or painted surfaces of the vehicle. Flush contacted areas immediately with plenty of water.

Windshield washer fluid

Refer to illustration 4.14

14   Fluid for the windshield washer system is stored in a plastic reservoir which is located in the right front corner (passenger side) of the engine compartment **(see illustration)**. In milder climates, plain water can be used to top up the reservoir, but the reservoir should be kept no more than two-thirds full to allow for expansion should the water freeze. In colder climates, the use of a specially designed windshield washer fluid, available at your dealer and any auto parts store, will help lower the freezing point of the fluid. Mix the solution with water in accordance with the manufacturer's directions on the container. Do not use regular antifreeze. It will damage the vehicle's paint.

Battery electrolyte

Refer to illustration 4.15

15   On models not equipped with a sealed battery, detach the battery hold down bracket and remove the filler/vent caps. Check the electrolyte level **(see illustration)** of all six battery cells. The fluid level is correct when it is approximately 1/4 inch above the battery plates. If the level is low, add distilled water to bring the fluid to the correct level. Install and securely re-tighten the vent caps. **Caution:** *Overfilling the cells may cause electrolyte to spill over during periods of heavy charging, causing corrosion or damage.*

Brake fluid

Refer to illustration 4.17

16   The brake master cylinder is mounted on the front of the power booster unit on the drivers side of the engine compartment.

17   To check the fluid level of the brake master cylinder, simply look at the MIN and MAX marks on the side of the reservoir **(see illustration)**. The fluid level is correct or OK when it is between the MIN and MAX marks on the side of the reservoir.

18   If the level is low or at the MIN marks, wipe the top of the reservoir cover with a clean rag to prevent contamination of the brake system before lifting the cover.

19   Add only the specified brake fluid to the reservoir (refer to *Recommended lubricants and fluids* at the front of this Chapter or to your owner's manual). Mixing different types of brake fluid can damage the system. Fill the brake master cylinder reservoir to the base of the filler

neck on 1998 and 1989 models or to the MAX mark on 1990 and later models. DO NOT fill the reservoir above the MAX mark or brake fluid may be expelled from the reservoir. **Warning:** *Use caution when filling the reservoir - brake fluid can harm your eyes and damage painted surfaces. Do not use brake fluid that has been opened for more than one year or has been left open. Brake fluid absorbs moisture from the air. Moisture in the hydraulic system can cause a dangerous loss of braking.*

20   While the reservoir cap is removed, inspect the master cylinder reservoir for contamination. If deposits, dirt particles or water droplets are present, the system should be drained and refilled.

21   After filling the reservoir to the proper level, make sure the lid is properly seated to prevent fluid leakage and/or system pressure loss.

22   The fluid in the brake master cylinder will drop slightly as the brake pads at each wheel wear down during normal operation. If either master cylinder requires repeated replenishing to keep it at the proper level, this is an indication of leakage in the brake or clutch system, which should be corrected immediately. If the brake system shows an indication of leakage check all brake lines and connections, along with the calipers, wheel cylinders and booster (see Section 15 for more information). If the hydraulic clutch system shows an indication of leakage check all clutch lines and connections, along with the clutch slave cylinder (see Chapter 8 for more information).

23   If, upon checking the brake or clutch master cylinder fluid level, you discover one or both reservoirs empty or nearly empty, the systems should be bled (see Chapter 9).

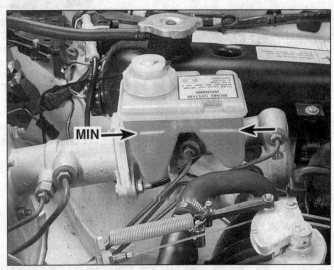

4.17 The brake fluid level should be kept above the MIN marks on the translucent plastic reservoir

5   Tire and tire pressure checks (every 250 miles or weekly)

Refer to illustrations 5.2, 5.3, 5.4a, 5.4b and 5.8

1   Periodic inspection of the tires may spare you from the inconvenience of being stranded with a flat tire. It can also provide you with vital information regarding possible problems in the steering and suspension systems before major damage occurs.

2   Normal tread wear can be monitored with a simple, inexpensive device known as a tread depth indicator **(see illustration)**. When the tread depth reaches the specified minimum, replace the tire(s).

3   Note any abnormal tread wear **(see illustration)**. Tread pattern irregularities such as cupping, flat spots and more wear on one side than the other are indications of front end alignment and/or balance problems. If any of these conditions are noted, take the vehicle to a tire shop or service station to correct the problem.

4   Look closely for cuts, punctures and embedded nails or tacks. Sometimes a tire will hold its air pressure for a short time or leak down very slowly even after a nail has embedded itself into the tread. If a slow leak persists, check the valve stem core to make sure it is tight **(see illustration)**. Examine the tread for an object that may have embedded itself into the tire or for a "plug" that may have begun to leak (radial tire punctures are repaired with a plug that is installed in a puncture). If a puncture is suspected, it can be easily verified by spraying a solution of soapy water onto the puncture area **(see illustration)**. The soapy solution will bubble if there is a leak. Unless the puncture is inordinately large, a tire shop or gas station can usually repair the

5.2 A tire tread depth indicator should be used to monitor tire wear - they are available at auto parts stores and service stations and cost very little

punctured tire.

5   Carefully inspect the inner sidewall of each tire for evidence of brake fluid leakage. If you see any, inspect the brakes immediately.

6   Correct tire air pressure adds miles to the life span of the tires, improves mileage and enhances overall ride quality. Tire pressure cannot be accurately estimated by looking at a tire, particularly if it is a

UNDERINFLATION

CUPPING

Cupping may be caused by:
- **Underinflation and/or mechanical irregularities such as out-of-balance condition of wheel and/or tire, and bent or damaged wheel.**
- **Loose or worn steering tie-rod or steering idler arm.**
- **Loose, damaged or worn front suspension parts.**

OVERINFLATION

INCORRECT TOE-IN OR EXTREME CAMBER

FEATHERING DUE TO MISALIGNMENT

5.3 This chart will help you determine the condition of your tires, the probable cause(s) of abnormal wear and the corrective action necessary

5.4a If a tire loses air on a steady basis, check the valve core first to make sure it's snug (special inexpensive wrenches are commonly available at auto parts stores)

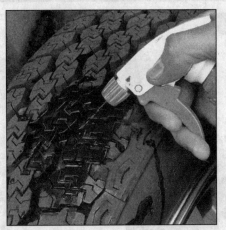

5.4b If the valve core is tight, raise the corner of the vehicle with the low tire and spray a soapy water solution onto the tread as the tire is turned slowly - slow leaks will cause small bubbles to appear

5.8 To extend the life of your tires, check the air pressure at least once a week with an accurate gauge (don't forget the spare!)

radial. A tire pressure gauge is therefore essential. Keep an accurate gauge in the glove box. The pressure gauges fitted to the nozzles of air hoses at gas stations are often inaccurate.

7   Always check tire pressure when the tires are cold. "Cold," in this case, means the vehicle has not been driven over a mile in the three hours preceding a tire pressure check. A pressure rise of four to eight pounds is not uncommon once the tires are warm.

8   Unscrew the valve cap protruding from the wheel or hubcap and push the gauge firmly onto the valve **(see illustration)**. Note the reading on the gauge and compare this figure to the recommended tire pressure shown on the tire placard on the left door. Be sure to reinstall the valve cap to keep dirt and moisture out of the valve stem mechanism. Check all four tires and, if necessary, add enough air to bring them up to the recommended pressure levels.

9   Don't forget to keep the spare tire inflated to the specified pressure (consult your owner's manual). Note that the air pressure specified for a compact spare (if equipped) is significantly higher than the pressure of the regular tires.

6   Automatic transmission fluid level check (every 3000 miles or 3 months)

Refer to illustrations 6.4a and 6.4b

1   The level of the automatic transmission fluid should be carefully maintained. Low fluid level can lead to slipping or loss of drive, while overfilling can cause foaming, loss of fluid and transmission damage.

2   The transmission fluid level should only be checked when the transmission is hot (at its normal operating temperature). If the vehicle has just been driven over 10 miles (15 miles in a frigid climate), and the fluid temperature is 160 to 175-degrees F, the transmission is hot. **Caution:** *If the vehicle has just been driven for a long time at high speed or in city traffic in hot weather, or if it has been pulling a trailer, an accurate fluid level reading cannot be obtained. Allow the fluid to cool down for about 30 minutes.*

3   If the vehicle has not been driven, park the vehicle on level ground, set the parking brake, then start the engine and bring it to operating temperature. While the engine is idling, depress the brake pedal and move the selector lever through all the gear ranges, beginning and ending in Park.

4   With the engine still idling, remove the dipstick from its tube **(see illustration)**. Check the level of the fluid on the dipstick **(see illustration)** and note its condition.

5   Wipe the fluid from the dipstick with a clean rag and reinsert it back into the filler tube until the cap seats.

6   Pull the dipstick out again and note the fluid level. If the transmis-

sion is cold, the level should be in the COLD or COOL range on the dipstick. If it is hot, the fluid level should be in the HOT range. If the level is at the low side of either range, add the specified automatic transmission fluid through the dipstick tube with a funnel.

7   Add just enough of the recommended fluid to fill the transmission to the proper level. It takes about one pint to raise the level from the low mark to the high mark when the fluid is hot, so add the fluid a little

6.4a The automatic transmission dipstick (arrow) is located in a tube which extends forward from the transmission

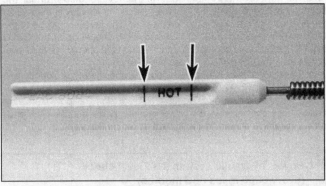

6.4b Check the automatic transmission fluid with the engine idling at operating temperature and the gear selector in Park, then add fluid to bring the level to the upper mark

7.6 The power steering fluid is checked with a dipstick which is part of the cap - the fluid level varies with temperature, so the fluid can be checked hot or cold

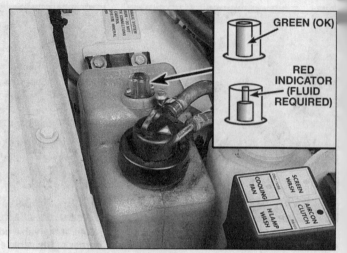

8.2 The power hydraulic system reservoir is located on the right side inner fender panel - to check the fluid level on 1988 and 1989 models simply look through the sight glass and note the color of the indicator

at a time and keep checking the level until it is correct.

8   The condition of the fluid should also be checked along with the level. If the fluid at the end of the dipstick is black or a dark reddish brown color, or if it emits a burned smell, the fluid should be changed (see Section 30). If you are in doubt about the condition of the fluid, purchase some new fluid and compare the two for color and smell.

7   Power steering fluid level check (every 3000 miles or 3 months)

Refer to illustration 7.6

Note: *On 1990 and later models the power steering system and the power hydraulic system reservoir are combined as one - use Castrol hydraulic system mineral oil only.*

1   Unlike manual steering, the power steering system relies on fluid which may, over a period of time, require replenishing.

2   The fluid reservoir for the power steering pump is located on the right inner fenderwell near the shock tower.

3   For the check, the front wheels should be pointed straight ahead and the engine should be off.

4   Use a clean rag to wipe off the reservoir cap and the area around the cap. This will help prevent any foreign matter from entering the reservoir during the check.

5   Twist off the cap (clockwise) and check the temperature of the fluid at the end of the dipstick with your finger.

6   Wipe off the fluid with a clean rag, reinsert it, then withdraw it and read the fluid level **(see illustration)**. The level should be near the upper mark on the dipstick. On some models the dipstick is marked so the fluid can be checked either cold or hot. The level should be at the HOT mark if the fluid was hot to the touch. It should be at the COLD mark if the fluid was cool to the touch. At no time should the fluid level drop below the lower mark for each heat range.

7   If additional fluid is required, pour the specified type directly into the reservoir, using a funnel to prevent spills.

8   If the reservoir requires frequent fluid additions, all power steering hoses, hose connections, the power steering pump and the rack-and-pinion assembly should be carefully checked for leaks.

8   Power hydraulic system fluid level check (every 3000 miles or 3 months)

Refer to illustrations 8.2 and 8.3
Caution: *Use only Castrol 5966 hydraulic system mineral oil in the*

power hydraulic system (available at Jaguar dealer service departments).

1   The power hydraulic system controls the ride leveling and the brake booster systems. The level of the fluid should be carefully maintained. Low fluid levels can adversely affect the riding and braking capabilities of your vehicle. The power hydraulic system fluid reservoir is located on the right inner fenderwell of the engine compartment.

1988 and 1989 models

2   The fluid level can easily be checked by viewing the reservoir sight glass. A green indicator in the sight glass indicates an OK condition, while a red indicator in the sight glass requires fluid to be added **(see illustration)**.

3   If additional fluid is required, pop open the plastic tab located on top of the reservoir cap **(see illustration)**. **Note:** *Castrol hydraulic system mineral oil is supplied in half-liter containers which are equipped with a special dispensing tube that is required to fill the hydraulic system.*

4   Insert the mineral oil dispensing tube into the reservoir filler hole. Push downward and turn until the dispensing tube is locked in place.

5   Add fluid until the green indicator in the sight glass appears, then release the dispensing tube by pushing downward and turning the opposite direction of installation.

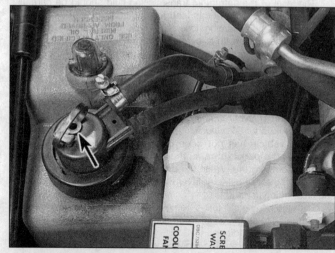

8.3 To add fluid, remove the filler hole dust cap (arrow)

8.7 On 1990 and later models remove the cap and check the level of fluid on the dipstick

1990 through 1994 models

Refer to illustration 8.7

6   The fluid level can be checked by removing the cap and observing the level of fluid on the dipstick.

7   Wipe off the fluid with a clean rag, reinsert it, then withdraw it and read the fluid level **(see illustration)**. The dipstick is marked so the fluid can be checked either cold or hot. The level should be at the HOT mark if the fluid was hot to the touch. It should be at the COLD mark if the fluid was cool to the touch. At no time should the fluid level drop below the add mark.

8   If additional fluid is required, pour the specified type directly into the reservoir, using a funnel to prevent spills.

9   Engine oil and oil filter change (every 3000 miles or 3 months)

Refer to illustrations 9.2, 9.7, 9.13 and 9.15

Note: *Some models may have a second drain plug located at the front oil pan sump. Be sure to drain the oil from both locations.*

1   Frequent oil changes are the best preventive maintenance the home mechanic can give the engine, because aging oil becomes diluted and contaminated, which leads to premature engine wear.

2   Make sure that you have all the necessary tools before you begin this procedure **(see illustration)**. You should also have plenty of rags or newspapers handy for mopping up any spills.

3   Access to the underside of the vehicle is greatly improved if the vehicle can be lifted on a hoist, driven onto ramps or supported by jackstands.

4   If this is your first oil change, get under the vehicle and familiarize yourself with the location of the oil drain plug. The engine and exhaust components will be warm during the actual work, so try to anticipate any potential problems before the engine and accessories are hot.

5   Park the vehicle on a level spot. Start the engine and allow it to reach its normal operating temperature (the needle on the temperature gauge should be at least above the bottom mark). Warm oil and contaminates will flow out more easily. Turn off the engine when it's warmed up. Remove the oil filler cap located next to the valve cover.

6   Raise the vehicle and support it on jackstands. **Warning:** *To avoid personal injury, never get beneath the vehicle when it is supported by only by a jack. The jack provided with your vehicle is designed solely for raising the vehicle to remove and replace the wheels. Always use jackstands to support the vehicle when it becomes necessary to place your body underneath the vehicle.*

7   Being careful not to touch the hot exhaust components, place the drain pan under the drain plug in the bottom of the pan and remove the plug **(see illustration)**. You may want to wear gloves while unscrewing the plug the final few turns if the engine is really hot.

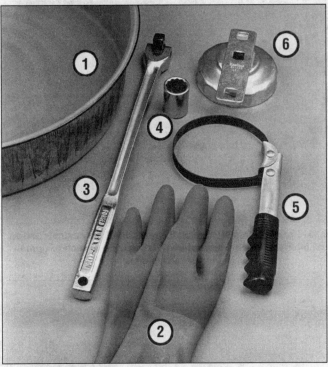

9.2 These tools are required when changing the engine oil and filter

1   ***Drain pan*** *- It should be fairly shallow in depth, but wide in order to prevent spills*

2   ***Rubber gloves*** *- When removing the drain plug and filter, it is inevitable that you will get oil on your hands (the gloves will prevent burns)*

3   ***Breaker bar*** *- Sometimes the oil drain plug is pretty tight and a long breaker bar is needed to loosen it*

4   ***Socket*** *– To be used with the breaker bar or a ratchet (must be the correct size to fit the drain plug)*

5   ***Filter wrench*** *- This is a metal band-type wrench, which requires clearance around the filter to be effective*

6   ***Filter wrench*** *- This type fits on the bottom of the filter and can be turned with a ratchet or breaker bar (different size wrenches are available for different types of filters)*

9.7 The oil drain plug (arrow) is located at the rear of the oil pan - use a box-end wrench or socket to remove it (some models may have a second drain plug at the front of the oil pan)

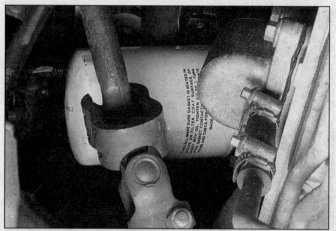

9.13 The oil filter is located on the left side of the engine - use an oil filter wrench for removal (DO NOT use the wrench to tighten the new filter)

9.15 Lubricate the oil filter gasket with clean engine oil before installing the filter on the engine

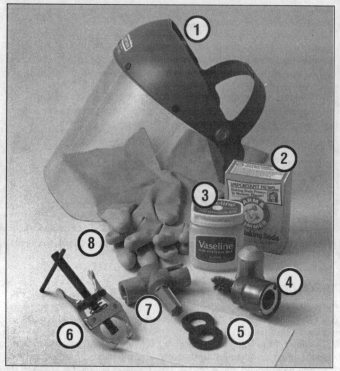

10.1 Tools and materials required for battery maintenance

1   *Face shield/safety goggles* - When removing corrosion with a brush, the acidic particles can easily fly up into your eyes
2   *Baking soda* - A solution of baking soda and water can be used to neutralize corrosion
3   *Petroleum jelly* - A layer of this on the battery posts will help prevent corrosion
4   *Battery post/cable cleaner* - This wire brush cleaning tool will remove all traces of corrosion from the battery posts and cable clamps
5   *Treated felt washers* - Placing one of these on each post, directly under the cable clamps, will help prevent corrosion
6   *Puller* - Sometimes the cable clamps are very difficult to pull off the posts, even after the nut/bolt has been completely loosened. This tool pulls the clamp straight up and off the post without damage
7   *Battery post/cable cleaner* - Here is another cleaning tool which is a slightly different version of number 4 above, but it does the same thing
8   *Rubber gloves* - Another safety item to consider when servicing the battery; remember that's acid inside the battery

8   Allow the old oil to drain into the pan. It may be necessary to move the pan farther under the engine as the oil flow slows to a trickle. Inspect the old oil for the presence of metal shavings and chips.
9   After all the oil has drained, wipe off the drain plug with a clean rag. Even minute metal particles clinging to the plug would immediately contaminate the new oil.
10   Clean the area around the drain plug opening, reinstall the plug and tighten it securely, but do not strip the threads.
11   Move the drain pan into position under the oil filter.
12   Remove all tools, rags, etc. from under the vehicle, being careful not to spill the oil in the drain pan, then lower the vehicle.
13   Loosen the oil filter **(see illustration)** by turning it counterclockwise with the filter wrench. Any standard filter wrench should work. Once the filter is loose, use your hands to unscrew it from the block. Just as the filter is detached from the block, immediately tilt the open end up to prevent the oil inside the filter from spilling out. **Warning:** *The engine exhaust pipes may still be hot, so be careful.*
14   With a clean rag, wipe off the mounting surface on the block. If a residue of old oil is allowed to remain, it will smoke when the block is heated up. It will also prevent the new filter from seating properly. Also make sure that the none of the old gasket remains stuck to the mounting surface. It can be removed with a scraper if necessary.
15   Compare the old filter with the new one to make sure they are the same type. Smear some engine oil on the rubber gasket of the new fil-

ter and screw it into place **(see illustration)**. Because over-tightening the filter will damage the gasket, do not use a filter wrench to tighten the filter. Tighten it by hand until the gasket contacts the seating surface. Then seat the filter by giving it an additional 3/4-turn.
16   Add new oil to the engine through the oil filler cap next to the valve cover. Use a spout or funnel to prevent oil from spilling onto the top of the engine. Pour three quarts of fresh oil into the engine. Wait a few minutes to allow the oil to drain into the pan, then check the level on the oil dipstick (see Section 4 if necessary). If the oil level is at or near the H mark, install the filler cap hand tight, start the engine and allow the new oil to circulate.
17   Allow the engine to run for about a minute. While the engine is running, look under the vehicle and check for leaks at the oil pan drain plug and around the oil filter. If either is leaking, stop the engine and tighten the plug or filter slightly.
18   Wait a few minutes to allow the oil to trickle down into the pan, then recheck the level on the dipstick and, if necessary, add enough oil to bring the level to the H mark.

10.6a Battery terminal corrosion usually appears as light, fluffy powder

10.6b Removing a cable from the battery post with a wrench - sometimes special battery pliers are required for this procedure if corrosion has caused deterioration of the nut hex (always remove the ground cable first and hook it up last!)

10.7a When cleaning the cable clamps, all corrosion must be removed (the inside of the clamp is tapered to match the taper on the post, so don't remove too much material)

19 During the first few trips after an oil change, make it a point to check frequently for leaks and proper oil level.

20 The old oil drained from the engine cannot be reused in its present state and should be disposed of. Check with your local refuse disposal company, disposal facility or environmental agency to see whether they will accept the oil for recycling. Don't pour used oil into drains or onto the ground. After the oil has cooled, it can be drained into a suitable container (capped plastic jugs, topped bottles, milk cartons, etc.) for transport to one of these disposal sites.

10 Battery check, maintenance and charging (every 6000 miles or 6 months)

Refer to illustrations 10.1, 10.6a, 10.6b, 10.7a and 10.7b

Warning: *Certain precautions must be followed when checking and servicing the battery. Hydrogen gas, which is highly flammable, is always present in the battery cells, so keep lighted tobacco and all other open flames and sparks away from the battery. The electrolyte inside the battery is actually dilute sulfuric acid, which will cause injury if splashed on your skin or in your eyes. It will also ruin clothes and painted surfaces. When removing the battery cables, always detach the negative cable first and hook it up last!*

1 A routine preventive maintenance program for the battery in your vehicle is the only way to ensure quick and reliable starts. But before performing any battery maintenance, make sure that you have the proper equipment necessary to work safely around the battery **(see illustration)**.

2 There are also several precautions that should be taken whenever battery maintenance is performed. Before servicing the battery, always turn the engine and all accessories off and disconnect the cable from the negative terminal of the battery.

3 The battery produces hydrogen gas, which is both flammable and explosive. Never create a spark, smoke or light a match around the battery. Always charge the battery in a ventilated area.

4 Electrolyte contains poisonous and corrosive sulfuric acid. Do not allow it to get in your eyes, on your skin or on your clothes. Never ingest it. Wear protective safety glasses when working near the battery. Keep children away from the battery.

5 Note the external condition of the battery. If the positive terminal and cable clamp on your vehicle's battery is equipped with a rubber protector, make sure it isn't torn or damaged. It should completely cover the terminal. Look for any corroded or loose connections, cracks in the case or cover or loose hold-down clamps. Also check the entire

10.7b Regardless of the type of tool used to clean the battery posts, a clean, shiny surface should be the result

length of each cable for cracks and frayed conductors.

6 If corrosion, which looks like white, fluffy deposits **(see illustration)** is evident, particularly around the terminals, the battery should be removed for cleaning. Loosen the cable clamp bolts, being careful to remove the ground cable first, and slide them off the terminals **(see illustration)**. Then disconnect the hold-down clamp bolt and nut, remove the clamp and lift the battery from the engine compartment.

7 Clean the cable clamps thoroughly with a battery brush or a terminal cleaner and a solution of warm water and baking soda **(see illustration)**. Wash the terminals and the top of the battery case with the same solution but make sure that the solution doesn't get into the battery. When cleaning the cables, terminals and battery top, wear safety goggles and rubber gloves to prevent any solution from coming in contact with your eyes or hands. Wear old clothes too - even diluted, sulfuric acid splashed onto clothes will burn holes in them. If the terminals have been extensively corroded, clean them up with a terminal cleaner **(see illustration)**. Thoroughly wash all cleaned areas with plain water.

8 Make sure the battery tray is in good condition and the hold-down clamp bolt or nut is tight. If the battery is removed from the tray, make sure no parts remain in the bottom of the tray when the battery is reinstalled. When reinstalling the hold-down clamp bolt or nut, do not over-tighten it.

9 Information on removing and installing the battery can be found in

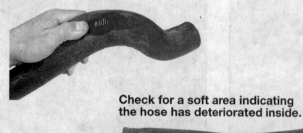

Check for a chafed area that could fail prematurely.

Check for a soft area indicating the hose has deteriorated inside.

Overtightening the clamp on a hardened hose will damage the hose and cause a leak.

Check each hose for swelling and oil-soaked ends. Cracks and breaks can be located by squeezing the hose.

11.4   Hoses, like drivebelts, have a habit of failing at the worst possible time - to prevent the inconvenience of a blown radiator or heater hose, inspect them carefully as shown here

Chapter 5. Information on jump starting can be found at the front of this manual. For more detailed battery checking procedures, refer to the *Haynes Automotive Electrical Manual*.

Cleaning

10   Corrosion on the hold-down components, battery case and surrounding areas can be removed with a solution of water and baking soda. Thoroughly rinse all cleaned areas with plain water.

11   Any metal parts of the vehicle damaged by corrosion should be covered with a zinc-based primer, then painted.

Charging

Warning: *When batteries are being charged, hydrogen gas, which is very explosive and flammable, is produced. Do not smoke or allow open flames near a charging or a recently charged battery. Wear eye protection when near the battery during charging. Also, make sure the charger is unplugged before connecting or disconnecting the battery from the charger.*

12   Slow-rate charging is the best way to restore a battery that's discharged to the point where it will not start the engine. It's also a good way to maintain the battery charge in a vehicle that's only driven a few

miles between starts. Maintaining the battery charge is particularly important in the winter when the battery must work harder to start the engine and electrical accessories that drain the battery are in greater use.

13   It's best to use a one or two-amp battery charger (sometimes called a "trickle" charger). They are the safest and put the least strain on the battery. They are also the least expensive. For a faster charge, you can use a higher amperage charger, but don't use one rated more than 1/10th the amp/hour rating of the battery. Rapid boost charges that claim to restore the power of the battery in one to two hours are hardest on the battery and can damage batteries not in good condition. This type of charging should only be used in emergency situations.

14   The average time necessary to charge a battery should be listed in the instructions that come with the charger. As a general rule, a trickle charger will charge a battery in 12 to 16 hours.

11   Cooling system check (every 6000 miles or 6 months)

Refer to illustration 11.4

1   Many major engine failures can be attributed to a faulty cooling system. If the vehicle is equipped with an automatic transmission, the cooling system also cools the transmission fluid and thus plays an important role in prolonging transmission life.

2   The cooling system should be checked with the engine cold. Do this before the vehicle is driven for the day or after the engine has been shut off for at least three hours.

3   Remove the cap from the coolant reservoir (expansion tank) by turning it to the left until it reaches a stop. If you hear a hissing sound (indicating there is still pressure in the system), wait until it stops. Now press down on the cap with the palm of your hand and continue turning to the left until the cap can be removed. Thoroughly clean the cap, inside and out, with clean water. Also clean the filler neck on the reservoir. All traces of corrosion should be removed. The coolant inside the radiator should be relatively transparent. If it's rust colored, the system should be drained and refilled (see Section 28). If the coolant level isn't up to the base of the filler neck, add additional antifreeze/coolant mixture (see Section 4).

4   Carefully check the large upper and lower radiator hoses along with the smaller diameter heater hoses which run from the engine to the firewall. Inspect each hose along its entire length, replacing any hose which is cracked, swollen or shows signs of deterioration. Cracks may become more apparent if the hose is squeezed **(see illustration)**. Regardless of condition, it's a good idea to replace hoses with new ones every two years.

5   Make sure that all hose connections are tight. A leak in the cooling system will usually show up as white or rust colored deposits on the areas adjoining the leak. If wire-type clamps are used at the ends of the hoses, it may be a good idea to replace them with more secure screw-type clamps.

6   Use compressed air or a soft brush to remove bugs, leaves, etc. from the front of the radiator or air conditioning condenser. Be careful not to damage the delicate cooling fins or cut yourself on them.

7   Every other inspection, or at the first indication of cooling system problems, have the cap and system pressure tested. If you don't have a pressure tester, most gas stations and repair shops will do this for a minimal charge.

12   Underhood hose check and replacement (every 6000 miles or 6 months)

Caution: *Replacement of air conditioning hoses must be left to a dealer service department or air conditioning shop that has the equipment to depressurize the system safely. Never remove air conditioning components or hoses until the system has been depressurized.*

General

1   High temperatures in the engine compartment can cause the deterioration of the rubber and plastic hoses used for engine, accessory and emission systems operation. Periodic inspection should be made for cracks, loose clamps, material hardening and leaks.

2   Information specific to the cooling system hoses can be found in Section 11.

3   Some, but not all, hoses are secured to the fittings with clamps. Where clamps are used, check to be sure they haven't lost their tension, allowing the hose to leak. If clamps aren't used, make sure the hose has not expanded and/or hardened where it slips over the fitting, allowing it to leak.

Vacuum hoses

4   It's quite common for vacuum hoses, especially those in the emissions system, to be color coded or identified by colored stripes molded into them. Various systems require hoses with different wall thickness, collapse resistance and temperature resistance. When replacing hoses, be sure the new ones are made of the same material.

5   Often the only effective way to check a hose is to remove it completely from the vehicle. If more than one hose is removed, be sure to label the hoses and fittings to ensure correct installation.

6   When checking vacuum hoses, be sure to include any plastic T-fittings in the check. Inspect the fittings for cracks and the hose where it fits over the fitting for distortion, which could cause leakage.

7   A small piece of vacuum hose (1/4-inch inside diameter) can be used as a stethoscope to detect vacuum leaks. Hold one end of the hose to your ear and probe around vacuum hoses and fittings, listening for the "hissing" sound characteristic of a vacuum leak. **Warning:** *When probing with the vacuum hose stethoscope, be very careful not to come into contact with moving engine components such as the drivebelts, cooling fan, etc.*

Fuel hose

Warning: *There are certain precautions which must be taken when inspecting or servicing fuel system components. Work in a well ventilated area and do not allow open flames (cigarettes, appliance pilot lights, etc.) or bare light bulbs near the work area. Mop up any spills immediately and do not store fuel-soaked rags where they could ignite. Since gasoline is carcinogenic, wear latex gloves. If any fuel contacts your skin, rinse it off immediately with soap and water. The fuel system is under pressure, so if any fuel lines are to be disconnected, the pressure in the system must be relieved first. When you perform any kind of work on the fuel system, wear safety glasses and have a Class B type fire extinguisher on hand.*

8   Check all rubber fuel lines for deterioration and chafing. Check especially for cracks in areas where the hose bends and just before fittings, such as where a hose attaches to the fuel filter.

9   High quality fuel line, meeting the manufacturer's original specifications, should be used for fuel line replacement. Never, under any circumstances, use unreinforced vacuum line, clear plastic tubing or water hose for fuel lines.

10   Spring-type clamps are commonly used on fuel lines. These clamps often lose their tension over a period of time, and can be "sprung" during removal. Replace all spring-type clamps with screw clamps whenever a hose is replaced.

Metal lines

11   Sections of metal line are often used for fuel line between the fuel pump and carburetor or fuel injection unit. Check carefully to be sure the line has not been bent or crimped and that cracks have not started in the line.

12   If a section of metal fuel line must be replaced, only seamless steel tubing should be used, since copper and aluminum tubing don't have the strength necessary to withstand normal vibrations.

13   Check the metal brake lines where they enter the master cylinder and brake proportioning unit (if used) for cracks in the lines or loose fittings. Any sign of brake fluid leakage calls for an immediate thorough inspection of the brake system.

13   Windshield wiper blade inspection and replacement (every 6000 miles or 6 months)

Refer to illustrations 13.3, 13.5 and 13.6

1   The windshield wiper and blade assembly should be inspected periodically for damage, loose components and cracked or worn blade elements.

2   Road film can build up on the wiper blades and affect their efficiency, so they should be washed regularly with a mild detergent solution.

3   The action of the wiping mechanism can loosen bolts, nuts and fasteners, so they should be checked and tightened, as necessary **(see illustration)**, at the same time the wiper blades are checked.

4   If the wiper blade elements are cracked, worn or warped, or no longer clean adequately, they should be replaced with new ones.

5   Lift the arm assembly away from the glass for clearance, press on the release lever, then slide the wiper blade assembly out of the hook in the end of the arm **(see illustration)**.

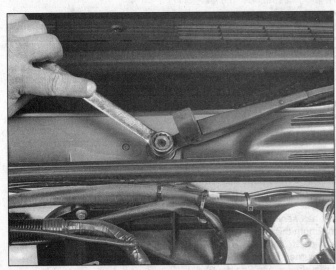

13.3 Tilt the trim cap back and check the tightness of the wiper arm retaining nuts

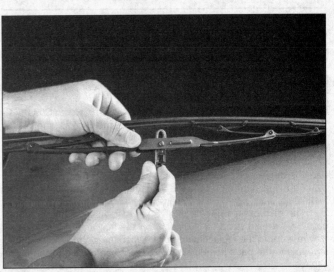

13.5 Press on the release tab and push the blade assembly down and away from the hook in the arm

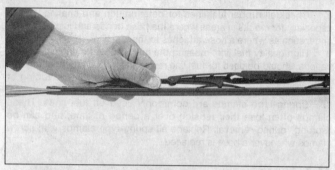

13.6 Use needle-nose pliers to compress the rubber element, then slide the element out - slide the new element in and lock the blade assembly fingers into the notches of the wiper element

6   Use needle-nose pliers to compress the blade element, then slide the element out of the frame and discard it **(see illustration)**.
7   Installation is the reverse of removal.

14   Tire rotation (every 6000 miles or 6 months)

Refer to illustration 14.2
1   The tires should be rotated at the specified intervals and whenever uneven wear is noticed. Since the vehicle will be raised and the tires removed anyway, check the brakes (see Section 15) at this time.
2   Radial tires must be rotated in a specific pattern **(see illustration)**.
3   Refer to the information in *Jacking and towing* at the front of this manual for the proper procedures to follow when raising the vehicle and changing a tire. If the brakes are to be checked, do not apply the parking brake as stated. Make sure the tires are blocked to prevent the vehicle from rolling.
4   Preferably, the entire vehicle should be raised at the same time. This can be done on a hoist or by jacking up each corner and then lowering the vehicle onto jackstands placed under the frame rails. Always use four jackstands and make sure the vehicle is firmly supported.
5   After rotation, check and adjust the tire pressures as necessary and be sure to check the lug nut tightness.
6   For further information on the wheels and tires, refer to Chapter 10.

15   Brake check (every 6000 miles or 6 months)

Warning: *The dust created by the brake system may contain asbestos, which is harmful to your health. Never blow it out with compressed air and don't inhale any of it. An approved filtering mask should be worn when working on the brakes. Do not, under any circumstances, use petroleum-based solvents to clean brake parts. Use brake system cleaner only! Try to use non-asbestos replacement parts whenever possible.*
Note: *For detailed photographs of the brake system, refer to Chapter 9.*
1   In addition to the specified intervals, the brakes should be inspected every time the wheels are removed or whenever a defect is suspected. Any of the following symptoms could indicate a potential brake system defect: The vehicle pulls to one side when the brake pedal is depressed; the brakes make squealing or dragging noises when applied; brake pedal travel is excessive; the pedal pulsates; brake fluid leaks, usually onto the inside of the tire or wheel.
2   The disc brakes have built-in electrical wear indicators which cause a warning lamp to illuminate on the instrument panel when they're worn to the replacement point. When the warning light comes on, replace the pads immediately or expensive damage to the discs can result.
3   Loosen the wheel lug nuts.
4   Raise the vehicle and place it securely on jackstands.

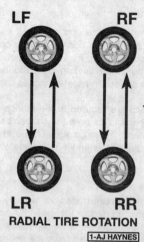

14.2 The recommended tire rotation pattern for these vehicles

15.6 You will find an inspection hole like this in each caliper - placing a ruler across the hole should enable you to determine the thickness of remaining pad material for both inner and outer pads

5   Remove the wheels (see *Jacking and towing* at the front of this book, or your owner's manual, if necessary).

Disc brakes

Refer to illustrations 15.6 and 15.11
6   There are two pads (an outer and an inner) in each caliper. The pads are visible through inspection holes in each caliper **(see illustration)**.
7   Check the pad thickness by looking at each end of the caliper and through the inspection hole in the caliper body. If the lining material is less than the thickness listed in this Chapter's Specifications, replace the pads. **Note:** *Keep in mind that the lining material is riveted or bonded to a metal backing plate and the metal portion is not included in this measurement.*
8   If it is difficult to determine the exact thickness of the remaining pad material by the above method, or if you are at all concerned about the condition of the pads, remove the caliper(s), then remove the pads from the calipers for further inspection (see Chapter 9).
9   Once the pads are removed from the calipers, clean them with brake cleaner and re-measure them with a ruler or a vernier caliper.
10   Measure the disc thickness with a micrometer to make sure that it still has service life remaining. If any disc is thinner than the specified minimum thickness, replace it (refer to Chapter 9). Even if the disc has service life remaining, check its condition. Look for scoring, gouging and burned spots. If these conditions exist, remove the disc and have it resurfaced (see Chapter 9).
11   Before installing the wheels, check all brake lines and hoses for damage, wear, deformation, cracks, corrosion, leakage, bends and

15.11 Check along the brake hoses and at each fitting (arrow) for deterioration and cracks

15.22 Measure the parking brake shoe lining thickness from the outer surface to the metal shoe

twists, particularly in the vicinity of the rubber hoses at the calipers **(see illustration)**. Check the clamps for tightness and the connections for leakage. Make sure that all hoses and lines are clear of sharp edges, moving parts and the exhaust system. If any of the above conditions are noted, repair, reroute or replace the lines and/or fittings as necessary (see Chapter 9).

Hydraulic brake booster check

12   Sit in the driver's seat and perform the following sequence of tests.
13   Start the engine, run it for about a minute and turn it off. Firmly depress the brake several times - the pedal travel should decrease with each application.
14   With the brake fully depressed, start the engine - the pedal should move down a little when the engine starts.
15   Depress the brake, stop the engine and hold the pedal in for about 30 seconds - the pedal should neither sink nor rise.
16   If your brakes do not operate as described above when the preceding tests are performed, the brake booster is either in need of repair or has failed. Refer to Chapter 9 for the removal procedure.

Parking brake

Refer to illustration 15.22
17   Slowly pull up on the parking brake and count the number of clicks you hear until the handle is up as far as it will go. The adjustment should be within the specified number of clicks listed in this Chapter's Specifications. If you hear more or fewer clicks, it's time to adjust the parking brake (refer to Chapter 9).
18   An alternative method of checking the parking brake is to park the vehicle on a steep hill with the parking brake set and the transmission in Neutral (be sure to stay in the vehicle during this check!). If the parking brake cannot prevent the vehicle from rolling, it is in need of adjustment (see Chapter 9).
19   However, every 24 months (or whenever a fault is suspected), the parking brake assembly itself should be visually inspected.
20   With the vehicle raised and supported on jackstands, remove the rear wheels.
21   Remove the rear discs as outlined in Chapter 9. Support the caliper assemblies with a coat hanger or heavy wire and do not disconnect the brake line from the caliper.
22   With the disc removed, the parking brake components are visible and can be inspected for wear and damage. The linings should last the life of the vehicle. However, they can wear down if the parking brake system has been improperly adjusted. There is no minimum thickness specification for the parking brake shoes, but as a rule of thumb, if the shoe material is less 1/32-inch thick, you should replace them **(see illustration)**. Also check the springs and adjuster mechanism and inspect the disc for deep scratches and other damage. For more information on the brake system see Chapter 9.

16   Fuel system check (every 6000 miles or 6 months)

Refer to illustrations 16.4 and 16.6
Warning: *Gasoline is extremely flammable, so take extra precautions when you work on any part of the fuel system. Don't smoke or allow open flames or bare light bulbs near the work area, and don't work in a garage where a natural gas-type appliance (such as a water heater or clothes dryer) with a pilot light is present. Since gasoline is carcinogenic, wear latex gloves when there's a possibility of being exposed to fuel, and, if you spill any fuel on your skin, rinse it off immediately with soap and water. Mop up any spills immediately and do not store fuel-soaked rags where they could ignite. The fuel system is under constant pressure, so, if any fuel lines are to be disconnected, the fuel pressure in the system must be relieved first (see Chapter 4 for more information). When you perform any kind of work on the fuel system, wear safety glasses and have a Class B type fire extinguisher on hand.*
1   If you smell gasoline while driving or after the vehicle has been sitting in the sun, inspect the fuel system immediately.
2   Remove the fuel filler cap and inspect it for damage and corrosion. The gasket should have an unbroken sealing imprint. If the gasket is damaged or corroded, install a new cap.
3   Working inside the engine compartment, inspect the fuel feed and return lines for cracks. Make sure that the threaded flare nut type connectors or hose clamps which secure the fuel lines to the fuel injection system are tight. **Warning:** *The fuel system pressure must be relieved before servicing fuel system components. The fuel system pressure relief procedure is outlined in Chapter 4.*
4   The fuel tank can be inspected from inside the rear trunk com-

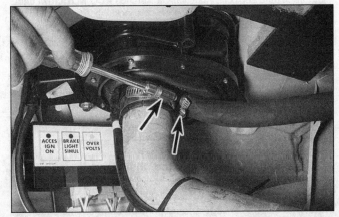

16.4 Inspect the fuel filler neck-to-body seal and the fuel vent hoses for cracks and deterioration - make sure the clamps are tight (arrows)

16.6 Carefully inspect any fuel lines that are routed through the rear suspension carrier for chafing

17.2 The differential check/fill plug is located on the rear of the differential housing - place your finger in the filler plug hole to make sure the lubricant level is even with the bottom of the hole

18.8a Check the steering gear boots for cracks and leaking steering fluid

partment. Inspect the gas tank and filler neck for punctures, cracks or other damage. The connection between the filler neck and the body is particularly critical. Sometimes the rubber seal around the filler neck will leak because of loose clamps or deteriorated rubber **(see illustration)**. Inspect all fuel tank mounting brackets and straps to be sure the tank is securely attached to the vehicle. **Warning:** *Do not, under any circumstances, try to repair a fuel tank (except rubber components). A welding torch or any open flame can easily cause fuel vapors inside the tank to explode.*

5   Since some of the components in the fuel system are located underneath the vehicle - the fuel filter, fuel pump and the majority of the fuel feed and return lines, for example - they can be inspected easier with the vehicle raised on a hoist or supported on jackstands.

6   With the vehicle raised and safely supported, Carefully check all flexible hoses and metal lines leading away from the fuel tank. Check for loose connections, deteriorated hoses, crimped lines and other damage **(see illustration)**. Repair or replace damaged sections as necessary (see Chapter 4)

---

17 Differential lubricant level check (every 6,000 miles or 6 months)

Refer to illustration 17.2

1   The differential has a check/fill plug which must be removed to check the lubricant level. If the vehicle is raised to gain access to the plug, be sure to support it safely on jackstands - DO NOT crawl under the vehicle when it's supported only by the jack!

2   Remove the lubricant check/fill plug from the differential **(see illustration)**. Use a 3/8-inch drive ratchet and a short extension to unscrew the plug.

3   Use your little finger as a dipstick to make sure the lubricant level is even with the bottom of the plug hole. If not, use a syringe or squeeze bottle to add the recommended lubricant until it just starts to run out of the opening.

4   Install the plug and tighten it securely.

---

18 Steering and suspension check (every 12,000 miles or 12 months)

Refer to illustrations 18.8a, 18.8b and 18.10
Note: *The steering linkage and suspension components should be checked periodically. Worn or damaged suspension and steering linkage components can result in excessive and abnormal tire wear, poor ride quality and vehicle handling and reduced fuel economy. For*

detailed illustrations of the steering and suspension components, refer to Chapter 10.

With the wheels on the ground

1   Park the vehicle on level ground, turn the engine off and set the parking brake. Check the tire pressures.

2   Push down at one corner of the vehicle, then release it while noting the movement of the body. It should stop moving and come to rest in a level position with one or two bounces. When bouncing the vehicle up and down, listen for squeaks and noises from the suspension components.

3   If the vehicle continues to move up-and-down or if it fails to return to its original position, a worn or weak shock absorber is probably the reason.

4   Repeat the above check at each of the three remaining corners of the vehicle.

Under the vehicle

5   Raise the vehicle with a floor jack and support it securely on jackstands. See *jacking and towing* at the front of this book for proper jacking points.

6   Check the shock absorbers for evidence of fluid leakage. Make sure that any fluid noted is from the shocks and not from any other source. Also check the rubber mounts at each end for deterioration. If the shock absorbers fail these tests, replace the shocks as a set.

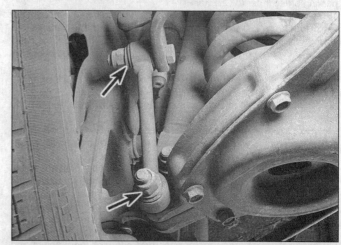

18.8b Check the stabilizer bar bushings (arrows) for deterioration (check all of the other suspension bushings, too)

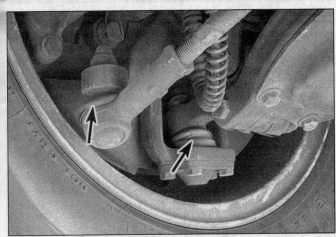

18.10 Inspect the balljoint and tie-rod end boots for tears - tears or damage in either boot will allow contamination of the grease which will lead to premature failure

7   Check the tires for irregular wear patterns and proper inflation. See Section 5 in this Chapter for information regarding tire wear.
8   Inspect the universal joint between the steering shaft and the steering gear housing. Check the steering gear housing for grease leakage. Make sure that the boots are not damaged and that the boot clamps are not loose **(see illustration)**. Check the steering linkage for looseness or damage. Look for loose bolts, broken or disconnected parts and deteriorated rubber bushings on all suspension and steering components **(see illustration)**. While an assistant turns the steering wheel from side to side, check the steering components for free movement, chafing and binding. If the steering components do not seem to be reacting with the movement of the steering wheel, try to determine where the slack is located.
9   Check the balljoints moving each lower arm up and down with a prybar to ensure that its balljoint has no play. If any balljoint does have play, replace it. See Chapter 10 for the front balljoint replacement procedure. Check the tie-rod ends for excessive play.
10   Inspect the balljoint and tie-rod end boots for damage and leaking grease **(see illustration)**. Replace the balljoints and tie-rod ends with new ones if they are damaged (see Chapter 10).

19   Chassis lubrication (every 12,000 miles or 12 months)

Refer to illustrations 19.1 and 19.6
1   Refer to *Recommended lubricants and fluids* at the front of this Chapter to obtain the correct types of lubricating grease. You'll also need a grease gun and other materials to properly lubricate the chassis **(see illustration)**. Occasionally plugs will be installed rather than grease fittings. If so, grease fittings will have to be purchased and installed.
2   Look under the vehicle and see if grease fittings or plugs are installed. If there are plugs, remove them and buy grease fittings, which will thread into the component. A dealer or auto parts store will be able to supply the correct fittings. Straight, as well as angled, fittings are available.
3   For easier access under the vehicle, raise it with a jack and place jackstands under the frame. Make sure it's safely supported by the stands. If the wheels are to be removed at this interval for tire rotation or brake inspection, loosen the lug nuts slightly while the vehicle is still on the ground.
4   Before beginning, force a little grease out of the nozzle to remove any dirt from the end of the gun. Wipe the nozzle clean with a rag.
5   With the grease gun and plenty of clean rags, crawl under the vehicle and begin lubricating all the front suspension components that are equipped with a grease fitting.
6   Lubricate the rear drive axles **(see illustration)**. Wipe the grease

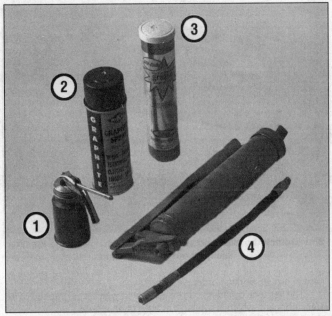

19.1 Materials required for chassis and body lubrication

1   *Engine oil* - Light engine oil in a can like this can be used for door and hood hinges
2   *Graphite spray* - Used to lubricate lock cylinders
3   *Grease* - Grease, in a variety of types and weights, is available for use in a grease gun. Check the Specifications for your requirements
4   *Grease gun* - A common grease gun, shown here with a detachable hose and nozzle, is needed for chassis lubrication. After use, clean it thoroughly

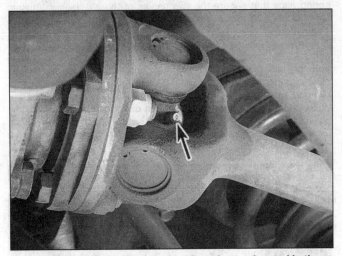

19.6 Grease fittings for the rear driveaxles are located in the center on each U-joint

fittings clean and push the nozzle firmly over it. Pump the gun until grease expels from the U-joint cap seal.
7   Wipe the excess grease from the components and the grease fitting. Repeat the procedure for the remaining fittings.
8   Clean and lubricate the parking brake cable, along with the cable guides and levers. This can be done by smearing some of the chassis grease onto the cable and its related parts with your fingers.
9   Open the hood and smear a little chassis grease on the hood latch mechanism. Have an assistant pull the hood release lever from inside the vehicle as you lubricate the cable at the latch.
10   Lubricate all the hinges (door, hood, etc.) with engine oil to keep

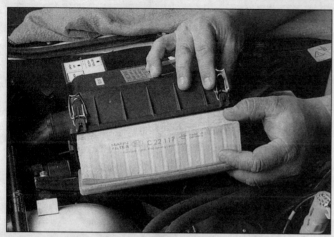

20.1 Detach the clips and separate the cover, then slide the filter element out of the housing

them in proper working order.
11   The key lock cylinders can be lubricated with spray graphite or sil-icone lubricant, which is available at auto parts stores.
12   Lubricate the door weather-stripping with silicone spray. This will reduce chafing and retard wear.

20   Air filter check and replacement (every 12,000 miles or 12 months)

Refer to illustration 20.1
1   The air filter is located inside a housing at the left (driver's) side of the engine compartment. To remove the air filter, release the four spring clips that secure the two halves of the air cleaner housing together, then lift the cover up and remove the air filter element **(see illustration)**.
2   Inspect the outer surface of the filter element. If it is dirty, replace it. If it is only moderately dusty, it can be reused by blowing it clean from the back to the front surface with compressed air. Because it is a pleated paper type filter, it cannot be washed or oiled. If it cannot be cleaned satisfactorily with compressed air, discard and replace it. While the cover is off, be careful not to drop anything down into the housing. **Caution:** *Never drive the vehicle with the air cleaner removed. Excessive engine wear could result and backfiring could even cause a fire under the hood.*

21.6 Dislodge the dust cap by working around the outer circumference with a hammer and chisel

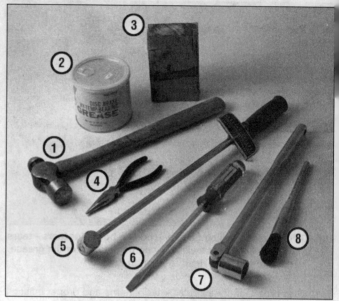

21.1 Tools and materials needed for front wheel bearing maintenance

1   **Hammer** - *A common hammer will do just fine*
2   **Grease** - *High-temperature grease that is formulated specially for front wheel bearings should be used*
3   **Wood block** - *If you have a scrap piece of 2x4, it can be used to drive the new seal into the hub*
4   **Needle-nose pliers** - *Used to straighten and remove the cotter pin in the spindle*
5   **Torque wrench** - *This is very important in this procedure; if the bearing is too tight, the wheel won't turn freely - if it's too loose, the wheel will "wobble" on the spindle. Either way, it could mean extensive damage*
6   **Screwdriver** - *Used to remove the seal from the hub (a long screwdriver is preferred)*
7   **Socket/breaker bar** - *Needed to loosen the nut on the spindle if it's extremely tight*
8   **Brush** - *Together with some clean solvent, this will be used to remove old grease from the hub and spindle*

3   Wipe out the inside of the air cleaner housing.
4   Place the new filter into the air cleaner housing, making sure it seats properly.
5   Installation of the cover is the reverse of removal.

21   Front wheel bearing check, repack and adjustment (every 12,000 miles or 12 months)

Check and repack
Refer to illustrations 21.1, 21.6, 21.7, 21.9, 21.15, 21.17, 21.19 and 21.20
1   In most cases the front wheel bearings will not need servicing until the brake pads are changed. However, the bearings should be checked whenever the front of the vehicle is raised for any reason. Several items, including a torque wrench and special grease, are required for this procedure **(see illustration)**.
2   With the vehicle securely supported on jackstands, spin each wheel and check for noise, rolling resistance and freeplay.
3   Grasp the top of each tire with one hand and the bottom with the other. Move the wheel in-and-out on the spindle. If there's any notice-able movement, the bearings should be checked and then repacked with grease or replaced if necessary.
4   Remove the wheel.

21.7 Remove the cotter pin and discard it - use a new one when the hub is reinstalled

21.9 Pull the hub assembly forward slightly - then push it back into position to dislodge the outer wheel bearing

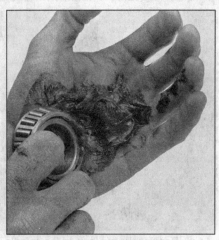

21.15 Work the grease completely into the bearing rollers

5   Remove the brake caliper (see Chapter 9) and hang it out of the way on a piece of wire. A wood block of the appropriate width can be slid between the brake pads to keep them separated, if necessary. Also remove the brake disc.

6   Pry the dust cap out of the hub using a screwdriver or a hammer and chisel **(see illustration)**.

7   Straighten the bent ends of the cotter pin, then pull the cotter pin out of the nut lock **(see illustration)**. Discard the cotter pin and use a new one during reassembly.

8   Remove the nut lock, nut and washer from the end of the spindle.

9   Pull the hub out slightly, then push it back into its original position. This should force the outer bearing off the spindle enough so it can be removed **(see illustration)**.

10   Pull the hub off the spindle. **Note:** *Sometimes the inner wheel bearing and grease seal remain attached to the spindle. Grasp the back of the seal with both hands and pull forward to remove them.*

11   If the grease seal is not already detached from the hub, use a screwdriver to pry the seal out of the rear of the hub. As this is done, note how the seal is installed.

12   If the inner wheel bearing is not already detached from the hub, remove it at this time.

13   Use solvent to remove all traces of the old grease from the bearings, hub and spindle. A small brush may prove helpful; however make sure no bristles from the brush embed themselves inside the bearing rollers. Allow the parts to air dry.

14   Carefully inspect the bearings for cracks, heat discoloration, worn rollers, etc. Check the bearing races inside the hub for wear and damage. If the bearing races are defective, the hubs should be taken to a machine shop with the facilities to remove the old races and press new ones in. Note that the bearings and races come as matched sets and old bearings should never be installed on new races.

15   Use high-temperature front wheel bearing grease to pack the bearings. Work the grease completely into the bearings, forcing it between the rollers, cone and cage from the back side **(see illustration)**.

16   Apply a thin coat of grease to the spindle at the outer bearing seat, inner bearing seat, shoulder and seal seat.

17   Put a small quantity of grease inboard of each bearing race inside the hub. Using your finger, form a dam at these points to provide extra grease availability and to keep thinned grease from flowing out of the bearing **(see illustration)**.

18   Place the grease-packed inner bearing into the rear of the hub and put a little more grease outboard of the bearing.

19   Place a new seal over the inner bearing and tap the seal evenly into place until it's flush with the hub **(see illustration)**.

20   Carefully place the hub assembly onto the spindle and push the grease-packed outer bearing into position **(see illustration)**.

Adjustment

Refer to illustration 21.23

21   Install the washer and spindle nut. Tighten the nut only slightly (no more than 12 ft-lbs of torque).

21.17 Apply a thin layer of grease to the inner and outer bearing races

21.19 After installing the inner wheel bearing into the hub - press the grease seal into place

21.20 Install the hub assembly onto the spindle - then push the grease-packed outer bearing into position

21.23 Position the nut lock on the spindle nut so that it lines up with the cotter pin hole - DO NOT loosen the spindle nut from its snug position

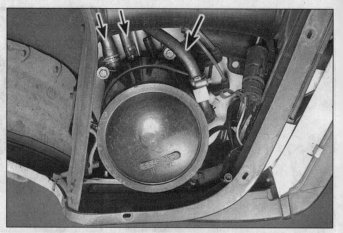

23.3 Check the charcoal canister for damage and the hoses (arrows) for deterioration

22   Spin the hub in a forward direction while tightening the spindle nut to approximately 20 ft-lbs to seat the bearings and remove any grease or burrs which could cause excessive bearing play later.
23   Loosen the spindle nut 1/4-turn, then using your hand (not a wrench of any kind), tighten the nut until it's snug. Install the nut lock and a new cotter pin through the hole in the spindle and the slots in the nut lock. If the nut lock slots don't line up, remove the nut lock and turn it slightly until they do **(see illustration)**.
24   Bend the ends of the cotter pin until they're flat against the nut. Cut off any extra length which could interfere with the dust cap.
25   Install the dust cap, tapping it into place with a hammer.
26   Install the brake disc and caliper in the reverse order of removal (see Chapter 9).
27   Install the wheel on the hub and tighten the lug nuts.
28   Grasp the top and bottom of the tire and check the bearings in the manner described earlier in this Section.
29   Lower the vehicle and tighten the lug nuts to the torque listed in this Chapter's Specifications.

22   Seat belt check (every 12,000 miles or 12 months)

1   Check the seat belts, buckles, latch plates and guide loops for any obvious damage or signs of wear.
2   Make sure the seat belt reminder light comes on when the key is turned on.
3   The seat belts are designed to lock up during a sudden stop or impact, yet allow free movement during normal driving. The retractors should hold the belt against your chest while driving and rewind the belt when the buckle is unlatched.
4   If any of the above checks reveal problems with the seat-belt system, replace parts as necessary. **Note:** *Check with your local dealer service department; the seat belt system should be covered under the factory warranty.*

23   Evaporative emissions control system check (every 24,000 miles or 24 months)

Refer to illustration 23.3
1   The function of the evaporative emissions control system is to draw fuel vapors from the gas tank and fuel system, store them in a charcoal canister and then burn them during normal engine operation.
2   The most common symptom of a fault in the evaporative emissions system is a strong fuel odor in the engine compartment. If a fuel odor is detected, inspect the charcoal canister.
3   The charcoal canister is located between the front bumper and

the left front fenderwell. Remove the front spoiler lower cover (see Chapter 11). Then check the canister and all hoses for damage and deterioration **(see illustration)**.
4   The evaporative emissions control system is explained in more detail in Chapter 6.

24   Fuel filter replacement (every 24,000 miles or 24 months)

Refer to illustrations 24.3 and 24.4
Warning: *Gasoline is extremely flammable, so take extra precautions when you work on any part of the fuel system. Don't smoke or allow open flames or bare light bulbs near the work area, and don't work in a garage where a natural gas-type appliance (such as a water heater or clothes dryer) with a pilot light is present. Since gasoline is carcinogenic, wear latex gloves when there's a possibility of being exposed to fuel, and, if you spill any fuel on your skin, rinse it off immediately with soap and water. Mop up any spills immediately and do not store fuel-soaked rags where they could ignite. The fuel system is under constant pressure, so, if any fuel lines are to be disconnected, the fuel pressure in the system must be relieved first (see Chapter 4 for more information). When you perform any kind of work on the fuel system, wear safety glasses and have a Class B type fire extinguisher on hand.*
1   The canister type filter is mounted underneath the vehicle on the left side frame rail just in front of the rear tire.
2   Depressurize the fuel system (see Chapter 4), then disconnect the cable from the negative terminal of the battery.
3   On 1988 through 1990 models, detach the banjo bolt from the

24.3 Remove the banjo bolt from the outlet side (B), detach the fitting from the inlet side (A) and unscrew the filter mounting bolt (C)

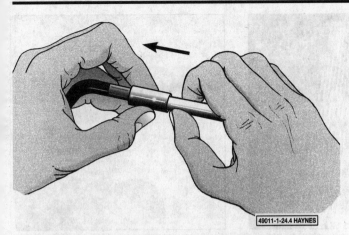

24.4 On 1991 through 1994 models, slide back the locking collars and remove the inlet and outlet fuel lines

outlet side of the filter then remove the union from the inlet side of the filter. Unscrew the filter mounting bolt and remove the filter **(see illustration)**.

4   On 1991 through 1994 models, the fuel filter has quick-disconnect fittings that do not require hand tools to remove. Simply slide back the locking collars and remove the inlet and outlet fuel lines **(see illustration)**. Detach the filter mounting bracket and discard the old filter in a proper container.

5   Note the direction of the arrow on the outside of the filter; it should be pointed towards the front of the vehicle. Make sure the new filter is installed so that it's facing the proper direction. **Note:** *Always install new copper washers where equipped.*

6   Install the inlet and outlet fittings then tighten the filter mounting bracket. Reconnect the battery cable, start the engine and check for leaks.

25 Spark plug check and replacement (every 24,000 miles or 24 months)

Refer to illustrations 25.1, 25.4a and 25.4b

1   Spark plug replacement requires a spark plug socket which fits onto a ratchet wrench. This socket is lined with a rubber grommet to protect the porcelain insulator of the spark plug and to hold the plug while you insert it into the spark plug hole. You will also need a wire-type feeler

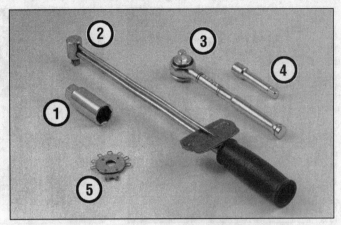

25.1 Tools required for changing spark plugs

1   **Spark plug socket** - *This will have special padding inside to protect the spark plug porcelain insulator*
2   **Torque wrench** - *Although not mandatory, use of this tool is the best way to ensure that the plugs are tightened properly*
3   **Ratchet** - *Standard hand tool to fit the plug socket*
4   **Extension** - *Depending on model and accessories, you may need special extensions and universal joints to reach one or more of the plugs*
5   **Spark plug gap gauge** - *This gauge for checking the gap comes in a variety of styles. Make sure the gap for your engine is included*

gauge to check and adjust the spark plug gap and a torque wrench to tighten the new plugs to the specified torque **(see illustration)**.

2   If you are replacing the plugs, purchase the new plugs, adjust them to the proper gap and then replace each plug one at a time. **Note:** *When buying new spark plugs, it's essential that you obtain the correct plugs for your specific vehicle. This information can be found in the Specifications Section at the beginning of this Chapter, on the Vehicle Emissions Control Information (VECI) label located on the underside of the hood or in the owner's manual. If these sources specify different plugs, purchase the spark plug type specified on the VECI label because that information is provided specifically for your engine.*

3   Inspect each of the new plugs for defects. If there are any signs of cracks in the porcelain insulator of a plug, don't use it.

4   Check the electrode gaps of the new plugs. Check the gap by inserting the wire gauge of the proper thickness between the electrodes at the tip of the plug **(see illustration)**. The gap between the

25.4a Spark plug manufacturers recommend using a wire-type gauge when checking the gap - if the wire does not slide between the electrodes with a slight drag, adjustment is required

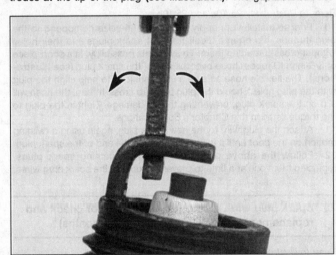

25.4b To change the gap, bend the side electrode only, as indicated by the arrows, and be very careful not to crack or chip the porcelain insulator surrounding the center electrode

25.6 When removing the spark plug wires, grasp only the boot and use a twisting/pulling motion

25.8 Use a spark plug socket with a long extension to unscrew the spark plugs

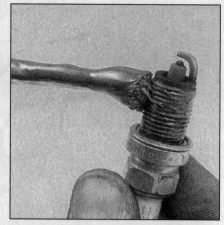

25.10a Apply a coat of anti-seize compound to the spark plug threads

electrodes should be identical to that listed in this Chapter's Specifications or on the VECI label. If the gap is incorrect, use the notched adjuster on the feeler gauge body to bend the curved side electrode slightly **(see illustration)**.

5   If the side electrode is not exactly over the center electrode, use the notched adjuster to align them. **Caution:** *If the gap of a new plug must be adjusted, bend only the base of the ground electrode - do not touch the tip.*

Removal

Refer to illustrations 25.6 and 25.8

6   To prevent the possibility of mixing up spark plug wires, work on one spark plug at a time. Remove the wire and boot from one spark plug. Grasp the boot - not the cable - as shown, give it a half twisting motion and pull straight up **(see illustration)**.

7   If compressed air is available, blow any dirt or foreign material away from the spark plug area before proceeding (a common bicycle pump will also work).

8   Remove the spark plug **(see illustration)**.

9   Whether you are replacing the plugs at this time or intend to reuse the old plugs, compare each old spark plug with the chart shown on the inside back cover of this manual to determine the overall running condition of the engine.

Installation

Refer to illustrations 25.10a and 25.10b

10   Prior to installation, apply a coat of anti-seize compound to the plug threads. It's often difficult to insert spark plugs into their holes without cross-threading them. To avoid this possibility, fit a short piece of 3/8-inch ID rubber hose over the end of the spark plug **(see illustrations)**. The flexible hose acts as a universal joint to help align the plug with the plug hole. Should the plug begin to cross-thread, the hose will slip on the spark plug, preventing thread damage. Tighten the plug to the torque listed in this Chapter's Specifications.

11   Attach the plug wire to the new spark plug, again using a twisting motion on the boot until it is firmly seated on the end of the spark plug.

12   Follow the above procedure for the remaining spark plugs, replacing them one at a time to prevent mixing up the spark plug wires.

---

26   Spark plug wire, distributor cap and rotor check and replacement (every 24,000 miles or 24 months)

Refer to illustrations 26.11a, 26.11b, 26.12a and 26.12b

1   The spark plug wires should be checked whenever new spark plugs are installed.

2   Begin this procedure by making a visual check of the spark plug

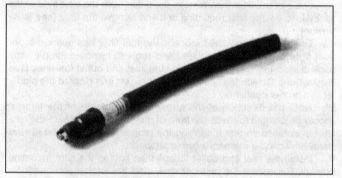

25.10b A length of 3/8-inch ID rubber hose will save time and prevent damaged threads when installing the spark plugs

wires while the engine is running. In a darkened garage (make sure there is adequate ventilation) start the engine and observe each plug wire. Be careful not to come into contact with any moving engine parts. If there is a break in the wire, you will see arcing or a small spark at the damaged area. If arcing is noticed, make a note to obtain new wires, then allow the engine to cool and check the distributor cap and rotor.

3   The spark plug wires should be inspected one at a time to prevent mixing up the order, which is essential for proper engine operation. Each original plug wire should be numbered to help identify its location. If the number is illegible, a piece of tape can be marked with the correct number and wrapped around the plug wire.

4   Disconnect the plug wire from the spark plug. A removal tool can be used for this purpose or you can grasp the rubber boot, twist the boot half a turn and pull the boot free. Do not pull on the wire itself.

5   Check inside the boot for corrosion, which will look like a white crusty powder.

6   Push the wire and boot back onto the end of the spark plug. It should fit tightly onto the end of the plug. If it doesn't, remove the wire and use pliers to carefully crimp the metal connector inside the wire boot until the fit is snug.

7   Using a clean rag, wipe the entire length of the wire to remove built-up dirt and grease. Once the wire is clean, check for burns, cracks and other damage. Do not bend the wire sharply, because the conductor might break.

8   Disconnect the spark plug wire from the distributor cap. Again, pull only on the rubber boot. Check for corrosion and a tight fit. Reinsert the wire in the distributor cap.

9   Inspect the remaining spark plug wires, making sure that each one is securely fastened at the distributor and spark plug when the check is complete.

10   If new spark plug wires are required, purchase a set for your spe-

26.11a Unsnap the distributor cap retaining clips - pull the cap up and away to access the rotor

cific engine model. Remove and replace the wires one at a time to avoid mix-ups in the firing order.

11   Detach the distributor cap by unsnapping the cap retaining clips. Look inside it for cracks, carbon tracks and worn, burned or loose contacts **(see illustrations)**.

12   Pull the rotor off the distributor shaft and examine it for cracks and carbon tracks **(see illustrations)**. Replace the cap and rotor if any damage or defects are noted.

13   It is common practice to install a new cap and rotor whenever new spark plug wires are installed. When installing a new cap, remove the wires from the old cap one at a time and attach them to the new cap in the exact same location **Note:** *If an accidental mix-up occurs, refer to the firing order Specifications at the beginning of this Chapter.*

27   Drivebelt check, adjustment and replacement (every 24,000 miles or 24 months)

Refer to illustrations 27.3a, 27.3b, 27.4, 27.6a, 27.6b and 27.11

Check

1   The drivebelts, or V-belts as they are sometimes called, are located at the front of the engine and play an important role in the

26.12a Pull off the rotor and inspect it thoroughly

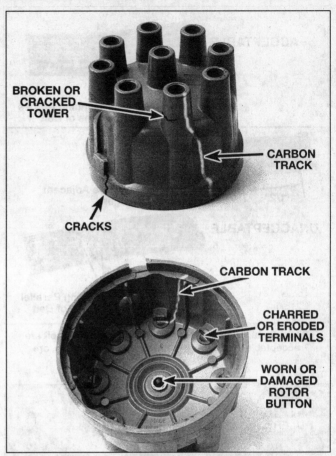

26.11b Shown here are some of the common defects to look for when inspecting the distributor cap (if in doubt about its condition, install a new one)

overall operation of the vehicle and its components. Due to their function and material make-up, the belts are prone to failure after a period of time and should be inspected and adjusted periodically to prevent major engine damage.

2   The number of belts used on a particular vehicle depends on the accessories installed. The main belt transmits power from the

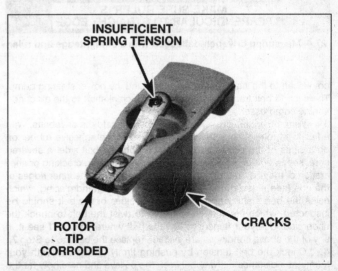

26.12b The ignition rotor should be checked for wear and corrosion as indicated here (if in doubt about its condition, buy a new one)

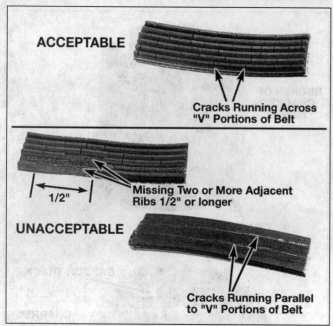

27.3a Small cracks in the underside of a V-ribbed belt are acceptable - lengthwise cracks, or missing pieces, are cause for replacement

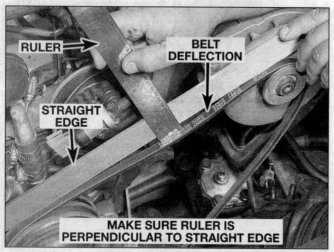

27.4 Measuring drivebelt deflection with a straightedge and ruler

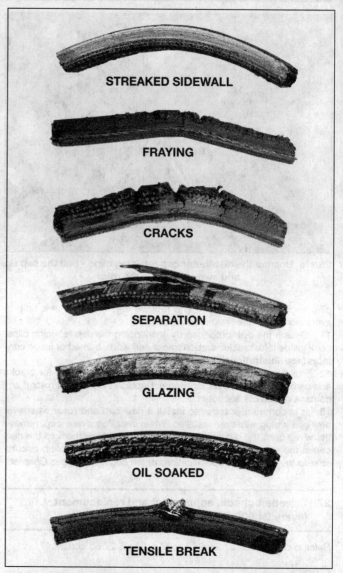

27.3b Here are some of the more common problems associated with V-belts (check the belts very carefully to prevent an untimely breakdown)

crankshaft to the water pump, alternator and the power steering pump. The second belt transmits power from the crankshaft to the air conditioning compressor.

3   With the engine off, open the hood and locate the drivebelts. With a flashlight, check each belt for separation of the adhesive rubber on both sides of the core, core separation from the belt side, a severed core, separation of the ribs from the adhesive rubber, cracking or separation of the ribs, and torn or worn ribs or cracks in the inner ridges of the ribs **(see illustrations)**. Also check for fraying and glazing, which gives the belt a shiny appearance. Both sides of the belt should be inspected, which means you will have to twist the belt to check the underside. Use your fingers to feel the belt where you can't see it. If any of the above conditions are evident, replace the belt (go to Step 7).

4   Check the belt tension by pushing firmly on the belt with your thumb at a distance halfway between the pulleys and note how far the belt can be pushed (deflected). Measure this deflection with a ruler **(see illustration)**. As a rule of thumb, if the distance from pulley cen-ter-to- pulley center is between 7 and 11 inches, the belt should deflect 1/4-inch. If the belt travels between pulleys spaced 12 to 16 inches apart, the belt should deflect 1/2-inch for a V-belt or 1/4-inch for a V-ribbed belt.

Adjustment

5   There are two belt tensioning mechanisms. The first one adjusts the air conditioning compressor belt which is accessible from underneath the vehicle. The second tensioning mechanism is located above the alternator - it adjusts the tension on the main belt (the water pump, alternator and power steering pump belt).

6   The air conditioning compressor and the alternator each have a belt tensioning mechanism and pivot bolt(s) which must be loosened slightly to enable you to move the component **(see illustrations)**.

7   After the bolts have been loosened, belt tension can be adjusted by either loosening or tightening the locknuts on the belt tensioning adjustment rod **(see illustration 27.6a and b)**. Move the component away from the engine to tighten the belt or toward the engine to loosen the belt.

8   Measure the belt tension using the method described in Step 4. Repeat this procedure until the drivebelt is adjusted properly.

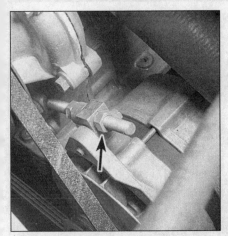

27.6a To adjust the alternator/power steering drivebelt, loosen the outer locknut (arrow) and the pivot bolt - turn the inner locknut counterclockwise to loosen or clockwise to tighten the belt

27.6b To adjust the air conditioning compressor drivebelt, loosen the outer locknut (arrow) and the pivot bolts - turn the inner locknut counterclockwise to loosen or clockwise to tighten the belt

27.11 When installing V-ribbed drivebelts, make sure the belt is centered between the pulley edges (arrows) - it must not overlap either edge of the pulley

Replacement

9   To replace a belt, loosen the drivebelt adjustment rod and pivot bolt as described above, slip the belt off the crankshaft pulley and remove it. If you are replacing the alternator/power steering pump belt, you'll have to remove the air conditioning compressor belt first because of the way they are arranged on the crankshaft pulley. Because of this and because belts tend to wear out more or less together, it is a good idea to replace both belts at the same time. Mark each belt and its appropriate pulley groove so the replacement belts can be installed in their proper positions.

10   Take the old belts to the parts store in order to make a direct comparison for length, width and design.

11   After replacing ribbed drivebelts, make sure that it fits properly in the ribbed grooves in the pulleys (see illustration). It is essential that the belt be properly centered.

12   Adjust the belt(s) in accordance with the procedure outlined above.

28   Cooling system servicing (draining, flushing and refilling) (every 24,000 miles or 24 months)

Warning: *Do not allow engine coolant (antifreeze) to come in contact with your skin or painted surfaces of the vehicle. Rinse off spills immediately with plenty of water. Antifreeze is highly toxic if ingested. Never leave antifreeze laying around in an open container or in puddles on the floor; children and pets are attracted by it's sweet smell and may drink it. Check with local authorities about disposing of used antifreeze. Many communities have collection centers which will see that antifreeze is disposed of safely.*

1   Periodically, the cooling system should be drained, flushed and refilled to replenish the antifreeze mixture and prevent formation of rust and corrosion, which can impair the performance of the cooling system and cause engine damage. When the cooling system is serviced, all hoses and the radiator cap should be checked and replaced if necessary.

Draining

Refer to illustrations 28.3, 28.4 and 28.5

2   Apply the parking brake and block the wheels. If the vehicle has just been driven, wait several hours to allow the engine to cool down before beginning this procedure.

3   Remove the expansion tank pressure cap (see illustration).

4   Move a large container under the radiator drain to catch the coolant. Then using a large screwdriver, open the radiator drain plug and direct the coolant into the container (see illustration).

28.3 Push the expansion tank pressure cap downward and rotate counterclockwise - never remove it when the engine is hot!

28.4 The radiator drain fitting (arrow) located at the bottom of the radiator

28.5 The block drain plug is located on the right side of the block (exhaust manifolds removed for clarity)

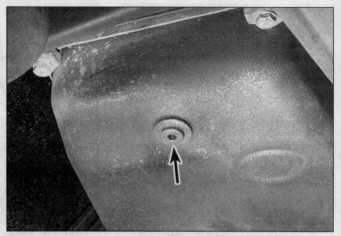

30.5 Using an Allen wrench remove the drain plug located in the bottom of the transmission pan

30.6a Unscrew the dipstick tube collar

5   After the coolant stops flowing out of the radiator, move the container under the engine block drain plug. Remove the plug and allow the coolant in the block to drain **(see illustration)**.

6   While the coolant is draining from the engine block, check the condition of the radiator hoses, heater hoses and clamps (refer to Section 11 if necessary).

7   Replace any damaged clamps or hoses (see Chapter 3).

Flushing

8   Once the system is completely drained, flush the radiator with fresh water from a garden hose until water runs clear at the drain. The flushing action of the water will remove sediments from the radiator but will not remove rust and scale from the engine and cooling tube surfaces.

9   These deposits can be removed by the chemical action of a cleaner. Follow the procedure outlined in the manufacturer's instructions. If the radiator is severely corroded, damaged or leaking, it should be removed (see Chapter 3) and taken to a radiator repair shop.

10   On 1988 and 1989 models remove the overflow hose from the coolant recovery reservoir. Drain the reservoir and flush it with clean water, then reconnect the hose (see Chapter 3).

Refilling

11   Close and tighten the radiator drain. Install and tighten the engine block drain plugs.

12   Make sure the heater temperature control is in the maximum heat position.

13   Slowly refill the expansion tank with a 55/45 mixture of antifreeze and water until the coolant reaches the base of the filler neck.

14   Leave the expansion tank pressure cap off and run the engine in a well-ventilated area until the thermostat opens (coolant will begin flowing through the radiator and the upper radiator hose will become hot). Race the engine two or three times under no load.

15   Turn the engine off and let it cool. Add more coolant mixture to bring the level back up to the base of the filler neck.

16   Squeeze the upper radiator hose to expel air, then add more coolant mixture if necessary. Reinstall the expansion tank pressure cap.

17   Start the engine, allow it to reach normal operating temperature and check for leaks.

29   Brake fluid change (every 24,000 miles or 24 months)

Warning: *Brake fluid can harm your eyes and damage painted surfaces, so use extreme caution when handling or pouring it. Do not use brake fluid that has been standing open or is more than one year old.*

Brake fluid absorbs moisture from the air. Excess moisture can cause a dangerous loss of braking effectiveness.

1   At the specified time intervals, the brake fluid should be drained and replaced. Since the brake fluid may drip or splash when pouring it, place plenty of rags around the master cylinder to protect any surrounding painted surfaces.

2   Before beginning work, purchase the specified brake fluid (see *Recommended lubricants and fluids* at the beginning of this Chapter).

3   Remove the cap from the master cylinder reservoir.

4   Using a hand suction pump or similar device, withdraw the fluid from the master cylinder reservoir.

5   Add new fluid to the master cylinder until it rises to the base of the filler neck.

6   Bleed the brake system as described in Chapter 9 at all four brakes until new and uncontaminated fluid flows from the bleeder screw.

7   Refill the master cylinder with fluid and check the operation of the brakes. The pedal should feel solid when depressed, with no sponginess. **Warning:** *Do not operate the vehicle if you are in doubt about the effectiveness of the brake system.*

30   Automatic transmission fluid and filter change (every 24,000 miles or 24 months)

Refer to illustrations 30.5, 30.6a, 30.6b, 30.7, 30.8, 30.10a, 30.10b and 30.10c

1   At the specified time intervals, the transmission fluid should be

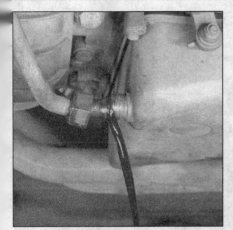

30.6b Detach the tube and let the remaining fluid drain

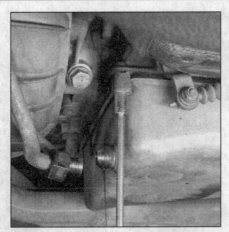

30.7 Use a socket and extension to remove the transmission pan bolts and brackets

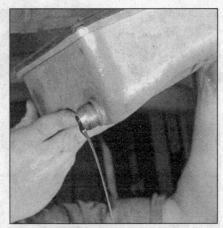

30.8 Lower the pan from the transmission

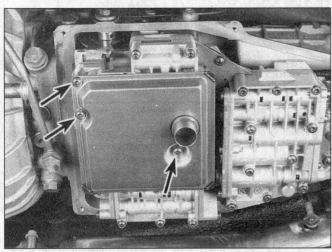

30.10a Use a Torx-head driver to remove the filter bolts (arrows) . . .

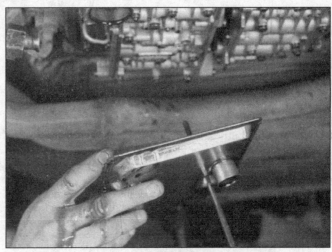

30.10b . . . then remove the fluid filter from the transmission

drained and replaced. Since the fluid will remain hot long after driving, perform this procedure only after the engine has cooled down completely.

2   Before beginning work, purchase the specified transmission fluid (see *Recommended lubricants and fluids* at the beginning of this Chapter) and a new filter.

3   Other tools necessary for this job include jackstands to support the vehicle in a raised position, a drain pan capable of holding at least eight pints, newspapers and clean rags.

4   Raise the vehicle and support it securely on jackstands.

5   Place the drain pan under the drain plug in the bottom of the transmission pan. Remove the plug and allow the fluid to drain **(see illustration)**.

6   Reinstall the drain plug, then move the drain pan underneath the dipstick tube. Loosen the dipstick tube collar and let the remaining fluid drain **(see illustrations)**.

7   Remove the pan mounting bolts and brackets **(see illustration)**.

8   Detach the pan from the transmission and lower it, being careful not to spill the remaining fluid **(see illustration)**.

9   Drain the remaining fluid from the transmission pan, clean it with solvent and dry it with compressed air. Be sure to clean the metal filings from the magnet, if equipped.

10   Remove the screws and detach the filter from the valve body **(see illustrations)**.

11   Install the new O-ring and filter, being sure to tighten the bolts securely.

12   Carefully clean the fluid pan-to-transmission sealing surface.

30.10c Be sure to remove the old O-ring from the transmission - always use a new O-ring when replacing the filter

13   Make sure the gasket surface on the transmission pan is clean, then install the gasket. Put the pan in place against the transmission and install the brackets and bolts. working around the pan, tighten each bolt a little at a time until the torque listed in this Chapter's Specifications is reached. Don't overtighten the bolts! Connect the dipstick tube and tighten the collar securely.

31.4 The differential drain plug (arrow) is accessible through a hole located in the middle of the differential support brace

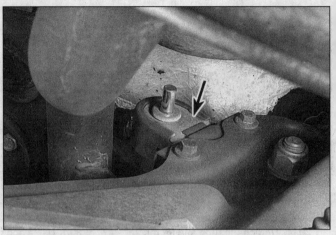

32.2 Check the exhaust system hangers (arrow) for damage and cracks

14   Lower the vehicle and add the specified amount of fluid through the filler tube (see Section 6).
15   With the transmission in Park and the parking brake set, run the engine at fast idle, but don't race it.
16   Move the gear selector through each range and back to Park. Check the fluid level.
17   Check under the vehicle for leaks after the first few miles of driving.

31   Differential lubricant change (every 24,000 miles or 24 months)

Refer to illustration 31.4
1   Drive the vehicle for several miles to warm up the differential lubricant, then raise the vehicle and support it securely on jackstands.
2   Move a drain pan, rags, newspapers and the required tools under the vehicle.
3   Remove the check/fill plug from the differential. If necessary refer to Section 17 for the check/fill plug location.
4   With the drain pan under the differential, use a ratchet and socket to loosen the drain plug **(see illustration)**. Note: *A special pipe plug socket may be required to complete this procedure.*
5   Once loosened, carefully unscrew it with your fingers until you can remove it from the case. Since the lubricant will be hot, wear a rubber glove to prevent burns.
6   Allow all of the oil to drain into the pan, then replace the drain plug and tighten it securely.
7   Refer to Section 17 and fill the differential with lubricant.
8   Reinstall the fill plug and tighten it securely.

9   Lower the vehicle. Check for leaks at the drain plug after the first few miles of driving.

32   Exhaust system check (every 48,000 miles or 48 months)

Refer to illustration 32.2
1   With the engine cold (at least three hours after the vehicle has been driven), check the complete exhaust system from its starting point at the engine to the end of the tailpipe. This should be done on a hoist where unrestricted access is available.
2   Check the pipes and connections for evidence of leaks, severe corrosion or damage. Make sure that all brackets and hangers are in good condition and tight **(see illustration)**.
3   At the same time, inspect the underside of the body for holes, corrosion, open seams, etc. which may allow exhaust gases to enter the passenger compartment. Seal all body openings with silicone or body putty.
4   Rattles and other noises can often be traced to the exhaust system, especially the mounts and hangers. Try to move the pipes, muffler and catalytic converter. If the components can come in contact with the body or suspension parts, secure the exhaust system with new mounts.
5   Check the running condition of the engine by inspecting inside the end of the tailpipe. The exhaust deposits here are an indication of engine state-of-tune. If the pipe is black and sooty or coated with white deposits, the engine is in need of a tune-up, including a thorough fuel system inspection.

Chapter 2 Part A Engines

Contents

Specifications

General
Cylinder numbers (front to rear)	1-2-3-4-5-6
Firing order	1-5-3-6-2-4
Displacement	
3.6L	3.6 liters (219 cu. in.)
4.0L	4.0 liters (243 cu. in.)

Camshafts and lifters
Journal diameter	26.9370 to 26.9494 mm (1.0605 to 1.0610 inches)
Bearing oil clearance	0.037 to 0.063 mm (0.0014 to 0.0024 inch)
Runout limit	0.0406 mm (0.0016 inch)
Lobe lift (maximum variation between lobes)	0.0127 mm (0.005 inch)
Valve lifter	
Diameter	33.34 to 33.35 mm (1.3126 to 1.3130 inches)
Oil clearance	0.020 to 0.050 mm (0.0008 to 0.0020 inch)
Valve lash/clearance	0.30 to 0.36 mm (0.012 to 0.014 inch)

Oil pump
Outer rotor to body clearance, maximum	0.2 mm (0.0079 inch)
Outer rotor OD	69.774 to 69.825 mm (2.7470 to 2.7490 inches)
Rotor thickness, inner and outer	27.962 to 27.975 mm (1.1008 to 1.1013 inches)
Clearance over rotors, maximum	0.1 mm (0.0039 inch)

Torque specifications*

	Nm	Ft-lbs (unless otherwise indicated)
Camshaft bearing cap bolts	23 to 27	16 to 20
Camshaft sprocket bolts	23 to 27	16 to 20
Crankshaft damper-to-crankshaft bolt		
3.6L	204	151
4.0L	180 to 220	133 to 162
Crankshaft pulley to damper bolts	23 to 27	16 to 20
Crankshaft rear oil seal retainer bolts	23 to 27	16 to 20
Crankshaft sensor bolts	23 to 27	16 to 20
Cylinder head bolts		
Step 1	60	44
Step 2	Tighten an additional 90-degrees (1/4 turn)	
Driveplate bolts	123 to 149	91 to 110
Engine mounts		
To engine block	49 to 66	36 to 39
To chassis	22 to 24	16 to 18
Exhaust manifold heat shield fasteners	23 to 27	16 to 20
Exhaust manifold nuts	23 to 27	16 to 20
Intake manifold nuts	23 to 27	16 to 20
Oil pump bolts	23 to 27	16 to 20
Oil pan bolts	23 to 27	16 to 20
Oil pan bolts, adapter to pan	49 to 54	36 to 40
Timing chain cover	23 to 27	16 to 20
Valve cover screws	10 to 12	89 to 106 in-lbs

*Note: Refer to Part B for additional specifications

1   General information

This Part of Chapter 2 is devoted to in-vehicle repair procedures for the inline six-cylinder engines. All information concerning engine removal and installation and engine block and cylinder head overhaul can be found in Part B of this Chapter.

The following repair procedures are based on the assumption that the engine is installed in the vehicle. If the engine has been removed from the vehicle and mounted on a stand, many of the steps outlined in this Part of Chapter 2 will not apply. We have photographed some in-car engine procedures with the engine on a stand for photographic purposes.

The Specifications included in this Part of Chapter 2 apply only to the procedures contained in this Part. Part B of Chapter 2 contains the Specifications necessary for cylinder head and engine block rebuilding.

During the years covered by this manual, two six-cylinder engines were installed in XJ-6 models, they include; the 3.6L (1988 and 1989) and the 4.0L engine (1990 through 1994). The two engines are almost identical (only the crankshaft stroke is longer on the 4.0L), and both incorporate dual overhead camshafts (DOHC) and four valves per cylinder.

2   Repair operations possible with the engine in the vehicle

Many repair operations can be accomplished without removing the engine from the vehicle.

Clean the engine compartment and the exterior of the engine with some type of degreaser before any work is done. It will make the job easier and help keep dirt out of the internal areas of the engine.

Depending on the components involved, it may be helpful to remove the hood to improve access to the engine as repairs are performed (refer to Chapter 11 if necessary). Cover the fenders to prevent damage to the paint. Special pads are available, but an old bedspread or blanket will also work.

If vacuum, exhaust, oil or coolant leaks develop, indicating a need for gasket or seal replacement, the repairs can generally be made with the engine in the vehicle. The intake and exhaust manifold gaskets, crankshaft oil seals and cylinder head gasket are all accessible with the engine in place (although rear oil seal replacement involves

removal of the transmission). The oil pan is difficult for a home mechanic to replace without a hoist and other specialized equipment, since the front suspension, steering and crossmember must be lowered to allow enough clearance for oil pan removal. If such equipment is not available, the alternative would be to remove the engine for replacement of the oil pan or oil pump. Note: We assume that the home mechanic does not have access to the specialized equipment, and have photographed our subject engine out of the car for some procedures.

Exterior engine components, such as the intake and exhaust manifolds, the water pump, the starter motor, the alternator, the distributor and the fuel system components can be removed for repair with the engine in place.

Since the cylinder head can be removed with the engine in-vehicle, camshaft and valve component servicing can also be accomplished. Replacement of the timing chains and sprockets is also possible with the engine in-vehicle provided the oil pan can be removed (see above).

3   Top Dead Center (TDC) for number one piston - locating

Refer to illustration 3.8

Note: The following procedure is based on the assumption that the distributor is correctly installed. If you are trying to locate TDC to install the distributor correctly, piston position must be determined by feeling for compression at the number one spark plug hole, then aligning the ignition timing marks as described in step 8.

1   Top Dead Center (TDC) is the highest point in the cylinder that each piston reaches as it travels up the cylinder bore. Each piston reaches TDC on the compression stroke and again on the exhaust stroke, but TDC generally refers to piston position on the compression stroke.

2   Positioning the piston(s) at TDC is an essential part of many procedures such as camshaft and timing chain/sprocket removal and distributor removal.

3   Before beginning this procedure, be sure to place the transmission in Neutral and apply the parking brake or block the rear wheels. Also, disable the ignition system by detaching the coil wire from the center terminal of the distributor cap and grounding it on the engine block with a jumper wire. Remove the spark plugs (see Chapter 1).

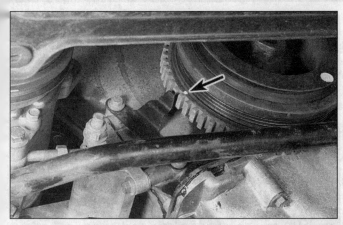

3.8 Align the mark on the crankshaft sensor ring (arrow) with the bottom edge of the pointer on the front cover

4   In order to bring any piston to TDC, the crankshaft must be turned using one of the methods outlined below. When looking at the timing chain end of the engine, normal crankshaft rotation is clockwise.

  a) *The preferred method is to turn the crankshaft with a socket and ratchet attached to the bolt threaded into the front of the crankshaft. Apply pressure on the bolt in a clockwise direction only. Never turn the bolt counterclockwise.*

  b) *A remote starter switch, which may save some time, can also be used. Follow the instructions included with the switch. Once the piston is close to TDC, use a socket and ratchet as described in the previous paragraph.*

  c) *If an assistant is available to turn the ignition switch to the Start position in short bursts, you can get the piston close to TDC without a remote starter switch. Make sure your assistant is out of the vehicle, away from the ignition switch, then use a socket and ratchet as described in Paragraph a) to complete the procedure.*

5   Note the position of the terminal for the number one spark plug wire on the distributor cap. If the terminal isn't marked, follow the plug wire from the number one cylinder spark plug to the cap.

6   Use a felt-tip pen or chalk to make a mark on the distributor body directly under the number one terminal (see Chapter 5).

7   Detach the cap from the distributor and set it aside (see Chapter 1 if necessary).

8   Turn the crankshaft until the small triangle cast into the front edge of the crankshaft sensor ring is aligned with the bottom edge of the timing pointer located at the front of the engine **(see illustration)**.

9   Look at the distributor rotor - it should be pointing directly at the mark you made on the distributor body. If so, you are at TDC for number 1 cylinder.

10   If the rotor is 180-degrees off, the number one piston is at TDC on the exhaust stroke.

11   To get the piston to TDC on the compression stroke, turn the crankshaft one complete revolution (360-degrees) clockwise. The rotor should now be pointing at the mark on the distributor. When the rotor is pointing at the number one spark plug wire terminal in the distributor cap and the ignition timing marks are aligned, the number one piston is at TDC on the compression stroke. **Note:** *If it's impossible to align the ignition timing marks when the rotor is pointing at the mark on the distributor body, the timing chain may have jumped the teeth or the pulleys may have been installed incorrectly.*

12   After the number one piston has been positioned at TDC on the compression stroke, TDC for any of the remaining cylinders can be located by turning the crankshaft and following the firing order. Mark the remaining spark plug wire terminal locations on the distributor body just like you did for the number one terminal, then number the marks to correspond with the cylinder numbers. As you turn the crankshaft, the rotor will also turn. When it's pointing directly at one of the marks on the distributor, the piston for that particular cylinder is at TDC on the compression stroke.

---

4   Valve cover - removal and installation

Refer to illustrations 4.2, 4.6, and 4.7

Removal

1   Disconnect the negative cable from the battery. **Caution:** *If the stereo in your vehicle is equipped with an anti-theft system, make sure you have the correct activation code before disconnecting the battery.*

2   Detach the PCV hose from the valve cover **(see illustration)**.

3   Remove the spark plug wires from the spark plugs, handling them by the boots and not pulling on the wires.

4   Remove the valve cover mounting screws, then detach the valve cover and gasket from the cylinder head. If the valve cover is stuck to the cylinder head, bump the end with a wood block and a hammer to jar it loose. If that doesn't work, try to slip a flexible putty knife between the cylinder head and valve cover to break the seal. **Caution:** *Don't pry at the valve cover-to-cylinder head joint or damage to the sealing surfaces may occur, leading to oil leaks after the valve cover is reinstalled.*

Installation

5   The mating surfaces of the cylinder head and valve cover must be clean when the valve cover is installed. If there's residue or oil on the mating surfaces when the valve cover is installed, oil leaks may develop.

6   Apply RTV sealant around the two half-circle rubber plugs at the rear of the cylinder head **(see illustration)**.

4.2 Disconnect the PCV hose (arrow) from the valve cover, then pull the spark plug wires out by their boots, not the wires

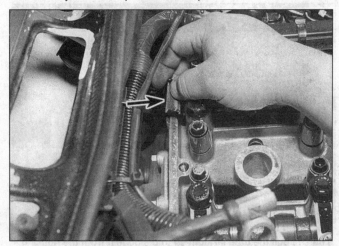

4.6 Apply a thin coat of RTV sealant to the half-circle plugs and insert them into the cylinder head before installing the valve cover

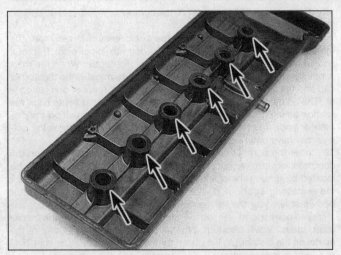

4.7 Press the valve cover gasket into the groove around the perimeter of the valve cover and install a new set of spark plug tube seals (arrows)

7   Using a new gasket and spark plug tube seals, install the valve cover **(see illustration).**
8   Tighten the screws to the torque listed in this Chapter's Specifications in three or four equal steps.
9   Reinstall the remaining components, start the engine and check for oil leaks.

---

5   Intake manifold - removal and installation

Refer to illustrations 5.3, 5.6a, 5.6b, 5.7a and 5.7b

Removal

1   Disconnect the negative cable from the battery. **Caution:** *If the stereo in your vehicle is equipped with an anti-theft system, make sure you have the correct activation code before disconnecting the battery.*
2   Refer to Chapter 4 to remove the accelerator and cruise-control linkage, safely relieve the fuel system pressure, and disconnect the fuel supply lines.
3   Label or mark and detach the PCV and vacuum hoses connected to the intake manifold, **(see illustration).**
4   The intake manifold can be removed with the injectors and fuel rail still in place. Simply disconnect the wiring connectors at each injector (label them first for reassembly). If the injectors are to be removed from the intake manifold, refer to Chapter 4.

5.3 The various hoses should be marked to ensure correct reinstallation

5.6a Remove the oil filler tube bracket nuts (arrows) . . .

5   Refer to Chapter 4 and remove the throttle body.
6   Remove the three nuts retaining the oil filler tube bracket, then pull the tube up as far as possible **(see illustrations).**
7   Remove the ground strap and intake manifold mounting nuts/bolts, then detach the intake manifold from the engine **(see illustrations).**

5.6b . . . pull the tube straight up to dislodge it from the housing - it won't come all the way out, but can be removed with the intake manifold

5.7a Remove the ground strap from the front stud (arrow), and the engine wiring harness clips from the other studs

5.7b Remove the intake manifold bolts/nuts and remove the intake manifold - the upper fasteners are studs/nuts, while the lower row are bolts (arrows indicate two showing here)

5.9 Install the new intake manifold gasket over the studs (arrows) install the manifold

Installation

Refer to illustration 5.9

8   Clean the mating surfaces of the intake manifold and the cylinder head mounting surface with lacquer thinner or acetone. If the gasket shows signs of leaking, have the manifold checked for warpage at an automotive machine shop and resurfaced if necessary.

9   Install a new gasket, then position the intake manifold on cylinder head and install the nuts/bolts **(see illustration)**.

10   Tighten the nuts/bolts in three or four equal steps to the torque listed in this Chapter's Specifications. Work from the center out towards the ends to avoid warping the manifold.

11   Install the remaining parts in the reverse order of removal.

12   Before starting the engine, check the throttle linkage for smooth operation.

13   Run the engine and check for coolant and vacuum leaks.

14   Road test the vehicle and check for proper operation of all accessories, including the cruise control system.

6   Exhaust manifolds - removal and installation

Refer to illustrations 6.3, 6.4 and 6.6
Warning: *The engine must be completely cool before beginning this procedure.*

Removal

1   Disconnect the negative cable from the battery. **Caution:** *If the stereo in your vehicle is equipped with an anti-theft system, make sure you have the correct activation code before disconnecting the battery.*

2   On 1990 and later models, disconnect the EGR pipe and remove the EGR valve from the top of the exhaust manifold (see Chapter 6).

3   Apply penetrating oil to the exhaust manifold mounting nuts/bolts, and the nuts retaining the exhaust pipes to the manifolds. After the nuts have soaked, remove the nuts retaining the exhaust pipes to the manifolds and the lower bolt from the heat shield **(see illustration)**.

4   Remove the heat shield from the exhaust manifolds **(see illustration)**.

5   Disconnect the electrical connector to the oxygen sensor. Unless the oxygen sensor is being replaced, leave the sensor in place.

6   Remove the nuts/bolts and detach the manifolds and gaskets **(see illustration)**.

Installation

Refer to illustration 6.8

7   Use a scraper to remove all traces of old gasket material and carbon deposits from the manifold and cylinder head mating surfaces. If the gasket was leaking, have the manifold checked for warpage at an automotive machine shop and resurfaced if necessary.

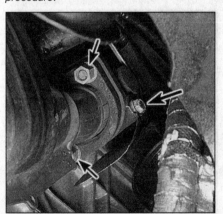

6.3 Remove the nuts (small arrows) retaining the exhaust pipe to the front and rear manifold flanges, there are two for each pipe - larger arrow indicates one heat shield bolt accessible from below

6.4 Remove the upper heat shield bolts (arrows)

6.6 Remove the bolts and nuts and remove the front and rear exhaust manifolds

6.8 Install new gaskets in position over the studs with the markings facing out

7.4 Use a large breaker bar and the appropriate size socket to remove the crankshaft pulley bolt

8   Position new gaskets over the cylinder head studs **(see illustration)**. **Note:** *The marks on the gasket should face out (away from the cylinder head) and the arrow should point toward the rear of the engine.*
9   Install the manifolds and thread the mounting nuts/bolts into place.
10   Working from the center out, tighten the nuts/bolts to the torque listed in this Chapter's Specifications in three or four equal steps.
11   Reinstall the remaining parts in the reverse order of removal.
12   Run the engine and check for exhaust leaks.

7   Crankshaft front oil seal - replacement

Refer to illustrations 7.4, 7.5, 7.7, 7.8, 7.9 and 7.11
1   Disconnect the negative battery cable. **Caution:** *If the stereo in your vehicle is equipped with an anti-theft system, make sure you have the correct activation code before disconnecting the battery.*
2   Refer to Chapter 1 and remove the accessory drive belts.
3   Refer to Chapter 3 and remove the fan shroud and fan clutch assembly.
4   Remove the crankshaft damper bolt with a socket and large breaker bar **(see illustration)**. To hold the crankshaft stationary, remove the flywheel inspection cover (see Chapter 8) and wedge a large screwdriver into the flywheel ring gear teeth. **Warning:** *The damper bolt is under considerable torque, so be sure the socket is firmly in place and that your hands are not in danger of hitting anything sharp.*
5   Use a bolt-type damper puller (available at most auto parts stores) to remove the crankshaft damper **(see illustration)**.

7   Remove the Woodruff key from the crankshaft keyway **(see illustration)**.
8   Carefully pry the seal out of the front cover with a screwdriver or seal-removal tool **(see illustration)**. Don't scratch the bore or damage the crankshaft in the process (if the crankshaft is damaged, the new seal will end up leaking).
9   The crankshaft seal rides on a spacer that slips over the front of the crankshaft. Slip the spacer off and clean the varnish off the seal surface **(see illustration)**.
10   Clean the bore in the cover and coat the outer edge of the new seal with engine oil or multi-purpose grease. Apply moly-base grease to the seal lip.
11   Lubricate the spacer with clean engine oil and install it onto the crankshaft. Using a socket with an outside diameter slightly smaller than the outside diameter of the seal, carefully drive the new seal into place with a hammer **(see illustration)**. Make sure it's installed squarely and driven in to the same depth as the original. If a socket isn't available, a short section of large-diameter pipe will also work. **Note:** *The new seal comes with a plastic installer guide. Do not remove this guide until installation is completed. The guide keeps the seal lip properly oriented over the crankshaft.*
12   Reinstall the Woodruff key, then install the damper. Tighten the damper bolt to the torque listed in this Chapter's Specifications. **Note:** *The damper bolt can be used to pull the damper back onto the crankshaft, but make sure the damper is perfectly aligned with the Woodruff key.*
13   The rest of the assembly is the reverse of the removal procedure.
14   Run the engine and check for oil leaks at the front seal.

7.5 After removing the center bolt, remove the crankshaft damper with a two-bolt puller - be careful not to damage the sensor ring

7.7 Carefully tap one end the Woodruff key up and out of the crankshaft keyway, then grasp it with a pair of locking pliers and pull it the rest of the way out - be careful not to damage the key or keyway

7.8 Remove the crankshaft seal with a screwdriver or seal puller - there are two slots (arrows) in the cover which allow you to pry behind the seal

7.9 Remove the spacer from the end of the crankshaft and clean it thoroughly

7.11 Drive the new seal squarely into the front cover with a large socket or section of pipe - do not remove the plastic installation guide (arrow) until the seal is installed

8   Timing chains and sprockets - removal, inspection and installation

Caution: *If the timing chain broke during engine operation, the valves may have come in contact with the pistons, causing damage. Check the valve clearance (see Section 10) before removal of the cylinder head - bent valves usually will have excessive clearance, indicating damage that will require machine shop work to repair.*

Note 1: *This procedure requires that the oil pan be removed (see Section 12). In a professional shop, this would be performed as an in-car procedure with specialized tools to remove the front suspension. Given the equipment available to the average home mechanic, this alternate procedure requires removal of the engine from the vehicle.*

Note 2: *If your engine is a 4.0L, built after serial number 9J160552, and you're experiencing an engine rattle on cold starts that disappears after the engine is warmed up, the problem could be a defective upper tensioner. A newly designed replacement upper tensioner is available from the dealer and should solve the problem. It can be installed easily without pulling the cylinder head or front cover, or can be installed during a chain removal procedure.*

Removal

Refer to illustrations 8.7, 8.9a, 8.9b, 8.10, 8.11, 8.12, 8.13, 8.15 and 8.16

1   Disconnect the negative cable from the battery. **Caution:** *If the stereo in your vehicle is equipped with an anti-theft system, make sure you have the correct activation code before disconnecting the battery.*

2   Block the rear wheels and set the parking brake.

3   Refer to Part B of this Chapter for engine removal procedures.

4   Refer to Section 4 and remove the valve cover.

5   Refer to Section 3 and position the engine at TDC for cylinder number 1, then mark and remove the distributor (see Chapter 5).

6   Refer to Section 11 and remove the cylinder head. After cylinder head removal, the upper timing chain will be loosely retained by the two upper chain guides, which are retained by installing a large rubber band (see Section 10). **Caution:** *Do not rotate the crankshaft with the upper timing chain disconnected and the cylinder head and camshafts in place, or damage could result from piston-to-valve contact.*

7   Some models may be equipped with a hydraulic pump used for the brake booster/hydraulic self-leveling suspension system. If equipped, it will be mounted to the front cover. Models not equipped with this option will have a flat block-off plate over the hole. If equipped with the pump, refer to Chapters 9 and 10 for procedures to reduce the high pressure in the brake booster system and to depressurize the self-leveling system. Before removing the engine, unbolt the pump from the front cover and set it aside without disconnecting the hoses **(see illustration)**.

8   Refer to Section 7 and remove the crankshaft pulley and damper. Refer to Section 12 for removal of the oil pan.

9   If equipped with the hydraulic pump, remove the coupling disc and unbolt the drive coupling from the intermediate shaft **(see illustrations)**.

8.7 Unbolt the hydraulic pump (arrow) from the front cover, without disconnecting the hoses

8.9a Pull the hydraulic pump coupling disc (arrow) off the drive coupling . . .

8.9b . . . and unbolt the drive coupling (arrow) from the intermediate shaft

10   Remove the front cover-to-engine block bolts **(see illustration)**. **Note:** *Two of the front cover bolts are water pump assembly bolts. Refer to Chapter 3 for water pump removal, although only the two bolts that attach to the engine block need be removed.*

11   Release the rubber band from the upper tensioners and remove the upper timing chain **(see illustration)**.

12   Remove the upper chain guides **(see illustration)**.

13   Unbolt and remove the lower timing chain tensioner **(see illustration)**.

14   Refer to Section 13 for removal of the oil pump sprocket and drive chain.

15   Remove the lower timing chain from the intermediate sprocket, auxiliary shaft sprocket and the crankshaft sprocket **(see illustration)**.

16   Before proceeding any further, apply timing marks on the crankshaft and the engine block, allowing you to locate TDC position without the crankshaft pulley in place **(see illustration)**.

Inspection

17   Examine the sprockets for signs of wear or damage. Replace the timing chain if obvious wear or damage is noted or if it is the least bit questionable. **Note:** *If there is wear or damage noticed in any of the sprockets or chains, the entire set must be replaced, i.e. new chains and new sprockets.*

18   Correct any problems which contributed to chain failure prior to installation of a new chain.

19   Check the chain guides for grooves, chips or wear in the contact surface. Clean and inspect the upper and lower tensioners.

8.10 Remove the front cover-to-engine block and oil pan-to-cover bolts (arrows)

Installation

Refer to illustrations 8.23a, 8.23b, 8.28a, 8.28b and 8.29

20   Remove all dirt, oil and grease from the timing chain area at the front of the engine.

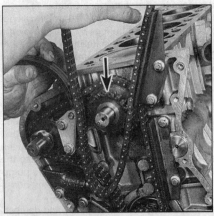

8.11 Remove the upper timing chain from the intermediate sprocket (arrow)

8.12 Unbolt and remove the upper chain guide (right arrow) and the upper chain tensioner guide (left arrow)

8.13 Remove the two bolts and remove the lower timing chain tensioner (arrow)

8.15 Remove the lower timing chain from the intermediate sprocket (A), the auxiliary shaft sprocket (B) and the crankshaft sprocket (C)

8.16 Apply paint marks on the crankshaft, crankshaft sprocket and the engine block (arrow) to indicate TDC position

8.23a Add oil to the reservoir in the lower tensioner . . .

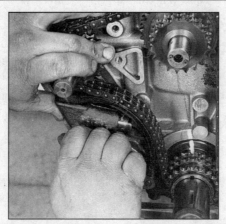

8.23b . . . and install the tensioner against the guide - after it's installed, push the tensioner guide back and forth a few times to prime the tensioner

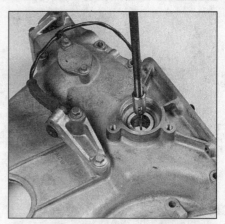

8.28a Drill a small hole in the intermediate shaft seal, thread a sheet metal screw into it and use a small slide-hammer pull the seal out of the cover

21   Recheck the crankshaft timing marks to be sure they are properly aligned **(see illustration 8.16)**.

22   Install the lower timing chain on the crankshaft, intermediate-shaft and auxiliary-shaft sprockets. The chain should be lubricated with engine oil.

23   Clean and lubricate the lower tensioner, fill the lower tensioner oil reservoir with engine oil and install it on the engine block, aligning the notch in the tensioner with the lug on the back of the guide **(see illustrations)**. This should remove all slack from the lower timing chain. If not, push the lower tensioner guide back and forth a few times to prime the tensioner.

24   Install the upper chain tensioner guide and mounting bracket to the engine block. **Caution:** *Before fully tightening the mounting bracket to the engine block, make sure the mount and chain guide are clear of the lower chain, auxiliary sprocket and intermediate sprocket. If necessary, position the mount for clearance before tightening the mounting bolts.*

25   Reinstall the oil pump drive chain and sprocket to the crankshaft (see Section 13).

26   Reinstall the upper chain fixed guide to the engine block and place the upper timing chain over the intermediate sprocket and auxiliary shaft sprocket, draping the excess chain over the top of the fixed guide. Lubricate the chain and sprockets with clean engine oil.

27   Gather the loose portion of the upper timing chain and place it

between the upper guides. Use a large rubber band to hold the two guides snugly around the chain (see Section 11).

28   If necessary, replace the intermediate shaft seal **(see illustrations)**.

29   Apply a thin coat of RTV sealant to the engine side of the front cover and RTV sealant to the oil-pan mating surface (bottom of the front cover), then install the front cover. **Note:** *Make sure the top surface of the cover aligns with the top surface of the engine block, by checking with a straightedge* **(see illustration)**.

30   Refer to Section 11 for installation of the cylinder head and Section 10 for installation of the camshafts and connection of the upper timing chain to the two camshaft sprockets.

31   The remainder of the installation is the reverse of the removal procedure. If your vehicle is equipped with the hydraulic/self-leveling suspension, install the drive coupling and coupling disc to the intermediate shaft **(see illustrations 8.9a and 8.9b)**. Coat the mounting surface of the pump with RTV sealant and make sure the tang on the pump aligns with the slot in the intermediate shaft before bolting the pump to the front cover. Refer to Section 7 for installation of the crankshaft spacer, damper and pulley. **Caution:** *DO NOT start the engine until you're absolutely certain that the timing chains are installed correctly. Serious and costly engine damage could occur if the chains are installed wrong.*

32   Run the engine and check for proper operation.

8.28b Drive the new seal in with a seal-driver or socket, to the same depth as the original seal

8.29 Bolt the front cover finger tight to the engine block, use a straightedge to make sure the cover's top surface is level with the top of the engine block, then tighten the cover bolts

9.3 Use a screwdriver to hold the drive coupling (arrow) stationary while removing the bolt

9.4 Remove the auxiliary shaft seal with a small slide-hammer puller

9.5 Use snap-ring pliers to remove the snap ring (arrow) from the shaft - note the three internal hex-head bolts retaining the housing to the engine block

9   Auxiliary shaft - replacement

Refer to illustrations 9.3, 9.4, 9.5, 9.8, 9.9, 9.10 and 9.11

Caution: *If the stereo in your vehicle is equipped with an anti-theft system, make sure you have the correct activation code before disconnecting the battery.*

1   Refer to Chapter 10 and remove the power steering pump, without disconnecting the hoses. Remove the plastic power steering pump drive coupling disc.

2   Refer to Section 8 and remove the front cover and upper and lower timing chains.

3   Remove the power steering drive coupling from the auxiliary shaft **(see illustration)**.

4   Use a small drill to drill holes in the oil seal, then use a slide-hammer puller to remove the seal from the rear of the auxiliary shaft housing **(see illustration)**. **Caution:** *Drill straight and carefully to avoid damaging the auxiliary shaft.*

5   Use a pair of snap-ring pliers to remove the snap ring from the rear of the auxiliary shaft **(see illustration)**.

6   Pull the auxiliary shaft out toward the front of the engine.

7   Remove the three internal hex-head bolts and the auxiliary shaft housing.

8   Examine the surface of the auxiliary shaft, it's sprocket, and the distributor drive-gear. If there is noticeable wear or damage, replace the auxiliary shaft assembly with a new one **(see illustration)**.

9   If the auxiliary shaft housing has been removed, clean it, scrape away the old gasket material from the housing and the engine block and install the housing with a new gasket **(see illustration)**.

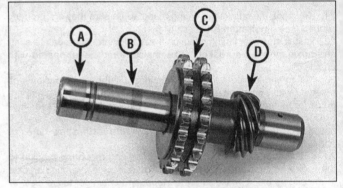

9.8 Inspect these areas of the auxiliary shaft for wear

A Oil seal surface	C Sprocket
B Bearing journal	D Distributor drive-gear

10   Clean the auxiliary shaft, lubricate it with engine oil and install it through the front of the engine block, then install the washer **(see illustration)**. Reinstall the snap-ring **(see illustration 9.4)**.

11   The new oil seal for the rear of the auxiliary shaft should come with a plastic installation sleeve that keeps the seal lip from folding back during installation. Keep this sleeve in place until the seal is fully installed. Tap the new seal into the housing with a hammer and appropriate-size socket until the seal is flush, then remove the plastic sleeve **(see illustration)**.

9.9 Install the auxiliary shaft rear housing with a new gasket, aligning the oil slot (arrow) with the housing

9.10 Install the washer before replacing the snap-ring

9.11 Tap the seal squarely into the bore with a socket until the seal is flush with the housing, then remove the plastic installation sleeve

10.4   Measure the valve clearance with a feeler gauge inserted between the heel of the camshaft lobe and the lifter

10.5   Position the camshaft alignment tool over each camshaft - the projection on the tool only fits into the slot on the camshafts when they are at TDC - flip the tool over to check the other camshaft

12   The remainder of the installation is the reverse of removal. **Note:** *When reinstalling the distributor* (see Chapter 5), *use a new O-ring to prevent oil leaks at the distributor.*
13   Run the engine and check for oil leaks at the power steering pump-to-housing interface.

---

10   Camshafts and valve lifters - removal, inspection and installation

---

Removal

Refer to illustrations 10.4, 10.5, 10.7, 10.10a, 10.10b, 10.11a, 10.11b, 10.12, 10.13, 10.14, 12.17 and 10.18
Note: *The replacement of the camshafts requires the use of several special tools. Read through the procedure and acquire the special tools, or their equivalent, before beginning work.*
1   Remove the valve cover as described in Section 4.
2   Refer to Section 3 and position the engine at TDC for number 1 cylinder.
3   Refer to Chapter 5 and remove the distributor cap and set it aside along with the spark plug wires. Mark the positions of the distributor body and rotor.
4   Using a feeler gauge, measure and record the clearance between the intake and exhaust camshaft lobes and the lifters for cylinder number 1 **(see illustration)**. Rotate the crankshaft until the next cylinder in the firing order is at TDC and check and record the valve clearance for that cylinder. Following the firing order, check and record the valve clearance for the remaining valves with the appropriate cylinder at TDC.

5   Return the engine to TDC for cylinder number 1. Using the special tool (Jaguar tool no. 18G 1433), check the position of each camshaft to ensure that they are truly at TDC **(see illustration)**. It may be necessary to rotate the crankshaft slightly, to allow the tool to fit into the slot. Once the camshafts are positioned, DO NOT rotate the crankshaft further.
6   Check the TDC marks made on the distributor body and refer to Chapter 5 for removal of the distributor. **Note:** *Plug the distributor hole with a rag or duct tape to keep out dirt.*
7   Locate the upper timing chain tensioner on the right front of the cylinder head. Loosen the bolt on the clamp and swing the clamp away from the tensioner return valve, then remove the valve **(see illustration)**.
8   Remove the tensioner bolts and pull out the tensioner.
9   The camshaft bearing caps are each retained by three bolts (the two front caps on each camshaft have only two bolts), of which one is a cylinder head bolt that threads into the engine block. If the camshafts are being removed as a step in cylinder head removal, the following steps involving spacer blocks are not required, just remove the bolts and caps, then remove the camshafts. If the procedure is being used for camshaft removal or adjustment of the lifter shims, the procedure must be followed exactly to maintain the cylinder head gasket seal.
10   To maintain a good seal on the cylinder head gasket, if the cylinder head is not being removed, a spacer block (Jaguar tool no. 18G 1435) is used to replace each camshaft bearing cap as it is removed. Begin by unbolting and removing intake cap no. 2. Remove the large cylinder head bolt first, then the cap bolts. Without delay, install a spacer block, with the cylinder head bolt, and tighten it to 53 Nm (39 ft-lbs) **(see illustrations)**.

10.7   Loosen this bolt (arrow) and swing the clamp away from the tensioner, then use pliers to pull the valve out

10.10a   As each cap is removed . . .

10.10b   . . . replace it with the special spacer block (arrow) and tighten the cylinder head bolt to 53 Nm (39 ft-lbs)

10.11a Each of the camshaft bearing caps are stamped with I (intake) or E (exhaust) and a number (arrows)

10.11b After the number 2 cap is replaced with a spacer, repeat the procedure for the remainder of the caps in the sequence shown - after cap 5 in the sequence, loosen caps 6 and 7 alternately until valve spring pressure is relieved from the camshaft

11   Repeat Step 10 with the remainder of the intake camshaft caps in sequence **(see illustrations)**. **Note:** *No spacer blocks are required with the number 1 camshaft caps.*

12   Remove the four bolts in each camshaft inner sprocket **(see illustration)**. The bolts are secured by sheetmetal "washer" plates. Bend down the locking tabs with a hammer and screwdriver tip to remove the bolts. **Caution:** *Stuff rags below the sprockets while removing the bolts to prevent a bolt from falling down into the front cover.*

13   Remove the two bolts retaining the upper chain guide to the cylinder head **(see illustration)**.

10.12 Bend back the locking tabs (arrows) and remove the camshaft sprocket bolts

14   Pull the inner sprockets from each camshaft **(see illustration)**. Each camshaft sprocket is comprised of an inner and outer, each with a set of fine splines that lock them together. The outer sprockets, with the teeth, can rotate on the camshafts until the inner sprocket bolts are tightened.

15   Pull the outer sprockets from the camshafts and allow the chain to slacken.

16   At this point the camshafts can be carefully lifted straight up and off the cylinder head. Take care not to nick any of the lobes or journals during removal.

17   Use a magnet to remove the lifters, keeping them in order in a divided, numbered box **(see illustration)**. They <u>must</u> be returned to their original location if reusing the original camshafts!

18   Removing the lifters exposes the adjusting shims, sitting in a pocket in each valve spring retainer **(see illustration)**. Keep the shims with their matching lifters. Measure the thickness of each shim with a micrometer and record the measurements.

Inspection

Refer to illustrations 10.20, 10.21a and 10.21b

19   After the camshaft has been removed from the engine, cleaned with solvent and dried, inspect the bearing journals for uneven wear, pitting and evidence of seizure. If the journals are damaged, the bearing surfaces in the cylinder head and caps may be damaged as well, requiring replacement of the cylinder head.

20   Measure the bearing journals with a micrometer to determine if they are excessively worn or out-of-round **(see illustration)**. Compare the measurements to Specifications.

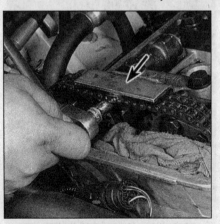

10.13 Remove the two bolts and the upper timing chain guide (arrow)

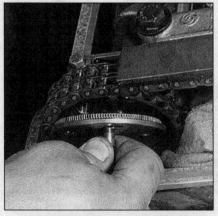

10.14 Pull the inner sprocket from the outer sprocket of each camshaft

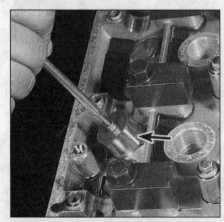

10.17 A magnet can be used to remove the lifters (arrow)

10.18 The valve adjustment shims (arrow) fit into a pocket in the valve spring retainer - use a magnet to remove the shims and keep them with their respective lifters

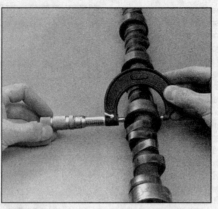

10.20 Measure the bearing journals with a micrometer to check diameter - measure at several places around the journal to check for taper or out-of-round

10.21a Measure the camshaft lobe at its greatest dimension . . .

21   Check the camshaft lobes for heat discoloration, score marks, chipped areas, pitting and uneven wear. Measure the lobe heights with a micrometer and record the measurements (see illustrations). If there is variance of more than 0.005-inch, the camshaft and lifters must be replaced. If the lobes are in good condition, the camshaft can be reused.
22   Inspect the top, bottom and side surfaces of the lifters for wear, grooving or scoring. If the lifters are damaged, the camshaft and its lifters must be replaced as a set.

Installation

Refer to illustrations 10.27a, 10.27b, 10.28 and 10.30

23   If the valve clearance for any valve is incorrect, as measured in Step 4, install a thicker or thinner shim on that valve. For example, if the clearance had been too large by 0.004-inch (compared to the recommended clearance in the Specifications), replace the existing shim with a new one that is 0.004-inch thicker. If the clearance was too tight, use a shim that is thinner than the original. Shims are identified alphabetically, in sizes from 0.085-inch (designated size A, the thinnest) to 0.108-inch (designated size X, the thickest).
24   Lubricate the lifters with a thin coat of moly-based lubricant on the top, bottom and sides and install them in their original positions.
25   Lubricate the camshafts with moly-based lube on the journals and lobes and lay them carefully in their bearing saddles.
26   Using NEW cylinder head bolts, replace the spacers, one at a time, with the bearing caps and bolts. Tighten the cap bolts, then the cylinder head bolts to the torque listed in this Chapter's Specifications. The front cap should be installed first, then cap number 7. Alternately tighten the first and last caps to bring the camshaft down evenly. Next, install cap numbers 4, 2, 3, 5, and 6.

27   Align the intake camshaft with the special camshaft positioning tool as described in Step 5. Engage the outer sprocket with the chain, slip the sprocket over the end of the camshaft, then turn it until there is no slack in the chain to the right of the camshaft sprocket (facing the front of the engine). Now align the inner sprocket with the camshaft until the bolt holes align and mesh the splines between the two sprocket halves (see illustrations). Tighten the inner sprocket bolts to the camshaft and bend the locking sheetmetal tabs over the bolts.

10.21b . . . and subtract the camshaft lobe diameter at its smallest dimension to obtain the lobe lift

10.27a Each camshaft sprocket is comprised of two sections, an inner (A) and outer (B) that are splined together

10.27b Push the outer sprocket over the intake camshaft until it locks in place - then turn the sprocket left to remove chain slack at the right

28   Keeping the slack in the chain to the left of the exhaust camshaft, install the exhaust camshaft outer sprocket, meshed with the chain, over the end of the exhaust camshaft. Insert the timing chain tensioner tool (Jaguar tool no. 18G 1436) at the upper tensioner mounting point **(see illustration)**. **Note:** *The chain tensioner tool applies pressure to the upper timing chain to simulate the effect of the tensioner, which is operated by engine oil pressure when the engine is running.*
29   Align the exhaust camshaft to TDC with the special timing gauge tool. Tighten the center bolt in the tensioner tool to 4 to 6 Nm (36 to 48 inch-pounds). When the chain is tensioned, align the inner exhaust sprocket with the bolt holes in the camshaft, engage the splines between the two sprocket halves and secure the sprocket with the bolts and locking tabs. Install the clip to secure the two sprocket halves together.
30   Clean the tensioner gasket surface and install a new gasket and O-ring. Push the ratchet down and twist it to maintain the fully retracted position, and install the tensioner in place of the tensioning tool **(see illustration)**. **Note:** *Align the slot in the end of the tensioner straight up and down to fit over the tang on the back of the chain tensioner guide. At this stage only tighten the front retaining bolt, leaving the remaining bolt and clamp loose.*
31   Insert an Allen key through the tensioner and release the snail ratchet by turning it counterclockwise. This will move the plunger against the timing chain under the force of the internal spring.
32   Clean the tensioner return valve and fit two new O-rings, then lubricate with engine oil and locate the valve in the tensioner body. Position the clamp over the valve and fully tighten both tensioner retaining bolts.
33   Rotate the engine and recheck that all valve clearance measurements are now correct (see Step 4).
34   The remainder of installation is the reverse of removal. **Note:** *When installing the distributor, use a new O-ring where it fits into the engine block.*

11   Cylinder head - removal and installation

Note: *The engine must be completely cool before beginning this procedure.*

Removal

Refer to illustrations 11.10, and 11.11

1   Disconnect the negative cable from the battery. **Caution:** *If the stereo in your vehicle is equipped with an anti-theft system, make sure you have the correct activation code before disconnecting the battery.*
2   Drain the coolant from the engine block and radiator (see Chapter 1).
3   Drain the engine oil and remove the oil filter (see Chapter 1).
4   Remove the hood for easier access, if necessary (see Chapter 11).
5   Remove the intake manifold (see Section 5).
6   Remove the exhaust manifolds (see Section 6).
7   Remove the valve cover (see Section 4).
8   Refer to Section 3 and position the engine at TDC for cylinder

10.28 The special tensioning tool simulates the operation of the oil-driven tensioner - apply 4 to 6 Nm (36 to 48 inch-pounds) pressure on the center bolt (arrow)

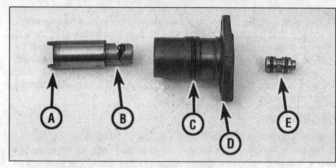

10.30 Upper timing chain tension components

A Notch (to align with tang on guide)	C O-ring
	D Gasket
B Tensioner ratchet	E Valve (with O-rings)

number 1. Remove the distributor (see Chapter 5).
9   Remove the camshafts and sprockets (see Section 10). Place the upper chain between the two upper chain guides and wrap a large rubber band around the two guides, retaining the chain and guides.
10   Remove the coolant housing from the cylinder head **(see illustration)**.
11   Remove the cylinder head-to-front cover bolts **(see illustration)**.
12   Using a socket and breaker bar, loosen the cylinder head bolts in 1/4-turn increments until they can be removed by hand. Loosen the cylinder head bolts opposite of the recommended tightening sequence **(see illustration 11.23)** to avoid warping or cracking the cylinder head.

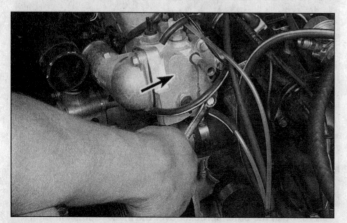

11.10 Disconnect the hoses and remove the bolts to separate the coolant housing (arrow) from the cylinder head

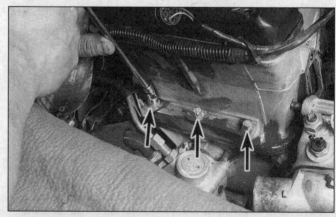

11.11 Remove the bolts (arrows) securing the cylinder head to the front cover

11.19 Remove the rear cover from the cylinder head, clean the gasket surfaces and reinstall the cover with a new gasket (arrow) - note that the side of the gasket with the printed-on sealer bead is placed against the cylinder head

11.20 Fabricate two alignment studs from old cylinder head bolts and install them in the engine block - after the cylinder head is installed, remove the two studs

13   Lift the cylinder head off the engine block. If it's stuck, very carefully pry up at the transmission end, beyond the gasket surface. **Caution:** *Though the cylinder head is aluminum, it is still heavy, large and awkward to handle. To avoid damaging the body during removal, use an engine hoist to lift the cylinder head out of the engine compartment, or have an assistant help you.*

14   With the cylinder head on a workbench, remove all external components from the cylinder head to allow for thorough cleaning and inspection. See Chapter 2, Part B, for cylinder head servicing procedures.

Installation

Refer to illustrations 11.19, 11.20, 11.21a, 11.21b and 11.23

15   The mating surfaces of the cylinder head and engine block must be perfectly clean when the cylinder head is installed.

16   Use a gasket scraper to remove all traces of carbon and old gasket material, then clean the mating surfaces with lacquer thinner or acetone. If there's oil on the mating surfaces when the cylinder head is installed, the gasket may not seal correctly and leaks could develop. When working on the engine block, stuff the cylinders with clean shop rags to keep out debris. Use a vacuum cleaner to remove material that falls into the cylinders. **Caution:** *Use care when cleaning the cylinder head gasket surface. The cylinder head and engine block are aluminum and can be easily damaged by sharp scraping tools. Gasket removal solvents are available from auto parts stores and are recommended for safe removal of gasket material.*

17   Check the engine block and cylinder head mating surface for nicks, deep scratches and damage from coolant corrosion. If damage is slight, it can be removed with a file; if it's excessive, machining may be the only alternative. See Part B of this Chapter for procedures and criteria concerning the repair of corrosion damage.

18   Use a tap of the correct size to chase the threads in the cylinder head bolt holes, then clean the holes with compressed air - make sure that nothing remains in the holes. **Warning:** *Wear eye protection when using compressed air!*

19   Remove the rear cover from the cylinder head. Clean the gasket surface and install the cover with a new gasket **(see illustration)**. Place the side of the gasket with the sealer bead against the cylinder head, do not use sealant on this gasket.

20   Fabricate two alignment studs from the old head bolts. Cut off the heads, then slot the ends with a hacksaw **(see illustration)**. New head bolts must be used to reinstall the cylinder head.

21   **Caution:** *There are variations in cooling holes in some models. Before installing the cylinder head gasket, carefully check all of the passages and bolt holes in the new cylinder head gasket to be sure it matches your engine block. Also make sure the new cylinder head gasket you're using is equipped with the improved oil transfer hole seal* **(see illustration)**. Position the cylinder head gasket over the dowel pins in the engine block, make sure TOP is facing up **(see illustration)**.

22   Carefully place the cylinder head on the engine block without disturbing the gasket.

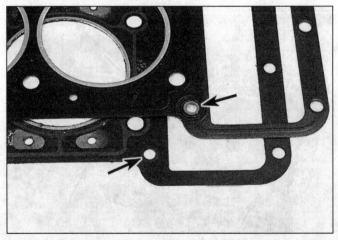

11.21a Only use a cylinder head gasket with the improved oil transfer seal (right arrow) - the older style (left arrow) is prone to oil leaks

11.21b Place the new cylinder head gasket over the dowels in the engine block - note the markings for UP or TOP printed on the gasket

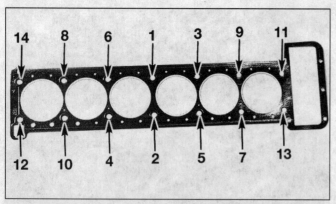

11.23 Cylinder head bolt TIGHTENING sequence

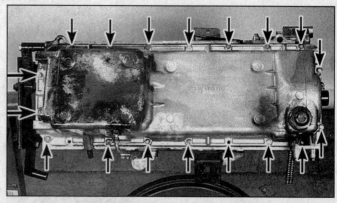

12.3 Remove the oil pan bolts (arrows)

23   Install NEW cylinder head bolts and following the recommended sequence, tighten the bolts in two steps to the torque listed in this Chapter's Specifications **(see illustration)**. Step 2 of the tightening sequence requires the bolts to be tightened and additional 90 degrees. An angle-torque attachment for your torque wrench is available at auto parts stores. This tool provides precision when the angle-torque method is required and its use is highly recommended. If the tool is not available, paint a mark on the edge of each cylinder head bolt and tighten the bolt until the mark is 90 degrees from the starting point. After the cylinder head bolts are tightened, tighten the cylinder head-to-timing-cover bolts.

24   The remaining installation steps are the reverse of removal. Refer to Section 10 for replacing the camshaft sprockets and adjusting the timing chain and tensioner. Refill the cooling system (see Chapter 1).

25   Run the engine and check for oil or coolant leaks. Adjust the ignition timing (see Chapter 5) and road test the vehicle.

12   Oil pan - removal and installation

Removal

Refer to illustrations 12.3 and 12.4

1   **Note:** *The oil pan cannot be removed with the engine in the chassis without lowering the front suspension and crossmember. This is a difficult procedure for the home mechanic without a vehicle hoist and some other specialized tools. The other alternative requires the engine be removed from the vehicle and mounted on a stand, as we have illustrated here. Refer to Part B of this Chapter for engine removal procedures.*

2   Drain the engine oil and remove the oil filter (see Chapter 1).

3   Remove the bolts and detach the oil pan **(see illustration)**.

4   If it's stuck, pry it loose very carefully with a small screwdriver or putty knife **(see illustration)**. Don't damage the mating surfaces of the pan and engine block or oil leaks could develop.

Installation

Refer to illustrations 12.8, 12.9 and 12.10

5   Remove all traces of old gasket material and sealant from the engine block and oil pan. Clean the mating surface with lacquer thinner or acetone. **Caution:** *Do not use a sharp scraping tool. Both the oil pan and the engine block are aluminum and could be easily damaged.*

6   Make sure the threaded bolt holes in the engine block and bell-housing are clean.

7   Inspect the flange of the oil pan for any cracks, pits or scratches that could cause an oil leak.

8   Remove the baffle plate at the rear of the oil pan **(see illustration)**. Clean the sump area and the baffle, then reinstall the baffle.

9   Inspect the oil pump pickup tube for cracks, or foreign material blocking the screen **(see illustration)**.

10   Apply a bead of RTV sealant to the oil pan flange **(see illustration)**. **Note:** *The oil pan must be installed within 5 minutes of sealer application.*

11   Carefully position the oil pan on the engine block and push it toward the transmission adapter plate as you press it against the engine block. Loosely install four bolts, two on each side of the oil pan. Tighten the four bolts in a criss-cross pattern to the torque listed in this Chapter's Specifications, then loosen each bolt 90-degrees.

12   Install the two engine adapter-to-oil pan bolts. Tighten the two bolts to the torque listed in this Chapter's Specifications, then loosen each one 180-degrees.

12.4 Pry at the recess in the front of the oil pan to break the gasket seal - insert a putty knife, if necessary, between the oil pan and engine block

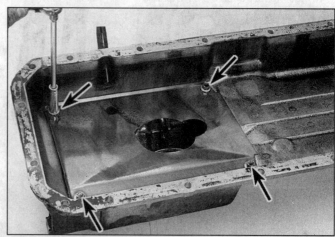

12.8 Remove the bolts (arrows) and the sheetmetal baffle plate - clean the sump area of the oil pan with the baffle removed

13 Install the remainder of the oil pan-to-engine block bolts hand tight until all are installed, then tighten them to the torque listed in this Chapter's Specifications. Lastly, tighten the two adapter-to-oil pan bolts to the torque listed in this Chapter's Specifications. **Caution:** *Failure to follow this tightening procedure could stress or possibly crack the adapter plate.*

14 The remainder of installation is the reverse of removal. Be sure to add oil and install a new oil filter.

15 Run the engine and check for oil pressure and leaks.

13 Oil pump - removal, inspection and installation

Removal

Refer to illustrations 13.2, 13.4, 13.7a and 13.7b

1 Remove the oil pan (see Section 12).

2 Unbolt the oil pickup tube and oil transfer housing from the engine block **(see illustration)**. **Note:** *Have a drain pan handy under the transfer housing, as oil may drip out when the housing is loosened from the engine block.*

3 Pull the transfer housing and transfer tubes to the rear to separate them from the oil pump body.

4 Bend back the locking tabs and remove the three bolts retaining the oil pump drive sprocket to the oil pump **(see illustration)**. Pull the chain and sprocket from the front of the pump. **Note:** *There are shims between the sprocket and the pump. Collect them while pulling off the sprocket.*

12.9 Lubrication system components

A	Oil pump	C	Transfer housing
B	Transfer tubes	D	Oil pump pickup

5 Remove the bolts and detach the oil pump from the engine.

6 Remove all traces of sealant and old gasket material from the oil pump body and engine block, then clean the mating surfaces with lacquer thinner or acetone.

7 Remove the screws and separate the front and rear pump covers from the body. Lift out the drive and driven rotors **(see illustrations)**. **Note:** *Mark the front face of each rotor before removing them.*

12.10 Apply a bead of RTV sealant around the perimeter of the oil pan mounting flange, be sure to run the bead around the outside of all the bolt holes

13.2 Unbolt the oil pump pickup (A) and the bolts (B) retaining the transfer assembly (C) to the engine block

13.4 Pry back the locking tabs and remove the three bolts retaining the oil pump drive sprocket to the pump

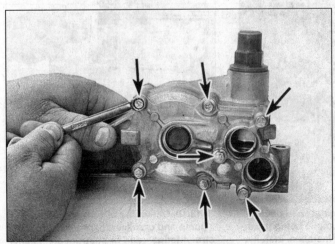

13.7a Remove the bolts and separate the front and rear pump covers

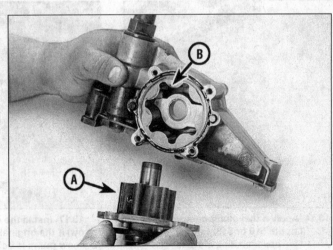

13.7b Remove the outer rotor (A) and inner rotor (B)

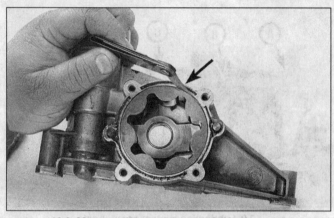

**13.9 Measure the outer rotor-to-body clearance
with feeler gauges (arrow)**

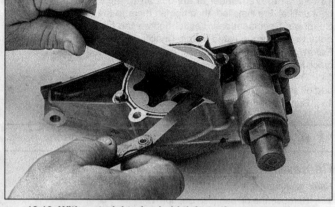

**13.10 With a straightedge held tight to the pump surface,
measure the clearance over the rotors with feeler gauges**

Inspection

Refer to illustrations 13.9, 13.10 and 13.11

8   Clean and dry the pump body and both rotors. Measure the outside diameter of the outer rotor and thickness of both rotors.

9   Place the outer rotor into the pump body and use feeler gauges to measure the clearance between the outer rotor and the body **(see illustration)**.

10   Place a straightedge across the pump body and measure between the straightedge and the rotors to check the over-the-rotor clearance **(see illustration)**. Compare your measurements to this Chapter's Specifications and replace the oil pump if any are beyond the maximum allowable.

11   Remove the oil pressure relief valve cap. Remove and clean the relief valve components **(see illustration)**.

12   Clean all components with solvent and inspect them for wear and damage. If excessive wear, damage or if any clearance is beyond the Specifications, replace the entire pump as an assembly.

13   Check the oil pressure relief valve piston sliding surface and valve spring. If either the spring or the valve is damaged, they must be replaced as a set.

Installation

Refer to illustrations 13.14, 13.17 and 13.18

14   Lubricate the drive and driven rotors with clean engine oil and place them in the case with the marks facing out. Apply a thin coat of anaerobic sealant (Loctite 510 or 518) to the gasket flange and install the cover **(see illustration)**.

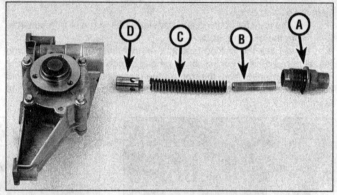

13.11 Oil pressure relief valve components

A *Relief valve cap*	C *Spring*
B *Tube*	D *Valve*

15   Lubricate the oil pressure relief valve piston with clean engine oil and reinstall the valve components into the oil pump body **(see illustration 13.11)**.

16   Apply a thin coat of anaerobic sealant (Loctite 510 or 518) to the oil pump-to-engine block-mounting surface, position the oil pump body against the engine block and install the mounting bolts, tightening the bolts to the torque listed in this Chapter's Specifications. Follow a criss-cross pattern when tightening the bolts to avoid warping the oil pump body.

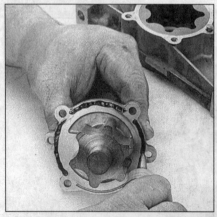

**13.14 Apply a thin coat anaerobic sealant
(Loctite 510 or 518) to the pump
cover sealing surface**

**13.17 Install the original shim pack
(arrow) if the original pump is being used -
if a new pump is being installed, install a
0.38 mm (0.015-inch) shim pack**

**13.18 Check the alignment of the oil
pump and crankshaft sprockets with a
straightedge - add or subtract shims until
the sprockets are aligned for smooth
operation of the chain**

14.2 Mark the driveplate and the crankshaft so they can be reassembled in the same relative position

14.3 Use a screwdriver to secure the flywheel while the bolts are removed

14.4 Pry off the driveplate spacer (arrow) - if a driveplate is replaced, the spacer should be replaced also

17   If using the original oil pump, install the original sprocket shim pack **(see illustration)**. If a new pump is installed, start with a 0.38 mm (0.015-inch) thick shim pack, install the drive sprocket and align the sprocket as follows:

18   Use a straightedge to check the alignment of the oil pump sprocket with the crankshaft sprocket **(see illustration)**. If they are not aligned, increase or decrease the shim pack at the oil pump sprocket until alignment is correct, then secure the oil pump sprocket bolts by bending up the sheetmetal tabs. **Note:** *You may be able to use all or part of the original shim pack from the original oil pump (if the pump is being replaced with a new unit). If necessary, shims are available in 0.127 mm (0.005 inch), 0.254 mm (0.010 inch) and 0.508 mm (0.020 inch) sizes.*

19   Install new O-rings to each end of the transfer tubes and install the tubes into the transfer housing. **Note:** *Use petroleum jelly to lubricate the O-rings.*

20   Apply a thin coat of RTV sealant to the engine block-mounting surface of the transfer housing. Lift the transfer housing and tubes into place and push the front of the tubes into the back of the oil pump, until you can start the transfer housing-to-engine block bolts. Tighten the bolts to the torque listed in this Chapter's Specifications.

21   Reinstall the remaining parts in the reverse order of removal.

22   Add oil, start the engine and check for oil pressure and leaks.

23   Recheck the engine oil level.

14   Driveplate - removal and installation

Refer to illustrations 14.2, 14.3 and 14.4

Removal

1   Raise the vehicle and support it securely on jackstands, then refer to Chapter 7 and remove the transmission. If it's leaking, now would be a very good time to replace the front pump seal/O-ring.

2   Use a center punch or paint to make alignment marks on the driveplate and crankshaft to ensure correct alignment during reinstallation **(see illustration)**.

3   Remove the bolts that secure the driveplate to the crankshaft. If the crankshaft turns, wedge a screwdriver through a hole in the driveplate to keep it from turning **(see illustration)**.

4   Remove the driveplate from the crankshaft. A spacer is located behind the driveplate **(see illustration)**. Pry it off and store it with the driveplate. **Warning:** *The ring-gear teeth may be sharp, wear gloves to protect your hands when handling the driveplate.*

Installation

5   Clean the driveplate to remove grease and oil. Inspect the surface for cracks. Check for cracked and broken ring gear teeth. **Note:** *If there is any damage to the driveplate, replace the driveplate with a new*

driveplate, a new spacer and new bolts. Improved parts are available as a set from the dealer.

6   Clean and inspect the mating surfaces of the driveplate and the crankshaft. If the crankshaft rear seal is leaking, replace it before reinstalling the driveplate (see Section 15).

7   Position the driveplate against the crankshaft. Be sure to align the marks made during removal. Some models may have an alignment dowel or staggered bolt holes to ensure correct installation. Before installing the bolts, apply thread-locking compound to the bolt threads.

8   Wedge a screwdriver in the ring gear teeth to keep the driveplate from turning and tighten the bolts to the torque listed in this Chapter's Specifications. Follow a criss-cross pattern and work up to the final torque in three or four steps.

9   The remainder of installation is the reverse of the removal procedure.

15   Crankshaft rear oil seal - replacement

Refer to illustrations 15.2, 15.3, 15.4, 15.5 and 15.6

1   The transmission, adapter plate and driveplate must be removed from the vehicle for this procedure (see Chapter 7).

2   Remove the bolts and detach the oil seal retainer. Remove the gasket material from the engine block and the seal retainer **(see illustration)**.

3   Position the oil seal and retainer assembly between two wood blocks on a workbench and drive the old seal out from the backside **(see illustration)**.

15.2 Remove the bolts (arrows) and the crankshaft rear oil seal retainer from the back of the engine block

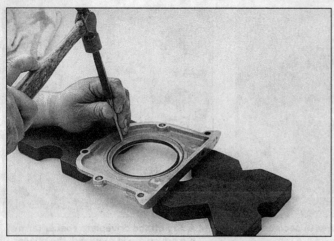

15.3 After removing the retainer assembly from the engine block, support it between two wood blocks and drive out the old seal with a drift punch and hammer

15.4 Drive the new seal into the retainer with a wood block

4   The new seal must be driven into the retainer plate from the engine side. Drive the new seal into the retainer with a wood block or a section of pipe slightly smaller in diameter than the outside diameter of the seal **(see illustration)**. The seal should be driven in only until it is flush with the transmission side of the retainer. **Caution:** *The new seal comes with a special plastic installation sleeve inserted in the seal. It is designed to allow the seal to slide over the end of the crankshaft without displacing the seal lip. Do NOT remove this plastic sleeve until the retainer and seal have been installed on the engine.*

5   Lubricate seal area of the crankshaft with engine oil. Apply a bead of RTV sealant to the sealing surface of the retainer **(see illustration)**.

6   Slowly and carefully press the seal and retainer squarely onto the crankshaft **(see illustration)**. The plastic sleeve may be pushed out as the retainer seats on the engine block. Remove the plastic sleeve.

7   Install and tighten the retainer bolts to the torque listed in this Chapter's Specifications.

8   The remaining steps are the reverse of removal.

16 Engine mounts - check and replacement

Refer to illustration 16.9

1   Engine mounts seldom require attention, but broken or deteriorated mounts should be replaced immediately or the added strain placed on the driveline components may cause damage or wear.

Check

2   During the check, the engine must be raised slightly to remove the weight from the mounts.

3   Raise the vehicle and support it securely on jackstands, then position a jack under the engine oil pan. Place a large wood block between the jack head and the oil pan, then carefully raise the engine just enough to take the weight off the mounts. Do not position the wood block under the drain plug. **Warning:** *DO NOT place any part of your body under the engine when it's supported only by a jack!*

4   Check the front mounts to see if the rubber is cracked, hardened or separated from the metal plates. Sometimes the rubber will split down the center.

5   Check for relative movement between the mount plates and the engine or frame (use a large screwdriver or pry bar to attempt to move the mounts). If movement is noted, lower the engine and tighten the mount fasteners.

6   Rubber preservative should be applied to the mounts to slow deterioration.

Replacement

7   Disconnect the negative cable from the battery. **Caution:** *If the stereo in your vehicle is equipped with an anti-theft system, make sure you have the correct activation code before disconnecting the battery.*

8   Raise the vehicle and support it securely on jackstands. Support the engine as described in Step 3. **Caution:** *Watch the mechanical cooling fan to ensure that it doesn't hit the shroud as the engine is raised.*

9   To remove either engine mount, remove the nut from the engine bracket, then raise the engine **(see illustration)**.

10   From underneath the vehicle, lower the steering gear (see Chapter 10) for access to the nut retaining the insulator to the chassis bracket.

11   Installation is the reverse of removal. Use thread-locking compound on the mount bolts/nuts and be sure to tighten them securely.

12   See Chapter 7 for transmission mount replacement.

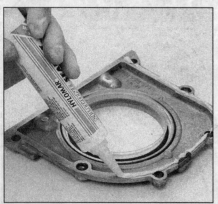

15.5 Apply RTV sealant to the sealing surface

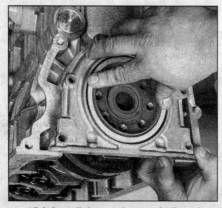

15.6 Install the retainer and oil seal onto the crankshaft

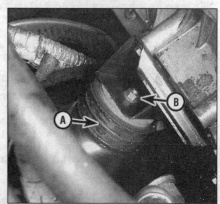

16.9 Front engine mount (A) and retaining nut to engine bracket (B)

Chapter 2 Part B
General engine overhaul procedures

Contents

Specifications

General

Displacement	
3.6	3.6 liters (219 cu. in.)
4.0	4 liters (243 cu. in.)
Cylinder compression pressure @ 300 rpm, warm	
Standard...	150 to 160 psi
High compression models	160 to 170 psi
Maximum variation between cylinders..........................	10 psi
Oil pressure (engine warm)	
At idle	30 psi minimum
At 4000 rpm..	70 psi minimum

Cylinder head

Resurfacing limit	0.010 inch maximum
Minimum thickness (see text)	
3.6L	5.101 inches
4.0L	5.108 inches

Valves and related components

Valve stem-to-guide clearance	0.0015 to 0.0030 inch
Valve springs, free length	1.580 inches
Valve lifter	
Diameter...	1.3126 to 1.3130 inches
Lifter-to-bore clearance	0.0008 to 0.0020 inch

Crankshaft and connecting rods

Connecting rod journal	
Diameter	2.0856 to 2.0861 inches
Taper and out-of-round limits	0.0003 inch
Bearing oil clearance	
3.6L	0.0016 to 0.0033 inch
4.0L	0.0010 to 0.0027 inches
Connecting rod side clearance (endplay)	0.005 to 0.009 inch
Main bearing journal	
Diameter	3.0007 to 3.0012 inches
Taper and out-of-round limits	0.0003 inch
Bearing oil clearance	0.0016 to 0.0033 inch
Crankshaft endplay	
Standard	0.004 to 010 inch

Engine block

Deck warpage limit	0.003 inch
Cylinder bore diameter	
Standard	
A	3.5823 to 3.5828 inches
B	3.5829 to 3.5834 inches
Oversize	
0.010 inch OS	3.5929 to 3.5934 inches
0.020 inch OS	3.6029 to 3.6034 inches

Pistons and rings

Piston-to-bore clearance	0.0007 to 0.0017 inch
Piston ring end gap	
No. 1 (top) compression ring	0.016 to 0.026 inch
No. 2 (middle) compression ring	0.016 to 0.026 inch
Oil ring	0.012 to 0.022 inch
Piston ring groove clearance	
No. 1 (top) compression ring	0.0016 to 0.0030 inch
No. 2 (middle) compression ring	0.0016 to 0.0030 inch

Torque specifications

	Nm	Ft-lbs
Main bearing cap bolts	136 to 142	100 to 105
Connecting rod cap nuts	50 to 60	37 to 44

* **Note:** *Refer to Part A for additional torque specifications.*

1   General information

Included in this portion of Chapter 2 are the general overhaul procedures for the cylinder head and internal engine components.

The information ranges from advice concerning preparation for an overhaul and the purchase of replacement parts to detailed, step-by-step procedures covering removal and installation of internal engine components and the inspection of parts.

The following Sections have been written based on the assumption that the engine has been removed from the vehicle. For information concerning in-vehicle engine repair, as well as removal and installation of the external components necessary for the overhaul, see Part A of this Chapter.

The Specifications included in this Part are only those necessary for the inspection and overhaul procedures which follow. Refer to Part A for additional Specifications.

2   Engine overhaul - general information

Refer to illustrations 2.4a and 2.4b

It's not always easy to determine when, or if, an engine should be completely overhauled, as a number of factors must be considered.

High mileage is not necessarily an indication that an overhaul is needed, while low mileage doesn't preclude the need for an overhaul.

Frequency of servicing is probably the most important consideration. An engine that's had regular and frequent oil and filter changes, as well as other required maintenance, will most likely give many thousands of miles of reliable service. Conversely, a neglected engine may require an overhaul very early in its life.

Excessive oil consumption is an indication that piston rings, valve seals and/or valve guides are in need of attention. Make sure that oil leaks aren't responsible before deciding that the rings and/or guides are bad. Perform a cylinder compression check to determine the extent of the work required (see Section 4). Also check the vacuum readings under various conditions (see Section 3).

Check the oil pressure with a gauge installed in place of the oil pressure sending unit **(see illustrations)** and compare it to this Chapter's Specifications. If it's extremely low, the bearings and/or oil pump are probably worn out.

Loss of power, rough running, knocking or metallic engine noises, excessive valve train noise and high fuel consumption rates may also point to the need for an overhaul, especially if they're all present at the same time. If a complete tune-up doesn't remedy the situation, major mechanical work is the only solution.

An engine overhaul involves restoring the internal parts to the specifications of a new engine. During an overhaul, the piston rings are replaced and the cylinder walls are reconditioned (rebored and/or honed). If a rebore is done by an automotive machine shop, new oversize pistons will also be installed. The main bearings, connecting rod bearings and camshaft bearings are generally replaced with new ones and, if necessary, the crankshaft may be reground to restore the jour-

2.4a The oil pressure sending unit (arrow) is located on the left front corner of the engine block, near the oil filter

2.4b The oil pressure can be checked by removing the sending unit and installing a pressure gauge in its place

3.4 The vacuum gauge is easily attached to a port on the intake manifold, and can tell a lot about an engine's state of tune

nals. Generally, the valves are serviced as well, since they're usually in less-than-perfect condition at this point. While the engine is being overhauled, other components, such as the distributor, starter and alternator, can be rebuilt as well. The end result should be a like new engine that will give many trouble free miles. **Note:** *Critical cooling system components such as the hoses, drivebelts, thermostat and water pump should be replaced with new parts when an engine is overhauled. The radiator should be checked carefully to ensure that it isn't clogged or leaking (see Chapter 3). If you purchase a rebuilt engine or short block, some rebuilders will not warranty their engines unless the radiator has been professionally flushed. Also, we don't recommend overhauling the oil pump - always install a new one when an engine is rebuilt.*

Before beginning the engine overhaul, read through the entire procedure to familiarize yourself with the scope and requirements of the job. Overhauling an engine isn't difficult, but it is time consuming. Plan on the vehicle being tied up for a minimum of two weeks, especially if parts must be taken to an automotive machine shop for repair or reconditioning. Check on availability of parts and make sure that any necessary special tools and equipment are obtained in advance. Most work can be done with typical hand tools, although a number of precision measuring tools are required for inspecting parts to determine if they must be replaced. Often an automotive machine shop will handle the inspection of parts and offer advice concerning reconditioning and replacement. **Note:** *Always wait until the engine has been completely disassembled and all components, especially the engine block, have been inspected before deciding what service and repair operations must be performed by an automotive machine shop.* Since the engine block's condition will be the major factor to consider when determining whether to overhaul the original engine or buy a rebuilt one, never purchase parts or have machine work done on other components until the engine block has been thoroughly inspected. As a general rule, time is the primary cost of an overhaul, so it doesn't pay to install worn or substandard parts.

If it turns out that a number of major components are beyond reconditioning, it may be cost effective to buy a factory-rebuilt engine from a Jaguar dealership.

As a final note, to ensure maximum life and minimum trouble from a rebuilt engine, everything must be assembled with care in a spotlessly-clean environment.

3   Vacuum gauge diagnostic checks

Refer to illustration 3.4

A vacuum gauge provides valuable information about what is going on in the engine at a low cost. You can check for worn rings or cylinder walls, leaking cylinder head or intake manifold gaskets, incor-

rect carburetor adjustments, restricted exhaust, stuck or burned valves, weak valve springs, improper ignition or valve timing and ignition problems.

Unfortunately, vacuum gauge readings are easy to misinterpret, so they should be used in conjunction with other tests to confirm the diagnosis.

Both the absolute readings and the rate of needle movement are important for accurate interpretation. Most gauges measure vacuum in inches of mercury (in-Hg). As vacuum increases (or atmospheric pressure decreases), the reading will decrease. Also, for every 1,000 foot increase in elevation above sea level; the gauge readings will decrease about one inch of mercury.

Connect the vacuum gauge directly to intake manifold vacuum, not to ported (above the throttle plate) vacuum **(see illustration)**. Be sure no hoses are left disconnected during the test or false readings will result.

Before you begin the test, allow the engine to warm up completely. Block the wheels and set the parking brake. With the transmission in Park, start the engine and allow it to run at normal idle speed. **Warning:** *Carefully inspect the fan blades for cracks or damage before starting the engine. Keep your hands and the vacuum tester clear of the fan and do not stand in front of the vehicle or in line with the fan when the engine is running.*

Read the vacuum gauge; an average, healthy engine should normally produce between 17 and 22 inches of vacuum with a fairly steady needle.

Refer to the following vacuum gauge readings and what they indicate about the engines condition:

1　A low steady reading usually indicates a leaking gasket between the intake manifold and carburetor or throttle body, a leaky vacuum hose, late ignition timing or incorrect camshaft timing. Check ignition timing with a timing light and eliminate all other possible causes, utilizing the tests provided in this Chapter before you remove the timing belt cover to check the timing marks.

2　If the reading is three to eight inches below normal and it fluctuates at that low reading, suspect an intake manifold gasket leak at an intake port or a faulty injector.

3　If the needle has regular drops of about two to four inches at a steady rate the valves are probably leaking. Perform a compression or leak-down test to confirm this.

4　An irregular drop or down-flick of the needle can be caused by a sticking valve or an ignition misfire. Perform a compression or leak-down test and read the spark plugs.

5　A rapid vibration of about four in-Hg vibration at idle combined with exhaust smoke indicates worn valve guides. Perform a leak-down test to confirm this. If the rapid vibration occurs with an increase in engine speed, check for a leaking intake manifold gasket or cylinder head gasket, weak valve springs, burned valves or ignition misfire.

6　A slight fluctuation, say one inch up and down, may mean ignition problems. Check all the usual tune-up items and, if necessary, run the engine on an ignition analyzer.

7　If there is a large fluctuation, perform a compression or leak-down test to look for a weak or dead cylinder or a blown cylinder head gasket.

8　If the needle moves slowly through a wide range, check for a clogged PCV system, incorrect idle fuel mixture, throttle body or intake manifold gasket leaks.

9　Check for a slow return after revving the engine by quickly snapping the throttle open until the engine reaches about 2,500 rpm and let it shut. Normally the reading should drop to near zero, rise above normal idle reading (about 5 in.-Hg over) and then return to the previous idle reading. If the vacuum returns slowly and doesn't peak when the throttle is snapped shut, the rings may be worn. If there is a long delay, look for a restricted exhaust system (often the muffler or catalytic converter). An easy way to check this is to temporarily disconnect the exhaust ahead of the suspected part and redo the test.

4　Cylinder compression check

Refer to illustration 4.6

1　A compression check will tell you what mechanical condition the upper end (pistons, rings, valves, cylinder head gasket) of your engine is in. Specifically, it can tell you if the compression is down due to leakage caused by worn piston rings, defective valves and seats or a blown cylinder head gasket. **Note:** *The engine must be at normal operating temperature and the battery must be fully charged for this check.*

2　Begin by cleaning the area around the spark plugs before you remove them (compressed air should be used, if available, otherwise a small brush or even a bicycle tire pump will work). The idea is to prevent dirt from getting into the cylinders as the compression check is being done.

3　Remove all of the spark plugs from the engine (see Chapter 1).

4　Block the throttle wide open.

5　Detach the coil wire from the center of the distributor cap and ground it on the engine block. Use a jumper wire with alligator clips on each end to ensure a good ground. Also, remove the fuel pump relay (see Chapter 4) to disable the fuel pump during the compression test.

6　Install the compression gauge in the spark plug hole (**see illustration**).

7　Crank the engine over at least seven compression strokes and watch the gauge. The compression should build up quickly in a healthy engine. Low compression on the first stroke, followed by gradually increasing pressure on successive strokes, indicates worn piston rings. A low compression reading on the first stroke, which doesn't

4.6 A compression gauge with a threaded fitting for the spark plug hole is preferred over the type that requires hand pressure to maintain the seal - be sure to block open the throttle valve as far as possible during the compression check!

build up during successive strokes, indicates leaking valves or a blown cylinder head gasket (a cracked cylinder head could also be the cause). Deposits on the undersides of the valve heads can also cause low compression. Record the highest gauge reading obtained.

8　Repeat the procedure for the remaining cylinders and compare the results to this Chapter's Specifications.

9　Add some engine oil (about three squirts from a plunger-type oil can) to each cylinder, through the spark plug hole, and repeat the test.

10　If the compression increases after the oil is added, the piston rings are definitely worn. If the compression doesn't increase significantly, the leakage is occurring at the valves or cylinder head gasket. Leakage past the valves may be caused by burned valve seats and/or faces or warped, cracked or bent valves.

11　If two adjacent cylinders have equally low compression, there's a strong possibility that the cylinder head gasket between them is blown. The appearance of coolant in the combustion chambers or the crankcase would verify this condition.

12　If one cylinder is 20 percent lower than the others, and the engine has a slightly rough idle, a worn exhaust lobe on the camshaft could be the cause.

13　If the compression is unusually high, the combustion chambers are probably coated with carbon deposits. If that's the case, the cylinder head(s) should be removed and decarbonized.

14　If compression is way down or varies greatly between cylinders, it would be a good idea to have a leak-down test performed by an automotive repair shop. This test will pinpoint exactly where the leakage is occurring and how severe it is.

5　Engine removal - methods and precautions

If you've decided that an engine must be removed for overhaul or major repair work, several preliminary steps should be taken.

Locating a suitable place to work is extremely important. Adequate work space, along with storage space for the vehicle, will be needed. If a shop or garage isn't available, at the very least a flat, level, clean work surface made of concrete or asphalt is required.

Cleaning the engine compartment and engine before beginning the removal procedure will help keep tools clean and organized.

An engine hoist or A-frame will also be necessary. Make sure the equipment is rated in excess of the combined weight of the engine and transmission. Safety is of primary importance, considering the potential hazards involved in lifting the engine out of the vehicle.

If the engine is being removed by a novice, a helper should be

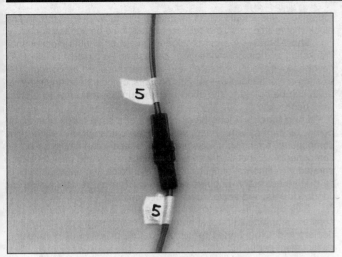

6.7 Label both ends of each wire and hose before disconnecting it

6.20 Lift the engine high enough to clear the vehicle, tilting it up at the front to clear the front crossmember, then move it away and lower the hoist

available. Advice and aid from someone more experienced would also be helpful. There are many instances when one person cannot simultaneously perform all of the operations required when lifting the engine out of the vehicle.

Plan the operation ahead of time. Arrange for or obtain all of the tools and equipment you'll need prior to beginning the job. Some of the equipment necessary to perform engine removal and installation safely and with relative ease are (in addition to an engine hoist) a heavy duty floor jack, complete sets of wrenches and sockets as described in the front of this manual, wooden blocks and plenty of rags and cleaning solvent for mopping up spilled oil, coolant and gasoline. If the hoist must be rented, make sure that you arrange for it in advance and perform all of the operations possible without it beforehand. This will save you money and time.

Plan for the vehicle to be out of use for quite a while. A machine shop will be required to perform some of the work which the do-it-yourselfer can't accomplish without special equipment. These shops often have a busy schedule, so it would be a good idea to consult them before removing the engine in order to accurately estimate the amount of time required to rebuild or repair components that may need work.

Always be extremely careful when removing and installing the engine. Serious injury can result from careless actions. Plan ahead, take your time and a job of this nature, although major, can be accomplished successfully.

6   Engine - removal and installation

Refer to illustrations 6.7, 6.20 and 6.21
Note: *Read through the entire Section before beginning this procedure. It is recommended to remove the engine and transmission from the top as a unit, then separate the engine from the transmission on the shop floor. If the transmission is not being serviced, it is possible to leave the transmission in the vehicle and remove the engine from the top by itself, by removing the crankshaft damper and tilting up the front end of the engine for clearance, but access to the upper bellhousing bolts is only practical when the rear transmission mount and driveshaft have been removed and the transmission is angled down with a floor-jack.*

Removal

1   Relieve the fuel system pressure (see Chapter 4).
2   Disconnect the negative cable from the battery. **Caution:** *If the stereo in your vehicle is equipped with an anti-theft system, make sure you have the correct activation code before disconnecting the battery.*

3   Place protective covers on the fenders and cowl and remove the hood (see Chapter 11).
4   Remove the battery and battery tray.
5   Remove the air cleaner assembly (see Chapter 4).
6   Raise the vehicle and support it securely on jackstands. Drain the cooling system and engine oil and remove the drivebelts (see Chapter 1).
7   Clearly label, then disconnect all vacuum lines, coolant and emissions hoses, wiring harness connectors and ground straps. Masking tape and/or a touch up paint applicator work well for marking items **(see illustration).** Take instant photos or sketch the locations of components and brackets.
8   Remove the cooling fan(s) and radiator (see Chapter 3).
9   Disconnect the heater hoses.
10   Release the residual fuel pressure in the tank by removing the gas cap, then detach the fuel lines connecting the engine to the chassis (see Chapter 4). Plug or cap all open fittings.
11   Disconnect the throttle linkage, transmission linkage (and dipstick tube) and speed control cable, if equipped, from the engine (see Chapters 4 and 7).
12   Refer to Part A of this Chapter and remove the intake and exhaust manifolds.
13   Unbolt the power steering pump (see Chapter 10). Tie the pump aside without disconnecting the hoses. Refer to Part A for removal of the hydraulic pump (if equipped) from the timing chain cover.
14   On air-conditioned models, unbolt the compressor and set it aside. Do not disconnect the refrigerant hoses. **Note:** *Wire the compressor out of the way with a coat hanger, don't let the compressor hang on the hoses.*
15   Refer to Part A of this Chapter and remove the drivebelts, water pump pulley and crankshaft pulley.
16   Attach a lifting sling to the engine. Position a hoist and connect the sling to it. Take up the slack until there is slight tension on the hoist.
17   With a floor jack and piece of wood supporting the bottom of the transmission oil pan, refer to Chapter 8 and remove the driveshaft and rear transmission mount. **Warning:** *Do not place any part of your body under the engine/transmission when it's supported only by a hoist or other lifting device.*
18   With the hoist taking the weight of the engine, unbolt the engine mounts (see Part A of this Chapter).
19   Recheck to be sure nothing is still connecting the engine or transmission to the vehicle. Disconnect and label anything still remaining.
20   Slowly lift the engine/transmission out of the vehicle **(see illustration).** It may be necessary to pry the mounts away from the frame brackets.
21   Move the engine away from the vehicle and carefully lower the

6.21 With the engine on the floor but still supported by the hoist, remove the four large bolts (arrows) and pull off the transmission adapter plate

hoist until the engine/transmission can be set on the floor. Refer to Chapter 7 and remove the transmission and torque converter. Refer to Part A of this Chapter for removal of the flywheel. With the flywheel removed, remove the four large bolts and the transmission adapter plate from the engine **(see illustration)**.

22   Refer to Part A of this Chapter for removal of the rear main seal retainer plate from the back of the engine, then lift the engine to a position where it can be attached to a sturdy engine stand.

Installation

23   Check the engine/transmission mounts. If they're worn or damaged, replace them.

24   Attach the hoist and remove the engine from the stand. Refer to Part A of this Chapter and replace the rear main seal and retainer plate, then reattach the transmission adapter plate and refer to Chapter 7 for mounting the torque converter and transmission.

25   Carefully lower the engine into the vehicle with the hoist. An assistant is helpful to guide the engine clear of accessories in the engine compartment as the engine is lowered into place.

26   Install the engine mount bolts and tighten them securely. Raise the back of the transmission with the floor jack and reattach the transmission mount, driveshaft and shift linkage.

27   Reinstall the remaining components and fasteners in the reverse order of removal.

28   Add coolant, oil, power steering and transmission fluids as needed (see Chapter 1).

29   Run the engine and check for proper operation and leaks. Shut off the engine and recheck the fluid levels.

7   Engine rebuilding alternatives

The do-it-yourselfer is faced with a number of options when performing an engine overhaul. The decision to replace the engine block, piston/connecting rod assemblies and crankshaft depends on a number of factors, with the number one consideration being the condition of the engine block. Other considerations are cost, access to machine shop facilities, parts availability, time required to complete the project and the extent of prior mechanical experience on the part of the do-it-yourselfer.

Some of the rebuilding alternatives include:

Individual parts - If the inspection procedures reveal that the engine block and most engine components are in reusable condition, purchasing individual parts may be the most economical alternative. The engine block, cylinder head, crankshaft, and piston/connecting

rod assemblies should all be inspected carefully. Even if the engine block shows little wear, the cylinder bores should be surface honed.

Short block - A short block consists of an engine block with a crankshaft and piston/connecting rod assemblies already installed. All new bearings are incorporated and all clearances will be correct. The existing camshafts, valve train components, cylinder head and external parts can be bolted to the short block with little or no machine shop work necessary.

Long block - A long block consists of a short block plus an oil pump, oil pan, cylinder head, valve cover, camshaft and valve train components, timing sprockets and chain or gears and timing cover. All components are installed with new bearings, seals and gaskets incorporated throughout. The installation of manifolds and external parts is all that's necessary. Engines in this rebuilt form are available from Jaguar dealers, and some independent rebuilders.

Give careful thought to which alternative is best for you and discuss the situation with local automotive machine shops, auto parts dealers and experienced rebuilders before ordering or purchasing replacement parts.

8   Engine overhaul - disassembly sequence

1   It's much easier to disassemble and work on the engine if it's mounted on a portable engine stand. A stand can often be rented quite cheaply from an equipment rental yard. Before the engine is mounted on a stand, the driveplate and rear oil seal retainer should be removed from the engine.

2   If a stand isn't available, it's possible to disassemble the engine with it blocked up on the floor. Be extra careful not to tip or drop the engine when working without a stand.

3   If you're going to obtain a rebuilt engine, all external components must come off first, to be transferred to the replacement engine, just as they will if you're doing a complete engine overhaul yourself. These include:

Alternator and brackets
Emissions control components
Distributor, spark plug wires and spark plugs
Thermostat and housing cover
Water pump
EFI components
Intake/exhaust manifolds
Oil filter
Engine mounts
Driveplate
Transmission adapter plate

Note: *When removing the external components from the engine, pay close attention to details that may be helpful or important during installation. Note the installed position of gaskets, seals, spacers, pins, brackets, washers, bolts and other small items.*

4   If you're obtaining a short block, which consists of the engine block, crankshaft, pistons and connecting rods all assembled, then the cylinder head, oil pan and oil pump will have to be removed as well from your engine so that your short-block can be turned in to the rebuilder as a core. See *Engine rebuilding alternatives* for additional information regarding the different possibilities to be considered.

5   If you're planning a complete overhaul, the engine must be disassembled and the internal components removed in the following order:

Intake and exhaust manifolds
Valve cover
Upper timing chain and camshaft sprockets
Camshafts
Timing chain cover
Cylinder head
Oil pan
Oil pump
Piston/connecting rod assemblies
Crankshaft rear oil seal retainer
Crankshaft and main bearings

9.2 A small plastic bag, with an appropriate label, can be used to store the valve train components so they can be kept together and reinstalled in the correct guide

9.3 Compress the spring until the keepers can be removed with a small magnetic screwdriver or needle-nose pliers - you must use a valve spring compressor with an adapter such as the one shown (arrow) for removal of the keepers

6   Before beginning the disassembly and overhaul procedures, make sure the following items are available. Also, refer to Section 21 for a list of tools and materials needed for engine reassembly.

Common hand tools
Small cardboard boxes or plastic bags for storing parts
Gasket scraper
Ridge reamer
Micrometers
Telescoping gauges
Dial indicator set
Valve spring compressor
Cylinder surfacing hone
Piston ring groove-cleaning tool
Electric drill motor
Tap and die set
Wire brushes
Oil gallery brushes
Cleaning solvent

Special Jaguar tools
Engine lifting brackets (18G 1465)
Timing damper simulator (18E 1436)
Camshaft TDC tool (18G 1433)

9   Cylinder head - disassembly

Refer to illustrations 9.2 and 9.3
Note: *New and rebuilt cylinder heads are available from Jaguar and some independent rebuilders. Due to the fact that some specialized tools are necessary for the disassembly and inspection procedures, and replacement parts may not be readily available, it may be more practical and economical for the home mechanic to purchase a replacement cylinder head rather than taking the time to disassemble, inspect and recondition the original.*

1   Cylinder head disassembly involves removal of the intake and exhaust valves and related components. It's assumed that the lifters and camshafts have already been removed (see Part A as needed).
2   Before the valves are removed, arrange to label and store them, along with their related components, so they can be kept separate and reinstalled in the same valve guides they are removed from **(see illustration)**.
3   Compress the springs on the first valve with a spring compressor and remove the keepers **(see illustration)**. Carefully release the valve spring compressor and remove the retainer, the spring and the spring seat (if used). **Caution:** *Be very careful not to nick or otherwise damage the lifter bores when compressing the valve springs.* **Note:** *If your*

spring compressor does not have an end (such as the one shown) with cutouts on the side, an adapter is available to use with a standard spring compressor.
4   Pull the valve out of the cylinder head, then remove the oil seal from the guide. If the valve binds in the guide (won't pull through), push it back into the cylinder head and deburr the area around the keeper groove with a fine file or whetstone.
5   Repeat the procedure for the remaining valves. Remember to keep all the parts for each valve together so they can be reinstalled in the same locations.
6   Once the valves and related components have been removed and stored in an organized manner, the cylinder head should be thoroughly cleaned and inspected. If a complete engine overhaul is being done, finish the engine disassembly procedures before beginning the cylinder head cleaning and inspection process.

10   Cylinder head - cleaning and inspection

Refer to illustrations 10.12, 10.13, 10.15, 10.17, 10.18 and 10.19
1   Thorough cleaning of the cylinder head(s) and related valve train components, followed by a detailed inspection, will enable you to decide how much valve service work must be done during the engine overhaul. **Note:** *If the engine was severely overheated, the cylinder head is probably warped (see Step 12).*

Cleaning
2   Scrape all traces of old gasket material and sealing compound off the cylinder head gasket, intake manifold and exhaust manifold sealing surfaces. Be very careful not to gouge the cylinder head. Special gasket-removal solvents that soften gaskets and make removal much easier are available at auto parts stores.
3   Remove all built up scale from the coolant passages.
4   Run a stiff wire brush through the various holes to remove deposits that may have formed in them. If there are heavy deposits in the water passages, the bare head should be professionally cleaned at a machine shop.
5   Run an appropriate-size tap into each of the threaded holes to remove corrosion and thread sealant that may be present. If compressed air is available, use it to clear the holes of debris produced by this operation. **Warning:** *Wear eye protection when using compressed air!*
6   Clean the exhaust and intake manifold stud threads with a wire brush.
7   Clean the cylinder head with solvent and dry it thoroughly. Compressed air will speed the drying process and ensure that all holes and

10.12 Using a new head gasket, trace around the cylinder head and engine block water passages and bolt holes - make sure there is no erosion of the aluminum beyond these lines

10.13 Check the cylinder head and engine block gasket surfaces for warpage by trying to slip a feeler gauge under a precision straightedge (see the Specifications for the maximum warpage allowed and use a feeler gauge of that thickness) - check both the cylinder head and engine block (shown)

recessed areas are clean. **Note:** *Decarbonizing chemicals are available and may prove very useful when cleaning cylinder heads and valve train components. They are very caustic and should be used with caution. Be sure to follow the instructions on the container.*

8   Clean the lifters with solvent and dry them thoroughly. Compressed air will speed the drying process and can be used to clean out the oil passages. Don't mix them up during the cleaning process, keep them in a box with numbered compartments.

9   Clean all the valve springs, spring seats, keepers and retainers with solvent and dry them thoroughly. Work on the components from one valve at a time to avoid mixing up the parts.

10   Scrape off any heavy deposits that may have formed on the valves, then use a motorized wire brush to remove deposits from the valve heads and stems. Again, make sure the valves don't get mixed up.

Inspection

Note: *Be sure to perform all of the following inspection procedures before concluding that machine shop work is required.* Make a list of the items that need attention. The inspection procedures for the lifters and camshafts, can be found in Part A.

Cylinder head

11   Inspect the cylinder head very carefully for cracks, evidence of coolant leakage and other damage. If cracks are found, check with an automotive machine shop concerning repair. If repair isn't possible, a new cylinder head should be obtained.

12   A common problem on aluminum engines is erosion of the cylinder head or engine block coolant passages due to improper sealing. Using a new cylinder head gasket held against the cylinder head, trace the bolt holes and coolant passage outlines in pencil on the cylinder head. Use the gasket to trace the same on the top of the engine block **(see illustration)**. If the top of the engine block has eroded *outside* of the pattern around the water passages or cylinder head bolt holes, the engine block must be replaced; the manufacturer doesn't recommend resurfacing it. If the cylinder head has eroded outside of the water passage holes but the erosion is *away from* the combustion chamber, the eroded area can be built up with metal-impregnated epoxy and machined flat again.

13   Using a straightedge and feeler gauge, check the cylinder head gasket mating surface (on the engine block and cylinder head) for warpage **(see illustration)**. If the warpage exceeds the limit found in this Chapter's Specifications, it can be resurfaced at an automotive machine shop, but no more then 0.010-inch of material should be removed. If the cylinder head had been overheated, take it to the machinist for inspection before proceeding further. It's possible that the overheating could have annealed (softened) the aluminum of the

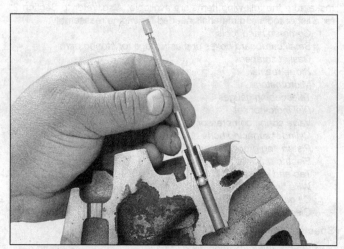

10.15 Use a small dial bore gauge to determine the inside diameter of the valve guides - subtract the measured valve stem diameter to determine the stem-to-guide clearance

cylinder head, making it unsuitable for machine work. In this case, a new cylinder head is required.

Note 1: *To check if a cylinder head has been machined previously, measure the height between the cylinder head gasket surface and the valve cover mounting surface with a large micrometer or vernier caliper and compare with Specifications.*

Note 2: *Jaguar aluminum cylinder heads require precision machine work. It is best to find a machine shop that has considerable experience in servicing Jaguar cylinder heads.*

14   Examine the valve seats in each of the combustion chambers. If they're pitted, cracked or burned, the cylinder head will require valve service that's beyond the scope of the home mechanic.

15   Check the valve stem-to-guide clearance with a small hole gauge and micrometer, or a small dial bore gauge **(see illustration)**. Also, check the valve stem deflection with a dial indicator attached securely to the cylinder head. The valve must be in the guide and approximately 1/16-inch off the seat. The total valve stem movement indicated by the gauge needle must be noted, then divided by two to obtain the actual clearance value. If it exceeds the stem-to-guide clearance limit found in this Chapter's Specifications, the valve guides should be replaced. After this is done, if there's still some doubt regarding the condition of the valve guides they should be checked by an automotive machine shop (the cost should be minimal).

Valves

16   Carefully inspect each valve face for uneven wear, deformation, cracks, pits and burned areas. Check the valve stem for scuffing and galling and the neck for cracks. Rotate the valve and check for any obvious indication that it's bent. Look for pits and excessive wear on the end of the stem. The presence of any of these conditions indicates the need for valve service by an automotive machine shop.

17   Measure the margin width on each valve (see illustration). Any valve with a margin narrower than 1/32-inch will have to be replaced with a new valve.

Valve components

18   Check each valve spring for wear (on the ends) and pits. Measure the free length and compare it to this Chapter's Specifications (see illustration). Any springs that are shorter than specified have sagged and should not be re-used. The tension of all springs should be pressure checked with a special fixture before deciding that they're suitable for use in a rebuilt engine (take the springs to an automotive machine shop for this check). Note: *If any valve springs are found broken on 1988 or 1989 engines, all springs should be replaced with the improved springs used in 1990 (after VIN 9EPCLA120245) and later engines. They are identified with a white stripe. If your engine has springs with white-stripes, they have already been replaced, and only broken ones need be replaced.*

19   Stand each spring on a flat surface and check it for squareness (see illustration). If any of the springs are distorted or sagged, replace all of the springs.

20   Check the spring retainers and keepers for obvious wear and cracks. Any questionable parts should be renewed, as extensive damage will occur if they fail during engine operation.

21   If the inspection process indicates that the valve components are in generally poor condition and worn beyond the limits specified, which is usually the case in an engine that's being overhauled, reassemble the valves in the cylinder head and refer to Section 11 for valve servicing recommendations.

11   Valves - servicing

1   Because of the complex nature of the job and the special tools and equipment needed, servicing of the valves, the valve seats and the valve guides, commonly known as a valve job, should be done by a professional.

2   The home mechanic can remove and disassemble the cylinder head(s), do the initial cleaning and inspection, then reassemble and deliver them to a dealer service department or an automotive machine shop for the actual service work. Doing the inspection will enable you to see what condition the cylinder head(s) and valvetrain components

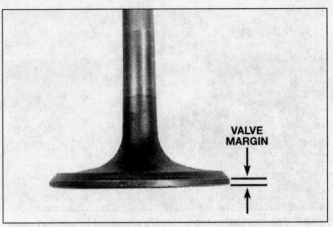

10.17 The margin width on each valve must be as specified (if no margin exists, the valve cannot be re-used)

are in and will ensure that you know what work and new parts are required when dealing with an automotive machine shop.

3   The dealer service department, or automotive machine shop, will remove the valves and springs, recondition or replace the valves and valve seats, recondition the valve guides, check and replace the valve springs, spring retainers and keepers (as necessary), replace the valve seals with new ones, reassemble the valve components and make sure the installed spring height is correct. The cylinder head gasket surface will also be resurfaced if it's warped.

4   After the valve job has been performed by a professional, the cylinder head(s) will be in like new condition. When the cylinder heads are returned, be sure to clean them again before installation on the engine to remove any metal particles and abrasive grit that may still be present from the valve service or cylinder head resurfacing operations. Use compressed air, if available, to blow out all the oil holes and passages.

12   Cylinder head - reassembly

Refer to illustration 12.6

1   Regardless of whether or not the cylinder head was sent to an automotive machine shop for valve servicing, make sure it's clean before beginning reassembly. Replace the cylinder head rear plate gasket anytime the engine is overhauled or the cylinder head is reconditioned (see Part A of this Chapter for replacement procedure).

2   If the cylinder head was sent out for valve servicing, the valves

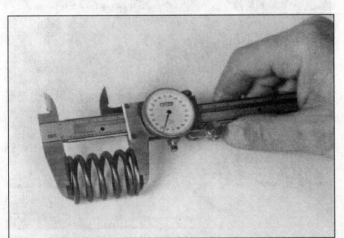

10.18 Measure the free length of each valve spring with a dial or vernier caliper

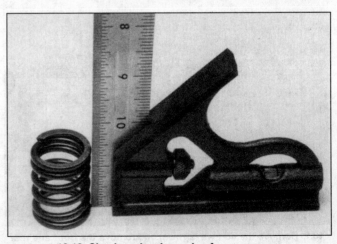

10.19 Check each valve spring for squareness

12.6 The small valve stem keepers are easier to position when coated with grease

and related components will already be in place. Begin the reassembly procedure with Step 8.

3   Install new seals on each of the valve guides. Gently push each valve seal into place until it's seated on the guide. **Caution:** *Don't hammer on the valve seals once they're seated or you may damage them. Don't twist or cock the seals during installation or they won't seat properly on the valve stems.*

4   Beginning at one end of the cylinder head, lubricate and install the first valve. Apply moly-base grease or clean engine oil to the valve stem.

5   Place the spring seat or shim(s) over the valve guide and set the valve spring and retainer in place.

6   Compress the springs with a valve spring compressor and carefully install the keepers in the upper groove, then slowly release the compressor and make sure the keepers seat properly. Apply a small dab of grease to each keeper to hold it in place if necessary **(see illustration)**.

7   Repeat the procedure for the remaining valves. Be sure to return the components to their original locations - don't mix them up!

13   Pistons/connecting rods - removal

Refer to illustrations 13.1, 13.2, 13.3, 13.4 and 13.6

Note : *Prior to removing the piston/connecting rod assemblies, remove the cylinder head(s), the oil pan and the oil pump transfer tubes by referring to the appropriate Sections in Chapter 2A.*

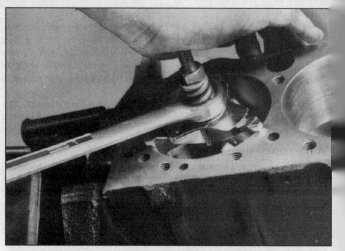

13.1 A ridge reamer is required to remove the ridge from the top of each cylinder - do this before removing the pistons!

1   Use your fingernail to feel if a ridge has formed at the upper limit of ring travel (about 1/4-inch down from the top of each cylinder). If carbon deposits or cylinder wear have produced ridges, they must be completely removed with a special tool **(see illustration)**. Follow the manufacturer's instructions provided with the tool. Failure to remove the ridges before attempting to remove the piston/connecting rod assemblies may result in piston damage.

2   After the cylinder ridges have been removed, turn the engine upside-down so the crankshaft is facing up. Remove the screws and the front and rear windage trays from the bottom of the engine block **(see illustration)**.

3   Before the connecting rods are removed, check the endplay with a feeler gauge. Slide the blade between the first connecting rod and the crankshaft throw until the play is removed **(see illustration)**. The endplay is equal to the thickness of the feeler gauge(s). If the endplay exceeds the specified service limit, new connecting rods will be required. If new rods (or a new crankshaft) are installed, the endplay may fall under the service limit (if it does, the rods will have to be machined to restore it - consult an automotive machine shop for advice if necessary). Repeat the procedure for the remaining connecting rods.

4   Check the connecting rods and caps for identification marks. If they aren't plainly marked, use a small center punch to make the appropriate number of indentations on each rod and cap (1, 2, 3, etc.,

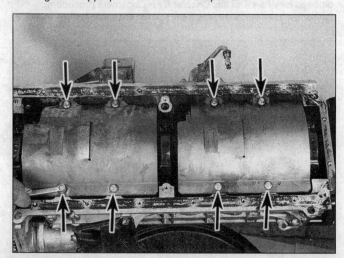

13.2 Remove the screws (arrows) and remove the front and rear windage trays

13.3 Check the connecting rod side clearance with a feeler gauge as shown here

13.4 The connecting rods and caps should be marked to indicate which cylinder they're installed in - if they aren't, mark them with a center punch to avoid confusion during reassembly

13.6 To prevent damage to the crankshaft journals and cylinder walls, slip sections of hose over the connecting rod bolts before removing the pistons

depending on the cylinder they're associated with) **(see illustration)**.

5   Loosen each of the connecting rod cap nuts 1/2-turn at a time until they can be removed by hand. Remove the number one connecting rod cap and bearing insert. Don't drop the bearing insert out of the cap. **Note:** *These engines use special connecting rod and main bearing cap bolts that are designed to be used one time only. They can be used during Plastigage checks, but must be replaced with new bolts when the engine is finally reassembled.*

6   Slip a short length of plastic or rubber hose over each connecting rod cap bolt to protect the crankshaft journal and cylinder wall as the piston is removed **(see illustration)**.

7   Remove the bearing insert and push the connecting rod/piston assembly out through the top of the engine. Use a wooden hammer handle to push on the upper bearing surface in the connecting rod. If resistance is felt, double-check to make sure that all of the ridge was removed from the cylinder.

8   Repeat the procedure for the remaining cylinders. **Note:** *Turn the crankshaft as needed to position the piston/connecting rod assembly to be removed close to parallel with the cylinder bore; i.e. don't try to drive it out while at a large angle to the bore.*

9   After removal, reassemble the connecting rod caps and bearing inserts in their respective connecting rods and install the cap nuts/bolts finger tight. Leaving the old bearing inserts in place until reassembly will help prevent the connecting rod bearing surfaces from being accidentally nicked or gouged.

10   Don't separate the pistons from the connecting rods (see Section 18 for additional information).

14   Crankshaft - removal

Refer to illustrations 14.1, 14.3 and 14.5

Note: *The rear main oil seal and retainer must be removed from the engine block before proceeding with crankshaft removal (see Part A of this Chapter).*

1   Before the crankshaft is removed, check the endplay. Mount a dial indicator to the front of the engine with the stem in line with and touching the end of the crankshaft **(see illustration)**.

2   Push the crankshaft all the way to the rear and zero the dial indicator. Next, pry the crankshaft to the front as far as possible and check the reading on the dial indicator. The distance that it moves is the endplay. If it's greater than that specified in this Chapter's Specifications, check the crankshaft thrust surfaces for wear. If no wear is evident, new thrust washers should correct the endplay.

3   If a dial indicator isn't available, feeler gauges can be used. Gently pry or push the crankshaft all the way to the front of the engine. Slip feeler gauges between the crankshaft and the front face of the number 4 (thrust) main bearing to determine the clearance **(see illustration)**.

4   Check the main bearing caps to see if they're marked to indicate their locations. They should be numbered consecutively from the front of the engine to the rear. If they aren't, mark them with number stamping dies or a center punch. Main bearing caps generally have a cast-in arrow, which points to the front of the engine. Loosen the main bearing cap bolts 1/4-turn at a time each, starting at the ends and working

14.1 Checking crankshaft endplay with a dial indicator

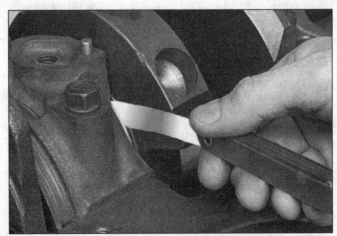

14.3 Checking crankshaft endplay with a feeler gauge

14.5 The right side of each main bearing cap is stamped with a number (left arrow) that corresponds to the stamped number on the pan rail (right arrow)

15.1a A hammer and a large punch can be used to knock the core plugs sideways in their bores

15.1b Pull the core plugs from the engine block with pliers

toward the center, until they can be removed by hand.

5   The main bearing caps are numbered on the right side with corresponding numbers stamped into the oil pan rail on the same side **(see illustration)**. Gently tap the caps with a soft-face hammer, then separate them from the engine block. If necessary, use the bolts as levers to remove the main bearing caps. Try not to drop the bearing inserts if they come out with the caps. **Note:** *The number four main bearing is the thrust bearing and is not numbered.*

6   Carefully lift the crankshaft out of the engine. It may be a good idea to have an assistant available, since the crankshaft is quite heavy. With the bearing inserts in place in the engine block and main bearing caps, return the main bearing caps to their respective locations on the engine block and tighten the bolts finger tight.

15   Engine block - cleaning

Refer to illustrations 15.1a, 15.1b, 15.8 and 15.10

Caution: *The core plugs (also known as freeze or soft plugs) may be difficult or impossible to retrieve if they're driven completely into the engine block coolant passages.*

1   Using the blunt end of a punch, tap in on the outer edge of the core plug to turn the plug sideways in the bore. Then using pliers, pull the core plug from the engine block **(see illustrations)**.

2   Using a gasket scraper, remove all traces of gasket material from the engine block. Be very careful not to nick or gouge the gasket sealing surfaces.

3   Remove the main bearing caps and separate the bearing inserts from the caps and the engine block. Tag the bearings, indicating which cylinder they were removed from and whether they were in the cap or the engine block, then set them aside.

4   Remove all of the threaded oil gallery plugs from the engine block. The plugs are usually very tight - they may have to be drilled out and the holes retapped. Use new plugs when the engine is reassembled.

5   If the engine is extremely dirty, it should be taken to an automotive machine shop to be steam cleaned or hot tanked.

6   After the engine block is returned, clean all oil holes and oil galleries one more time. Brushes specifically designed for this purpose are available at most auto parts stores. Flush the passages with warm water until the water runs clear, dry the engine block thoroughly and wipe all machined surfaces with a light, rust preventive oil. If you have access to compressed air, use it to speed the drying process and to blow out all the oil holes and galleries. **Warning:** *Wear eye protection when using compressed air!*

7   If the engine block isn't extremely dirty or sludged up, you can do

15.8 All bolt holes in the engine block - particularly the main bearing cap and cylinder head bolt holes - should be cleaned and restored with a tap (be sure to remove debris from the holes after this is done)

an adequate cleaning job with hot soapy water and a stiff brush. Take plenty of time and do a thorough job. Regardless of the cleaning method used, be sure to clean all oil holes and galleries very thoroughly, dry the engine block completely and coat all machined surfaces with light oil.

8   The threaded holes in the engine block must be clean to ensure accurate torque readings during reassembly. Run the proper size tap into each of the holes to remove rust, corrosion, thread sealant or sludge and restore damaged threads **(see illustration)**. If possible, use compressed air to clear the holes of debris produced by this operation.

9   Reinstall the main bearing caps and tighten the bolts finger tight.

10   After coating the sealing surfaces of the new core plugs with Permatex no. 2 sealant, install them in the engine block **(see illustration)**. Make sure they're driven in straight and seated properly or leakage could result. Special tools are available for this purpose, but a large socket, with an outside diameter that will just slip into the core plug, a 1/2-inch drive extension and a hammer will work just as well.

11   Apply non-hardening sealant (such as Permatex no. 2 or Teflon pipe sealant) to the new oil gallery plugs and thread them into the holes in the engine block. Make sure they're tightened securely.

12   If the engine isn't going to be reassembled right away, cover it with a large plastic trash bag to keep it clean.

15.10 A large socket on an extension can be used to drive the new core plugs into the bores

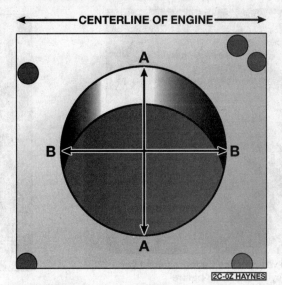

16.4a Measure the diameter of each cylinder at a right angle to engine centerline (A), and parallel to engine centerline (B) - out-of-round is the difference between A and B; taper is the difference between A and B at the top of the cylinder and A and B at the bottom of the cylinder

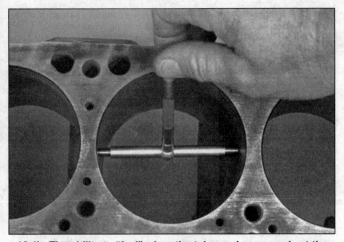

16.4b The ability to "feel" when the telescoping gauge is at the correct point will be developed over time, so work slowly and repeat the check until you're satisfied that the bore measurement is accurate

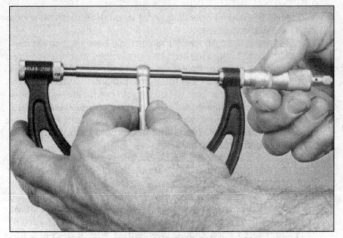

16.4c The gauge is then measured with a micrometer to determine the bore size

16 Engine block - inspection

Refer to illustrations 16.4a, 16.4b and 16.4c

1   Before the engine block is inspected, it should be cleaned as described in Section 15.

2   Visually check the engine block for cracks, rust and corrosion (see illustration 10.12). Look for stripped threads in the threaded holes. It's also a good idea to have the engine block checked for hidden cracks by an automotive machine shop that has the special equipment to do this type of work, especially if the vehicle had a history of overheating or using coolant. If defects are found, have the engine block repaired, if possible, or replaced. If the top of the engine block has been eroded by coolant leakage and the erosion is near the cylinder bores, the engine block must be replaced.

3   Check the cylinder bores for scuffing and scoring.

4   Check the cylinders for taper and out-of-round conditions as follows (see illustrations):

5   Measure the diameter of each cylinder at the top (just under the ridge area), center and bottom of the cylinder bore, parallel to the crankshaft axis.

6   Next, measure each cylinder's diameter at the same three locations perpendicular to the crankshaft axis.

7   The taper of each cylinder is the difference between the bore diameter at the top of the cylinder and the diameter at the bottom. The out-of-round specification of the cylinder bore is the difference between the parallel and perpendicular readings. Compare your results to this Chapter's Specifications.

8   If the cylinder walls are badly scuffed or scored, or if they're out-of-round or tapered beyond the limits given in this Chapter's Specifications, have the engine block rebored and honed at an automotive machine shop. If a rebore is done, oversize pistons and rings will be required.

9   Using a precision straightedge and feeler gauge, check the engine block deck (the surface that mates with the cylinder head) for distortion (see illustration 10.13). If it's distorted beyond the specified limit, it can be resurfaced by an automotive machine shop.

10   If the cylinders are in reasonably good condition and not worn to the outside of the limits, and if the piston-to-cylinder clearances can be maintained properly, then they don't have to be rebored. Honing is all that's necessary (refer to Section 17).

17 Cylinder honing

Refer to illustrations 17.3a and 17.3b

1   Prior to engine reassembly, the cylinder bores must be honed so the new piston rings will seat correctly and provide the best possible combustion chamber seal. **Note:** *If you don't have the tools or don't*

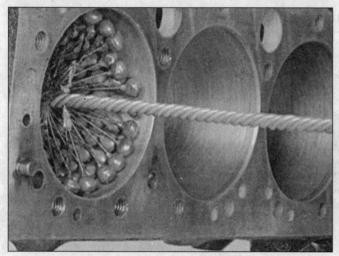

17.3a A "bottle brush" hone will produce better results if you have never done cylinder honing before

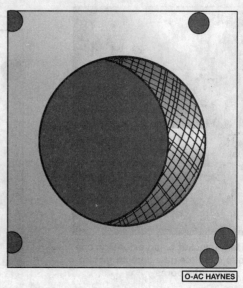

O-AC HAYNES

17.3b The cylinder hone should leave a smooth, crosshatch pattern with the lines intersecting at approximately a 60-degree angle

want to tackle the honing operation, most automotive machine shops will do it for a reasonable fee.

2   Before honing the cylinders, install the main bearing caps (without bearing inserts) and tighten the bolts to the specified torque.

3   Two types of cylinder hones are commonly available - the flex hone or "bottle brush" type and the more traditional surfacing hone with spring-loaded stones. Both will do the job, but for the less-experienced mechanic the "bottle brush" hone will probably be easier to use. You'll also need some kerosene or honing oil, rags and a variable-speed electric drill motor. The drill motor should be operated at a steady, slow speed. Proceed as follows:

a) *Mount the hone in the drill motor, compress the stones and slip it into the first cylinder* (see illustration). **Warning:** *Be sure to wear safety goggles or a face shield!*

b) *Lubricate the cylinder with plenty of honing oil, turn on the drill and move the hone up-and-down in the cylinder at a pace that will produce a fine crosshatch pattern on the cylinder walls. Ideally, the crosshatch lines should intersect at approximately a 60-degree angle* (see illustration). *Be sure to use plenty of lubricant and don't take off any more material than is absolutely necessary to produce the desired finish.* **Note:** *Piston ring manufacturers may specify a smaller crosshatch angle than the traditional 60-degrees - read and follow any instructions included with the new rings.*

c) *Don't withdraw the hone from the cylinder while it's running. Instead, shut off the drill and continue moving the hone up-and-down in the cylinder until it comes to a complete stop, then compress the stones and withdraw the hone. If you're using a "bottle brush" type hone, stop the drill motor, then turn the chuck in the normal direction of rotation while withdrawing the hone from the cylinder.*

d) *Wipe the oil out of the cylinder and repeat the procedure for the remaining cylinders.*

4   After the honing job is complete, chamfer the top edges of the cylinder bores with a small file so the rings won't catch when the pistons are installed. Be very careful not to nick the cylinder walls with the end of the file.

5   The entire engine block must be washed again very thoroughly with warm, soapy water to remove all traces of the abrasive grit produced during the honing operation. **Note:** *The bores can be considered clean when a lint-free white cloth - dampened with clean engine oil - used to wipe them out doesn't pick up any more honing residue, which will show up as gray areas on the cloth. Be sure to run a brush through all oil holes and galleries and flush them with running water.*

6   After rinsing, dry the engine block and apply a coat of light rust preventive oil to all machined surfaces. Wrap the engine block in a plastic trash bag to keep it clean and set it aside until reassembly.

18   Pistons/connecting rods - inspection

Refer to illustrations 18.4a, 18.4b, 18.10 and 18.11

1   Before the inspection process can be carried out, the piston/connecting rod assemblies must be cleaned and the original piston rings removed from the pistons. **Note:** *Always use new piston rings when the engine is reassembled.*

2   Using a piston ring installation tool, carefully remove the rings from the pistons. Be careful not to nick or gouge the pistons in the process.

3   Scrape all traces of carbon from the top of the piston. A hand-held wire brush or a piece of fine emery cloth can be used once the majority of the deposits have been scraped away. Do not, under any circumstances, use a wire brush mounted in a drill motor to remove deposits from the pistons. The piston material is soft and may be eroded away by the wire brush.

4   Use a piston ring groove-cleaning tool to remove carbon deposits from the ring grooves. If a tool isn't available, a piece broken off the old ring will do the job. Be very careful to remove only the carbon deposits - don't remove any metal and do not nick or scratch the sides of the ring grooves (see illustrations).

18.4a The piston ring grooves can be cleaned with a special tool, as shown here . . .

18.4b . . . or a section of a broken ring

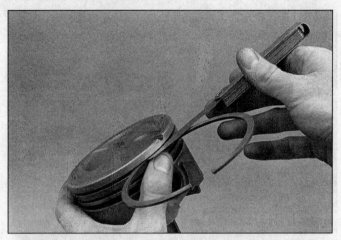

18.10 Check the ring groove clearance with a feeler gauge at several points around the groove

5   Once the deposits have been removed, clean the piston/connecting rod assemblies with solvent and dry them with compressed air (if available). Make sure the oil return holes in the back sides of the ring grooves and the oil hole in the lower end of each rod are clear.

6   If the pistons and cylinder walls aren't damaged or worn excessively, and if the engine block is not rebored, new pistons won't be necessary. Normal piston wear appears as even vertical wear on the piston thrust surfaces and slight looseness of the top ring in its groove. New piston rings, however, should always be used when an engine is rebuilt.

7   Carefully inspect each piston for cracks around the skirt, at the pin bosses and at the ring lands. **Caution:** *Some early 1988 3.6L engines (before engine no. 9D 121113) have incorrectly-stamped pistons. On these, the word FRONT is actually stamped on the rear of the pistons. Correct pistons will have the cast arrows on the inside of the skirt to your* **left** *when facing the word FRONT.*

8   Look for scoring and scuffing on the thrust faces of the skirt, holes in the piston crown and burned areas at the edge of the crown. If the skirt is scored or scuffed, the engine may have been suffering from overheating and/or abnormal combustion, which caused excessively high operating temperatures. The cooling and lubrication systems should be checked thoroughly. A hole in the piston crown is an indication that abnormal combustion (preignition) was occurring. Burned areas at the edge of the piston crown are usually evidence of spark knock (detonation). If any of the above problems exist, the causes

must be corrected or the damage will occur again. The causes may include intake air leaks, incorrect air/fuel mixture, incorrect ignition timing and EGR system malfunctions.

9   Corrosion of the piston, in the form of small pits, indicates that coolant is leaking into the combustion chamber and/or the crankcase. Again, the cause must be corrected or the problem may persist in the rebuilt engine.

10   Measure the piston ring groove clearance by laying a new piston ring in each ring groove and slipping a feeler gauge in beside it **(see illustration)**. Check the clearance at three or four locations around each groove. Be sure to use the correct ring for each groove - they are different. If the clearance is greater than that listed in this Chapter's Specifications, new pistons will have to be used.

11   Check the piston-to-bore clearance by measuring the bore (see Section 16) and the piston diameter. Make sure the pistons and bores are correctly matched. Measure the piston across the skirt, at a 90-degree angle to the piston pin **(see illustration)**. Subtract the piston diameter from the bore diameter to obtain the clearance. If it's greater than specified, the engine block will have to be rebored and new pistons and rings installed.

12   Check the piston-to-rod clearance by twisting the piston and rod in opposite directions. Any noticeable play indicates excessive wear, which must be corrected.

13   If the pistons must be removed from the connecting rods for any reason, the rods should be taken to an automotive machine shop, to be checked for bend and twist, since automotive machine shops have special equipment for this purpose.

14   Check the connecting rods for cracks and other damage. Temporarily remove the rod caps, lift out the old bearing inserts, wipe the connecting rod and cap bearing surfaces clean and inspect them for nicks, gouges and scratches. After checking the connecting rods, replace the old bearings, slip the caps into place and tighten the nuts finger tight. **Note:** *If the engine is being rebuilt because of a connecting rod knock, be sure to install new rods.*

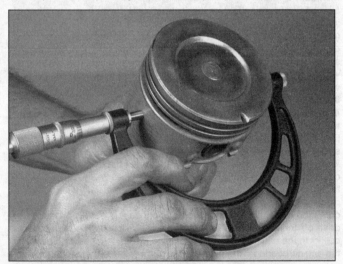

18.11 Measure the piston diameter at a 90-degree angle to the piston pin, at the bottom of the piston pin area - a precision caliper may be used if a micrometer isn't available

19 Crankshaft - inspection

Refer to illustration 19.5

1   Clean the crankshaft with solvent and dry it with compressed air (if available). Be sure to clean the oil holes with a stiff brush and flush them with solvent.

2   Check the main and connecting rod bearing journals for uneven wear, scoring, pits and cracks.

3   Remove all burrs from the crankshaft oil holes with a stone, file or scraper.

4   Check the remainder of the crankshaft for cracks and other damage. It should be magnafluxed to reveal hidden cracks - an automotive

19.5 Measure the diameter of each crankshaft journal at several points to detect taper and out-of-round conditions

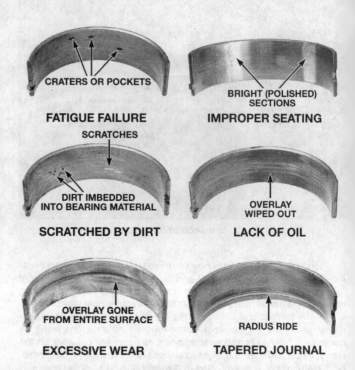

20.1 When inspecting the main and connecting rod bearings, look for these problems

machine shop will handle the procedure.

5   Using a micrometer, measure the diameter of the main and connecting rod journals and compare the results to this Chapter's Specifications **(see illustration)**. By measuring the diameter at a number of points around each journal's circumference, you'll be able to determine whether or not the journal is out-of-round. Take the measurement at each end of the journal, near the crank throws, to determine if the journal is tapered. Crankshaft runout should be checked also, but large V-blocks and a dial indicator are needed to do it correctly. If you don't have the equipment, have a machine shop check the runout.

6   If the crankshaft journals are damaged, tapered, out-of-round or worn beyond the limits given in the Specifications, have the crankshaft reground by an automotive machine shop. Be sure to use the correct size bearing inserts if the crankshaft is reconditioned.

7   Check the oil seal journals at each end of the crankshaft for wear and damage. If the seal has worn a groove in the journal, or if it's nicked or scratched, the new seal may leak when the engine is reassembled. In some cases, an automotive machine shop may be able to repair the journal by pressing on a thin sleeve. If repair isn't feasible, a new or different crankshaft should be installed.

8   Refer to Section 20 and examine the main and rod bearing inserts.

20   Main and connecting rod bearings - inspection and selection

Inspection

Refer to illustration 20.1

1   Even though the main and connecting rod bearings should be replaced with new ones during the engine overhaul, the old bearings should be retained for close examination, as they may reveal valuable information about the condition of the engine **(see illustration)**.

2   Bearing failure occurs because of lack of lubrication, the presence of dirt or other foreign particles, overloading the engine and corrosion. Regardless of the cause of bearing failure, it must be corrected before the engine is reassembled to prevent it from happening again.

3   When examining the bearings, remove them from the engine block, the main bearing caps, the connecting rods and the rod caps and lay them out on a clean surface in the same general position as their location in the engine. This will enable you to match any bearing problems with the corresponding crankshaft journal.

4   Dirt and other foreign particles get into the engine in a variety of ways. It may be left in the engine during assembly, or it may pass through filters or the PCV system. It may get into the oil, and from there

into the bearings. Metal chips from machining operations and normal engine wear are often present. Abrasives are sometimes left in engine components after reconditioning, especially when parts are not thoroughly cleaned using the proper cleaning methods. Whatever the source, these foreign objects often end up embedded in the soft bearing material and are easily recognized. Large particles will not embed in the bearing and will score or gouge the bearing and journal. The best prevention for this cause of bearing failure is to clean all parts thoroughly and keep everything spotlessly clean during engine assembly. Frequent and regular engine oil and filter changes are also recommended.

5   Lack of lubrication (or lubrication breakdown) has a number of interrelated causes. Excessive heat (which thins the oil), overloading (which squeezes the oil from the bearing face) and oil leakage or throw off (from excessive bearing clearances, worn oil pump or high engine speeds) all contribute to lubrication breakdown. Blocked oil passages, which usually are the result of misaligned oil holes in a bearing shell, will also oil starve a bearing and destroy it. When lack of lubrication is the cause of bearing failure, the bearing material is wiped or extruded from the steel backing of the bearing. Temperatures may increase to the point where the steel backing turns blue from overheating.

6   Driving habits can have a definite effect on bearing life. Low speed operation in too high a gear (lugging the engine) puts very high loads on bearings, which tends to squeeze out the oil film. These loads cause the bearings to flex, which produces fine cracks in the bearing face (fatigue failure). Eventually the bearing material will loosen in pieces and tear away from the steel backing. Short trip driving leads to corrosion of bearings because insufficient engine heat is produced to drive off the condensed water and corrosive gases. These products collect in the engine oil, forming acid and sludge. As the oil is carried to the engine bearings, the acid attacks and corrodes the bearing material.

7   Incorrect bearing installation during engine assembly will lead to bearing failure as well. Tight-fitting bearings leave insufficient bearing oil clearance and will result in oil starvation. Dirt or foreign particles

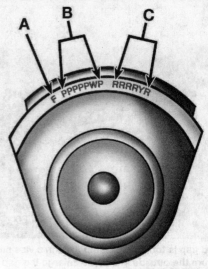

49011-2B-20.9 HAYNES

20.9 Later model 4.0L engines have graded journals and bearings, with the markings indicated on the front throw of the crankshaft - "A" indicates the front of the engine, "B" indicates the codes for the main journals/bearings, and "C" indicates the connecting rod journal grades

trapped behind a bearing insert result in high spots on the bearing which lead to failure.

Selection

Refer to illustration 20.9

8   If the original bearings are worn or damaged, or if the oil clearances are incorrect (see Sections 23 or 25), the following procedures should be used to select the correct new bearings for engine reassembly. However, if the crankshaft has been reground, new undersize bearings must be installed - the following procedure should not be used if undersize bearings are required! The automotive machine shop that reconditions the crankshaft will provide or help you select the correct-size bearings. Regardless of how the bearing sizes are determined, use the oil clearance, measured with Plastigage, as a guide to ensure the bearings are the right size.

9   If you need to use a STANDARD size main or rod bearing, install one that has the same number as the original bearing. **Note:** *4.0L engines after #164637 have sized crankshafts and bearings in three grades, indicated by color and letter. The codes are stamped into the front throw of the crankshaft* (see illustration). *Match replacement bearings by the color codes: pink (P), white (W) or green (G) for main bearings; red (R), yellow (Y) or blue (B) for the three grades of connecting rod bearings.*

10   Remember, the oil clearance is the final judge when selecting new bearing sizes. If you have any questions or are unsure which bearings to use, get help from a dealer parts or service department.

21 Engine overhaul - reassembly sequence

1   Before beginning engine reassembly, make sure you have all the necessary new parts, gaskets and seals as well as the following items on hand:

Common hand tools
A 1/2-inch drive torque wrench
Piston ring installation tool
Piston ring compressor
Short lengths of rubber or plastic hose
* to fit over connecting rod bolts*

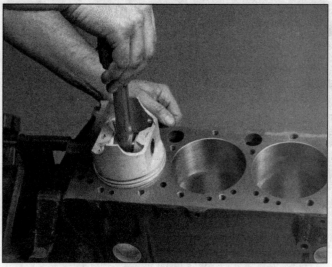

22.3 When checking piston ring end gap, the ring must be square in the cylinder bore (this is done by pushing the ring down with the top of a piston as shown)

Plastigage
Feeler gauges
A fine-tooth file
New engine oil
Engine assembly lube or moly-base grease
Gasket sealant
Thread locking compound

Special Jaguar tools

Engine lifting brackets (18G 1465)
Timing damper simulator (18E 1436)
Camshaft TDC tool (18G 1433)

2   In order to save time and avoid problems, engine reassembly must be done in the following general order:

Piston rings (Part B)
Crankshaft and main bearings (Part B)
Piston/connecting rod assemblies (Part B)
Rear main (crankshaft) oil seal (Part B)
Auxiliary shaft (Part A)
Timing chains and sprockets (Part A)
Oil pump (Part A)
Timing chain cover (Part A)
Cylinder head and lifters (Part A)
Camshafts (Part A)
Oil pick-up (Part A)
Oil pan (Part A)
Intake and exhaust manifolds (Part A)
Valve cover (Part A)
Flywheel/driveplate (Part A)

22 Piston rings - installation

Refer to illustrations 22.3, 22.4, 22.5, 22.9a, 22.9b and 22.12

1   Before installing the new piston rings, the ring end gaps must be checked. It's assumed that the piston ring groove clearance has been checked and verified correct (see Section 18).

2   Lay out the piston/connecting rod assemblies and the new ring sets so the ring sets will be matched with the same piston and cylinder during the end gap measurement and engine assembly.

3   Insert the top (number one) ring into the first cylinder and square it up with the cylinder walls by pushing it in with the top of the piston (see illustration). The ring should be near the bottom of the cylinder,

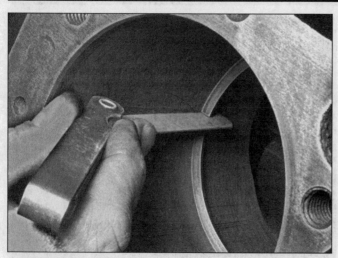

22.4 With the ring square in the cylinder, measure the end gap with a feeler gauge

22.5 If the end gap is too small, clamp a file in a vise and file the ring ends (from the outside in only) to enlarge the gap slightly

at the lower limit of ring travel.

4   To measure the end gap, slip feeler gauges between the ends of the ring until a gauge equal to the gap width is found **(see illustration)**. The feeler gauge should slide between the ring ends with a slight amount of drag. Compare the measurement to that found in this Chapter's Specifications. If the gap is larger or smaller than specified, double-check to make sure you have the correct rings before proceeding.

5   If the gap is too small, it must be enlarged or the ring ends may come in contact with each other during engine operation, which can cause serious damage to the engine. The end gap can be increased by filing the ring ends very carefully with a fine file. Mount the file in a vise equipped with soft jaws, slip the ring over the file with the ends contacting the file face and slowly move the ring to remove material from the ends **(see illustration)**. **Caution:** *When performing this operation, file only from the outside in, and after the correct gap is achieved, deburr the filed ends of the rings with a fine whetstone.*

6   Excess end gap isn't critical unless it's greater than Specifications. Again, double-check to make sure you have the correct rings for your engine.

7   Repeat the procedure for each ring that will be installed in the first cylinder and for each ring in the remaining cylinders. Remember to keep rings, pistons and cylinders matched.

8   Once the ring end gaps have been checked/corrected, the rings can be installed on the pistons.

9   The oil control ring (lowest one on the piston) is usually installed

first. It's composed of three separate components. Slip the spacer/expander into the groove **(see illustration)**. If an anti-rotation tang is used, make sure it's inserted into the drilled hole in the ring groove. Next, install the lower side rail. Don't use a piston ring installation tool on the oil ring side rails, as they may be damaged. Instead, place one end of the side rail into the groove between the spacer/expander and the ring land, hold it firmly in place and slide a finger around the piston while pushing the rail into the groove **(see illustrations)**. Next, install the upper side rail in the same manner.

10   After the three oil ring components have been installed, check to make sure that both the upper and lower side rails can be turned smoothly in the ring groove.

11   The number two (middle) ring is installed next. It's usually stamped with a mark which must face up, toward the top of the piston. **Note:** *Always follow the instructions printed on the ring package or box - different manufacturers may require different approaches. Do not mix up the top and middle rings, as they have different cross sections.*

12   Use a piston ring installation tool and make sure the ring's identification mark is facing the top of the piston, then slip the ring into the middle groove on the piston **(see illustration)**. Don't expand the ring any more than necessary to slide it over the piston.

13   Install the number one (top) ring in the same manner. Make sure the mark is facing up. Be careful not to confuse the number one and number two rings.

14   Repeat the procedure for the remaining pistons and rings.

22.9a Install the spacer/expander in the oil control ring groove

22.9b DO NOT use a piston ring installation tool when installing the oil ring side rails

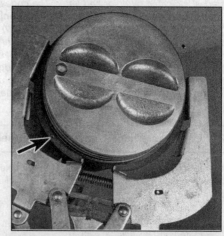

22.12 Install the compression rings with a ring expander - the mark must face up

23.10 Lay the Plastigage strips (arrow) on the main bearing journals, parallel to the crankshaft centerline

23.14 Compare the width of the crushed Plastigage to the scale on the envelope to determine the main bearing oil clearance (always take the measurement at the widest point of the Plastigage) - be sure to use the correct scale; standard and metric scales are included

23   Crankshaft - installation and main bearing oil clearance check

Refer to illustrations 23.10 and 23.14

1   Crankshaft installation is the first major step in engine reassembly. It's assumed at this point that the engine block and crankshaft have been cleaned, inspected and repaired or reconditioned.
2   Position the engine with the bottom facing up.
3   Remove the main bearing cap bolts and lift out the caps. Lay the caps out in the proper order.
4   If they're still in place, remove the old bearing inserts from the engine block and the main bearing caps. Wipe the main bearing surfaces of the engine block and caps with a clean, lint free cloth. They must be kept spotlessly clean!

Main bearing oil clearance check

5   Clean the back sides of the new main bearing inserts and lay the bearing half with the oil groove in each main bearing saddle in the engine block. Lay the other bearing half from each bearing set in the corresponding main bearing cap. Make sure the tab on each bearing insert fits into the recess in the engine block or cap. Also, the oil holes in the engine block must line up with the oil holes in the bearing insert. **Caution:** *Do not hammer the bearings into place and don't nick or gouge the bearing faces. No lubrication should be used at this time.*
6   The thrust bearings (washers) must be installed in the number four main bearing cap and saddle.
7   Clean the faces of the bearings in the engine block and the crankshaft main bearing journals with a clean, lint free cloth. Check or clean the oil holes in the crankshaft, as any dirt here can go only one way - straight through the new bearings.
8   Once you're certain the crankshaft is clean, carefully lay it in position in the main bearings.
9   Before the crankshaft can be permanently installed, the main bearing oil clearance must be checked.
10   Trim several pieces of the appropriate size Plastigage (they must be slightly shorter than the width of the main bearings) and place one piece on each crankshaft main bearing journal, parallel with the journal axis **(see illustration)**.
11   Clean the faces of the bearings in the caps and install the caps in their respective positions (don't mix them up) with the arrows pointing toward the front of the engine. Don't disturb the Plastigage. Apply a light coat of oil to the bolt threads and the undersides of the bolt heads, then install them. **Note:** *Use the old bolts for this step (save the new ones for final installation.*
12   Tighten the main bearing cap bolts, in three steps, to the torque listed in this Chapter's Specifications. Don't rotate the crankshaft at any time during this operation!

13   Remove the bolts and carefully lift off the main bearing caps or cap assembly. Keep them in order. Don't disturb the Plastigage or rotate the crankshaft. If any of the main bearing caps are difficult to remove, tap them gently from side-to-side with a soft-face hammer to loosen them.
14   Compare the width of the crushed Plastigage on each journal to the scale printed on the Plastigage envelope to obtain the main bearing oil clearance **(see illustration)**. Check the Specifications to make sure it's correct.
15   If the clearance is not as specified, the bearing inserts may be the wrong size (which means different ones will be required - see Section 20). Before deciding that different inserts are needed, make sure that no dirt or oil was between the bearing inserts and the caps or engine block when the clearance was measured. If the Plastigage is noticeably wider at one end than the other, the journal may be tapered (see Section 19).
16   Carefully scrape all traces of the Plastigage material off the main bearing journals and/or the bearing faces. Don't nick or scratch the bearing faces.

Final crankshaft installation

17   Carefully lift the crankshaft out of the engine. Clean the bearing faces in the engine block, then apply a thin, uniform layer of clean moly-base grease or engine assembly lube to each of the bearing surfaces. Coat the thrust washers as well.
18   Lubricate the crankshaft surfaces that contact the oil seals with moly-base grease, engine assembly lube or clean engine oil.
19   Make sure the crankshaft journals are clean, then lay the crankshaft back in place in the engine block. Clean the faces of the bearings in the main bearing caps, then apply lubricant to them. Install the main bearing caps in their respective positions with the arrows pointing toward the front of the engine. **Note:** *Be sure to install the thrust washers (lubricated) with the number 4 main journal.* The upper (block side) thrust washers can be rotated into position around the crankshaft with the crankshaft installed in the engine block, with the thrust washer grooves facing OUT. The lower thrust washers should be placed on the main bearing caps with their grooves OUT.
20   For the final assembly, use only **new** bolts, for both the main bearings and the connecting rods. Apply a light coat of oil to the bolt threads and the undersides of the bolt heads, then install them. Tighten all main bearing cap bolts to the torque listed in this Chapter's Specifications, starting in the center and working out to the ends.
21   Rotate the crankshaft a number of times by hand to check for any obvious binding.
22   Check the crankshaft endplay with a feeler gauge or a dial indica-

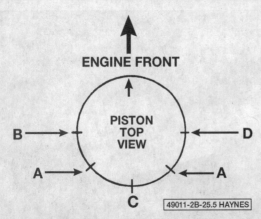

25.5 Stagger the ring end gaps around the piston, as shown, before installing the pistons

A	Oil ring rail gaps	C	Oil ring spacer gap
B	Second compression ring gap	D	Top compression ring gap

25.9 Pistons must be installed with the arrow (right arrow) or FRONT facing the front of the engine - left arrow indicates piston size letter

tor as described in Section 14. The endplay should be correct if the crankshaft thrust faces aren't worn or damaged and new thrust washers have been installed. **Note:** *If the endplay is too great, even with the new thrust bearings, oversized thrust bearings are available. There are two sizes, 0.005-inch and 0.010-inch oversize.*
23   Install a new rear main oil seal, then bolt the retainer to the engine block (see Section 24).

24   Rear main oil seal installation

1   The crankshaft must be installed first and the main bearing caps bolted in place, then the new seal should be installed in the retainer and the retainer bolted to the engine block.
2   Check the seal contact surface on the crankshaft very carefully for scratches and nicks that could damage the new seal lip and cause oil leaks. If the crankshaft is damaged, the only alternative is a new or different crankshaft.
3   Refer to Part A of this Chapter for installation of the new rear seal, using the plastic alignment tool supplied with the engine overhaul gasket set.

25   Pistons/connecting rods - installation and rod bearing oil clearance check

Refer to illustrations 25.5, 25.9, 25.11, 25.13 and 25.17
1   Before installing the piston/connecting rod assemblies, the cylinder walls must be perfectly clean, the top edge of each cylinder must be chamfered, and the crankshaft must be in place.
2   Remove the cap from the end of the number one connecting rod (refer to the marks made during removal). Remove the original bearing inserts and wipe the bearing surfaces of the connecting rod and cap with a clean, lint-free cloth. They must be kept spotlessly clean.

Connecting rod bearing oil clearance check

3   Clean the back side of the new upper bearing insert, then lay it in place in the connecting rod. Make sure the tab on the bearing fits into the recess in the rod so the oil holes line up. Don't hammer the bearing insert into place and be very careful not to nick or gouge the bearing face. Don't lubricate the bearing at this time.
4   Clean the back side of the other bearing insert and install it in the rod cap. Again, make sure the tab on the bearing fits into the recess in the cap, and don't apply any lubricant. It's critically important that the mating surfaces of the bearing and connecting rod are perfectly clean

and oil free when they're assembled.
5   Position the piston ring gaps at staggered intervals around the piston **(see illustration)**.
6   Slip a section of plastic or rubber hose over each connecting rod cap bolt.
7   Lubricate the piston and rings with clean engine oil and attach a piston ring compressor to the piston. Leave the skirt protruding about 1/4-inch to guide the piston into the cylinder. The rings must be compressed until they're flush with the piston.
8   Rotate the crankshaft until the number one connecting rod journal is at BDC (bottom dead center) and apply a coat of engine oil to the cylinder wall.
9   With the word FRONT (or the arrow) on top of the piston facing the front of the engine **(see illustration)**, gently insert the piston/connecting rod assembly into the number one cylinder bore and rest the bottom edge of the ring compressor on the engine block.
10   Tap the top edge of the ring compressor to make sure it's contacting the engine block around its entire circumference.
11   Gently tap on the top of the piston with the end of a wooden hammer handle **(see illustration)** while guiding the end of the connecting rod into place on the crankshaft journal. The piston rings may try to pop out of the ring compressor just before entering the cylinder bore, so keep some downward pressure on the ring compressor. Work slowly, and if any resistance is felt as the piston enters the cylinder,

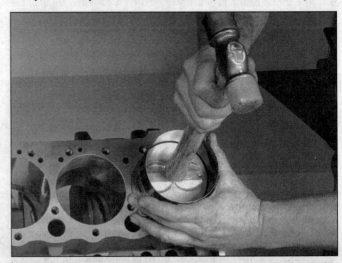

25.11 The piston can be driven (gently) into the cylinder bore with the end of a wooden or plastic hammer handle

25.13 Lay the Plastigage strips on each rod bearing journal, parallel to the crankshaft centerline

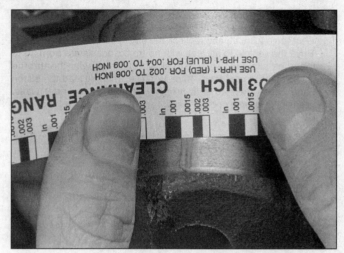

25.17 Measure the width of the crushed Plastigage to determine the rod bearing oil clearance (be sure to use the correct scale - standard and metric scales are included

stop immediately. Find out what's hanging up and fix it before proceeding. **Caution:** *Do not, for any reason, force the piston into the cylinder - you might break a ring and/or the piston.*

12   Once the piston/connecting rod assembly is installed, the connecting rod bearing oil clearance must be checked before the rod cap is permanently bolted in place.

13   Cut a piece of the appropriate size Plastigage slightly shorter than the width of the connecting rod bearing and lay it in place on the number one connecting rod journal, parallel with the journal axis **(see illustration)**.

14   Clean the connecting rod cap bearing face, remove the protective hoses from the connecting rod bolts and install the rod cap. Make sure the mating mark on the cap is on the same side as the mark on the connecting rod. Check the cap to make sure the front mark is facing the timing chain of the engine.

15   Apply a light coat of oil to the undersides of the nuts, then install and tighten them to the torque listed in this Chapter's Specifications, working up to it in three steps. **Note:** *Use the old nuts and bolts for this step (save the new ones for final installation).* Use a thin-wall socket to avoid erroneous torque readings that can result if the socket is wedged between the rod cap and nut. If the socket tends to wedge itself between the nut and the cap, lift up on it slightly until it no longer contacts the cap. Do not rotate the crankshaft at any time during this operation.

16   Remove the nuts and detach the rod cap, being very careful not to disturb the Plastigage.

17   Compare the width of the crushed Plastigage to the scale printed on the Plastigage envelope to obtain the oil clearance **(see illustration)**. Compare it to this Chapter's Specifications to make sure the clearance is correct.

18   If the clearance is not as specified, the bearing inserts may be the wrong size (which means different ones will be required). Before deciding that different inserts are needed, make sure that no dirt or oil was between the bearing inserts and the connecting rod or cap when the clearance was measured. Also, recheck the journal diameter. If the Plastigage was wider at one end than the other, the journal may be tapered (refer to Section 19).

Final connecting rod installation

19   Carefully scrape all traces of the Plastigage material off the rod journal and/or bearing face. Be very careful not to scratch the bearing, use your fingernail or the edge of a credit card to remove the Plastigage.

20   Make sure the bearing faces are perfectly clean, then apply a uniform layer of clean moly-base grease or engine assembly lube to both of them. You'll have to push the piston higher into the cylinder to expose the face of the bearing insert in the connecting rod, be sure to

slip the protective hoses over the connecting rod bolts first.

21   At this time, remove the original connecting rod bolts/nuts and replace them with new bolts/nuts. They are of a design which requires they be used only once. The old ones are OK for Plastigage checking, but for final assembly use only new connecting rod bolts/nuts. Install the rod cap and tighten the nuts to the torque listed in this Chapter's Specifications. Again, work up to the torque in three steps.

22   Repeat the entire procedure for the remaining pistons/connecting rod assemblies.

23   The important points to remember are:

a) *Keep the back sides of the bearing inserts and the insides of the connecting rods and caps perfectly clean when assembling them.*
b) *Make sure you have the correct piston/connecting rod assembly for each cylinder.*
c) *The dimple on the piston must face the front of the engine.*
d) *Lubricate the cylinder walls with clean oil.*
e) *Lubricate the bearing faces when installing the rod caps after the oil clearance has been checked.*

24   After all the piston/connecting rod assemblies have been properly installed, rotate the crankshaft a number of times by hand to check for any obvious binding.

25   As a final step, the connecting rod endplay must be checked. Refer to Section 13 for this procedure.

26   Compare the measured endplay to this Chapter's Specifications to make sure it's correct. If it was correct before disassembly and the original crankshaft and connecting rods were reinstalled, it should still be right. If new connecting rods or a new crankshaft were installed, the endplay may be inadequate. If so, the connecting rods will have to be removed and taken to an automotive machine shop for resizing.

26   Initial start-up and break-in after overhaul

Warning: *Have a fire extinguisher handy when starting the engine for the first time.*

1   Once the engine has been installed in the vehicle, double-check the engine oil and coolant levels.

2   With the spark plugs out of the engine and the ignition system and fuel pump disabled, crank the engine until oil pressure registers on the gauge or the light goes out.

3   Install the spark plugs, hook up the plug wires and restore the ignition system and fuel pump functions.

4   Start the engine. It may take a few moments for the fuel system to build up pressure, but the engine should start without a great deal of effort.

5   After the engine starts, it should be allowed to warm up to normal

operating temperature. While the engine is warming up, make a thorough check for fuel, oil and coolant leaks.

6   Shut the engine off and recheck the engine oil and coolant levels.

7   Drive the vehicle to an area with no traffic, accelerate from 30 to 50 mph, then allow the vehicle to slow to 30 mph with the throttle closed. Repeat the procedure 10 or 12 times. This will load the piston rings and cause them to seat properly against the cylinder walls. Check again for oil and coolant leaks.

8   Drive the vehicle gently for the first 500 miles (no sustained high speeds) and keep a constant check on the oil level. It is not unusual for an engine to use oil during the break-in period.

9   At approximately 500 to 600 miles, change the oil and filter.

10   For the next few hundred miles, drive the vehicle normally. Do not pamper it or abuse it.

11   After 2000 miles, change the oil and filter again and consider the engine broken in.

Chapter 3
Cooling, heating and air conditioning systems

Contents

Specifications

General

Radiator cap pressure rating	13.5 to 17.5 psi
Thermostat rating	180 to 207-degrees F

Torque specifications

	Nm	Ft-lbs (unless otherwise indicated)
Coolant pipe to block	22 to 28	16 to 21
Fan assembly-to-drive hub nuts....................................	22 to 28	16 to 21
Fan clutch-to-fan blade nuts	22 to 28	16 to 21
Thermostat cover bolts...	22 to 28	16 to 21
Thermostat housing-to-block bolts	22 to 28	16 to 21
Water pump bolts	22 to 28	16 to 21

1   General information

Engine cooling system

All vehicles covered by this manual employ a pressurized engine cooling system with thermostatically-controlled coolant circulation. An impeller type water pump mounted on the front of the block pumps coolant through the engine. The coolant flows around each cylinder and toward the rear of the engine. Cast-in coolant passages direct coolant around the intake and exhaust ports, near the spark plug areas and in proximity to the exhaust valve guides.

A wax-pellet type thermostat is located in the thermostat housing at the front of the engine. During warm up, the closed thermostat prevents coolant from circulating through the radiator. When the engine reaches normal operating temperature, the thermostat opens and allows hot coolant to travel through the radiator, where it is cooled before returning to the engine.

The cooling system is sealed by a pressure-type radiator cap. This raises the boiling point of the coolant, and the higher boiling point of the coolant increases the cooling efficiency of the radiator. If the system pressure exceeds the cap pressure-relief value, the excess pressure in the system forces the spring-loaded valve inside the cap off its seat and allows the coolant to escape through the overflow tube into a coolant reservoir. When the system cools, the excess coolant is automatically drawn from the reservoir back into the radiator. This type of cooling system is known as a closed design because coolant that escapes past the pressure cap is saved and reused.

The Jaguar cooling system on 1988 and 1989 models has both a header tank and a coolant recovery tank. The header tank is the highest point in the cooling system and is the location of the "radiator" cap (the cap is not on the radiator). The recovery tank down in the driver's fenderwell collects heated coolant as described above. Models from 1990 to 1994 do not have a coolant recovery tank, but have an enlarged header tank. In all models, the recovery tank has a sensor in it to detect a low coolant level, and the instrument panel has a warning light to that effect.

Heating system

The heating system consists of two blower fans, one under the dash on the right and one on the left, and a heater core located within the heater/air conditioning assembly which is under the dash and behind the console. Hoses connect the heater core to the engine cooling system. Heater function is controlled by the heater/air conditioning control head on the dashboard. Hot engine coolant is circulated through the heater core. When the heater mode is activated, a flap door opens to expose the heater box to the passenger compartment. A fan switch on the control head activates the blower motor, which forces air through the core, heating the air.

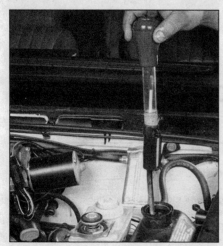

2.4 An inexpensive hydrometer can be used to test the condition of your coolant

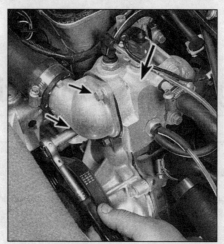

3.7 Remove the two bolts (small arrows) holding the thermostat cover to the housing (large arrow)

3.9 The thermostat is installed with the spring end towards the cylinder head - always use a new O-ring (A) and position the jiggle pin (B) up

Air conditioning system

The air conditioning system consists of a condenser mounted in front of the radiator, an evaporator mounted in the heater/air conditioning assembly behind the console and under the center of the dash, a compressor mounted on the engine, a filter-drier which contains a high pressure relief valve and the plumbing connecting all of the above.

A blower fan forces the warmer air of the passenger compartment through the evaporator core (sort of a radiator-in-reverse), transferring the heat from the air to the refrigerant. The liquid refrigerant boils off into low pressure vapor, taking the heat with it when it leaves the evaporator. The compressor keeps refrigerant circulating through the system, pumping the warmed coolant through the condenser where it is cooled and then circulated back to the evaporator.

2   Antifreeze/coolant - general information

Refer to illustration 2.4
Warning: *Do not allow antifreeze to come in contact with your skin or painted surfaces of the vehicle. Rinse off spills immediately with plenty of water. Antifreeze is highly toxic if ingested. Never leave antifreeze lying around in an open container or in puddles on the floor; children and pets are attracted by it's sweet smell and may drink it. Check with local authorities about disposing of used antifreeze. Many communities have collection centers which will see that antifreeze is disposed of safely. Never dump used antifreeze on the ground or into drains.*
Note: *Non-toxic antifreeze is now manufactured and available at local auto parts stores, but even these types should be disposed of properly.*

The cooling system should be filled with a water/ethylene-glycol based antifreeze solution, which will prevent freezing down to at least -20-degrees F, or lower if local climate requires it. It also provides protection against corrosion and increases the coolant boiling point.

The cooling system should be drained, flushed and refilled every 24,000 miles or every two years (see Chapter 1). The use of antifreeze solutions for periods of longer than two years is likely to cause damage and encourage the formation of rust and scale in the system. If your tap water is "hard", i.e. contains a lot of dissolved minerals, use distilled water with the antifreeze.

Before adding antifreeze to the system, check all hose connections, because antifreeze tends to leak through very minute openings. Engines do not normally consume coolant. Therefore, if the level goes down, find the cause and correct it.

The exact mixture of antifreeze-to-water you should use depends on the relative weather conditions. The mixture should contain at least 50-percent antifreeze, but should never contain more than 70-percent

antifreeze. Consult the mixture ratio chart on the antifreeze container before adding coolant. Hydrometers are available at most auto parts stores to test the ratio of antifreeze to water **(see illustration)**. Use antifreeze which meets the vehicle manufacturer's specifications.

3   Thermostat - check and replacement

Warning: *Do not attempt to remove the radiator cap, coolant or thermostat until the engine has cooled completely.*

Check

1   Before assuming the thermostat is responsible for a cooling system problem, check the coolant level (Chapter 1), drivebelt tension (Chapter 1) and temperature gauge (or light) operation.
2   If the engine takes a long time to warm up (as indicated by the temperature gauge or heater operation), the thermostat is probably stuck open. Replace the thermostat with a new one.
3   If the engine runs hot, use your hand to check the temperature of the lower radiator hose. **Warning:** *Do this check with the engine off. Do not get your hands near the fan blades.* If the hose is not hot, but the engine is, the thermostat is probably stuck in the closed position, preventing the coolant inside the engine from traveling through the radiator. Replace the thermostat. **Caution:** *Do not drive the vehicle without a thermostat. The computer may stay in open loop and emissions and fuel economy will suffer.*
4   If the lower radiator hose is hot, it means that the coolant is flowing and the thermostat is open. Consult the *Troubleshooting* section at the front of this manual for further diagnosis.

Replacement

Refer to illustrations 3.7 and 3.9
5   Disconnect the negative cable from the battery. **Caution:** *If the stereo in your vehicle is equipped with an anti-theft system, make sure you have the correct activation code before disconnecting the battery.*
6   Drain the coolant from the radiator (see Chapter 1).
7   Remove the bolts from the thermostat cover **(see illustration)**. If the cover doesn't pull loose, tap it with a soft-faced hammer. Do not use a screwdriver between the cover and the thermostat housing.
8   Remove the thermostat, noting the direction in which it was installed in the housing, and thoroughly clean the sealing surfaces.
9   Install a new O-ring onto the thermostat **(see illustration)**. Make sure it is evenly fitted all the way around.
10   Apply a bead of RTV sealant to the thermostat housing. Install the thermostat and housing, positioning the jiggle pin at the highest point.

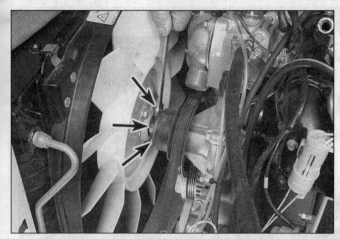

4.8 Remove the four nuts (arrows indicate three of them shown here) holding the fan/clutch assembly to the front of the water pump

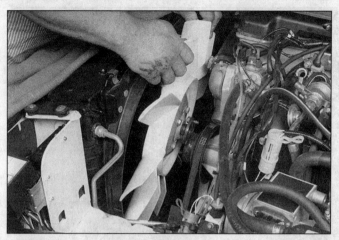

4.9 The fan can be removed with the shroud in place by angling it out of the shroud

Note: *The thermostat is usually marked TOP on the radiator side for proper orientation.*

11   Tighten the cover fasteners to the torque listed in this Chapter's Specifications.

12   Refill the cooling system, run the engine and check for leaks and proper operation.

4   Engine cooling fans - check and replacement

Mechanical fan (1988 to 1992 models)

Warning: *Keep hands, hair, tools and clothing away from the fan when the engine is running. To avoid injury or damage DO NOT operate the engine with a damaged fan. Do not attempt to repair fan blades - replace a damaged fan with a new one.*

Check

Warning: *In order to check the fan clutch, the engine will need to be at operating temperature, so while going through checks prior to Step 6 be careful that the engine is NOT running. Severe personal injury can result!*

1   Symptoms of failure of the fan clutch are continuous noisy operation, looseness, vibration and evidence of silicone fluid leaks.

2   Rock the fan back and forth by hand to check for excessive bearing play.

3   With the engine cold, turn the blades by hand. The fan should turn freely.

4   Visually inspect for substantial fluid leakage from the fan clutch assembly, a deformed bi-metal spring or grease leakage from the cooling fan bearing. If any of these conditions exist, replace the fan clutch.

5   When the engine is fully warmed up, turn off the ignition switch and disconnect the cable from the negative battery terminal. **Caution:** *If the stereo in your vehicle is equipped with an anti-theft system, make sure you have the correct activation code before disconnecting the battery.* Turn the fan by hand. Some resistance should be felt. If the fan turns easily, replace the fan clutch.

Removal and installation

Refer to illustrations 4.8, 4.9, 4.10 and 4.12

6   Leave the battery cable disconnected (see the Caution in Step 5).

7   Remove the fan's drivebelt (see Chapter 1).

8   Remove the nuts holding the fan assembly to the water pump **(see illustration)**. **Note:** *You'll have to "walk" the fan assembly forward as you loosen the nuts. There is not enough room to remove them all the way at one time.*

9   The fan can be removed without removing the shroud, if you are only replacing the fan or clutch **(see illustration)**. Be careful not to allow the blades contact the radiator fins.

10   Remove the two fan shroud mounting clips at the top of the shroud **(see illustration)**.

11   Lift the shroud up and out of the engine compartment. The bottom of the fan shroud does not have any fasteners. It has two tangs on

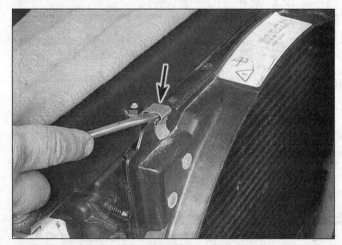

4.10 Pry out the two clips (arrow indicates the left one) at the top of the fan shroud and lift out the shroud

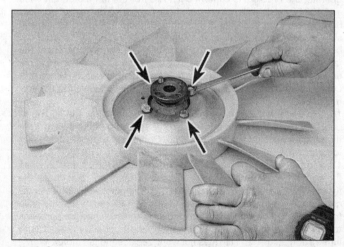

4.12 Separate the fan clutch from the fan by removing the four bolts (arrows)

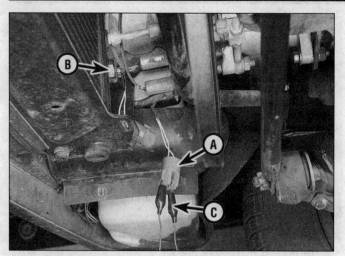

4.15 Disconnect the electrical connector (A) from the thermostatic switch (B) in the radiator and bypass it with a jumper wire (C) - the fan should operate now with the ignition on

4.17 Disconnect the fan wiring connector (arrow) and connect jumper wires from there directly to the positive and negative terminals of the battery - the purple wire's terminal should receive the battery power and the black wire's terminal should be grounded

the bottom that slip out of slots in the body when pulled up.

12   The fan clutch can be unbolted from the fan blade assembly for replacement **(see illustration)**. **Caution:** *To prevent silicone fluid from draining from the clutch assembly into the fan drive bearing and ruining the lubricant, DON'T place the clutch in a position with the rear pointing down. Store the clutch in its upright position if possible.*

13   Installation is the reverse of removal. Tighten the fan clutch-to-fan blade bolts and the fan assembly-to-drive hub nut to the torque listed in this Chapter's Specifications.

Electric fans

Check

Refer to illustrations 4.15 and 4.17

14   On 1988 through 1992 models, a single electric fan is mounted in front of the radiator, controlled by a thermostatic switch. Access to the fan is with the grille removed. The 1993 and 1994 models have a fan shroud assembly that includes two electric fans, and a "twin" thermostatic switch, with the assembly mounted on the engine side of the radiator.

15   If the electric fan does not come on at any time, bypass the thermostatic switch by disconnecting the electrical connector at the switch and connecting the two pins with a jumper wire **(see illustration)**. **Warning:** *Keep your hands or clothing away from the fan blades.* If the fan now operates, replace the thermostatic switch. If the fan doesn't operate, the problem is either the fan relay or the fan motor. On 1993 and 1994 models with twin electric fans, jumpering one set of connections in the plug from the switch should make both fans operate at slow speed (fans in series) and jumpering the other two should run both fans at higher speed (fans in parallel). In normal operation, the fans operate at the higher-speed only when the air conditioning is on, or when coolant temperature exceeds 212-degrees F. When the coolant cools down to below 200-degrees F, the fans revert to the normal speed.

16   To replace a defective thermostatic switch, allow the engine to cool and drain the coolant (see Chapter 1). Remove the switch from the radiator and install the new switch. Connect the electrical connector and test again for proper fan operation.

17   To test an inoperative fan motor (one that doesn't come on when the engine gets hot or when the air conditioner is on), first check the fuses and/or fusible links (see Chapter 12). Then disconnect the electrical connector at the motor (refer to Chapter 11 for removal of the grille for access on front-mounted-fan models) and use fused jumper wires to connect the fan directly to the battery and to chassis ground **(see illustration)**. If the fan still does not work, replace the fan motor. **Warning:** *Do not allow the test clips to contact each other or any metallic part of the vehicle.*

18   If the motor tested OK in the previous test but is still inoperative, then the fault lies in the relay, fuse, or wiring. The fan relay can be tested for continuity (see Chapter 12).

Replacement

Refer to illustration 4.20

19   Disconnect the negative battery cable. **Caution:** *If the stereo in your vehicle is equipped with an anti-theft system, make sure you have the correct activation code before disconnecting the battery.*

20   Access the 1988 through 1992 single electric fan with the grille removed (see Chapter 11 for grille removal). Disconnect the electrical connector and remove the bolts holding the fan assembly to the body **(see illustration)**.

21   On 1993 and 1994 models, remove the two bolts holding the fan shroud to the top of the radiator and lift the shroud/fans assembly from the vehicle.

22   If the fan on 1988 to 1992 models must be replaced, replace the fan, motor and shroud as a unit. The fan is separate from the shroud on later models.

23   Installation is the reverse of removal. If the thermostatic switch was replaced, refill the cooling system.

4.20 Disconnect the fan's electrical connector (large arrow) and remove the bolts (small arrows) on single-fan models - grille is removed here

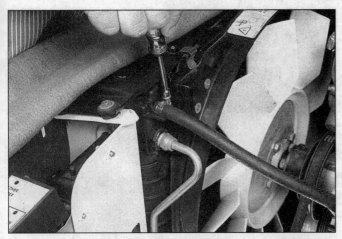

5.3 Remove the clamp and the hose going to the expansion tank

5.5a At the left side of the radiator, disconnect the automatic transmission cooler lines (small arrows) and the lower radiator hose (larger arrow)

5.5b Disconnect the power steering cooler lines (small arrows) at the right side of the radiator, and the upper radiator hose (large arrow)

5.6 Remove the bolts (arrows) and take off the radiator cowl panel

5 Radiator, expansion tank and coolant reservoir - removal and installation

Warning: *Do not start this procedure until the engine is completely cool.*

Radiator

Removal

Refer to illustrations 5.3, 5.5a, 5.5b, 5.6 and 5.8

1 Disconnect the negative battery cable. **Caution:** *If the stereo in your vehicle is equipped with an anti-theft system, make sure you have the correct activation code before disconnecting the battery.*
2 Drain the coolant into a container (see Chapter 1).
3 Remove both the upper and lower radiator hoses, and the small expansion tank hose from the top left of the radiator **(see illustration)**.
4 Remove the cooling fan and shroud (see Section 4).
5 Disconnect the automatic transmission cooler lines from the radiator **(see illustrations)**. Disconnect the cooling fan switch connector **(see illustration 4.15)**. Place a drip pan to catch the fluid and cap the fittings. **Note:** *The transmission oil cooler lines enter the radiator on the left, while the power steering cooler lines attach on the right side of the radiator. On 1993 and 1994 models, the cooler fittings require a spring-lock coupling tool, normally used on fuel lines or air conditioning lines.*
6 Remove the four bolts from the radiator cowl panel and take off the panel **(see illustration)**.
7 Lift out the radiator. Be aware of dripping fluids and the sharp

5.8 There are rubber mounts for the radiator and the condenser (arrows) - they must be in place when these components are reinstalled

fins. Take care not to damage the radiator fins by contact with other parts.
8 With the radiator removed, it can be inspected for leaks, damage and internal blockage. If in need of repairs, have a professional radiator shop or dealer service department perform the work as special techniques are required. Check the rubber mounting pads on the bottom of the radiator **(see illustration)**. If they're cracked or damaged, get replacement ones before installing the radiator.

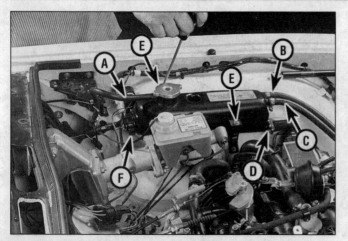

5.14 The expansion tank is located on the left fenderwell

    A   Hose to recovery tank (where applicable)
    B   Hose to radiator
    C   Hose to thermostat housing
    D   Hose to water pump housing
    E   Mounting screws
    F   Low-coolant-level sensor

5.16 The low-coolant-level sensor can be tested with an ohmmeter - resistance should be below 150 ohms - gently use a pair of long-neck pliers to move the sensor up and down in the tank to get a reading

9   Bugs and dirt can be cleaned from the radiator with compressed air and a soft brush. Don't bend the cooling fins as this is done. **Warning:** *Wear eye protection when using compressed air.*

Installation

10   Installation is the reverse of the removal procedure. Be sure the rubber mounts are in place on the bottom of the radiator.
11   After installation, fill the cooling system with the proper mixture of antifreeze and water. Refer to Chapter 1 if necessary.
12   Start the engine and check for leaks. Allow the engine to reach normal operating temperature, indicated by both radiator hoses becoming hot. Recheck the coolant level and add more if required.
13   On automatic transmission equipped models, check and add fluid as needed and check the power steering fluid level as well.

Expansion tank and coolant reservoir, removal and installation

Refer to illustrations 5.14, 5.16 and 5.17
14   The expansion tank is located at the top of the driver's side fenderwell. With the cooling system drained below the level of the expansion tank, remove the hoses, the coolant level probe and the two

screws mounting it to the body **(see illustration).**
15   Wash out and inspect the reservoir for cracks and chafing. Replace it if damaged.
16   If the low-coolant level light has been showing on the instrument panel, even when the coolant level is correct, disconnect the sensor's connector and test it with an ohmmeter **(see illustration).** The sensor should be replaced if the resistance at the connections is over 150 ohms. **Caution:** *Use of a long-necked funnel when adding coolant can damage the sensor, which is just below the expansion tank filler neck.*
17   A coolant recovery bottle is used on 1988 and 1989 models, located in the driver's fenderwell. The plastic inner fender splash shield must be removed for access to the recovery bottle (see Chapter 11). Disconnect the recovery hose and remove the mounting screws to replace the recovery bottle **(see illustration).** 1990 and later models do not have the recovery bottle, but do have a larger expansion tank.
18   Installation of either expansion tank or recovery bottle is the reverse of removal.

6   Engine oil cooler - replacement

Refer to illustrations 6.2 and 6.3
1   Models from 1988 through 1991 have a engine oil cooler, mounted ahead of the radiator. The engine's mechanical fan draws air

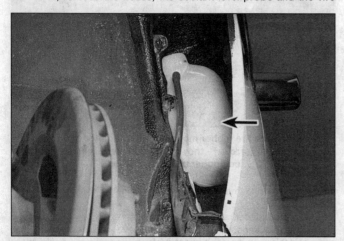

5.17 The recovery bottle (arrow) on 1988 and 1989 models is located in the fenderwell - disconnect the hoses and the two mounting screws

6.2 Disconnect the two metal oil lines (arrows) where they mount to the bottom of the cooler - use two wrenches

6.3 Remove the mounting nuts (arrows) to take the oil cooler out

7.3 Check the weep hole (arrow) for signs of leakage (pump removed for clarity) - a small amount of gray discoloration is normal, large brown stains indicates seal failure

8.4 Remove the water pump mounting bolts (arrows indicate five visible here)

through the oil cooler, cooling off hot engine oil that is circulated from the engine by steel tubes. Access to the cooler is with the grille removed (refer to Chapter 11 for grille removal).

2   To replace the oil cooler, first disconnect the two fittings connecting the lines to the cooler **(see illustration)**. **Caution:** *The engine should be cool for this procedure, and you should have a small drain pan handy because the fittings are on the bottom of the cooler and will probably drip some oil on disassembly.*

3   Remove the mounting nuts to take the cooler out of the vehicle **(see illustration)**.

4   The other ends of the oil cooler tubes mount to a block just below the oil filter. With a drain pan handy, remove the nut retaining both pipes to the block.

5   Installation of the oil cooler and oil lines is the reverse of removal. When reassembling the lines to the block or the cooler, use new O-rings.

7   Water pump - check

Refer to illustration 7.3

1   A failure in the water pump can cause serious engine damage due to overheating.

2   With the engine running and warmed to normal operating temperature, squeeze the upper radiator hose. If the water pump is working properly, a pressure surge should be felt as the hose is released. **Warning:** *Keep hands away from fan blades!*

3   Water pumps are equipped with weep or vent holes **(see illustration)**. If a failure occurs in the pump seal, coolant will leak from this hole. In most cases it will be necessary to use a flashlight to find the hole on the water pump by looking through the space behind the pulley just below the water pump shaft.

4   If the water pump shaft bearings fail there may be a howling sound at the front of the engine while it is running. Bearing wear can be felt if the water pump pulley is rocked up and down. Do not mistake drivebelt slippage, which causes a squealing sound, for water pump failure. Spray automotive drivebelt dressing on the belts to eliminate the belt as a possible cause of the noise.

8   Water pump and pipes - replacement

Refer to illustrations 8.4, 8.8a and 8.8b

Warning: *Do not start this procedure until the engine is completely cool.*

1   Disconnect the negative battery cable and drain the cooling system (see Chapter 1). **Caution:** *If the stereo in your vehicle is equipped*

with an anti-theft system, make sure you have the correct activation code before disconnecting the battery.

2   Refer to Section 4 to remove the mechanical fan and clutch (if applicable to your model).

3   Refer to Chapter 1 for removal of the drivebelts.

4   Remove the water pump mounting bolts **(see illustration)**. There are three different lengths of water pump bolts. The longer bolts retain the pump and rear housing to the engine **(see illustration 7.3)**. **Note:** *The water pump is sold as a complete assembly, including the rear housing with the hose connections. Unless the rear housing is corroded or cracked, many Jaguar mechanics only install the pump assembly itself, using the original rear housing with all its hoses intact. However, if the engine has a great deal of years or mileage on it, it would be a good idea to replace those hoses as well, in which case the new rear housing can be installed.*

5   If the pump doesn't come loose right away, tap it with a soft-faced hammer to break the gasket seal. Be careful not to hit the radiator fins with the pump during removal.

6   Thoroughly clean all sealing surfaces, removing all traces of gasket or sealant from the back of the pump and the face of the housing.

7   Apply a bead of RTV sealant to the sealing surface on the back of the pump. Install the pump and bolts, tightening the bolts to the torque listed in this Chapter's Specifications.

8   Install the remaining parts in the reverse order of removal. **Note:** *If the pump has been replaced after many miles of usage, it's a good idea to also replace the hoses connected to the water pump housing* **(see illustrations)**. *Refer to Chapter 2A for intake manifold removal to*

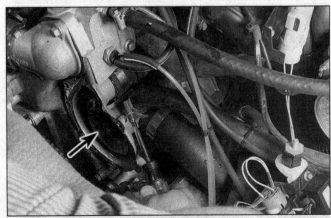

8.8a Once the water pump is removed, the rear housing (arrow) is held in place only by the hoses - they should be examined for leakage and condition whenever the pump is replaced

8.8b The water pipe (arrow) may need new gaskets where it meets the block - the pipe is best accessed from below or with the intake manifold removed

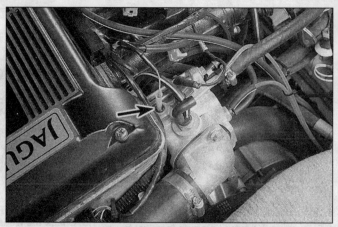

9.3 The coolant temperature sending unit (arrow) is located in the top of the thermostat housing - it is the sending unit with the single wire

access the coolant pipes and hoses. If you have noticed water leaks or stains on the left side of the engine, the leaks may be coming from these pipes and hoses.

9   Refill the cooling system (see Chapter 1), run the engine and check for leaks and proper operation.

9   Coolant temperature sending unit - check and replacement

Refer to illustration 9.3

Warning: *Do not start this procedure until the engine is completely cool.*

Check

1   If the coolant temperature gauge is inoperative, check the fuses first (see Chapter 12).
2   If the temperature gauge indicates excessive temperature after running awhile, see the *Troubleshooting* section in the front of the manual.
3   If the temperature gauge indicates Hot as soon as the engine is started cold, disconnect the wire at the coolant temperature sender **(see illustration)**. If the gauge reading drops, replace the sending unit. If the reading remains high, the wire to the gauge may be shorted to ground, or the gauge is faulty.
4   If the coolant temperature gauge fails to show any indication after the engine has been warmed up, (approx. 10 minutes) and the fuses

checked out OK, shut off the engine. Disconnect the wire at the sending unit and, using a jumper wire, connect the wire to a clean ground on the engine. Briefly turn on the ignition without starting the engine. If the gauge now indicates Hot, replace the sending unit.
5   If the gauge fails to respond, the circuit may be open or the gauge may be faulty - see Chapter 12 for additional information.

Replacement

6   Drain the coolant (see Chapter 1).
7   Disconnect the electrical connector from the sending unit.
8   Using a deep socket or a wrench, remove the sending unit.
9   Install the new unit and tighten it securely. Do not use thread sealant as it may electrically insulate the sending unit.
10   Reconnect the wiring connector, refill the cooling system and check for coolant leakage and proper gauge function.

10   Heating and air conditioning blower motors - circuit check and component replacement

Refer to illustrations 10.2a, 10.2b, 10.3a, 10.3b, 10.5, 10.6, 10.7, 10.10, 10.11a, 10.11b and 10.12

Warning: *Later model vehicles are equipped with airbags. To prevent accidental deployment of the airbag, which could cause personal injury or damage to the airbag system, DO NOT work in the vicinity of the steering wheel or instrument panel. The manufacturer recommends that, on airbag-equipped models, the following procedure should be*

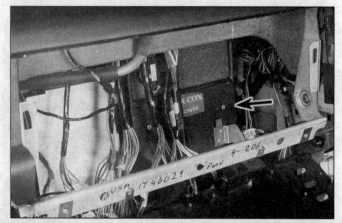

10.2a The right blower housing (arrow) is located behind the glove box area of the dash

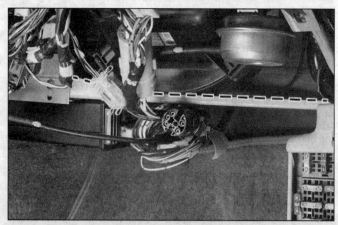

10.2b Apply heavy duct tape to the sharp edge of this brace (dotted line) when working behind the glove box area of the dash - the metal is very sharp

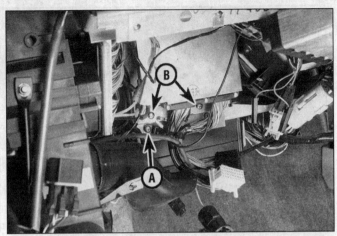

10.3a Remove the screw (A) holding the wiring harness in place, then remove the two lower cruise-control ECM screws (B) . . .

10.3b . . . then remove the upper ECM screw (arrow) and pull down the ECM, then remove the ECM mounting plate

10.5 Two bolts (arrow indicates the left bolt) retaining the top of the blower housing to the cowl

10.6 Pull down and out on the housing until it clears the sheet metal brace below it

left to a dealer service department or other repair shop because of the special tools and techniques required to disable the airbag system.

1   Disconnect the negative cable from the battery. **Caution:** *If the stereo in your vehicle is equipped with an anti-theft system, make sure you have the correct activation code before disconnecting the battery.*

2   There are two blower motors, one under the left side of the dash and one behind the glove compartment **(see illustration)**. If the blower doesn't work, check the fuse and all connections in the circuit for looseness and corrosion. Make sure the battery is fully charged. To access the right blower, remove the glove compartment liner, the glove compartment door and the right lower dash panel **(see Chapter 11)**. **Warning:** *When working around the area behind the glove box, watch out for a strip of sheet metal bracing that has a very sharp edge* **(see illustration)**. *Apply some heavy duct tape to the edge of the brace before beginning work in this area or you could injure your hands*.

3   Remove the screws holding the cruise-control ECM in place **(see illustrations)**, then remove the four screws holding the ECM mounting plate in place.

4   Disconnect the vacuum lines and electrical connectors at the blower housing, identifying each connection with marked masking tape for reassembly, or write down the color codes of the vacuum tubing. Remove the duct tape connecting the blower housing to the duct from the heater/air conditioning unit.

5   Remove the two bolts holding the top of the blower housing to the cowl **(see illustration)**.

6   Pull down and back on the housing until it squeezes past the metal brace below it **(see illustration)**. It will take some force at first.

7   To access the left blower motor, remove the left-hand brace rod

from the steering column forward to the body **(see illustration)**, then repeat Steps 4 and 5 on the left blower housing. The blower housing should now drop straight down and out.

8   If the blower motor does not operate, disconnect the electrical connectors at the blower motor and connect the black wire terminal to chassis ground, and the purple wire terminal to a fused source of battery voltage. If the blower doesn't operate, it should be replaced. If it does operate, there is a problem in the feed or ground circuit.

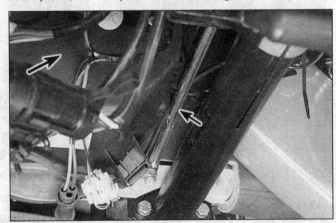

10.7 Remove this brace rod (small arrow) for clearance to remove the left blower motor housing (large arrow)

10.10 Remove the five clips (two shown here with arrows) and one screw holding the halves of the housing together

10.11a Separate the housing halves - the blower motor (arrow) is attached to a plastic plate sandwiched between the two housing halves

9   If the motor is good, but doesn't operate at any speed, the problem could be in the heater/air conditioning control assembly or the heating/air conditioning computer. Troubleshooting either of these electronic components is beyond the scope of the home mechanic, and should be referred to your Jaguar dealer or other qualified repair facility.

10   If either blower motor must be replaced, remove the five clips and one screw holding the blower housing halves together **(see illustration)**.

11   Separate the housing halves and pull up the plastic plate holding the motor and fan **(see illustration)**. The fan doesn't come off the motor, but loosen the clamp-bolt on the motor's mount bracket and slide the motor and fan out for replacement **(see illustration)**.

Note: Some 1988 models had problems with cracking of the fan blades and noise from the blowers. These blowers and fans have been superseded with improved parts, available from your Jaguar dealer.

12   When either blower housing is separated, you'll find two relays mounted inside **(see illustration)**. These are the blower isolation relay and blower relay. Before reinstalling the blower housing in the vehicle, refer to Chapter 12 for testing of these relays.

13   Installation is the reverse of removal. Check for proper operation.

11   Heater core - removal and installation

Refer to illustrations 11.2, 11.4, 11.5, 11.6a, 11.6b, 11.7, 11.8 and 11.9
Warning: *Later model vehicles are equipped with airbags. To prevent*

the accidental deployment of the airbag, which could cause personal injury or damage to the airbag system, DO NOT work in the vicinity of the steering wheel or instrument panel. The manufacturer recommends that, on airbag-equipped models, the following procedure should be left to a dealer service department or other repair shop because of the special tools and techniques required to disable the airbag system.

1   Disconnect the negative cable from the battery. **Caution:** *If the stereo in your vehicle is equipped with an anti-theft system, make sure you have the correct activation code before disconnecting the battery.*

2   Drain the cooling system (see Chapter 1). Disconnect the heater hoses where they enter the firewall **(see illustration)**. **Note:** *Use compressed air in one of the pipes to blow out any remaining coolant and collect it. This will prevent any spills on the carpeting when the heater core is removed.* Plug the pipes to prevent any remaining coolant from spilling out.

3   Refer to Chapter 11 for removal of the under-dash panels on both the driver and passenger sides, and removal of the glove box. **Warning:** *When working around the area behind the glove box, watch out for a strip of sheet metal bracing that has a very sharp edge* **(see illustration 10.2b)**. *Apply some heavy duct tape to the edge of the brace before beginning work in this area or you could injure your hands*.

4   On the driver's side, under the dash, remove the screws holding the plastic cover where the heater pipes enter the heater/air conditioning housing **(see illustration)**.

5   With the cover off, there is access to remove the four Allen bolts holding the two pipes to the heater core **(see illustration)**.

10.11b Loosen the clamp bolt (arrow) on the motor bracket and then pull the motor and fan out as an assembly

10.12 Inside the blower case are the blower and isolation relays (arrows) - while the case is apart, test these relays for proper operation

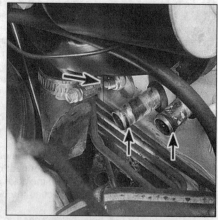

11.2 Disconnect the heater hoses from the pipes at the firewall (small arrows) - the large arrow indicates the evaporator case retaining nut

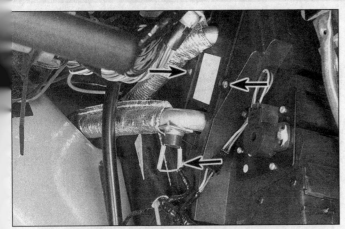

11.4 Remove these screws (arrows) to remove the plastic plate over the heater core pipes on the left side

11.5 With the cover off, remove the Allen bolts (arrows indicate three of the four) to pull the coolant pipes out of the left side of the heater core

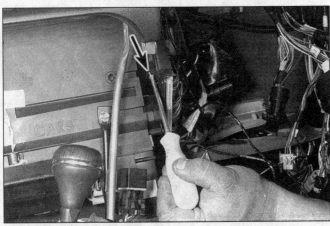

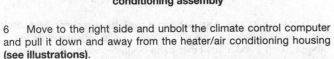

11.6a Remove three screws (arrow indicates one; there is also one at the top-back and one below) to take out the climate-control computer on the right side of the heater/air conditioning assembly

11.6b Pull away the climate control computer (arrow)

6　Move to the right side and unbolt the climate control computer and pull it down and away from the heater/air conditioning housing (see illustrations).

7　Remove the four small screws and remove the plastic plate over the heater core, right behind where the climate control computer had been (see illustration).

8　Carefully slide the heater core out from the right side of the heating/air conditioning housing (see illustration). Note: *Keep plenty of towels or rags on the carpeting to catch any coolant that may drip.*

9　Installation is the reverse order of removal. When reinstalling the heater core, make sure all of the foam insulation strips are in place and install new O-rings where the heater pipes enter the core (see illustration).

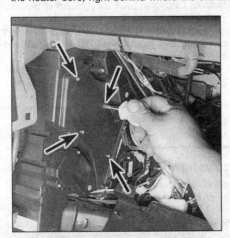

11.7 Remove the four screws (arrows) and the heater core cover plate

11.8 Pull the heater core out to the right

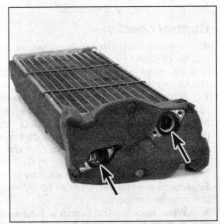

11.9 Retain the original foam insulation on the heater core or transfer to the new core, and replace the two O-rings (arrows)

12.3a Remove these six screws (arrows) to release the control panel/radio assembly from the console

12.3b Remove the four screws (three are shown here) holding the control assembly in the control/radio housing

10   Refill the cooling system, reconnect the battery and run the engine. Check for leaks and proper system operation.

12 Heater and air conditioning control assembly - check, removal and installation

Refer to illustrations 12.3a, 12.3b and 12.11
Warning: *Later model vehicles are equipped with airbags. To prevent the accidental deployment of the airbag, which could cause personal injury or damage to the airbag system, DO NOT work in the vicinity of the steering wheel or instrument panel. The manufacturer recommends that, on airbag-equipped models, the following procedure should be left to a dealer service department or other repair shop because of the special tools and techniques required to disable the airbag system.*

Removal and installation

1   Disconnect the negative cable from the battery. **Caution:** *If the stereo in your vehicle is equipped with an anti-theft system, make sure you have the correct activation code before disconnecting the battery.*
2   Refer to Chapter 11 for removal of the console heater control/radio assembly trim bezel.
3   Remove the mounting screws retaining the heater/air conditioning control assembly to the console **(see illustrations)**. Pull the assembly out and disconnect the electrical connectors.
4   Installation is the reverse of the removal procedure.
5   Run the engine and check for proper functioning of the heater (and air conditioning, if equipped).

Control checks

6   The climate-control system uses an all-electronic control panel that sends digital information to the climate control computer. There is little the home mechanic can do to troubleshoot or test the system. The factory recommends that diagnosis be performed at a dealership.
7   If there is a problem in just one area of climate control, put the controls through their entire range of operation and check the system responses, i.e. set the controls to COLD, the fan to low and the temperature to 65-degrees F. In this mode the Manual LED should be lit and the air conditioning compressor should engage. Try all of the fan speeds and try the temperature on HOT, then feel for warm air coming from the ducts. **Note:** *Between each try of the different controls, wait 20 seconds or so for the heater/air conditioning system to adjust before checking for a response.*
8   When each control button is pushed two times, it's LED light should go on or off. Replace the control assembly if any of the warning lights don't work.
9   On 1988 and 1989 models, if the climate controls do not respond to any driver input, check with your Jaguar dealer before replacing the

12.11 Check the operation of the vacuum servo motors; in this case, vacuum is applied to the servo on the right blower case - the flapper door (arrow) should operate

ECU or control panel. A service part is available (a resistor, #JLM 1901) that can be installed at one of the control panel terminals that may fix the problem without any other parts being replaced. Instructions are included with the part.
10   Check the vacuum lines to the several vacuum motors that operate the heater/air conditioning functions. Look for pinched or blocked hoses and leaks.
11   Each of the vacuum "servo motors" in the system can be checked with a hand-held vacuum pump **(see illustration)**. Apply vacuum and watch that the door or control it operates is working.
12   Further diagnosis of the controls or climate control ECU are best left to a Jaguar dealership or other qualified repair facility.

13 Air conditioning and heating system - check and maintenance

Air conditioning system

Warning: *The air conditioning system is under high pressure. Do not loosen any hose fittings or remove any components until the system has been discharged. Air conditioning refrigerant should be properly discharged into an EPA-approved recovery/recycling unit by a dealer service department or an automotive air conditioning repair facility. Always wear eye protection when disconnecting air conditioning system fittings.*

1   The following maintenance checks should be performed on a reg-

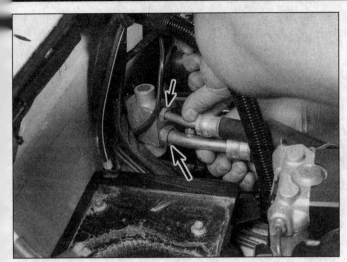

13.9 Feel the inlet (small arrow) and outlet (large arrow) pipes at the firewall leading to the air conditioning evaporator (battery removed for clarity)

13.11 The sight glass (arrow) is located on the top of the receiver/drier, to the right of the radiator

ular basis to ensure that the air conditioner continues to operate at peak efficiency:

   a) *Inspect the condition of the compressor drivebelt. If it is worn or deteriorated, replace it (see Chapter 1).*

   b) *Check the drivebelt tension and, if necessary, adjust it (see Chapter 1).*

   c) *Inspect the system hoses. Look for cracks, bubbles, hardening and deterioration. Inspect the hoses and all fittings for oil bubbles or seepage. If there is any evidence of wear, damage or leakage, replace the hose(s).*

   d) *Inspect the condenser fins for leaves, bugs and any other foreign material that may have embedded itself in the fins. Use a "fin comb" or compressed air to remove debris from the condenser.*

   e) *Make sure the system has the correct refrigerant charge.*

2   It's a good idea to operate the system for about ten minutes at least once a month. This is particularly important during the winter months because long term non-use can cause hardening, and subsequent failure, of the seals.

3   Leaks in the air conditioning system are best spotted when the system is brought up to operating temperature and pressure, by running the engine with the air conditioning ON for five minutes. Shut the engine off and inspect the air conditioning hoses and connections. Traces of oil usually indicate refrigerant leaks.

4   Because of the complexity of the air conditioning system and the special equipment required to effectively work on it, accurate troubleshooting of the system should be left to a professional technician.

5   If the air conditioning system doesn't operate at all, check the fuse panel and the air conditioning relay (refer to Chapter 12 for relay locations and testing). Refer to Sections 4 and 12 for electrical checks of heating/air conditioning system components.

6   The most common cause of poor cooling is simply a low system refrigerant charge. If a noticeable drop in cool air output occurs, the following quick check will help you determine if the refrigerant level is low. For more complete information on the air conditioning system, refer to the *Haynes Automotive Heating and Air Conditioning Manual.*

Checking the refrigerant charge

Refer to illustrations 13.9 and 13.11

7   Warm the engine up to normal operating temperature.

8   Place the air conditioning temperature selector at the coldest setting and put the blower at the highest setting. Open the doors (to make sure the air conditioning system doesn't cycle off as soon as it cools the passenger compartment).

9   With the compressor engaged - the clutch will make an audible click and the center of the clutch will rotate. After the system reaches operating temperature, feel the two pipes connected to the evaporator at the firewall **(see illustration)**.

10   The pipe (thinner tubing) leading from the condenser outlet to the evaporator should be cold, and the evaporator outlet line (the thicker tubing that leads back to the compressor) should be slightly colder (3 to 10-degrees F). If the evaporator outlet is considerably warmer than the inlet, the system needs a charge. Insert a thermometer in the center air distribution duct while operating the air conditioning system - the temperature of the output air should be 35 to 40-degrees F below the ambient air temperature (down to approximately 40-degrees F). If the ambient (outside) air temperature is very high, say 110-degrees F, the duct air temperature may be as high as 60-degrees F, but generally the air conditioning is 30 to 50-degrees F cooler than the ambient air. If the air isn't as cold as it used to be, the system probably needs a charge. Further inspection or testing of the system is beyond the scope of the home mechanic and should be left to a professional.

11   Inspect the sight glass **(see illustration)**. If the refrigerant looks foamy when running, it's low. When ambient temperatures are very hot, bubbles may show in the sight glass even with the proper amount of refrigerant. With the proper amount of refrigerant, when the air conditioning is turned off, the sight glass should show refrigerant that foams, then clears. **Note:** *1993 and 1994 models are equipped with R-134a refrigerant systems and do not have a sight glass.*

Adding refrigerant

Refer to illustration 13.12

Caution 1: *Refrigerant has changed from the use of R-12, through 1992 models, to the "environmentally friendly" R-134a used in 1993 and 1994 models. The two refrigerants are NOT compatible. Special fittings and manifold gauge sets are used on the different refrigerant types so that an accidental hook-up of the two systems cannot be made.*

Caution 2: *When replacing entire components, additional refrigerant oil should be added equal to the amount that is removed with the component being replaced. Refrigerant oils for the two systems, just like refrigerant R-12 vs. R-134a, are not compatible. Be sure to read the can before adding any oil to the system, to make sure it is compatible with the type of system being repaired.*

Note: *Because of Federal regulations by the Environmental Protection Agency, R-12 refrigerant is not available for home-mechanic use, however, cans of R-134a refrigerant are commonly available in auto parts stores. Models with R-12 systems will have to be serviced at a dealership or air conditioning shop. A special "R-134a retrofit kit" is available from Jaguar for models before 1993, to allow them to use modern R-134a refrigerant. The phased-out R12 is expensive and will eventually be unavailable, even to professional shops.*

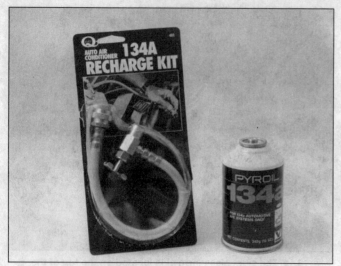

13.12 A basic charging kit is available at most auto parts stores - it must say R-134a and so must the cans of refrigerant you buy

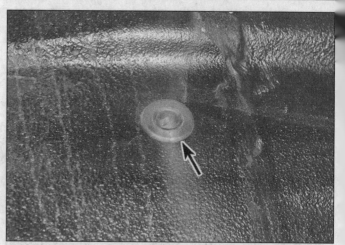

13.25 This drain hose (arrow) from the heater/air conditioning unit should be kept clear to allow drainage of condensation

12   Buy an automotive air conditioning charging kit at an auto parts store. A charging kit includes a 14-ounce can of R-134a refrigerant, a tap valve and a short section of hose that can be attached between the tap valve and the system low side service valve **(see illustration)**. Because one can of refrigerant may not be sufficient to bring the system charge up to the proper level, it's a good idea to buy a couple of additional cans. Try to find at least one can that contains red refrigerant dye. If the system is leaking, the red dye will leak out with the refrigerant and help you pinpoint the location of the leak.

13   Connect the charging kit by following the manufacturer's instructions.

14   Back off the valve handle on the charging kit and screw the kit onto the refrigerant can, making sure first that the O-ring or rubber seal inside the threaded portion of the kit is in place. **Warning:** *Wear protective eyewear when dealing with pressurized refrigerant cans.*

15   Remove the dust cap from the low-side charging port and attach the quick-connect fitting on the kit hose. **Warning:** *DO NOT hook the charging kit hose to the system high side! The fittings on the charging kit are designed to fit* **only** *on the low side of the system.*

16   Warm the engine to normal operating temperature and turn on the air conditioner. Keep the charging kit hose away from the fan and other moving parts.

17   Turn the valve handle on the kit until the stem pierces the can, then back the handle out to release the refrigerant. You should be able to hear the rush of gas. Add refrigerant to the low side of the system until both the outlet and the evaporator inlet pipe feel about the same temperature . Allow stabilization time between each addition. **Warning:** *Never add more than two cans of refrigerant to the system.* The can may tend to frost up, slowing the procedure. Wrap a shop towel wet with hot water around the bottom of the can to keep it from frosting.

18   If you have an accurate thermometer, you can place it in the center air conditioning duct inside the vehicle to monitor the air temperature. A charged system that is working properly, should output air down to approximately 40 degrees-F.

19   When the can is empty, turn the valve handle to the closed position and release the connection from the low-side port. Replace the dust cap.

20   Remove the charging kit from the can and store the kit for future use with the piercing valve in the UP position, to prevent inadvertently piercing the can on the next use.

Heating systems

Refer to illustration 13.25

21   If the air coming out of the heater vents isn't hot, the problem could stem from any of the following causes:

a) *The thermostat is stuck open, preventing the engine coolant from warming up enough to carry heat to the heater core. Replace the thermostat* (see Section 3).

b) *A heater hose is blocked, preventing the flow of coolant through the heater core. Feel both heater hoses at the firewall. They should be hot. If one of them is cold, there is an obstruction in one of the hoses or in the heater core, or the heater control valve is shut. Detach the hoses and back flush the heater core with a water hose. If the heater core is clear but circulation is impeded, remove the two hoses and flush them out with a water hose.*

c) *If flushing fails to remove the blockage from the heater core, the core must be replaced.* (see Section 11).

22   If the blower motor speed does not correspond to the setting selected on the blower switch, the problem could be a bad fuse, circuit, control panel or climate control computer (see Sections 10 and 12).

23   If there isn't any air coming out of the vents:

a) *Turn the ignition ON and activate the fan control. Place your ear at the heating/air conditioning register (vent) and listen. Most motors are audible. Can you hear the motor running?*

b) *If you can't (and have already verified that the blower switch and the blower motor resistor are good), the blower motor itself is probably bad (see Section 10).*

24   If the carpet under the heater core is damp, or if antifreeze vapor or steam is coming through the vents, the heater core is leaking. Remove it (see Section 11) and install a new unit (most radiator shops will not repair a leaking heater core).

25   Inspect the drain hose from the heater/air conditioning assembly at the right side of the firewall, make sure it is not clogged **(see illustration)**. If there is a humid mist coming from the system ducts, this hose may be plugged. In some early models, the hose may have been pinched during assembly or blocked with insulation or undercoating.

14   Air conditioning receiver/drier - removal and installation

Refer to illustration 14.2

Warning: *The air conditioning system is under high pressure. Do not loosen any hose fittings or remove any components until the system has been discharged. Air conditioning refrigerant should be properly discharged into an EPA-approved recovery/recycling unit by a dealer service department or an automotive air conditioning repair facility. Always wear eye protection when disconnecting air conditioning system fittings.*

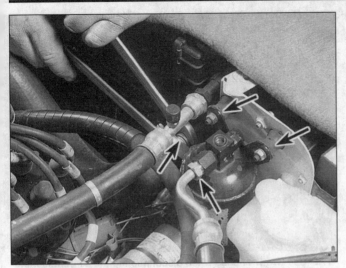

14.2 After the system has been discharged, unbolt the two refrigerant lines (left arrows) from the top of the receiver/drier and cap them - use two wrenches when loosening or tightening these lines - right arrows indicate the two top mounting bolts

1   Have the refrigerant discharged and recovered by an air conditioning technician.
2   Disconnect the refrigerant lines **(see illustration)** from the receiver/drier and cap the open fittings to prevent entry of moisture.
3   Remove the three nuts holding the receiver/drier to the radiator support and remove the receiver/drier. **Note:** *On 1993 and 1994 models, the receiver/drier is a long tubular style mounted to the top-front of the radiator support. The grille must be removed for access on these models* (refer to Chapter 11 for grille removal).
4   Installation is the reverse of removal.
5   Have the system evacuated, charged and leak tested by the shop that discharged it. If the receiver/drier was replaced, have them add about 28 cc (one ounce) of new refrigeration oil to the compressor. Use only the refrigerant oil compatible with the refrigerant of your system (R-12 or R-134a).

15   Air conditioning compressor - removal and installation

Refer to illustrations 15.4 and 15.5
Warning: *The air conditioning system is under high pressure. Do not loosen any hose fittings or remove any components until the system has been discharged. Air conditioning refrigerant should be properly discharged into an EPA-approved recovery/recycling unit by a dealer service department or an automotive air conditioning repair facility. Always wear eye protection when disconnecting air conditioning system fittings.*
1   Have the refrigerant discharged by an automotive air conditioning technician.
2   Disconnect the negative cable from the battery. **Caution:** *If the stereo in your vehicle is equipped with an anti-theft system, make sure you have the correct activation code before disconnecting the battery.*
3   Remove the drivebelt from the compressor (see Chapter 1).
4   Detach the electrical connector and disconnect the flexible refrigerant lines **(see illustration)**.
5   Unbolt the compressor and lift it from the vehicle **(see illustration)**.
6   If a new or rebuilt compressor is being installed, drain the fluid from the new unit by opening the drain plug and by tilting the compressor to the rear so that any remaining oil will come out the ports in the back normally covered by the plate and hard lines. Install the drain plug and end-plate and add 199 cc (7 fluid ounces) of new oil of a type compatible with the type refrigerant in your system.

15.4 Disconnect the electrical connector (small arrow) at the compressor, then disconnect the bolt (large arrow) at the retaining plate that holds the two hoses in place

15.5 Remove the lower mounting bolts and the adjuster bolt (arrows)

7   Installation is the reverse of removal. Replace any O-rings with new ones specifically made for the type of refrigerant in your system and lubricate them with refrigerant oil, also designed specifically for your refrigerant.
8   Have the system evacuated, recharged and leak tested by the shop that discharged it.

16   Air conditioning condenser - removal and installation

Refer to illustration 16.3
Warning: *The air conditioning system is under high pressure. Do not loosen any hose fittings or remove any components until the system has been discharged. Air conditioning refrigerant should be properly discharged into an EPA-approved recovery/recycling unit by a dealer service department or an automotive air conditioning repair facility. Always wear eye protection when disconnecting air conditioning system fittings.*
1   Have the refrigerant discharged and recovered by an air conditioning technician.
2   Remove the radiator cowl panel as described in Section 5.

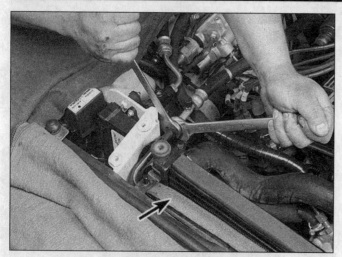

16.3 Disconnect the two lines, then pull up on the condenser (arrow)

17.2 Use two wrenches when disconnecting the air conditioning lines (arrows) at the firewall, on the backside of the expansion valve - one wrench holds the body of the expansion valve

3   Using two wrenches to avoid twisting the fittings, disconnect the inlet and outlet lines from the condenser (**see illustration**).

4   Pull the condenser straight up and out of the vehicle.

5   Installation is the reverse of removal. When reinstalling the condenser, be sure the rubber cushions fit on the mounting points and that any foam insulator strips are still in place or transferred to the new condenser.

6   Reconnect the refrigerant lines, using new O-rings. If a new condenser has been installed, add 84 cc (3 fluid ounces) of new refrigerant oil. **Note:** *The oil and O-rings must be compatible with the type of refrigerant you are using.*

7   Reinstall the remaining parts in the reverse order of removal.

8   Have the system evacuated, charged and leak tested by the shop that discharged it.

17   Air conditioning evaporator and expansion valve - removal and installation

Refer to illustrations 17.2, 17.4, 17.5, 17.9a, 17.9b and 17.13

Warning 1: *The air conditioning system is under high pressure. Do not loosen any hose fittings or remove any components until the system has been discharged. Air conditioning refrigerant should be properly*

discharged into an EPA-approved recovery/recycling unit by a dealer service department or an automotive air conditioning repair facility. Always wear eye protection when disconnecting air conditioning system fittings.

Warning 2: *Later model vehicles are equipped with airbags. To prevent the accidental deployment of the airbag, which could cause personal injury or damage to the airbag system, DO NOT work in the vicinity of the steering wheel or instrument panel. The manufacturer recommends that, on airbag-equipped models, the following procedure should be left to a dealer service department or other repair shop because of the special tools and techniques required to disable the airbag system.*

1   Refer to Chapter 11 for removal of the glove compartment, underdash panels and console. **Note:** *The removal of the heater/evaporator housing is difficult and time-consuming, much more so than the removal of the heater core (see Section 11). For some home mechanics, the job is better left to a Jaguar dealership or other qualified repair shop.*

2   Disconnect the air conditioning lines from the backside of the expansion valve (at the firewall, just to the right of the engine), using two wrenches (**see illustration**). Cap the open fittings and expansion valve after disassembly to prevent the entry of air or dirt.

3   Refer to Section 11 for moving the climate-control computer aside and disconnecting the heater core pipes.

17.4 Remove the housing retaining nut (arrow) on the engine side of the firewall, near the expansion valve - another nut is on the right, near the heater core pipes

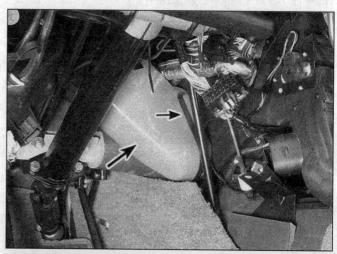

17.5 The left duct (large arrow) can be removed by pulling off the clip (small arrow) - the right duct pulls out without a clip

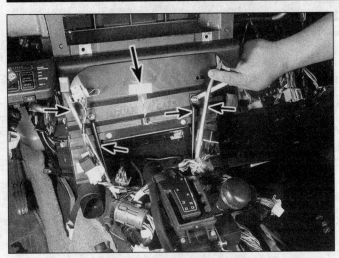

17.9a Unbolt the four support braces (small arrows) from the case (large arrow) and floor

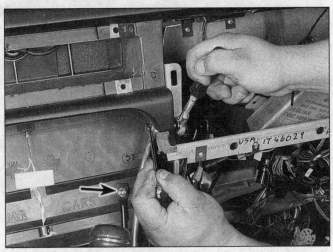

17.9b The black case-support rods are held to the case with nuts (arrow), while the gold dash-support rods are retained by a bolt/nut to the dash

4   From the engine side of the firewall, near the expansion valve, remove the nut retaining the heater/air conditioning assembly housing **(see illustration)**. Another mounting nut is on the left side, under the wiper motor **(see illustration 11.2)**.

5   Disconnect the defroster ducts on the left and right side of the evaporator housing **(see illustration)**.

6   Identify all of the vacuum motor lines with masking tape and a felt pen, then disconnect the lines. **Note:** *Most vacuum lines are color-coded. Make notes on which ones go to which devices.*

7   Tag and disconnect the wiring plugs connected to the heater/air conditioning housing.

8   At the bottom left and bottom right of the housing, pull off the rubber drain tubes that go into the flooring.

9   Remove the four rod-type support braces. Two support the dash, and two connect the case to the floor of the vehicle **(see illustrations)**.

10   With everything disconnected, pull the heater/air conditioning housing back and out from under the dash. **Caution:** *Do not force anything. If the unit gets stuck, determine where the interference is before a duct, wire or hose is broken.*

11   Pry off the series of black metal clips connecting the main housing to the evaporator case, then separate the evaporator case and pull out the evaporator core. **Note:** *When reinstalling the evaporator core into the case, be sure to reinstall the foam insulation in the same way it was installed originally.*

12   The evaporator core can be cleaned with a "fin comb" and blown off with compressed air.

13   The expansion valve is located on the right side of the firewall on the engine side. To replace it, remove the battery (see Chapter 5) for better access. Disconnect the lines from the back of the valve as in Step 2. Disconnect the high and low-pressure hoses from the *front* of the expansion valve **(see illustration)**.

14   If the evaporator core is replaced with a new unit, add 1.4 ounces

17.13 Disconnect the lines at the front of the expansion valve (located at the passenger side of the firewall (engine side) - always use two wrenches to avoid twisting a line - one wrench holds the body of the valve

of new refrigerant oil (make sure it is the oil compatible with your type of refrigerant) to the system.

15   The remainder of the installation is the reverse of the removal process. Be sure to use new O-rings, and new gaskets on the expansion valve.

16   Have the system evacuated, charged and leak tested by the shop that discharged it.

Notes

Chapter 4
Fuel and exhaust systems

Contents

Specifications

Fuel system

	kPa	psi
Fuel pressure		
Ignition ON, engine not running	260 to 300	38 to 44
Engine idling		
Vacuum hose detached from fuel pressure regulator	280 to 320	40 to 46
Vacuum hose attached to fuel pressure regulator	210 to 260	30 to 38
Fuel system hold pressure	145	21
Fuel injector resistance	2.0 to 3.0 ohms	

Idle speed

Must be set by authorized service department

Torque specification

	Nm	Ft-lbs (unless otherwise indicated)
Throttle body mounting bolts	19	14
Fuel rail mounting bolts	12	108 in-lbs

1   General information

The fuel system consists of a fuel tank, an electric fuel pump either located externally, next to the fuel tank (1988 through 1990 models) or in the fuel tank (1991 through 1994 models), an EFI fuel pump relay and main relay, an inertia switch, fuel injectors and fuel rail, an air cleaner assembly and a throttle body unit.

Multi Point Fuel Injection (MPFI) system

Multi point fuel injection uses timed impulses to sequentially inject the fuel directly into the intake port of each cylinder. The injectors are controlled by the Electronic Control Unit (ECU). The ECU monitors various engine parameters and delivers the exact amount of fuel, in the correct sequence, into the intake ports. The throttle body serves only to control the amount of air passing into the system. Because each cylinder is equipped with an injector mounted immediately adjacent to the intake valve, much better control of the fuel/air mixture ratio is possible.

Fuel pump and lines

Fuel is circulated from the fuel tank to the fuel injection system, and back to the fuel tank, through a pair of metal lines running along the underside of the vehicle. On early models (1988 through 1990), an electric fuel pump is attached to the chassis next to the fuel tank. On later models (1991 through 1994), the fuel pump and fuel level sending unit are located inside the fuel tank. A vapor return system routes all vapors and hot fuel back to the fuel tank through a separate return line.

The fuel pump will operate as long as the engine is cranking or running and the ECU is receiving ignition reference pulses from the electronic ignition system (see Chapter 5). If there are no reference pulses, the fuel pump will shut off after 2 or 3 seconds.

Inertia switch

These models are equipped with an inertia switch that is wired in the circuit between the fuel pump relay, the ignition switch and the fuel pump (refer to the wiring diagrams at the end of Chapter 12). The inertia switch is a special electrical device that provides circuit protection by switching off the ignition and fuel pump upon impact in the event of

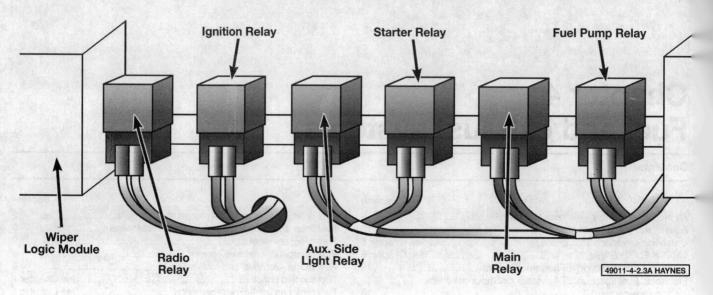

2.3a Relay locations on a 1988 model

vehicle collision. Later Jaguar models are equipped with an additional specialized inertia switch. This later device switches OFF all ignition fed circuits, locks the fuel filler cap, locks the trunk (only if doors are locked) and unlocks the doors if they are locked during the accident. All these functions are directed by the inertia switch. The inertia switch is located behind the left kick panel. Refer to Chapter 12 for more information.

Exhaust system

The exhaust system includes an exhaust manifold equipped with an exhaust oxygen sensor, a catalytic converter, an exhaust pipe, and a muffler.

The catalytic converter is an emission control device added to the exhaust system to reduce pollutants. A single-bed converter is used in combination with a three-way (reduction) catalyst. Refer to Chapter 6 for more information regarding the catalytic converter.

2   Fuel pressure relief

Refer to illustrations 2.3a, 2.3b and 2.3c
Warning: *Gasoline is extremely flammable, so take extra precautions when you work on any part of the fuel system. Don't smoke or allow open flames or bare light bulbs near the work area, and don't work in a garage where a natural gas-type appliance (such as a water heater or a clothes dryer) with a pilot light is present. Since gasoline is carcinogenic, wear latex gloves when there's a possibility of being exposed to fuel, and, if you spill any fuel on your skin, rinse it off immediately with soap and water. Mop up any spills immediately and do not store fuel-soaked rags where they could ignite. The fuel system is under constant pressure, so, if any fuel lines are to be disconnected, the fuel pressure in the system must be relieved first. When you perform any kind of work on the fuel system, wear safety glasses and have a Class B type fire extinguisher on hand.*

1   Before servicing any fuel system component, you must relieve the fuel pressure to minimize the risk of fire or personal injury.
2   Remove the fuel filler cap - this will relieve any pressure built up in the tank.
3   Remove the fuel pump relay from the main relay panel **(see illustrations)**. *Note: These models are equipped with a fuel pump relay that is located in various areas of the vehicle depending on the year. On 1988 and 1989 models, the fuel pump relay is under the glovebox. On 1990 through 1992 models, the fuel pump relay is in the engine compartment on the left side, attached to the brake pedal hanger. On 1993*

2.3b Relay locations on a 1989 model

2.3c On 1992 models, the fuel pump relay is located in the left rear corner of the engine compartment

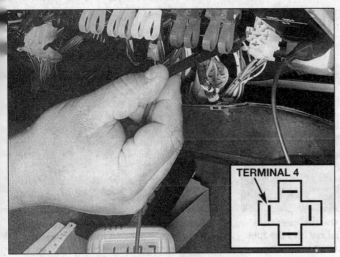

3.3a Checking for battery voltage at the fuel pump relay connector (1989 model)

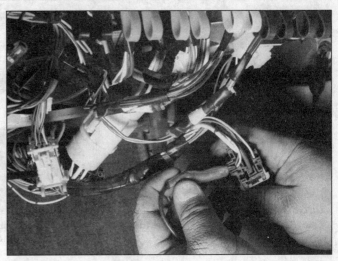

3.3b Checking for battery voltage to the main relay (1989 model)

models, the fuel pump relay is in the trunk. On 1994 models, it's in the engine compartment on the right side of the firewall. Refer to the relay location charts in Chapter 12 for additional information.

4   Start the engine and wait for the engine to stall, then turn the ignition key to Off. Disconnect the cable from the negative terminal of the battery before beginning any work on the fuel system. **Caution:** *If the stereo in your vehicle is equipped with an anti-theft system, make sure you have the correct activation code before disconnecting the battery.*

5   The fuel system is now depressurized. **Note:** *Place a rag around the fuel line before removing any hose clamp or fitting to prevent any residual fuel from spilling onto the engine.*

3   Fuel pump/fuel pressure - check

Warning: *Gasoline is extremely flammable, so take extra precautions when you work on any part of the fuel system. See the* **Warning** *in Section 2.*
Note 1: *To perform the fuel pressure test, you will need to obtain a fuel pressure gauge and adapter set (fuel line fittings).*
Note 2: *On 1988 through 1990 models, the fuel pump may chatter excessively and the engine may stall frequently during hot weather. If stalling occurs, the engine will restart after a cool-down period. Dual fuel pumps can be installed by a dealer service department or other qualified repair facility to remedy this problem.*

Preliminary inspection
Refer to illustrations 3.3a, 3.3b, 3.4a and 3.4b

1   Should the fuel system fail to deliver the proper amount of fuel, or any fuel at all, inspect it as follows. Remove the fuel filler cap. Have an assistant turn the ignition key to the ON position (engine not running) while you listen at the fuel filler opening. You should hear a whirring sound that lasts for a couple of seconds. On 1988 through 1990 models, listen behind the left rear wheel (external fuel pump) for the fuel pump sound.

2   If you don't hear anything, check the fuel pump relay **(see illustration 2.3a, b or c)** and circuit. If all circuits are intact and not damaged, check the inertia switch. **Note:** *The inertia switch is a special device that shuts down power to the ignition and the fuel pump in the event of an accident. Refer to Chapter 12 for checking and resetting procedures for the inertia switch.*

3   Remove the relay and check for battery voltage to the fuel pump relay connector **(see illustration)**. If there is battery voltage present, check the relay for proper operation. Refer to the relay checking procedure in Chapter 12. **Note:** *If battery voltage is not available, check for battery voltage to the main relay* **(see illustration)**. *Refer to the relay location diagrams in Chapter 12. The main relay, which is located next to the fuel pump relay, supplies voltage to the fuel pump and ignition system.*

4   If battery voltage is present, check for battery voltage directly at the fuel pump electrical connector **(see illustrations)**, within two sec-

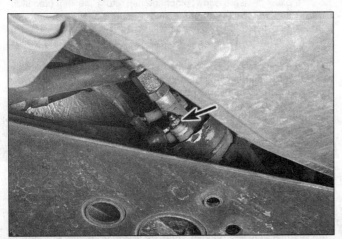

3.4a Remove the rubber boot from the fuel pump electrical connector and check for voltage while an assistant turns the ignition key (1989 model shown)

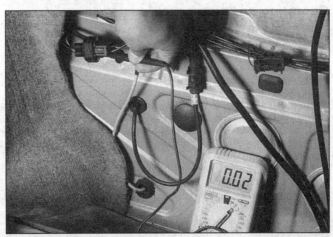

3.4b Check for battery voltage to the fuel pump on the harness connector near the fuel tank on models with in-tank fuel pumps

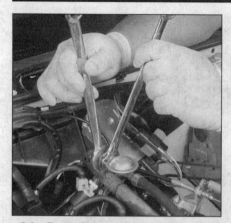
3.6a Remove the fuel line from the fuel pulsation damper . . .

3.6b . . . then install the fuel pressure gauge between the fuel rail and the fuel pressure damper using a T-fitting

3.9 First check the fuel pressure without vacuum applied to the fuel pressure regulator, then with vacuum applied; fuel pressure should DECREASE as vacuum INCREASES

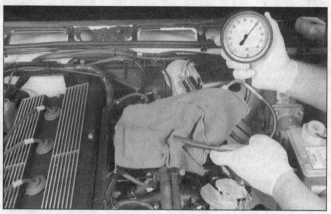
3.12 Using a pair of pliers, squeeze the return line and observe the fuel pressure increase (wrap a rag around the fuel line so you don't damage it)

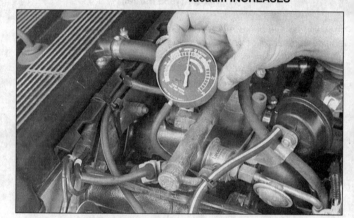
3.14 Connect a vacuum gauge to the vacuum line leading to the fuel pressure regulator and check the vacuum source. The fuel pressure regulator receives manifold vacuum that decreases (increases fuel pressure) when the engine speed is raised (acceleration)

onds of the ignition key being turned On. If there is no voltage, check the fuel pump circuit. If there is voltage present, replace the pump (see Section 4). **Note:** *It will be necessary to raise the vehicle and support it securely on jackstands to gain access to the fuel pump electrical connectors. Have an assistant operate the ignition key and be sure to block the front wheels to avoid any movement of the vehicle.*

Operating pressure check

Refer to illustrations 3.6a, 3.6b, 3.9, 3.12 and 3.14

5   Relieve the fuel system pressure (see Section 2). Detach the cable from the negative battery terminal. **Caution:** *If the stereo in your vehicle is equipped with an anti-theft system, make sure you have the correct activation code before disconnecting the battery.*

6   Detach the fuel line from the fuel rail and connect a fuel pressure gauge **(see illustrations)** between the fuel pulsation damper and the fuel rail. Tighten the hose clamps securely.

7   Attach the cable to the negative battery terminal. Start the engine.

8   Note the fuel pressure and compare it with the pressure listed in this Chapter's Specifications.

9   Disconnect the vacuum hose from the fuel pressure regulator and hook up a hand-held vacuum pump **(see illustration)** to the port on the fuel pressure regulator.

10   Read the fuel pressure gauge with vacuum applied to the pressure regulator and also with no vacuum applied. The fuel pressure should decrease as vacuum increases (and increase as vacuum decreases).

11   Reconnect the vacuum hose to the regulator and check the fuel pressure at idle, comparing your reading with the value listed in this

Chapter's Specifications. Disconnect the vacuum hose and watch the gauge - the pressure should jump up considerably as soon as the hose is disconnected. If it doesn't, check for a vacuum signal to the fuel pressure regulator (see Step 14).

12   If the fuel pressure is low, pinch the fuel return line shut **(see illustration)** and watch the gauge. If the pressure doesn't rise, the fuel pump is defective or there is a restriction or leak in the fuel feed line, or the pump is faulty. If the pressure rises sharply, replace the pressure regulator.

13   If the fuel pressure is too high, turn the engine off. Disconnect the fuel return line and blow through it to check for a blockage. If there is no blockage, replace the fuel pressure regulator.

14   Connect a vacuum gauge to the pressure regulator vacuum hose. Start the engine and check for vacuum **(see illustration)**. If there isn't vacuum present, check for a clogged hose or vacuum port. If the amount of vacuum is adequate but the pressure is too high, replace the fuel pressure regulator.

15   Turn the ignition switch to OFF, wait five minutes and recheck the pressure on the gauge. Compare the reading with the hold pressure listed in this Chapter's Specifications. If the hold pressure is less than specified:

  a) *The fuel lines may be leaking.*
  b) *The fuel pressure regulator may be allowing the fuel pressure to bleed through to the return line*
  c) *A fuel injector (or injectors) may be leaking.*
  d) *The fuel pump may be defective.*

4   Fuel pump - removal and installation

Warning: *Gasoline is extremely flammable, so take extra precautions when you work on any part of the fuel system. See the* **Warning** *in Section 2.*

Note 1: *On early models (1988 through 1990), an electric fuel pump is attached to the chassis next to the fuel tank. On later models (1991 through 1994), the fuel pump is located inside the fuel tank.*

Note 2: *On 1988 through 1990 models, the fuel pump may chatter excessively and the engine may stall frequently during hot weather. If stalling occurs, the engine will restart after a cool-down period. Dual fuel pumps can be installed by a dealer service department or other qualified repair facility to remedy this problem.*

1   Remove the fuel tank cap to relieve any pressure in the fuel tank. Relieve the fuel pressure (see Section 2).

2   Disconnect the cable from the negative terminal of the battery.

Caution: *If the stereo in your vehicle is equipped with an anti-theft system, make sure you have the correct activation code before disconnecting the battery.*

External fuel pumps

Refer to illustration 4.6

3   Raise the vehicle and support it securely on jackstands.

4   Disconnect the fuel lines from the fuel pump.

5   Disconnect the electrical connectors from the fuel pump **(see illustration 3.4a)**.

6   Remove the fuel pump bracket retaining nuts **(see illustration)**.

7   Carefully withdraw the fuel pump from the rubber case inside the fuel pump bracket and angle the fuel pump over the rear suspension

4.6 Remove the fuel pump mounting nuts (arrows) and slide the fuel pump out of the rubber casing (1989 model shown)

and out near the wheel on the left side of the vehicle.

8   Installation is the reverse of removal.

In-tank fuel pumps

Refer to illustration 4.12

9   Raise the vehicle and support it securely on jackstands.

10   Disconnect the fuel pump and fuel level sending unit electrical connectors and the fuel lines.

11   Remove the fuel tank from the trunk (see Section 7).

12   Disconnect the fuel lines from the evaporative flange **(see illustration)**. Remove the lock ring with a hammer and brass punch, tap-

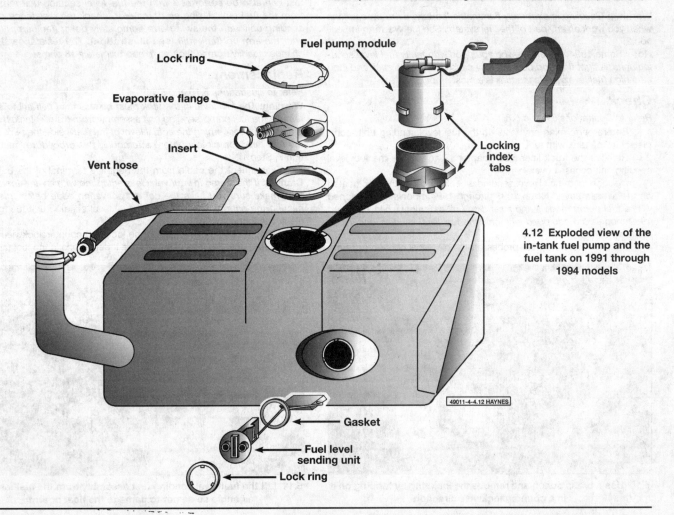

4.12 Exploded view of the in-tank fuel pump and the fuel tank on 1991 through 1994 models

Lock ring

Evaporative flange

Insert

Vent hose

Fuel pump module

Locking index tabs

Gasket

Fuel level sending unit

Lock ring

49011-4-4.12 HAYNES

5.4 Connect the probes of the ohmmeter to the fuel level sending unit terminals and check the resistance of the float assembly

ping the lock ring in a counterclockwise direction.

13   Withdraw the fuel pump module from the fuel tank. **Note:** *The fuel pump module is indexed near the bottom, therefore it will be necessary to turn the module slightly to unlock it from the rubber holder mounted on the bottom of the fuel tank.*

14   Replace the fuel pump module as a single unit.

15   Installation is the reverse of removal.

---

5   Fuel level sending unit - check and replacement

Warning: *Gasoline is extremely flammable, so take extra precautions when you work on any part of the fuel system. See the* **Warning** *in Section 2.*

Note: *Some 1994 models may be equipped with faulty fuel level sending units. A tight float rod bushing may cause the float to stick and indicate high fuel levels while the tank is almost empty.*

Check

Refer to illustrations 5.4 and 5.8

1   Before performing any tests on the fuel level sending unit, completely fill the tank with fuel.

2   Remove the trunk liner (see Chapter 12) to expose the fuel level sending unit access cover.

3   Disconnect the fuel level sending unit electrical connector located on the access cover. **Note:** *1991 through 1994 models are equipped with a fuel pump module and a sending unit assembly while 1988 and 1989 models are equipped with only the fuel level sending unit inside the tank.*

4   Position the ohmmeter probes on the electrical connector termi-

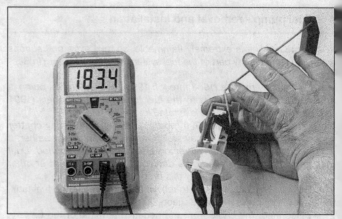

5.8 An accurate check of the sending unit can be made by removing it from the fuel tank and observing the resistance with the float down (empty) and then extended (full)

nals **(see illustration)** and check for resistance. Use the 200 ohm scale on the ohmmeter.

5   With the fuel tank completely full, the resistance should be about 18 to 20 ohms.

6   Reconnect the electrical connector and drive it until the tank is nearly empty.

7   Check the resistance. The resistance of the sending unit should be about 190 to 200 ohms.

8   If the readings are incorrect, replace the sending unit. **Note:** *The test can also be performed with the fuel level sending unit removed from the fuel tank. Using an ohmmeter, check the resistance of the sending unit with the swing arm completely down (tank empty) and with the arm up (tank full)* **(see illustration)**. *The resistance should change steadily from 200 ohms to approximately 18 ohms.*

Replacement

Refer to illustrations 5.10 and 5.11

Warning: *The fuel level in the tank must be less than half full to safely remove the fuel pump/sending unit assembly from the fuel tank. If there is any doubt concerning the actual level of the fuel inside the tank, drain the fuel tank completely before attempting this procedure (see Section 7, Step 1).*

9   Disconnect the cable from the negative terminal of the battery. **Caution:** *If the stereo in your vehicle is equipped with an anti-theft system, make sure you have the correct activation code before disconnecting the battery.* Disconnect the fuel level sending unit/fuel pump electrical connector.

10   Using a brass punch, tap on the lock ring counterclockwise **(see illustration)** until the tabs align with the indentations in the fuel tank.

5.10 Use a brass punch and remove the lock ring by tapping on it in a counterclockwise direction

5.11 Lift the fuel level sending unit assembly from the fuel tank at an angle so as not to damage the float or arm

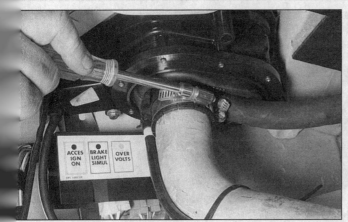

7.6 Remove the clamp that retains the fuel filler assembly to the filler neck

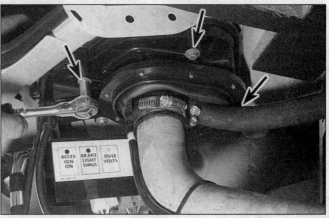

7.7a Remove the bolts (arrows) that retain the fuel filler assembly to the body and slide the assembly down the filler neck of the fuel tank

11   Carefully angle the sending unit out of the opening without damaging the fuel level float **(see illustration)**.
12   Installation is the reverse of removal.

---

6   Fuel lines and fittings - inspection and replacement

Warning: *Gasoline is extremely flammable, so take extra precautions when you work on any part of the fuel system. See the* **Warning** *in Section 2.*
Note: *If there is a distinct knocking noise coming from the dash when the engine is idling, the fuel feed hose may have hardened, restricting fuel flow and causing abnormal sounds. Replace the fuel inlet (feed) hose with a new one.*

Inspection

1   Once in a while, you will have to raise the vehicle to service or replace some component (an exhaust pipe hanger, for example). Whenever you work under the vehicle, always inspect fuel lines and all fittings and connections for damage or deterioration.
2   Check all hoses and pipes for cracks, kinks, deformation or obstructions.
3   Make sure all hoses and pipe clips attach their associated hoses or pipes securely to the underside of the vehicle.
4   Verify all hose clamps attaching rubber hoses to metal fuel lines or pipes are snug enough to assure a tight fit between the hoses and pipes.

Replacement

5   If you must replace any damaged sections, use original equipment replacement hoses or pipes constructed from exactly the same material as the section you are replacing. Do not install substitutes constructed from inferior or inappropriate material or you could cause a fuel leak or a fire.
6   Always, before detaching or disassembling any part of the fuel line system, note the routing of all hoses and pipes and the orientation of all clamps and clips to assure that replacement sections are installed in exactly the same manner.
7   Before detaching any part of the fuel system, be sure to relieve the pressure in the tank by removing the fuel tank cap, then relieve the fuel system pressure (see Section 2). Cover the fitting being disconnected with a rag to absorb any fuel that may leak out.

---

7   Fuel tank - removal and installation

Refer to illustrations 7.6, 7.7a, 7.7b, 7.8, 7.9a, 7.9b, 7.9c, 7.9d and 7.10
Warning: *Gasoline is extremely flammable, so take extra precautions*

7.7b Direct low pressure compressed air into the hole for the overflow line if it is clogged

when you work on any part of the fuel system. See the **Warning** *in Section 2.*
Note: *If the vehicle exhibits a fuel starvation condition when cornering sharply or under heavy braking with the fuel tank low, this condition is caused by a rubber fuel return hose falling off the grommet inside the fuel tank. This can be repaired while the fuel tank remains in the vehicle by draining all the fuel from the tank, removing the fuel level sending unit (see Section 5) and locating the return line connection with a flashlight. Loosen the clamp and pull the return hose through the opening of the fuel tank and install a stainless steel hose clamp. Secure the hose clamp and install the fuel level sending unit.*

1   This procedure is much easier to perform if the fuel tank is empty. Some models may have a drain plug for this purpose. If for some reason the drain plug can't be removed, postpone the job until the tank is empty or siphon the fuel into an approved container using a siphoning kit (available at most auto parts stores). **Warning:** *Do not start the siphoning action by mouth!*
2   Remove the fuel filler cap to relieve fuel tank pressure.
3   Detach the cable from the negative terminal of the battery.
Caution: *If the stereo in your vehicle is equipped with an anti-theft system, make sure you have the correct activation code before disconnecting the battery.*
4   If the tank is full or nearly full, drain the fuel into an approved container.
5   Raise the vehicle and place it securely on jackstands.
6   Remove the filler neck vent tube clamp **(see illustration)** and separate the tube from the fuel filler neck.
7   Remove the fuel filler assembly bolts **(see illustration)** and slide the large rubber boot down the neck of the fuel tank. **Note:** *These vehi-*

7.8 Remove the bolts (arrows) from the spare tire bracket and lift the assembly from the trunk

7.9a Disconnect the flexible fuel lines from the metal fuel lines

7.9b Disconnect the vapor return line from the fuel tank

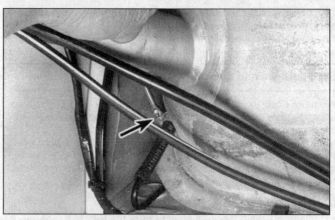

7.9c Disconnect the canister purge line from the fuel tank

cles are susceptible to clogging of the fuel overflow line. If this happens, excess fuel or water in the fuel filler cap recess could flow into the trunk, causing a dangerous condition and/or an unpleasant mess. To correct this condition, direct low-pressure compressed air into the overflow hole **(see illustration)**, which should clear any obstruction in the line.

8   Remove the spare tire and the spare tire bracket assembly **(see illustration)**.

9   Disconnect the fuel lines, the vapor return line and the canister vent line **(see illustrations)**. **Note:** Be sure to plug the hoses to prevent

leakage and contamination of the fuel system. Remove the driveline to gain access to the fuel line connectors next to the tank (see Chapter 8). Working under the vehicle, remove the pins using a needle-nose pliers, turn the connectors slightly to loosen them from the grommets and pull the fuel lines out of the tank. **Caution:** Remove all of the lines from the tank, including the metal lines, before removing the fuel tank or damage to the fittings could occur.

10   Remove the bolts from the fuel tank retaining straps **(see illustration)**.

11   Pull the fuel tank out into the trunk area. Be careful to angle the

7.9d Remove the clips (arrows) that retain the fuel lines to the fuel tank using needle-nose pliers

7.10 Remove the tank strap bolts (arrows) from the body

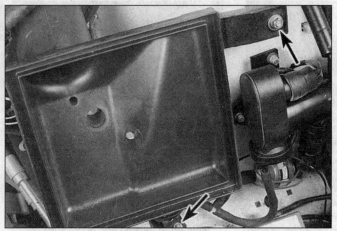

9.2a Remove the bolts (arrows) from the air cleaner assembly

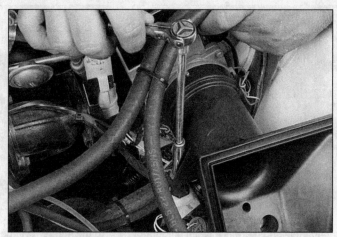

9.2b Also, remove the bolt that retains the air intake duct to the MAF sensor and lift the assembly from the compartment

10.2 Loosen the locknuts on the accelerator cable

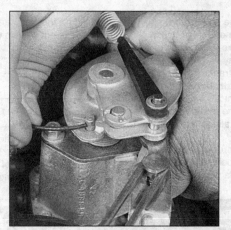

10.3 Rotate the bellcrank and remove the cable end from the slot

10.4 Remove the circlip (arrow) and separate the cable from the accelerator pedal assembly by pulling the pin from the pedal assembly

fuel filler neck away from the body.

12 Remove the tank from the vehicle.

13 Installation is the reverse of removal.

8 Fuel tank cleaning and repair - general information

1 Any repairs to the fuel tank or filler neck should be carried out by a professional who has experience in this critical and potentially dangerous work. Even after cleaning and flushing of the fuel system, explosive fumes can remain and ignite during repair of the tank.

2 If the fuel tank is removed from the vehicle, it should not be placed in an area where sparks or open flames could ignite the fumes coming out of the tank. Be especially careful inside garages where a natural gas-type appliance is located, because the pilot light could cause an explosion.

9 Air cleaner assembly - removal and installation

Refer to illustrations 9.2a and 9.2b

1 Detach the clips and remove the air filter cover and the filter element (see Chapter 1).

2 Remove the bolts and remove the air cleaner assembly from the engine compartment **(see illustrations).**

3 Installation is the reverse of removal.

10 Accelerator cable - removal, installation and adjustment

Removal

Refer to illustrations 10.2, 10.3 and 10.4

1 Detach the cable from the negative terminal of the battery. **Caution:** *If the stereo in your vehicle is equipped with an anti-theft system, make sure you have the correct activation code before disconnecting the battery.*

2 Loosen the locknut on the threaded portion of the throttle cable at the throttle body **(see illustration).**

3 Rotate the throttle lever, then slip the throttle cable end out of the slot in the lever **(see illustration).**

4 Detach the throttle cable from the accelerator pedal **(see illustration).**

5 From inside the vehicle, pull the cable through the firewall.

Installation and adjustment

Refer to illustrations 10.9, 10.10 and 10.11

6 Installation is the reverse of removal.

7 To adjust the cable, fully depress the accelerator pedal and check that the throttle is fully opened.

8 If not fully opened, loosen the locknuts, depress the accelerator pedal and adjust the cable until the throttle is fully open.

9 Tighten the locknuts and recheck the adjustment. Make sure the

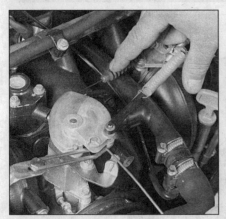

10.9 Make sure the throttle closes completely and there is a slight amount of flex in the cable

10.10 Attach a strong wire (coat hanger) to the master cylinder using a clamp and align it with the notch on the bellcrank

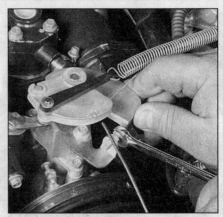

10.11 Rotate the bellcrank until it reaches wide open throttle and make sure the pointer aligns with the A on the bellcrank. Adjust if necessary

throttle closes fully when the pedal is released **(see illustration)**.

10   After the cable is adjusted, check the adjustment of the bellcrank. Use a small clamp and a straight rod or stiff wire (coat hanger) and attach it to the brake master cylinder in such a way that the tip acts as a pointer. Align the pointer with "A" (automatic transmission) or "M" (manual transmission) on the bellcrank **(see illustration)**, depending on what type of transmission is installed in the vehicle.

11   Slowly rotate the bellcrank until it reaches the throttle stop (wide open throttle) and check to make sure the pointer aligns with the notch in the bellcrank **(see illustration)**.

12   If necessary, adjust the position of the throttle stop using a wrench and turn the throttle stop screw until the bellcrank reaches the correct position. Lock the throttle stop screw in place.

13   Allow the bellcrank to return to the idle position and test the adjustment once again until the correct adjustment has been attained.

11   Electronic Fuel Injection (EFI) system - general information

Refer to illustration 11.1

1   These models are equipped with an Electronic Fuel Injection (EFI) system. This fuel injection system is designed by Bosch but licensed by Lucas and is called the Lucas LH Engine Management system. The EFI system is composed of three basic sub systems: fuel delivery system, air induction system and electronic control system **(see illustration)**.

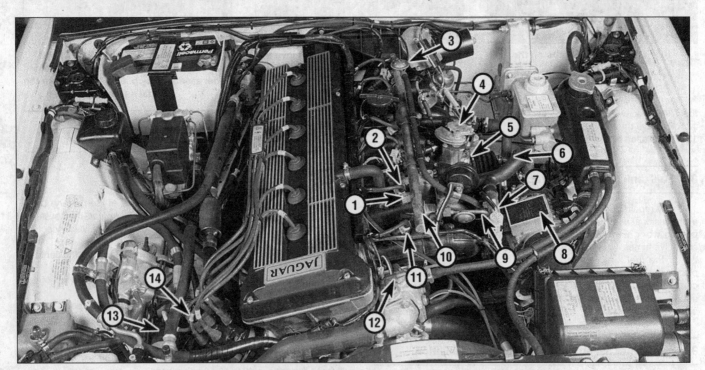

11.1 Fuel injection and emission control component locations for the 3.6L 1989 XJ6

1 Fuel pressure regulator (under fuel rail)	6 Intake Air Temperature (IAT) sensor	10 Fuel rail
2 Idle Speed Control (ISC) motor	7 Supplementary air valve	11 Fuel injector
3 Fuel pressure damper	8 Mass Airflow (MAF) sensor	13 Ignition amplifier (below block valve)
4 Bellcrank	9 Throttle potentiometer (under throttle body)	14 Distributor
5 Throttle body (below bellcrank)		

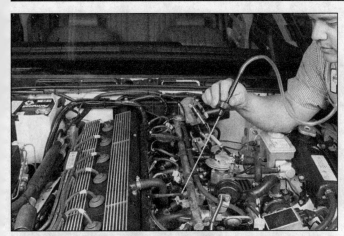

12.7 Use a stethoscope or a screwdriver to determine if the injectors are working properly - they should make a steady clicking sound that rises and falls with engine speed changes

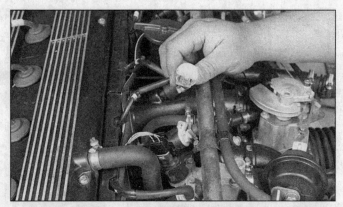

12.8 Install the "noid" light into the fuel injector electrical connector and check to see that it blinks with the engine running

12.9 Using an ohmmeter, measure the resistance across both terminals of the injector

Fuel system

2   An electric fuel pump is located on the chassis of the rear suspension (external) (1988 through 1990) or inside the fuel tank (1991 through 1994) The fuel pump supplies fuel under constant pressure to the fuel rail, which distributes fuel evenly to all injectors. From the fuel rail, fuel is injected into the intake ports, just above the intake valves, by fuel injectors. The amount of fuel supplied by the injectors is precisely controlled by an Electronic Control Unit (ECU). A pressure regulator controls system pressure in relation to intake manifold vacuum. A fuel filter between the fuel pump and the fuel rail filters fuel to protect the components of the system.

Air induction system

3   The air system consists of an air filter housing, a Mass Air Flow (MAF) sensor (airflow meter), Intake Air Temperature (IAT) sensor and a throttle body. The MAF sensor is an information gathering device for the ECU. A heated element determines the temperature differential by measuring the current changes which in turn measures the mass (weight and volume) of air entering the engine. This information helps the ECU determine the amount of fuel to be injected by the injectors. The throttle plate inside the throttle body is controlled by the driver. As the throttle plate opens, the amount of air that can pass through the system increases, so the potentiometer opens further and the ECU signals the injectors to increase the amount of fuel delivered to the intake ports. Refer to Chapter 6 for additional information on the fuel injection system sensors, test procedures and replacement procedures.

Electronic control system

4   The Computer Control System controls the EFI and other systems by means of an Electronic Control Unit (ECU), which employs a microcomputer. The ECU receives signals from a number of information sensors which monitor such variables as intake air volume, intake air temperature, coolant temperature, engine rpm, acceleration/deceleration and exhaust oxygen content. These signals help the ECU determine the injection duration necessary for the optimum air/fuel ratio. Some of these sensors and their corresponding ECU-controlled relays are not contained within EFI components, but are located throughout the engine compartment. For further information regarding the ECU and its relationship to the engine electrical and ignition system, see Chapter 6.

12 Electronic Fuel Injection (EFI) system - check

Refer to illustrations 12.7, 12.8 and 12.9

1   Check the ground wire connections for tightness. Check all wiring and electrical connectors that are related to the system. Loose electrical connectors and poor grounds can cause many problems that resemble more serious malfunctions.

2   Check to see that the battery is fully charged, as the control unit and sensors depend on an accurate supply voltage in order to properly meter the fuel.

3   Check the air filter element - a dirty or partially blocked filter will severely impede performance and economy (see Chapter 1).

4   If a blown fuse is found, replace it and see if it blows again. If it does, search for a grounded wire in the harness related to the system.

5   Check the air intake duct from the MAF sensor to the intake manifold for leaks, which will result in an excessively lean mixture. Also check the condition of the vacuum hoses connected to the intake manifold.

6   Remove the air intake duct from the throttle body and check for carbon and residue build-up. If it's dirty, clean it with aerosol carburetor cleaner (make sure the can says it's safe for use with oxygen sensors and catalytic converters) and a toothbrush.

7   With the engine running, place a stethoscope against each injector, one at a time, and listen for a clicking sound, indicating operation **(see illustration)**.

8   If there is a problem with an injector, purchase a special injector test light (noid light) and install it into the injector electrical connector **(see illustration)**. Start the engine and make sure that each injector connector flashes the noid light. This will test for the proper voltage signal to the injector. **Caution:** *If the engine will not start and the noid light indicates that each injector is receiving the proper signal, there is a good possibility that the injector(s) is stuck open and allowing fuel into the combustion chamber in excessive amounts. If the spark plugs are fouled, detach the primary (low voltage) wires from the ignition coil, disable the fuel pump by removing the fuel pump relay (see Section 2), remove the spark plugs and crank the engine over. If fuel sprays from the spark plug holes, the engine is flooded and the fuel must be removed from the combustion chambers.*

9   With the engine OFF and the fuel injector electrical connectors

13.7 Push up on the clip and remove the harness connector from the MAF sensor

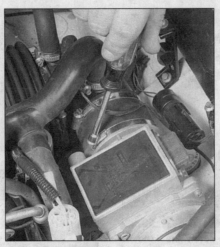

13.8 Remove the air intake duct clamp from the MAF sensor housing

13.9 Remove the bellcrank assembly bolts (arrows) and separate it from the throttle body

disconnected, measure the resistance of each injector **(see illustration)**. Each injector should measure about 2.0 to 3.0 ohms. If not, the injector is probably faulty.

10   The remainder of the system checks should be left to a Jaguar service department or other qualified repair shop, as there is a chance that the control unit may be damaged if not performed properly.

13   Electronic Fuel Injection (EFI) system - component check and replacement

Warning: *Gasoline is extremely flammable, so take extra precautions when you work on any part of the fuel system. See the* **Warning** *in Section 2.*

Caution: *If the stereo in your vehicle is equipped with an anti-theft system, make sure you have the correct activation code before disconnecting the battery.*

Throttle body

Check

1   Verify that the throttle linkage operates smoothly.
2   Start the engine, detach each vacuum hose and, using your finger, check the vacuum at each port on the throttle body with the engine at idle and above idle. The vacuum available from the throttle body is ported. Raise the engine rpm and watch as vacuum increases. It may be necessary to use a vacuum gauge. Refer to Chapter 2B for additional information concerning vacuum checks.

Replacement

Refer to illustrations 13.7, 13.8 and 13.9
Warning: *Wait until the engine is completely cool before beginning this procedure.*
3   Detach the cable from the negative terminal of the battery *(see the* **Caution** *at the beginning of this Section)*.
4   Drain the radiator (see Chapter 1).
5   Remove the air cleaner (see Chapter 1) and the air cleaner housing (see Section 9).
6   Remove the air intake duct.
7   Detach the electrical connector from the MAF sensor **(see illustration)**.
8   Remove the clamp that retains the MAF sensor to the air intake duct **(see illustration)** and lift the MAF sensor assembly from the engine compartment.
9   Detach the accelerator cable from the bellcrank (see Section 10), then remove the bellcrank assembly from the throttle body **(see illustration)**.

13.18 The area inside the throttle body near the throttle plate suffers from sludge build-up because the PCV hose vents vapor from the crankcase into the air intake duct

10   Detach the kickdown cable from the bellcrank and set the cable and brackets aside (see Chapter 7).
11   Clearly label, then detach, all vacuum and coolant hoses from the throttle body.
12   Disconnect the electrical connector from the throttle potentiometer.
13   Remove the four throttle body mounting bolts and detach the throttle body from the intake manifold.
14   Using a soft brush and carburetor cleaner, thoroughly clean the throttle body casting, then blow out all passages with compressed air.
Caution: *Do not clean the throttle position sensor with any solvents or sprays. Just wipe it off with a clean, soft cloth.*
15   Installation of the throttle body is the reverse of removal.
16   Be sure to tighten the throttle body mounting bolts to the torque listed in this Chapter's Specifications.

Adjustment

Refer to illustrations 13.18, 13.19 and 13.20
17   Remove the air intake duct to expose the throttle body and butterfly valve.
18   Make sure the throttle body is clean and free of burrs, nicks or carbon build-up **(see illustration)**.
19   Measure the clearance between the butterfly valve (throttle plate) and the wall of the throttle body **(see illustration)**. It should be 0.05 mm (0.002 inch).
20   If the gap is incorrect, loosen the throttle stop locknut **(see illus-**

13.19 Measure clearance between the butterfly valve and the throttle body

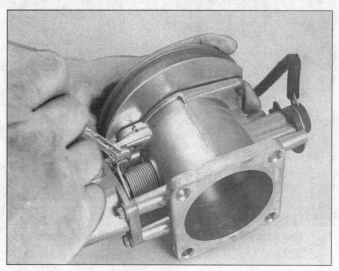

13.20 Adjust the butterfly angle by loosening the locknut on the throttle stop and turning the adjustment bolt

tration) and turn the throttle stop screw until the correct clearance is attained.

21   Install the air intake duct and surrounding components.

Throttle potentiometer

Refer to Chapter 6 for testing and removal procedures.

Idle Speed Control (ISC) motor

Note: *The minimum idle speed is pre-set at the factory and should not require adjustment under normal operating conditions; however if the throttle body has been replaced or you suspect the minimum idle speed has been tampered with (for example, if the idle speed screw was removed from the throttle body) have the vehicle checked by a dealer service department or a qualified automotive repair shop.*

Check

Refer to illustrations 13.23a and 13.23b

22   Start the engine and allow it to reach normal operating temperature. Switch on the headlights or heated rear window and confirm that the engine rpm decreases at first and then increases. This check mon-

itors the ISC motor as it is signaled by the computer to increase idle speed due to additional amperage required from the charging system. As the headlights draw current from the charging system, the alternator will create resistance on the belt as it works to produce the additional energy. If the rpm does not increase, check the ISC motor.

23   Check for approximately 11.2 volts to the ISC stepper motor **(see illustrations).** Disconnect the ISC harness connector and working on the harness side, check for 11.2 volts with the ignition key ON (engine not running). Also, check the corresponding terminals for the correct voltage amounts. If the correct voltage does not exist, check the wiring harness. Refer to the wiring diagrams at the end of Chapter 12.

24   The ISC motor or stepper motor can be checked for correct operation but a special tool is required to activate the internal coils. Have the stepper motor checked by a dealer service department or other qualified repair shop.

25   Reconnect the ISC motor electrical connector.

Replacement

Refer to illustration 13.27

26   Detach the cable from the negative terminal of the battery *(see* **Caution** *at the beginning of this Section).*

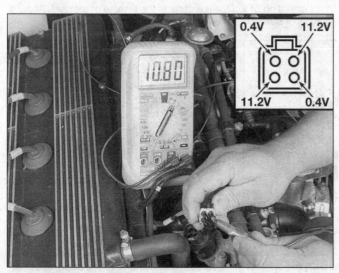

13.23a To check the ISC motor, turn the ignition key ON (engine not running) and check for the proper voltage amounts at the harness connector (1989 model shown)

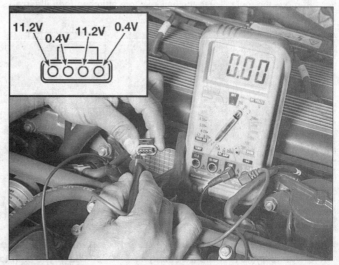

13.23b Later models are equipped with a different shape ISC connector but the voltage values should be the same as the early style

13.27 Use a large open end wrench to remove the ISC motor from the intake manifold

13.35 Remove the fuel rail mounting bolts (arrows) . . .

27   Use a large open-end wrench and unscrew the ISC motor from the housing **(see illustration)**.
28   Installation is the reverse of removal, but be sure to use a new gasket.

Fuel rail and fuel injectors

Note: *If there is a distinct knocking noise coming from the dash when the engine is idling, the fuel feed hose may have hardened restricting fuel flow and causing abnormal sounds. Replace the fuel inlet (feed) hose with a new part from the dealer parts department.*

Check

29   Refer to the fuel injection system checking procedure (see Section 12).

Replacement

Refer to illustrations 13.35, 13.36, 13.37, 13.38a and 13.38b
30   Relieve the fuel pressure (see Section 2).
31   Detach the cable from the negative terminal of the battery *(see* **Caution** *at the beginning of this Section).*
32   Disconnect the fuel injector electrical connectors and set the injector wire harness aside.
33   Detach the vacuum sensing hose from the fuel pressure regulator.
34   Disconnect the fuel lines from the fuel pressure regulator and the fuel rail **(see illustration 3.6a)**
35   Remove the fuel rail mounting bolts **(see illustration)**.
36   Remove the fuel rail with the fuel injectors attached **(see illustration)**.

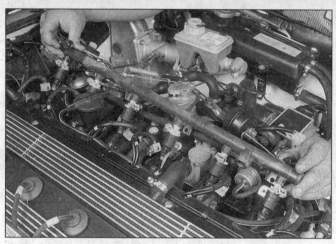

13.36 . . . and remove the fuel rail with the fuel injectors attached

37   Pry off the clips and remove the fuel injector(s) from the fuel rail **(see illustration)**.
38   If you are replacing the injector(s), discard the old injector. If you intend to re-use the same injectors, replace the grommets and O-rings **(see illustrations)**.
39   Installation of the fuel injectors is the reverse of removal. Apply a light film of clean engine oil to the O-rings before installing them.

13.37 Remove the fuel injector retaining clips from the fuel rail using a small screwdriver

13.38a If you plan to reinstall the original injectors, remove and discard the O-rings and grommets and replace them with new ones

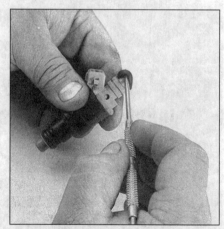

13.38b Use a sharp tipped screwdriver or pick to remove the old injector seal and make sure the injector body is not damaged in the process

13.45 Disconnect the fuel pressure regulator from the fuel return line

13.49 Check for battery voltage to the supplementary air valve

40   Tighten the fuel rail mounting bolts to the torque listed in this Chapter's Specifications.

Fuel pressure regulator

Check

41   Refer to the fuel pump/fuel pressure check procedure (see Section 3).

Replacement

Refer to illustration 13.45

42   Relieve the fuel pressure (see Section 2) and detach the cable from the negative terminal of the battery *(see the **Caution** at the beginning of this Section)*.
43   Detach the vacuum hose from the fuel pressure regulator.
44   Remove the fuel rail and the injectors as an assembly (see Steps 30 through 39).
45   Remove the fuel line from the fuel pressure regulator **(see illustration)**.
46   Remove the fuel pressure regulator mounting bolts and detach the pressure regulator from the engine.
47   The remainder of installation is the reverse of removal. Make sure the fuel lines are secure and there are no leaks before operating the vehicle.

Supplementary air valve

Check

Refer to illustration 13.49

48   The supplementary air valve provides additional throttle valve bypass air during cold starting and cold running conditions below 15-degrees F. This output actuator is controlled by the computer (ECU) in response to information received from the coolant temperature sensor, intake air temperature sensor and other information sensors working with the fuel injection system.
49   Check for battery voltage to the supplementary air valve. With the engine cold, backprobe the electrical connector using a long pin and check for battery voltage **(see illustration)**. Voltage should exist.
50   Because of the special tools required to test the supplementary air valve, have it tested by a dealer service department or other qualified repair facility.

Replacement

51   Remove the intake hoses, the mounting screws and detach the supplementary air valve from the engine.
52   Installation is the reverse of removal.
53   Be sure to use a new gasket when installing the idle-up valve.

Air intake plenum

Note: *The air intake plenum is removed and installed as a complete unit with the intake manifold. In the event of damage or leaks, remove the air intake plenum and intake manifold as a single unit and have it repaired by a dealer service department. Refer to Chapter 2 for removal and installation procedures.*

14   Exhaust system servicing - general information

Refer to illustrations 14.1a, 14.1b, 14.1c and 14.4
Warning: *Inspection and repair of exhaust system components should be done only after the system components have cooled completely.*
1   The exhaust system consists of the exhaust manifold, catalytic converter, the muffler, the tailpipe and all connecting pipes, brackets, hangers and clamps. The exhaust system is attached to the body with mounting brackets and rubber hangers **(see illustrations)**. If any of these parts are damaged or deteriorated, excessive noise and vibration will be transmitted to the body. **Note:** *The exhaust system configuration changes with later model updates. Earlier models (1988 and 1989) are equipped with a pre-catalytic converter near the exhaust manifold incorporating a single exhaust pipe to the muffler. Later models are equipped with dual exhaust pipes, dual catalytic converters and mufflers.*

14.1a The rear tailpipe section is fastened to the chassis with a special rubber mount (arrow) that pivots with road movement. Check them for deterioration and alignment

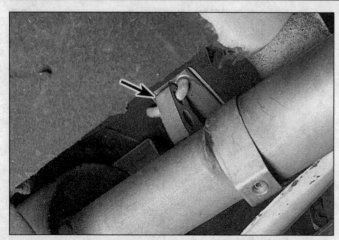

14.1b Check the condition of the flexible rubber mounts that hang the muffler to the chassis

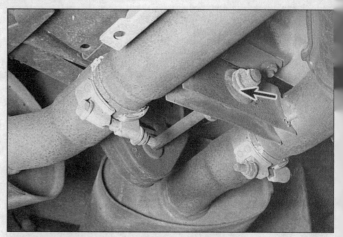

14.1c On dual muffler models, check the condition of the mount (arrow) and the clamps

2   Conducting regular inspections of the exhaust system will keep it safe and quiet. Look for any damaged or bent parts, open seams, holes, loose connections, excessive corrosion or other defects which could allow exhaust fumes to enter the vehicle. Deteriorated exhaust system components should not be repaired - they should be replaced with new parts.

3   If the exhaust system components are extremely corroded or rusted together, they will probably have to be cut from the exhaust system. The convenient way to accomplish this is to have a muffler repair shop remove the corroded sections with a cutting torch. If, however, you want to save money by doing it yourself and you don't have an oxy/acetylene welding outfit with a cutting torch, simply cut off the old components with a hacksaw. If you have compressed air, special pneumatic cutting chisels can also be used. If you do decide to tackle the job at home, be sure to wear eye protection to protect your eyes from metal chips and work gloves to protect your hands.

4   Here are some simple guidelines to apply when repairing the exhaust system:

a) *Work from the back to the front when removing exhaust system components.*

b) *Apply penetrating oil to the exhaust system component fasteners to make them easier to remove* **(see illustration)**.

c) *Use new gaskets, hangers and clamps when installing exhaust system components.*

d) *Apply anti-seize compound to the threads of all exhaust system fasteners during reassembly.*

e) *Be sure to allow sufficient clearance between newly installed parts and all points on the underbody to avoid overheating the floor pan*

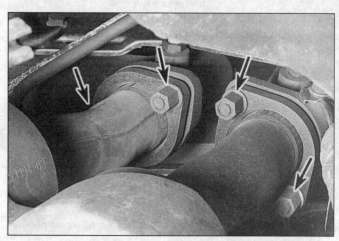

14.4 Use penetrating oil on the exhaust flange nuts before attempting to remove them

and possibly damaging the interior carpet and insulation. Pay particularly close attention to the catalytic converter and its heat shield. **Warning:** *The catalytic converter operates at very high temperatures and takes a long time to cool. Wait until it's completely cool before attempting to remove the converter. Failure to do so could result in serious burns.*

Chapter 5
Engine electrical systems

Contents

Specifications

Ignition system

Ignition timing (all models)	Not adjustable
Ignition coil resistance (at 68-degrees F)	
Primary resistance	0.4 to 0.5 ohms
Secondary resistance	6.0 to 6.5 K-ohms

Charging system

Charging voltage	13.9 to 15.1 volts
Standard amperage	
No load	less than 10 amps
Full load	30 amps or more

1   General information

The engine electrical systems include all ignition, charging and starting components. Because of their engine related functions, these components are discussed separately from chassis electrical devices such as the fuses, relays, lights, etc. (which are included in Chapter 12).

Always observe the following precautions when working on the electrical systems:

a) *Be extremely careful when servicing engine electrical components. They are easily damaged if checked, connected or handled improperly.*

b) *Never leave the ignition switch on for long periods of time (10 minutes maximum) with the engine off.*

c) *Don't disconnect the battery cables while the engine is running.*

d) *Maintain correct polarity when connecting a battery cable from another vehicle during jump starting.*

e) *Always disconnect the negative cable first and hook it up last or the battery may be shorted by the tool being used to loosen the cable clamps.*

It's also a good idea to review the safety-related information regarding the engine electrical systems located in the *Safety first* section near the front of this manual before beginning any operation included in this Chapter.

2   Battery - emergency jump starting

Refer to the *Booster battery (jump) starting* procedure at the front of this manual.

3   Battery - removal and installation

1   Disconnect the negative terminal, then the positive terminal from the battery. On 1989 through 1992 models, the battery is located in the engine compartment on the passenger side firewall and on 1993 and 1994 models, it is located in the trunk. **Caution:** *If the stereo in your vehicle is equipped with an anti-theft system, make sure you have the correct activation code before disconnecting the battery.*

2   Remove the battery hold-down clamp.
3   Lift out the battery. Be careful, it's heavy.
4   While the battery is out, inspect the carrier (tray) for corrosion.
5   If you are replacing the battery, make sure that you get one that's identical, with the same dimensions, amperage rating, cold cranking rating, etc. as the original.
6   Installation is the reverse of removal.

4   Battery cables - check and replacement

Caution: *If the stereo in your vehicle is equipped with an anti-theft system, make sure you have the correct activation code before disconnecting the battery.*
1   Periodically inspect the entire length of each battery cable for damage, cracked or burned insulation and corrosion. Poor battery cable connections can cause starting problems and decreased engine performance.
2   Check the cable-to-terminal connections at the ends of the cables for cracks, loose wire strands and corrosion. The presence of white, fluffy deposits under the insulation at the cable terminal connection is a sign that the cable is corroded and should be replaced. Check the terminals for distortion, missing mounting bolts and corrosion.
3   When removing the cables, always disconnect the negative cable first and hook it up last or the battery may be shorted by the tool used to loosen the cable clamps. Even if only the positive cable is being replaced, be sure to disconnect the negative cable from the battery first (see Chapter 1 for further information regarding battery cable removal).
4   Disconnect the cables from the battery, then trace each of them to their opposite ends and detach them from the starter solenoid and ground terminals. Note the routing of each cable to ensure correct installation.
5   If you are replacing either or both of the old cables, take them with you when buying new cables. It is vitally important that you replace the cables with identical parts. Cables have characteristics that make them easy to identify: positive cables are usually red, larger in cross-section and have a larger diameter battery post clamp; ground cables are usually black, smaller in cross-section and have a slightly smaller diameter clamp for the negative post.
6   Clean the threads of the solenoid or ground connection with a wire brush to remove rust and corrosion. Apply a light coat of battery terminal corrosion inhibitor, or petroleum jelly, to the threads to prevent future corrosion.
7   Attach the cable to the solenoid or ground connection and tighten the mounting nut/bolt securely.
8   Before connecting a new cable to the battery, make sure that it reaches the battery post without having to be stretched.
9   Connect the positive cable first, followed by the negative cable.

5   Ignition system - general information and precautions

1   All models are equipped with a computerized ignition system. The ignition system consists of the ignition coil, the crankshaft position sensor, the amplifier and the electronic control unit (ECU). The ignition ECU controls the ignition timing and advance characteristics for the engine. The ignition timing is not adjustable, therefore, changing the position of the distributor will not change the timing in any way. **Note:** *In the event the distributor must be removed from the engine, be sure to follow the precautions described in Section 9 and mark the engine and distributor with paint to ensure correct installation. If the distributor is not marked and the crankshaft is turned while the distributor is out of the engine, have the distributor installed by a dealer service department. The distributor must be installed using a special alignment tool.*
2   The distributor is driven by the intermediate shaft which also drives the power steering pump. The crankshaft position sensor is located on the front timing cover. It detects crank position by pulsing an electronic signal to the ECU. This signal is sent to the ECU to pro-

vide ignition timing specifications.
3   The computerized ignition system provides complete control of the ignition timing by determining the optimum timing in response to engine speed, coolant temperature, throttle position and vacuum pressure in the intake manifold. These parameters are relayed to the ECU by the crankshaft position sensor, throttle potentiometer, coolant temperature sensor and MAF sensor. Ignition timing is altered during warm-up, idling and warm running conditions by the ECU. This electronic ignition system also consists of the ignition switch, battery, coil, distributor, spark plug wires and spark plugs.
4   Refer to a dealer parts department or auto parts store for any questions concerning the availability of the distributor parts and assemblies. Testing the crankshaft position sensor is covered in Chapter 6.
5   When working on the ignition system, take the following precautions:

a)   *Do not keep the ignition switch on for more than 10 seconds if the engine will not start.*
b)   *Always connect a tachometer in accordance with the manufacturer's instructions. Some tachometers may be incompatible with this ignition system. Consult a dealer service department before buying a tachometer for use with this vehicle.*
c)   *Never allow the ignition coil terminals to touch ground. Grounding the coil could result in damage to the igniter and/or the ignition coil.*
d)   *Do not disconnect the battery when the engine is running.*

6   Ignition system - check

Refer to illustrations 6.3, 6.5, 6.9 and 6.11
Warning: *Because of the high voltage generated by the ignition system, extreme care should be taken whenever an operation is performed involving ignition components. This not only includes the amplifier, coil, distributor and spark plug wires, but related components such as connectors, tachometer and other test equipment also.*
1   With the ignition switch turned to the "ON" position, a "Battery" light or an "Oil Pressure" light is a basic check for ignition and battery supply to the ECU.
2   Check all ignition wiring connections for tightness, cuts, corrosion or any other signs of a bad connection.
3   Use a calibrated ignition tester to verify adequate secondary voltage (25,000 volts) at each spark plug **(see illustration)**. A faulty or poor connection at that plug could also result in a misfire. Also, check for carbon deposits inside the spark plug boot.

6.3 To use a calibrated ignition tester (available at most auto parts stores), remove a plug wire from a cylinder, connect the spark plug boot to the tester and clip the tester to a good ground - if there is enough voltage to fire the plug, sparks will be clearly visible between the electrode tip and the tester body

6.5 Check for battery voltage to the coil (+) terminal

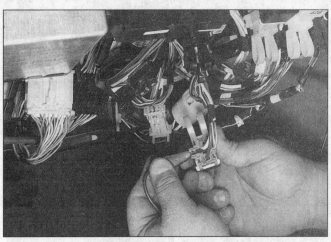

6.9 Check for battery voltage to the IGN ON relay

4   Check for carbon tracking on the coil. If carbon tracking is evident, replace the coil and be sure the secondary wires related to that coil are clean and tight. Excessive wire resistance or faulty connections could cause damage to the coil.
5   Check for battery voltage to the ignition coil **(see illustration)**. If battery voltage is available, check the ignition coil primary and secondary resistance (see Section 8).
6   Check the distributor cap for any obvious signs of carbon tracking, corroded terminals or cracks (see Chapter 1).
7   Using an ohmmeter, check the resistance of the spark plug wires. Each wire should measure less than 25,000 ohms.
8   Check for battery voltage to the ignition amplifier (see Section 7). If battery voltage does not exist, check the circuit from the ignition switch (refer to the wiring diagrams at the end of Chapter 12).
9   Check for battery voltage to the Ignition ON relay **(see illustration)**. If battery voltage does not exist, check the circuit from the ignition ON relay to the battery (refer to the wiring diagrams at the end of Chapter 12). **Note:** Refer to Chapter 12 for the location of the Ignition ON relay.
10   Check the operation of the crankshaft position sensor (see Chapter 6).
11   If all the checks are correct, check the voltage signal from the computer. Using an LED type test light, backprobe the coil power lead (negative terminal) on the ignition coil **(see illustration)**. Remove the coil secondary wire and ground the terminal to the engine. Now have an assistant crank the engine over and observe that the test light

pulses on and off. If there is no flashing from the test light, most likely the computer is damaged. Have the ECU diagnosed by a dealer service department.
12   Additional checks should be performed by a dealer service department or an automotive repair shop.

7   Amplifier - check and replacement

Warning: *Because of the high voltage generated by the ignition system, extreme care should be taken whenever an operation is performed involving ignition components. This not only includes the amplifier, coil, distributor and spark plug wires, but related components such as connectors, tachometer and other test equipment also.*
Note: *Because of the complexity and the special tools required to test the amplifier, the following procedure only describes a test to verify battery voltage is reaching the amplifier. If the wiring harness and the relays are working properly and battery voltage is available to the amplifier, have the ignition system and the ECU diagnosed by a dealer service department.*

Check
Refer to illustrations 7.1 and 7.2
1   Disconnect the amplifier electrical connector **(see illustration)**.
2   Turn the ignition key ON (engine not running), check for battery

6.11 Install the LED test light to the coil negative (-) terminal, crank the engine over and observe the light flash in response to the trigger signal from the computer

7.1 Remove the clip that retains the harness connector to the amplifier

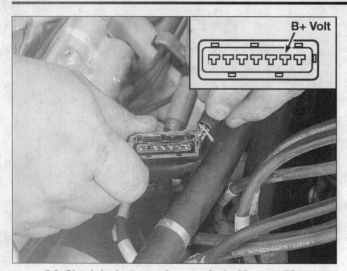

7.2 **Check for battery voltage to the ignition amplifier**

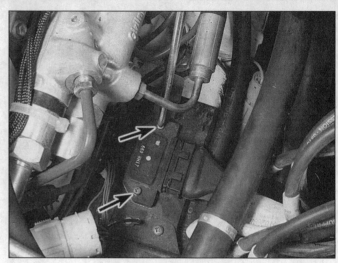

7.5 **Remove the amplifier mountings screws (arrows) and lift the unit from the engine compartment**

voltage **(see illustration)** to the amplifier.

3   If no battery voltage is present, check the harness from the ignition switch to the amplifier. Refer to the wiring diagrams at the end of Chapter 12.

Replacement

Refer to illustration 7.5

4   Remove the negative battery terminal. **Caution:** *If the stereo in your vehicle is equipped with an anti-theft system, make sure you have the correct activation code before disconnecting the battery.*

5   Remove the amplifier mounting screws **(see illustration)**.

6   Installation is the reverse of removal.

---

8   Ignition coil - check and replacement

Check

Refer to illustrations 8.3a and 8.3b

1   Detach the cable from the negative terminal of the battery. **Caution:** *If the stereo in your vehicle is equipped with an anti-theft system, make sure you have the correct activation code before disconnecting the battery.*

2   Disconnect the electrical connectors and the coil wire from the coil.

3   Using an ohmmeter, check the coil resistance:

a) *Measure the resistance between the positive and negative terminals* **(see illustration)**. *Compare your reading with the coil primary resistance listed in this Chapter's Specifications.*

b) *Measure the resistance between the positive terminal and the high tension terminal* **(see illustration)**. *Compare your reading with the coil secondary resistance listed in this Chapter's Specifications.*

4   If either of the above tests yield resistance values outside the specified amount, replace the coil.

Replacement

Refer to illustration 8.7

5   Detach the cable from the negative terminal of the battery. **Caution:** *If the stereo in your vehicle is equipped with an anti-theft system, make sure you have the correct activation code before disconnecting the battery.*

6   Label and disconnect the electrical wires from the coil terminals.

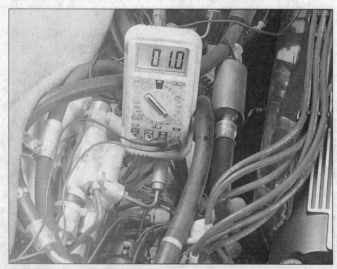

8.3a **To check the primary resistance of the coil, measure the resistance between the positive and the negative terminals**

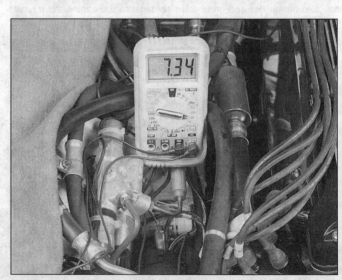

8.3b **To check the secondary resistance of the coil, measure the resistance between the positive terminal and the high tension terminal**

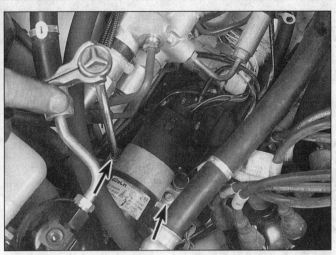

8.7 Remove the nuts from the coil mounting bracket (arrows)

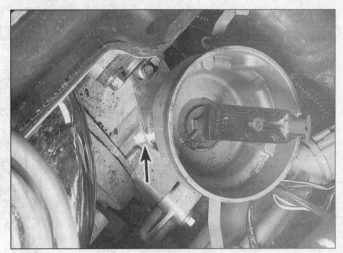

9.5a Paint or scribe a mark (arrow) on the edge of the distributor housing immediately below the rotor tip to ensure that the rotor is pointing in the same direction when the distributor is reinstalled

7   Remove the coil mounting fasteners **(see illustration)**.
8   Installation is the reverse of removal.

9   Distributor - removal and installation

Note: *The timing on this ignition system cannot be adjusted by turning the distributor. Ignition timing is maintained by the ECU at all times. In the event the distributor must be removed from the engine, be sure to follow the precautions described in this section and mark the engine and distributor with paint to ensure correct installation. If the distributor is not marked and the crankshaft is turned while the distributor is out of the engine, have the distributor installed by a dealer service department. The distributor must be installed using a special alignment tool.*

Removal

Refer to illustrations 9.5a and 9.5b
1   Detach the cable from the negative battery terminal. **Caution:** *If the stereo in your vehicle is equipped with an anti-theft system, make sure you have the correct activation code before disconnecting the battery.*
2   Disconnect the electrical connectors from the distributor.
3   Look for a raised "1" on the distributor cap. This marks the location for the number one cylinder spark plug wire terminal. If the cap does not have a mark for the number one terminal, locate the number one spark plug and trace the wire back to the terminal on the cap.
4   Remove the distributor cap (see Chapter 1) and rotate the engine until the rotor is pointing toward the number one spark plug terminal.
5   Make a mark on the edge of the distributor base directly below the rotor tip and in line with it. Also, mark the distributor base and the engine block to ensure that the distributor is installed correctly **(see illustrations)**.
6   Remove the distributor hold-down bolt, then pull the distributor straight out to remove it. **Caution:** *DO NOT turn the crankshaft while the distributor is out of the engine, or the alignment marks will be useless.*

Installation

7   Insert the distributor into the engine in exactly the same relationship to the block that it was in when removed.
8   If the distributor does not seat completely, recheck the alignment marks between the distributor base and the block to verify that the distributor is in the same position it was in before removal. Also check the rotor to see if it's aligned with the mark you made on the edge of the distributor base.
9   Install the distributor hold-down bolt(s).
10   The remainder of installation is the reverse of removal.

9.5b Paint or scribe another mark across the cylinder head and the distributor body (arrows) to ensure that the distributor is aligned correctly when it is reinstalled

10   Charging system - general information and precautions

Refer to illustration 10.1
    The charging system includes the alternator, an internal voltage regulator, a charge indicator light, load dump module, the battery, an ignition ON relay, an in-line fuse and the wiring between all the components **(see illustration on the following page)**. The charging system supplies electrical power for the ignition system, the lights, the radio, etc. The alternator is driven by a drivebelt at the front of the engine.
    The purpose of the voltage regulator is to limit the alternator's voltage to a preset value. This prevents power surges, circuit overloads, etc., during peak voltage output.
    The alternator load dump module protects the electrical circuits from excessive voltage surges. When the battery cables are removed large amounts of transient voltage is released through the electrical circuits. This device diverts up to 30 load volts of excess voltage to ground by way of a voltage dependent resistor.
    The in-line fuse is a special fuse installed into the circuit with the engine compartment wiring harness (see Chapter 12). The in-line fuse protects the electrical system in the event of excess voltage surges or

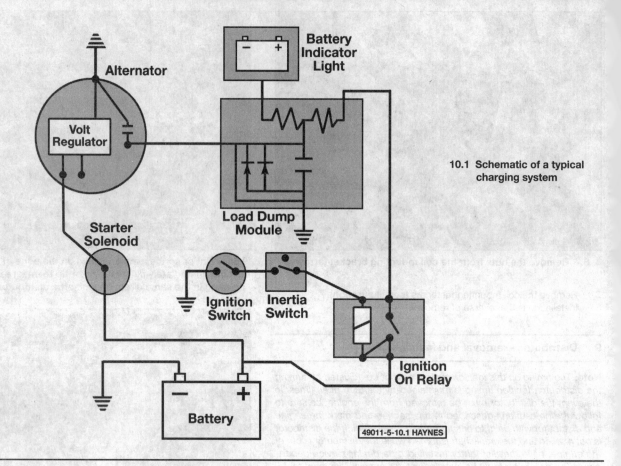

10.1 Schematic of a typical charging system

49011-5-10.1 HAYNES

a power-to-ground short circuit. Refer to Chapter 12 for additional information concerning the in-line fuses and their locations.

1993 and 1994 models are equipped with a Starter Logic Relay. This microprocessor (computer) gathers information from the ignition switch, linear gear position switch, park/neutral switch, the security switch and the electronic door lock system. If all the conditions are in order, the computer allows battery voltage to be transferred from the ignition switch to the starter/solenoid assembly.

The charging system doesn't ordinarily require periodic maintenance. However, the drivebelt, battery and wires and connections should be inspected at the intervals outlined in Chapter 1.

The dashboard warning light should come on when the ignition key is turned to Start, then should go off immediately. If it remains on, there is a malfunction in the charging system. Some vehicles are also equipped with a voltage gauge. If the voltage gauge indicates abnormally high or low voltage, check the charging system (see Section 11).

Be very careful when making electrical circuit connections to a vehicle equipped with an alternator and note the following:

a) When reconnecting wires to the alternator from the battery, be sure to note the polarity.
b) Before using arc welding equipment to repair any part of the vehicle, disconnect the wires from the alternator and the battery terminals.
c) Never start the engine with a battery charger connected.
d) Always disconnect both battery leads before using a battery charger.
e) The alternator is driven by an engine drivebelt which could cause serious injury if your hand, hair or clothes become entangled in it with the engine running.
f) Because the alternator is connected directly to the battery, it could arc or cause a fire if overloaded or shorted out.
g) Wrap a plastic bag over the alternator and secure it with rubber bands before steam cleaning the engine.

11   Charging system - check

Refer to illustrations 11.2 and 11.9
Note: *1993 and 1994 models are equipped with a Starter Logic Relay. This microprocessor (computer) gathers information from the ignition switch, linear gear position switch, park/neutral switch, the security switch and the electronic door lock system. If all the conditions are in order, the computer allows battery voltage to be transferred from the ignition switch to the starter/solenoid assembly. If all the components of the charging system are working properly and the system still does not charge properly, have the Starter Logic Relay diagnosed by a dealer service department.*

1   If a malfunction occurs in the charging circuit, don't automatically assume that the alternator is causing the problem. First check the following items:

a) *Check the drivebelt tension and its condition. Replace it if worn or deteriorated.*
b) *Make sure the alternator mounting and adjustment bolts are tight.*
c) *Inspect the alternator wiring harness and the electrical connectors at the alternator and voltage regulator. They must be in good condition and tight.*
d) *Check the fusible link (if equipped) located between the starter solenoid and the alternator or the large main fuses in the engine compartment. If it's burned, determine the cause, repair the circuit and replace the link or fuse (the vehicle won't start and/or the accessories won't work if the fusible link or fuse blows).*
e) *Check all the in-line fuses that are in series with the charging system circuit (see Chapter 12). The location of these fuses and fusible links may vary from year and model but the designations are the same. Refer to the wiring diagrams at the end of Chapter 12.*
f) *Start the engine and check the alternator for abnormal noises (a shrieking or squealing sound indicates a bad bushing).*

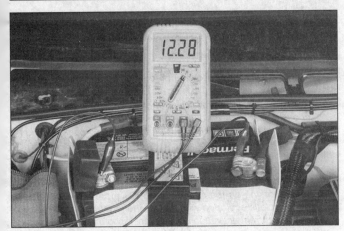

11.2 Connect the probes of a voltmeter to the battery terminals and observe battery voltage with the engine OFF and then with the engine running

11.9 The load dump module is located on the firewall next to the MAF sensor

g) *Check the specific gravity of the battery electrolyte. If it's low, charge the battery (doesn't apply to maintenance free batteries).*

h) *Make sure that the battery is fully charged (one bad cell in a battery can cause overcharging by the alternator).*

i) *Disconnect the battery cables (negative first, then positive).* **Caution:** *If the stereo in your vehicle is equipped with an anti-theft system, make sure you have the correct activation code before disconnecting the battery. Inspect the battery posts and the cable clamps for corrosion. Clean them thoroughly if necessary (see Chapter 1). Reconnect the positive cable, then the negative cable.*

2   Using a voltmeter, check the battery voltage with the engine off. It should be approximately 12 volts **(see illustration)**.

3   Start the engine and check the battery voltage again. It should now be approximately 13.5 to 15.1 volts.

4   Turn on the headlights. The voltage should drop and then come back up, if the charging system is working properly.

5   If the voltage reading is greater than the specified charging voltage, replace the alternator.

6   If you have an ammeter, connect it up to the charging system according to the manufacturers instructions. If you don't have a professional-type ammeter, you can also use an inductive-type current indicator. This device is inexpensive, readily available at auto parts stores and accurate enough to perform simple amperage checks like the following test.

7   With the engine running at 2,000 rpm, check the reading on the ammeter with all accessories and lights off (no load), then again with

the high-beam headlights on and the heater blower switch turned to the HI position (full load). Compare your readings to the standard amperage listed in this Chapter's Specifications.

8   If the ammeter reading is less than standard amperage, repair or replace the alternator.

9   If the alternator is working but the charging system still does function properly, check the operation of the load dump module **(see illustration)**. Have this component checked at a dealer service department.

12 Alternator - removal and installation

Refer to illustrations 12.3 and 12.4

Note: *If oil leaks are detected near the alternator bracket bolts, it will be necessary to remove the alternator and bracket assembly and seal the bolt threads. First use Loctite primer, wait until it dries and then apply Loctite thread sealer (number 545) to the threads. Be sure the engine block threads are clean and free of oil and debris.*

1   Detach the cable from the negative terminal of the battery. **Caution:** *If the stereo in your vehicle is equipped with an anti-theft system, make sure you have the correct activation code before disconnecting the battery.*

2   Detach the electrical connectors from the alternator.

3   Loosen the alternator adjustment and pivot bolts **(see illustration)** and detach the drivebelt.

4   Remove the adjustment and pivot bolts **(see illustration)** from the alternator adjustment bracket.

12.3 Loosen the lock bolt and back-off the adjustment bolt (arrow) to remove the drivebelt

12.4 Remove the pivot bolt and nut

5   If you are replacing the alternator, take the old alternator with you when purchasing a replacement unit. Make sure that the new/rebuilt unit is identical to the old alternator. Look at the terminals - they should be the same in number, size and locations as the terminals on the old alternator. Finally, look at the identification markings - they will be stamped in the housing or printed on a tag or plaque affixed to the housing. Make sure that these numbers are the same on both alternators.

6   Many new/rebuilt alternators do not have a pulley installed, so you may have to switch the pulley from the old unit to the new/rebuilt one. When buying an alternator, find out the shop's policy regarding installation of pulleys - some shops will perform this service free of charge.

7   Installation is the reverse of removal.

8   After the alternator is installed, adjust the drivebelt tension (see Chapter 1).

9   Check the charging voltage to verify proper operation of the alternator (see Section 11).

13   Starting system - general information and precautions

The sole function of the starting system is to crank the engine over quickly enough to allow it to start.

The starting system consists of the battery, the starter motor, the starter solenoid, the starter relay and the electrical circuit connecting the components. The solenoid is mounted directly on the starter motor.

The solenoid/starter motor assembly is installed on the upper part of the engine, next to the transmission bellhousing.

When the ignition key is turned to the START position, the starter solenoid is actuated through the starter control circuit. The starter solenoid then connects the battery to the starter. The battery supplies the electrical energy to the starter motor, which does the actual work of cranking the engine.

The starter on a vehicle equipped with an automatic transmission can be operated only when the transmission selector lever is in Park or Neutral.

These vehicles are equipped with either a Bosch or Lucas starter assembly. The Lucas unit is distinguished by the separate ground strap from the solenoid to the starter body. Bosch starter assemblies are equipped with a solid metal grounding bar.

The starting system circuit is equipped with a relay. The relay allows the ignition switch to power the starter solenoid.

1993 and 1994 models are equipped with a Starter Logic Relay. This microprocessor (computer) gathers information from the ignition switch, linear gear position switch, park/neutral switch, the security switch and the electronic door lock system. If all the conditions are in

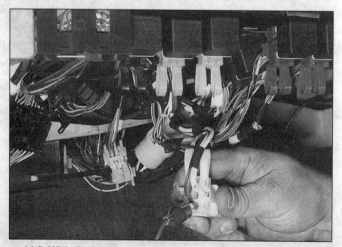

14.5 With the ignition key ON (engine not running), check for battery voltage to the starter relay

order, the computer allows battery voltage to be transferred from the ignition switch to the starter/solenoid assembly. If all the components of the starting and charging system are working properly and the system still will not start properly, have the Starter Logic Relay diagnosed by a dealer service department.

Always observe the following precautions when working on the starting system:

a)   *Excessive cranking of the starter motor can overheat it and cause serious damage. Never operate the starter motor for more than 15 seconds at a time without pausing to allow it to cool for at least two minutes.*

b)   *The starter is connected directly to the battery and could arc or cause a fire if mishandled, overloaded or short circuited.*

c)   *Always detach the cable from the negative terminal of the battery before working on the starting system.* **Caution:** *If the stereo in your vehicle is equipped with an anti-theft system, make sure you have the correct activation code before disconnecting the battery.*

14   Starter motor - testing in vehicle

Refer to illustration 14.5

Note: *1993 and 1994 models are equipped with a Starter Logic Relay. This microprocessor (computer) gathers information from the ignition switch, rotary switch, the security switch and the electronic door lock system. If all the conditions are in order, the computer allows battery voltage to be transferred from the ignition switch to the starter/solenoid assembly. If all the components of the starting and charging system are working and the system still will not start properly, have the Starter Logic Relay diagnosed by a dealer service department.*

1   Make sure that the battery is charged and that all cables, both at the battery and starter solenoid terminals, are clean and secure.

2   If the starter motor does not turn at all when the switch is operated, make sure that the shift lever is in Neutral or Park.

3   If the starter motor spins but the engine is not cranking, the over-running clutch in the starter motor is slipping and the starter motor must be replaced.

4   If, when the switch is actuated, the starter motor does not operate at all but the solenoid clicks, then the problem lies with either the battery, the main solenoid contacts or the starter motor itself (or the engine is seized).

5   If the solenoid plunger cannot be heard when the switch is actuated, the battery is bad, the in-line fuse is burned (the circuit is open), the starter relay **(see illustration)** is defective or the starter solenoid itself is defective.

6   To check the solenoid, connect a jumper lead between the battery (+) and the ignition switch terminal (the small terminal) on the solenoid. If the starter motor now operates, the solenoid is OK and the problem is in the ignition switch, linear switch (1988 through 1992), rotary switch (1993 and 1994) or in the wiring.

7   If the starter motor still does not operate, remove the starter/solenoid assembly for disassembly, testing and repair.

8   If the starter motor cranks the engine at an abnormally slow speed, first make sure that the battery is charged and that all terminal connections are tight. If the engine is partially seized, or has the wrong viscosity oil in it, it will crank slowly.

9   Run the engine until normal operating temperature is reached, then disconnect the coil wire from the distributor cap and ground it on the engine.

10   Connect a voltmeter positive lead to the battery positive post and connect the negative lead to the negative post.

11   Crank the engine and take the voltmeter readings as soon as a steady figure is indicated. Do not allow the starter motor to turn for more than 15 seconds at a time. A reading of nine volts or more, with the starter motor turning at normal cranking speed, is normal. If the reading is nine volts or more but the cranking speed is slow, the motor is faulty. If the reading is less than nine volts and the cranking speed is slow, the solenoid contacts are probably burned, the starter motor is bad, the battery is discharged or there is a bad connection.

15.4a Disconnect the solenoid electrical connector at the harness connector located near the firewall behind the cylinder head (arrow)

15.4b From underneath the vehicle, remove the battery terminal from the solenoid (cylinder head removed for clarity)

15 Starter motor - removal and installation

Refer to illustrations 15.4a, 15.4b and 15.5

1   Detach the cable from the negative terminal of the battery. **Caution:** *If the stereo in your vehicle is equipped with an anti-theft system, make sure you have the correct activation code before disconnecting the battery.*

2   Raise the vehicle and support it securely using jackstands.

3   Drain the transmission fluid (see Chapter 7) and remove the transmission fluid filler tube from the transmission.

4   Detach the electrical connectors from the starter/solenoid assembly **(see illustrations).**

5   Place a floorjack under the tail section of the transmission, remove the rear transmission mount (see Chapter 7) and lower the transmission slightly to gain access to the upper transmission bellhousing bolts. Using an extension with a swivel socket, remove the upper starter mounting bolt **(see illustration).**

6   Working forward of the transmission, reach up into the engine bellhousing area, under the intake manifold and remove the lower starter mounting bolt.

7   Tilt the starter down and carefully lower the starter assembly through the front, ahead of the transmission.

8   Installation is the reverse of removal.

15.5 The upper starter bolt can be reached from underneath the vehicle using a long extension and swivel socket (cylinder head removed for clarity)

16 Starter solenoid - removal and installation

Refer to illustration 16.4

1   Remove the starter motor (see Section 15).

2   Scribe or paint a mark across the starter motor and solenoid assembly.

3   Disconnect the strap from the solenoid to the starter motor terminal (if equipped).

4   Remove the screws which secure the solenoid to the starter drive end housing **(see illustration).**

5   Separate the solenoid from the starter.

6   Installation is the reverse of removal. Be sure to align the paint or scribe mark.

16.4 Remove the three solenoid mounting screws (arrows) and separate the solenoid from the starter assembly

Notes

Chapter 6
Emissions and engine control systems

Contents

Specifications

EGR gas temperature sensor resistance

212-degrees F	60 to 100 K-ohms
400-degrees F	3 to 8 K-ohms
662-degrees F	250 to 350 ohms

Torque specification

	Nm	Ft-lbs
Crankshaft sensor bolt	27	20

1   General information

Refer to illustrations 1.6a and 1.6b

To minimize pollution of the atmosphere from incompletely burned and evaporating gases and to maintain good driveability and fuel economy, a number of emission control systems are used on these vehicles. They include the:

Air Injection Reactor (AIR) system
Crankcase ventilation system
Exhaust Gas Recirculation (EGR) system
Electronic Fuel Injection (EFI) system

Evaporative Emission Control (EVAP) system
Three-way catalytic converter (TWC) system

The sections in this chapter include general descriptions, checking procedures within the scope of the home mechanic and component replacement procedures (when possible) for each of the systems listed above.

Before assuming an emissions control system is malfunctioning, check the fuel and ignition systems carefully (see Chapters 4 and 5). The diagnosis of some emission control devices requires specialized tools, equipment and training. If checking and servicing become too difficult or if a procedure is beyond the scope of your skills, consult your dealer service department or other repair shop.

This doesn't mean, however, that emission control systems are particularly difficult to maintain and repair. You can quickly and easily perform many checks and do most of the regular maintenance at home with common tune-up and hand tools. **Note:** *The most frequent cause of emission problems is simply a loose or broken electrical connector or vacuum hose, so always check the electrical connectors and vacuum hoses first.*

Pay close attention to any special precautions outlined in this chapter. It should be noted that the illustrations of the various systems may not exactly match the system installed on your vehicle because of changes made by the manufacturer during production or from year-to-year.

The Vehicle Emissions Control Information (VECI) label and a vacuum hose diagram are located under the hood **(see illustrations)**. These contain important emissions specifications and setting procedures, and a vacuum hose schematic with emissions components identified. When servicing the engine or emissions systems, the VECI label in your particular vehicle should always be checked for up-to-date information.

2   Electronic control system and ECU

General description

Note: *These models are susceptible to ECU damage if water is allowed to build up in the front cowl drain and overspill into the dash area near the computer. Inspect and clear the front cowl drain as a regular maintenance item to keep the water draining properly. Remove the duckbill-type rubber hose and inspect it for clogging, collapsing or deterioration.*

1   The Lucas LH Engine Management system controls the fuel injection system by means of a microcomputer known as the Electronic Control unit (ECU).

2   The ECU receives signals from various sensors which monitor changing engine operating conditions such as intake air mass, intake air temperature, coolant temperature, engine rpm, acceleration/deceleration, exhaust oxygen content, etc. These signals are utilized by the ECU to determine the correct injection duration.

3   The system is analogous to the central nervous system in the human body: The sensors (nerve endings) constantly relay signals to the ECU (brain), which processes the data and, if necessary, sends out a command to change the operating parameters of the engine (body).

4   Here's a specific example of how one portion of this system operates: An oxygen sensor, located in the exhaust manifold, constantly monitors the oxygen content of the exhaust gas. If the percentage of oxygen in the exhaust gas is incorrect, an electrical signal is sent to the ECU. The ECU takes this information, processes it and then sends a command to the fuel injection system telling it to change the air/fuel mixture. This happens in a fraction of a second and it goes on continuously when the engine is running. The end result is an air/fuel mixture ratio which is constantly maintained at a predetermined ratio, regardless of driving conditions.

5   In the event of a sensor malfunction, a backup circuit will take over to provide driveability until the problem is identified and fixed.

Precautions

6   Follow these steps:

a) *Always disconnect the power by either turning off the ignition switch or disconnecting the battery terminals before removing electrical connectors.* **Warning:** *Later models are equipped with airbags. To prevent the accidental deployment of the airbag, which could cause personal injury, DO NOT work in the vicinity of the steering column or instrument panel. The manufacturer recommends that, on airbag equipped models, the following procedure should be left to a dealer service department or other repair shop because of the special tools and techniques required to disable the airbag system.* **Caution:** *If the stereo in your vehicle is equipped with an anti-theft system, make sure you have the correct activation code before disconnecting the battery.*

b) *When installing a battery, be particularly careful to avoid reversing*

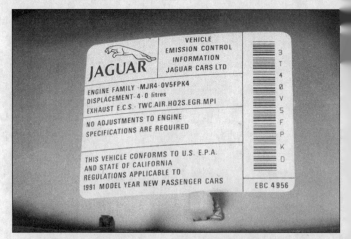

1.6a The Vehicle Emissions Control Information (VECI) label contains such essential information as the types of emission control systems installed, engine numeral designations and displacement (1992 model shown)

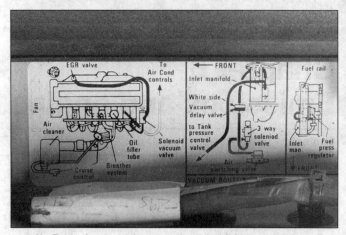

1.6b Typical vacuum hose routing label (1992 model shown)

the positive and negative battery cables. Also, make sure the ignition key is in the Off position when connecting or disconnecting the battery.

c) *Do not subject EFI components, emissions-related components or the ECU to severe impact during removal or installation.*

d) *Do not be careless during troubleshooting. Even slight terminal contact can invalidate a testing procedure and damage one of the numerous transistor circuits.*

e) *Never attempt to work on the ECU or open the ECU cover. The ECU is protected by a government-mandated extended warranty that will be nullified if you tamper with or damage the ECU.*

f) *If you are inspecting electronic control system components during rainy weather, make sure that water does not enter any part. When washing the engine compartment, do not spray these parts or their electrical connectors with water.*

g) *These models are susceptible to ECU damage if water is allowed to build up in the front cowl drain and overspill into the dash area. Inspect and clear the front cowl drain as a regular maintenance item to keep the water draining properly. Remove the duckbill type rubber hose and inspect it for clogging, collapsing or deterioration.*

ECU removal and installation

Refer to illustration 2.10

7   Disconnect the negative cable from the battery (see Chapter 5). **Warning:** *Later models are equipped with airbags. To prevent the accidental deployment of the airbag, which could cause personal injury, DO*

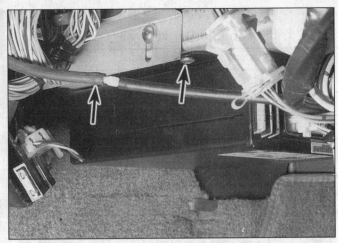

2.10 The ECU is located behind the passenger's side glovebox near the footrest area. Remove the mounting screws (arrows) and carefully lower the ECU

3.5 To access the self-diagnosis system trouble codes, locate the VCM button on the dash and with the ignition key ON (engine not running) press it to display the codes

NOT work in the vicinity of the steering column or instrument panel. The manufacturer recommends that, on airbag equipped models, the following procedure should be left to a dealer service department or other repair shop because of the special tools and techniques required to disable the airbag system. **Caution:** *If the stereo in your vehicle is equipped with an anti-theft system, make sure you have the correct activation code before disconnecting the battery.*

8   Remove the lower instrument panel on the passenger side under the glove compartment (see Chapter 11).

9   Remove the glove compartment from the passenger compartment (see Chapter 11).

10   Remove the screws from the ECU bracket **(see illustration)**.

11   Lower the ECU and unplug the electrical connectors.

12   Installation is the reverse of removal.

3   On Board Diagnosis (OBD) system - description and trouble code access

Note: *1990 and 1991 models may set Code 69 erroneously. If the battery voltage drops sufficiently and the ignition key is switched quickly from OFF to START, battery voltage will be lowered, causing a delayed park/neutral signal from the decoder module to the ECU. Check all the battery connections and the condition of the battery and then check the rotary switch adjustment in Chapter 7 to remedy this code.*

General information

1   The ECU contains a built-in self-diagnosis system which detects and identifies malfunctions occurring in the network. When the ECU detects a problem, three things happen: the CHECK ENGINE light comes on, the trouble is identified and a diagnostic code is recorded and stored. The ECU stores the failure code assigned to the specific problem area until the diagnosis system is canceled. **Note:** *1988 and 1989 models are not equipped with long term memory. It is possible to access the codes but the operator must remember to NOT turn the ignition key to the OFF position after the CHECK ENGINE light has been noticed. The codes will be lost and it will be necessary to start the engine and operate the vehicle through a complete drive cycle to allow the trouble code(s) to be set once again. Instead of turning the ignition key to the OFF position, simply stop at position II (key ON but engine not running) to retain the trouble codes.*

2   The CHECK ENGINE warning light, which is located on the instrument panel, comes on when the ignition switch is turned to ON and the engine is not running. When the engine is started, the warning light should go out. If the light remains on, the self-diagnosis system has detected a malfunction. **Note:** *The CHECK ENGINE light on early*

models is displayed on the dashboard VCM panel on the right side. Later models are equipped with a separate CHECK ENGINE light on the left side of the instrument cluster. **Note:** *Not all the codes will cause the CHECK ENGINE light to activate. When performing any fuel or emissions systems diagnosis, always check for codes that may be stored but not indicated by the CHECK ENGINE light.*

Obtaining diagnostic code output

Refer to illustration 3.5

3   To obtain an output of diagnostic codes, verify first that the battery voltage is above 11 volts, the throttle is fully closed, the transmission is in Park, the accessory switches are off and the engine is at normal operating temperature.

4   Turn the ignition switch to ON but don't start the engine (Position II). **Note:** *On 1988 and 1989 models, remember to turn the ignition switch to position II without turning the key to OFF.*

5   Press the VCM button on the display panel **(see illustration)** and observe the LED display on the dash for the designated codes. An asterisk next to the code indicates that there are multiple codes stored.

6   The numerical values will be displayed on the trip computer display on the dashboard.

7   If there are any malfunctions in the system, the corresponding trouble codes are displayed in numerical order, lowest to highest.

Canceling a diagnostic code

8   After the malfunctioning component has been repaired/replaced, the trouble code(s) stored in computer memory must be canceled.

A) On 1988 through 1991 vehicles, simply drive the vehicle faster than 19 mph and the computer will automatically erase the stored trouble code from memory.

B) On 1992 through 1994 models, disconnect the negative battery terminal for 30 seconds or more to erase the stored trouble codes. **Caution:** *If the stereo in your vehicle is equipped with an anti-theft system, make sure you have the correct activation code before disconnecting the battery.*

9   A stored code can also be canceled on early models by removing the cable from the battery negative terminal, but other items with memory (such as the clock and radio presets) will also be canceled. **Caution:** *If the stereo in your vehicle is equipped with an anti-theft system, make sure you have the correct activation code before disconnecting the battery.*

10   If the diagnosis code is not canceled, it will be stored by the ECU and appear with any new codes in the event of future trouble.

11   Should it become necessary to work on engine components requiring removal of the battery terminal, always check to see if a diagnostic code has been recorded before disconnecting the battery.

d 1989 models

	ffected	Probable Cause
	sor	Open oxygen sensor circuit
	or	Not in operating range
	perature sensor	Not in operating range
	sor	System indicates full rich
	entiometer/airflow sensor	Low throttle potentiometer signal with high airflow sensor signal
6	Throttle potentiometer/airflow sensor	High throttle potentiometer signal with low airflow sensor signal
7	Throttle potentiometer	Idle fuel adjustment failure
8	Intake air temperature sensor	Open or shorted circuit in IAT sensor harness

6-3

Trouble code chart for 1990 through 1994 models

Code	System Affected	Probable Cause
11	Idle potentiometer	Not in operating range
12	Airflow sensor	Not in operating range
14	Coolant temperature sensor	Not in operating range
16	Air temperature sensor	Not in operating range
17	Throttle potentiometer	Not in operating range
18	Throttle potentiometer/Airflow sensor	Signal resistance low at wide open throttle
19	Throttle potentiometer/Airflow sensor	Signal resistance high at idle
22	Heated oxygen sensor	Open or short circuit
22	Fuel pump circuit	Open or short circuit
23	Fuel supply	Rich exhaust indicated
24	Ignition amplifier circuit	Open or short circuit
26	Oxygen sensor circuit	Lean exhaust/vacuum leak
29	ECU	Self check
33	Fuel injector circuit	Open or short circuit
34	Fuel injector circuit	Faulty injector indicated
37	EGR solenoid circuit	Short or open circuit
39	EGR circuit	Faulty system operation
44	Oxygen sensor circuit	Rich or lean condition
46	Idle Speed Control valve - (Coil 1)	Open or short circuit
47	Idle Speed Control valve - (Coil 2)	Open or short circuit
48	Idle Speed Control valve	Not within specification
68	Road speed sensor	Incorrect signal voltage
69	Neutral safety switch circuit	Engine cranks in drive (adjust or replace switch)
89	Purge control valve circuit	Open or short circuit

4 Information sensors

Note 1: *Most of the components described in this section are protected by a Federally mandated extended warranty. See your dealer for the details regarding your vehicle.*
Note 2: *Refer to Chapters 4 and 5 for additional information on the location and the diagnostic procedures for the output actuators (ISC motor, air supplementary valve, distributor, amplifier, etc.) that are not directly covered in this section.*

Coolant temperature sensor

General description

1   The coolant temperature sensor is a thermistor (a resistor which varies the value of its voltage output in accordance with temperature changes) threaded into the thermostat housing. As the sensor temperature DECREASES, the resistance values will INCREASE. As the sensor temperature INCREASES, the resistance values will DECREASE. A failure in this sensor circuit should set a Code 3 (1988 and 1989) or 13 (1990 through 1994). This code indicates a failure in the coolant temperature sensor circuit, so in most cases the appropriate solution to the problem will be either repair of a connector or wire, or replacement of the sensor.

Check

Refer to illustrations 4.2 and 4.3
2   To check the sensor, measure its resistance value **(see illustration)** while it is completely cold (60 to 80-degrees F = 1,500 to 3,000 ohms). Next, start the engine and warm it up until it reaches operating temperature. The resistance should be lower (180 to 200-degrees F = 280 to 350 ohms).
3   If the resistance values of the coolant temperature sensor are correct, check the circuit for the proper signal voltage. Turn the ignition key ON (engine not running) and check for reference voltage with a high-impedance digital voltmeter **(see illustration)**. It should be approximately 5 volts.

Replacement

Warning: *Wait until the engine is completely cool before beginning this procedure.*
4   To remove the sensor, depress the locking tabs, unplug the electrical connector, then carefully unscrew the sensor. **Caution:** *Handle the coolant sensor with care. Damage to this sensor will affect the operation of the entire fuel injection system.*
5   Before installing the new sensor, wrap the threads with Teflon sealing tape to prevent leakage and thread corrosion.
6   Installation is the reverse of removal.

Oxygen sensor

Note: *An oxygen sensor splash shield is equipped on models from VIN 664941 (mid-1990) to present. This shield prevents the self-diagnosis system from setting an intermittent and erroneous code 44. Whenever replacing an oxygen sensor, make sure the splash shield is in place.*

General description

7   These models are equipped with a heated oxygen sensor system. The oxygen sensor is mounted ahead of the front catalytic converter and monitors the exhaust gases before they are changed. The electrical heating system incorporated into the oxygen sensor allows for quicker warm-up time and more efficient oxygen content monitoring. The oxygen sensor monitors the oxygen content of the exhaust gas stream. The oxygen content in the exhaust reacts with the oxygen sensor to produce a voltage output which varies from 0.1-volt (high oxygen, lean mixture) to 0.9-volts (low oxygen, rich mixture). The ECU constantly monitors this variable voltage output to determine the ratio of oxygen to fuel in the mixture. The ECU alters the air/fuel mixture ratio by controlling the pulse width (open time) of the fuel injectors. A mixture ratio of 14.7 parts air to 1 part fuel is the ideal mixture ratio for minimizing exhaust emissions, thus allowing the catalytic converter to operate at maximum efficiency. It is this ratio of 14.7 to 1 which the ECU and the oxygen sensor attempt to maintain at all times.

4.2 The coolant temperature sensor is located in the thermostat housing. To check the coolant temperature sensor, use an ohmmeter to measure the resistance between the two sensor terminals

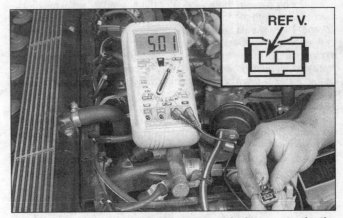

4.3 Check for reference voltage to the electrical connector for the coolant sensor with the ignition key ON (engine not running). It should be approximately 5.0 volts

8   The oxygen sensor produces no voltage when it is below its normal operating temperature of about 600-degrees F. During this initial period before warm-up, the ECU operates in open loop mode.
9   If the engine reaches normal operating temperature and/or has been running for two or more minutes, and if the oxygen sensor is producing a steady signal voltage below 0.45-volts at 1,500 or more rpm, the ECU will set a Code 4 (1988 and 1989) or 26 (1990 through 1994).
10   When there is a problem with the oxygen sensor or its circuit, the ECU operates in the open loop mode - that is, it controls fuel delivery in accordance with a programmed default value instead of feedback information from the oxygen sensor.
11   The proper operation of the oxygen sensor depends on four conditions:

a) *Electrical - The low voltages generated by the sensor depend upon good, clean connections which should be checked whenever a malfunction of the sensor is suspected or indicated.*

b) *Outside air supply - The sensor is designed to allow air circulation to the internal portion of the sensor. Whenever the sensor is removed and installed or replaced, make sure the air passages are not restricted.*

c) *Proper operating temperature - The ECU will not react to the sensor signal until the sensor reaches approximately 600-degrees F. This factor must be taken into consideration when evaluating the performance of the sensor.*

d) *Unleaded fuel - The use of unleaded fuel is essential for proper operation of the sensor. Make sure the fuel you are using is of this type.*

12   In addition to observing the above conditions, special care must be taken whenever the sensor is serviced.

 a) *The oxygen sensor has a permanently attached pigtail and electrical connector which should not be removed from the sensor. Damage to or removal of the pigtail or electrical connector can adversely affect operation of the sensor.*
 b) *Grease, dirt and other contaminants should be kept away from the electrical connector and the louvered end of the sensor.*
 c) *Do not use cleaning solvents of any kind on the oxygen sensor.*
 d) *Do not drop or roughly handle the sensor.*
 e) *The silicone boot must be installed in the correct position to prevent the boot from being melted and to allow the sensor to operate properly.*

Check

Refer to illustrations 4.13 and 4.15

13   Locate the oxygen sensor electrical connector and inspect the oxygen sensor heater. Disconnect the oxygen sensor electrical connector and connect an ohmmeter between the two terminals **(see illustration)**. It should measure approximately 5 to 6 ohms.

14   Also, check for proper supply voltage to the oxygen sensor heater. Measure the voltage with the electrical connector connected. Insert a long pin into the backside of the electrical connector on the correct wire. With the ignition key ON (engine not running), check for voltage. There should be approximately 12 volts. **Note:** *Battery voltage to the heater is supplied by the main relay (1988 through 1990) or the oxygen sensor relay (1991 through 1994). Check the oxygen sensor relay and the wiring harness if battery voltage is not available to the heater. Refer to the wiring diagrams at the end of Chapter 12 and the relay locator schematics also in Chapter 12.*

15   Next, check for a millivolt signal from the oxygen sensor. Locate the oxygen sensor electrical connector and insert a long pin into the oxygen sensor signal wire terminal **(see illustration).** The SIGNAL wire is the single wire with the rubber sheath covering its terminal.

16   Monitor the voltage signal (millivolts) as the engine goes from cold to warm.

17   The oxygen sensor will produce a steady voltage signal at first (open loop) of approximately 0.1 to 0.2 volts with the engine cold. After a period of approximately two minutes, the engine will reach operating temperature and the oxygen sensor will start to fluctuate between 0.1 to 0.9 volts (closed loop). If the oxygen sensor fails to reach the closed loop mode or there is a very long period of time until it does switch into closed loop mode, or if the voltage doesn't fluctuate well (indicating a "lazy" sensor), replace the oxygen sensor with a new part.

Replacement

Refer to illustration 4.21

Note: *Because it is installed in the exhaust manifold or pipe, which contracts when cool, the oxygen sensor may be very difficult to loosen when the engine is cold. Rather than risk damage to the sensor (assuming you are planning to reuse it in another manifold or pipe), start and run the engine for a minute or two, then shut it off. Be careful not to burn yourself during the following procedure.*

18   Disconnect the cable from the negative terminal of the battery. **Caution:** *If the stereo in your vehicle is equipped with an anti-theft system, make sure you have the correct activation code before disconnecting the battery.*

19   Raise the vehicle and place it securely on jackstands.

20   Disconnect the electrical connectors from the sensor pigtail lead.

21   Unscrew the oxygen sensor from the exhaust system **(see illustration). Caution:** *Excessive force may damage the threads.*

22   Anti-seize compound must be used on the threads of the sensor to facilitate future removal. The threads of new sensors will already be coated with this compound, but if an old sensor is removed and reinstalled, recoat the threads.

23   Install the sensor and tighten it securely.

24   Reconnect the electrical connectors to the main engine wiring harness.

25   Lower the vehicle and reconnect the cable to the negative terminal of the battery.

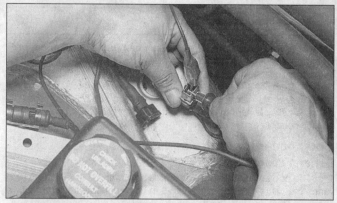

4.13 To test the oxygen sensor heater, disconnect the electrical connector, and working on the sensor side, check the resistance across the two terminals. Heater resistance should be 5 to 6 ohms

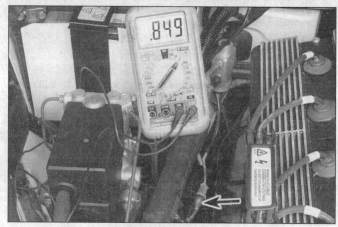

4.15 Install a pin into the backside of the oxygen sensor connector into the correct terminal and check for a millivolt output signal generated by the sensor as it warms up. The SIGNAL wire is easily recognized by the rubber sheath covering the terminal (arrow)

Throttle potentiometer

General description

26   The throttle potentiometer is located on the end of the throttle shaft on the bottom section of the throttle body. By monitoring the output voltage from the throttle potentiometer, the ECU can alter fuel delivery based on throttle valve angle (driver demand). A broken or loose throttle potentiometer will cause bursts of fuel from the injectors and an unstable idle because the ECU thinks the throttle is moving. Throttle body removal procedures are covered in Chapter 4.

4.21 Unscrew the oxygen sensor from the exhaust system

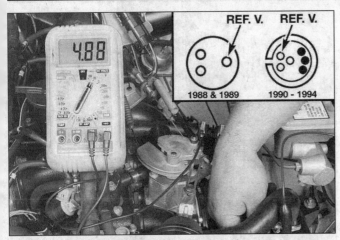

4.27 Backprobe the throttle potentiometer electrical connector with a pin and with the ignition key ON (engine not running) there should be 5.0 volts REFERENCE available

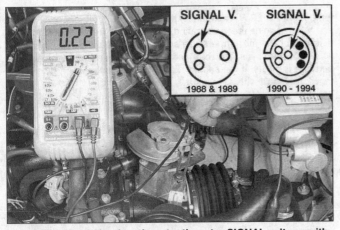

4.28 First check the throttle potentiometer SIGNAL voltage with the throttle closed (idle). It should be 0.2 to 0.5 volts . . .

Check

Refer to illustrations 4.27, 4.28 and 4.29

27   Check for the proper reference voltage to the throttle potentiometer. Carefully backprobe the throttle potentiometer electrical connector using a pin on the reference voltage wire and ground **(see illustration)**. With the ignition key ON (engine not running) the reference voltage should be approximately 5.0 volts.

28   Check the signal voltage from the potentiometer. Carefully backprobe the electrical connector on the signal voltage wire (-) with the ignition key ON (engine not running) **(see illustration)**. There should be approximately 0.5 volts.

29   Next, rotate the throttle lever manually and confirm that the reference voltage increases to approximately 4.8 volts **(see illustration)**.

30   If the voltage does not increase, replace the throttle potentiometer with a new part.

Replacement

31   Remove the throttle body from the intake manifold (see Chapter 4).

32   Remove the two mounting bolts and separate the throttle potentiometer from the throttle body. **Note:** *The throttle potentiometer is difficult to reach and adjustment requires that the home mechanic tighten the bolts after the final adjustment using a mirror. Be sure to mark the mounting position of the old throttle potentiometer before installing the new part.*

33   Installation is the reverse of removal.

Adjustment

34   Install the throttle body with the throttle potentiometer mounting bolts just loose enough to move the potentiometer. Be sure the bolts are tight and the potentiometer does not rotate easily.

35   Backprobe the signal wire and the ground wire (see Step 28) and with the throttle closed (idle position), rotate the potentiometer until the voltmeter reads between 0.2 and 0.5 volts. **Note:** *The throttle potentiometer is difficult to reach. Be sure to rotate the potentiometer slowly and do not interfere with the voltmeter and the electrical connectors to the gauge.*

36   Rotate the throttle lever and confirm that the voltage increases to approximately 4.8 volts. If the voltage range is correct, the throttle potentiometer is installed correctly.

37   Tighten the throttle potentiometer mounting bolts. If necessary, use a small mirror to locate the bolts.

Mass Airflow (MAF) sensor

General Information

Refer to illustrations 4.39 and 4.40

38   The Mass Airflow Sensor (MAF) is located on the air intake duct. This sensor uses a hot wire sensing element to measure the amount of air entering the engine. The air passing over the hot wire causes it to cool. Consequently, this change in temperature can be converted into an analog voltage signal to the ECU which in turn calculates the required fuel injector pulse width.

Check

39   Check for power to the MAF sensor. Backprobe the MAF sensor electrical connector. Working on the harness side with the ignition ON (engine not running), check for battery voltage on terminal number 5 **(see illustration)**.

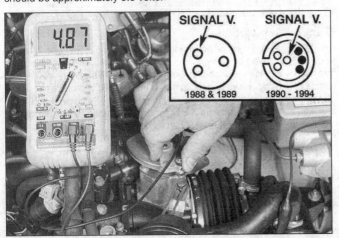

4.29 . . . then check the SIGNAL voltage with the throttle wide open. It should be between 4.5 and 5.0 volts

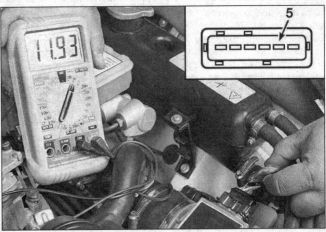

4.39 Check for battery voltage to the MAF sensor on terminal number 5

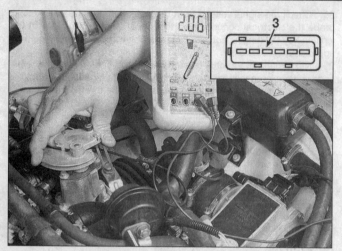

4.40 With the engine idling, raise the engine rpm and observe the voltage changes on terminal number 3

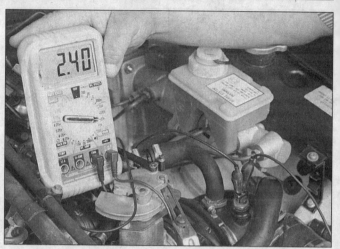

4.51 The air intake temperature sensor resistance will DECREASE when the temperature of the air INCREASES

40   Remove the pin and backprobe the MAF sensor electrical connector terminal number 3 with the voltmeter **(see illustration)**. The voltage should be less than 1.0 volt with the ignition switch ON (engine not running). Start the engine, raise the engine rpm. The signal voltage from the MAF sensor should increase to about 2.0 volts. It is impossible to simulate load conditions in the driveway but it is necessary to observe the voltmeter for a fluctuation in voltage as the engine speed is raised. The vehicle will not be under load conditions but MAF sensor voltage should vary slightly.

41   If the voltage readings are correct, check the wiring harness for open circuits or a damaged harness (see Chapter 12).

42   Also, check the reference voltage to the MAF sensor from the computer. Backprobe terminal number 6 and make sure approximately 5 volts is present.

Replacement

43   Disconnect the electrical connector from the MAF sensor.

44   Remove the air cleaner assembly (see Chapter 4).

45   Remove the four bolts and separate the MAF sensor from the air intake duct.

46   Installation is the reverse of removal.

Intake Air Temperature (IAT) sensor

General description

47   The intake air temperature sensor is located inside the air intake duct. This sensor acts as a resistor which changes value according to the temperature of the air entering the engine. Low temperatures produce a high resistance value (for example, at 68-degrees F the resistance is 2.0 to 2.6 K-ohms) while high temperatures produce low resistance values (at 176-degrees F the resistance is 260 to 330 ohms. The ECU supplies approximately 5-volts (reference voltage) to the air temperature sensor. The voltage will change according to the temperature of the incoming air. The voltage will be high when the air temperature is cold and low when the air temperature is warm. Any problems with the air temperature sensor will usually set a code 8 (1988 and 1989) or code 16 (1990 through 1994).

Check

Refer to illustration 4.51

48   To check the air temperature sensor, disconnect the two prong electrical connector and turn the ignition key ON but do not start the engine.

49   Measure the voltage (reference voltage). The meter should read approximately 5-volts.

50   If the voltage signal is not correct, have the ECU diagnosed by a dealer service department or other repair shop.

51   Measure the resistance across the air temperature sensor terminals **(see illustration)**. The resistance should be HIGH when the air

temperature is LOW. Next, start the engine and let it idle. Wait awhile and let the engine reach operating temperature. Turn the ignition OFF, disconnect the air temperature sensor and measure the resistance across the terminals. The resistance should be LOW when the air temperature is HIGH. If the sensor does not exhibit this change in resistance, replace it with a new part.

EGR gas temperature sensor (1991 through 1994 models)

General Description

52   The EGR gas temperature sensor is mounted in the exhaust gas transfer pipe. This sensor detects the temperature of the exhaust as it moves through the EGR valve. The information is sent to the ECU and in turn the EGR on/off time is regulated precisely and more efficiently.

Check

53   Disconnect the harness connector for the EGR gas temperature sensor and measure the resistance of the sensor at the various temperatures. Refer to the Specifications listed in this Chapter for a list of the temperatures and the resistance values.

Removal and installation

54   Disconnect the harness connector for the EGR gas temperature sensor and using an open-end wrench, remove the sensor from the EGR adapter under the intake manifold.

55   Installation is the reverse of removal.

Speed sensor

General description

56   The speed sensor is mounted on the differential housing and monitors vehicle speed by sensing the rotational speed of the rear axle. A problem with this sensor or circuit will set a code 68 and may also be the cause of an inoperative speedometer. If the speedometer doesn't work, the problem lies in the speed sensor, the instrument cluster, the ECU or the wiring in between. For further diagnosis, take the vehicle to a dealer service department or other qualified repair shop.

Crankshaft position sensor

Refer to illustration 4.57

Note 1: *If the vehicle exhibits constant hesitation under acceleration with inaccurate tachometer readings, most likely the crankshaft sensor gear is damaged or missing teeth. Check the crankshaft sensor gear and replace it if necessary.*

Note 2: *Another common problem associated with the crankshaft sensor is a NO START condition. The ignition system will not fire the spark plugs or display spark during an ignition system check (see Chapter 5).*

57 The crankshaft position sensor is located in the front timing cover near the crankshaft pulley (see illustration). The crankshaft position sensor relays a signal to the ECU to indicate the exact position (angle) of the crankshaft.

Check

58 The crankshaft sensor cannot be diagnosed without the proper tools. The Jaguar dealer uses a diagnostic scope/computer called the JDS. Have the crankshaft sensor diagnosed by the dealer service department or other qualified repair shop.

Replacement

59 To replace the sensor, disconnect the electrical connector and remove the bolt from the crankshaft position sensor. Installation is the reverse of removal.
60 To replace the crankshaft sensor gear, remove the front pulley (refer to Chapter 2A).
61 Be sure there is a small gap between the crankshaft sensor and the teeth on the gear. It should be between 0.46 to 1.07 mm (0.018 to 0.042 inch).
62 Installation is the reverse of removal. Tighten the crankshaft sensor bolt to the torque listed in this Chapter's Specifications.

5 Air Injector Reactor (AIR) system

General information

Refer to illustration 5.2
1 The air injection reactor system reduces carbon monoxide and hydrocarbon content in the exhaust gases by injecting fresh air into the hot exhaust gases leaving the exhaust ports. When fresh air is mixed with hot exhaust gases, oxidation is increased, reducing the concentration of hydrocarbons and carbon monoxide and converting them into harmless carbon dioxide and water.
2 The air injection system is composed of an air pump, diverter valve (bypass), check valve, air injection manifold, vacuum delay valve, vacuum control solenoid, air pump magnetic clutch, air pump clutch relay and hoses (see illustration). The air pump is driven by a belt from the crankshaft and supplies compressed air to the exhaust manifold(s). The check valve prevents the reverse flow of exhaust gases into the system. The vacuum operated (early models) or electrically operated (later models) air cut-off valve prevents air from being drawn into the exhaust when the air pump is switched off. System vacuum to the air

4.57 Location of the crankshaft position sensor

cut-off valve is controlled by the solenoid vacuum valve in parallel circuit with the air pump. A delay valve prevents vacuum loss to the solenoid valve during wide open throttle operation.
3 Injected air is controlled by the computer, the air pump clutch and the air pump clutch relay. The AIR system is used during warm-up (58 to 83-degrees F) to control emissions while the engine is running rich. The oxygen sensor feedback system cannot function while the AIR system is operating. The computer controls the operation of both systems during warm-up and normal operating temperatures. In the event of problems with the AIR system relay or circuit, the on-board diagnosis system will set a code 66.

Check

Refer to illustrations 5.5 and 5.6
4 Check the condition of the air pump drivebelt, the injection hoses and the injection manifold. Make sure that all components are intact and there are no leaks.
5 Check the operation of the air pump clutch relay (see illustration) and the air pump clutch. First remove the relay and check for battery voltage to the relay. Also, check the relay itself. Refer to the relay checking procedure in Chapter 12. Extract codes from the self-diagnosis system (see Section 3) and check for a code 66, AIR relay malfunction.

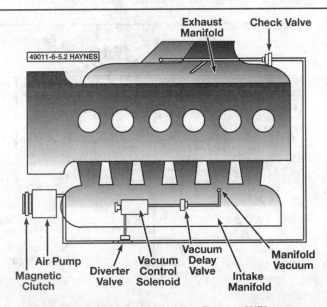

5.2 Schematic of the Air Injection Reactor (AIR) system

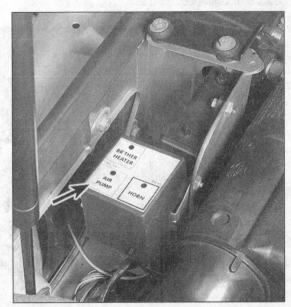

5.5 Location of the AIR pump relay on a 1992 model

6   Make sure the electrical connector is securely fastened to the diverter valve **(see illustration)**. If everything appears OK but a trouble code still sets, have the system diagnosed by a dealer service department or other qualified repair shop.

Air pump replacement

Refer to illustration 5.10

7   Disconnect the cable from the negative terminal of the battery. **Caution:** *If the stereo in your vehicle is equipped with an anti-theft system, make sure you have the correct activation code before disconnecting the battery.*

8   Disconnect the electrical connector from the air pump clutch.

9   Loosen the clips from the air inlet and outlet hose and separate them from the air injection pump.

10   Loosen the adjuster and pivot bolts **(see illustration)** and nuts but do not remove them from the air injection pump brackets.

11   Swing the pump toward the engine and remove the drivebelt from the pump.

12   Remove the link arm through-bolt.

13   Remove the pivot bolt and front spacer, rear cone and air injection pump from the engine compartment.

14   Remove the nut securing the front pulley on the air injection pump.

15   Remove the clutch snap-ring and the clutch.

16   Installation is the reverse of removal.

---

6   Exhaust Gas Recirculation (EGR) system

Refer to illustration 6.2

Note 1: *Some 1990 models have the EGR vacuum hose routed incorrectly through the firewall securing straps, thereby restricting the vacuum signal to the EGR valve. Remove the EGR vacuum hose from the firewall harness and install a new hose. Secure it to the engine compartment using tie-wraps and do not allow any restrictions in the hose.*

Note 2: *Some models have copper sealing washers that soften and leak around the EGR valve causing engine performance and starting problems. Install steel washers and pipe adapters into the EGR system. Contact a Jaguar dealer service department for the VIN numbers and years of the models that are affected by this defect.*

1   To reduce oxides of nitrogen emissions, some of the exhaust gases are recirculated through the EGR valve to the intake manifold to lower combustion temperatures.

5.6 Location of the AIR diverter valve on a 1992 model - check the hoses for cracking and the electrical connector for tightness

2   The EGR system consists of the EGR valve, an EGR solenoid, an EGR gas temperature sensor and the transfer pipe **(see illustration)**.

Check

EGR valve

Refer to illustrations 6.4 and 6.5

3   Start the engine and allow it to idle.

4   Detach the vacuum hose from the EGR valve and attach a hand vacuum pump in its place **(see illustration)**.

5   Apply vacuum to the EGR valve. Vacuum should remain steady and the engine should run poorly. **Note:** *This action will raise the pintle and allow exhaust gases to recirculate into the intake system and cause rough running condition at idle. Double-check the movement of the pintle by checking the diaphragm using the tip of your finger* **(see illustration)**. *If the EGR diaphragm moves smoothly and holds steady when vacuum is applied, the EGR valve is working properly.* **Warning:** *Be careful not to burn yourself during this check. If the EGR valve is hot, wear a glove or wait until it cools.*

a) *If the vacuum doesn't remain steady and the engine doesn't run poorly, replace the EGR valve and recheck it.*

5.10 Loosen the pivot bolt and then the adjustment nut to remove the drivebelt from the air pump. The adjustment nut has a lock bolt that must be loosened before the pump will move down the adjuster

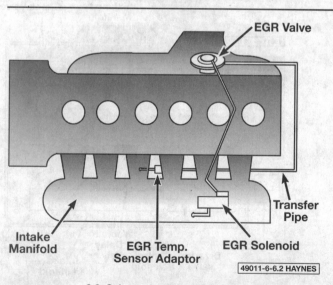

6.2 Schematic of the EGR system

6.4 Apply vacuum to the EGR valve and confirm that the valve opens and allows exhaust gases to circulate. Once it is activated, the EGR valve should hold steady (no loss in vacuum)

b) *If the vacuum remains steady but the engine doesn't run poorly, remove the EGR valve and check the valve and the intake manifold for blockage. Clean or replace parts as necessary and recheck.*

EGR system

Refer to illustrations 6.6 and 6.8

6   Disconnect the hose from the EGR valve, install a vacuum gauge and check for vacuum to the EGR valve. There should be vacuum present with the engine warmed to operating temperature (above 140-degrees F) and between 1,000 and 4,000 rpm **(see illustration)**.

7   Start the engine and observe the vacuum gauge. At idle, there should be no vacuum present. Raise the engine rpm and observe the vacuum increase. This is a ported vacuum source and therefore it should only register vacuum when throttled.

8   Check the operation of the EGR control solenoid. Check for battery voltage to the EGR control solenoid harness **(see illustration)**. If battery voltage is not available, check the harness. Refer to the wiring diagrams at the end of Chapter 12.

9   If battery voltage is available to the EGR control solenoid, have the EGR system diagnosed by a dealer service department or other qualified repair shop.

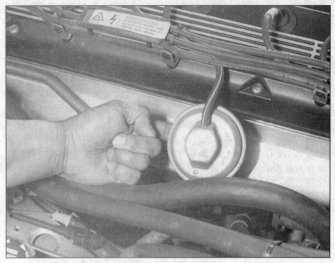

6.5 Use the tip of your finger to move the diaphragm inside the EGR valve

EGR valve replacement

10   Detach the vacuum hose, disconnect the fitting that attaches the EGR pipe to the EGR valve and remove the EGR valve from the exhaust manifold and check it for sticking and heavy carbon deposits. If the valve is sticking or clogged with deposits, clean or replace it.

11   Installation is the reverse of removal.

---

7   Evaporative Emission Control (EVAP) system

Note: *Some models may have charcoal canister vent plugs installed in the canister from the factory. These blanking plugs must be removed to allow proper pressure release within the EVAP system. Check the charcoal canister for these additional plugs and remove them. With the blanking plugs installed, the fuel tank will collapse causing rough running and hesitation and loss of power under load.*

General description

Refer to illustration 7.2

1   This system is designed to trap and store fuel that evaporates from the fuel tank, throttle body and intake manifold that would normally enter the atmosphere in the form of hydrocarbon (HC) emissions.

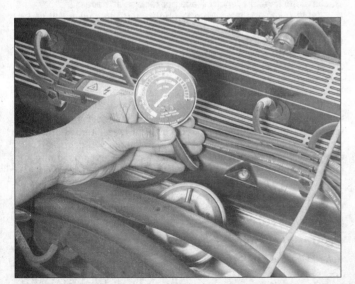

6.6 Check for vacuum to the EGR valve from the throttle body

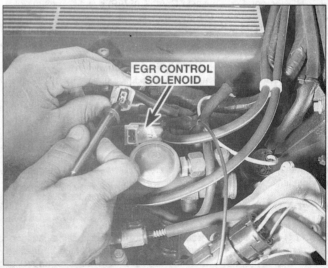

EGR CONTROL SOLENOID

6.8 Check for battery voltage to the EGR control solenoid

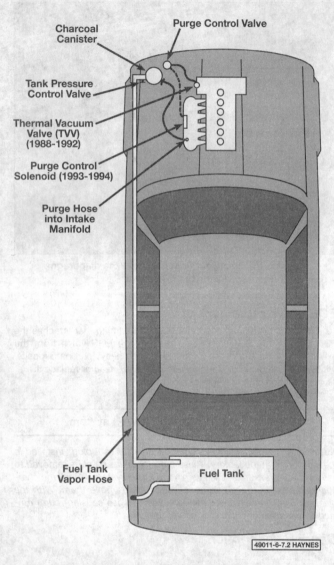

Charcoal
Canister

Purge Control Valve

Tank Pressure
Control Valve

Thermal Vacuum
Valve (TVV)
(1988-1992)

Purge Control
Solenoid (1993-1994)

Purge Hose
into Intake
Manifold

Fuel Tank
Vapor Hose

Fuel Tank

49011-6-7.2 HAYNES

7.2 Schematic of the EVAP system

7.11a Check for vacuum to the thermal vacuum valve (TVV)

**7.11b Check for vacuum from the TVV before and after the engine
has reached normal operating temperature**

2   The Evaporative Emission Control (EVAP) system consists of a charcoal-filled canister, the lines connecting the canister to the fuel tank, tank pressure control valve, purge control valve and thermal vacuum valve (TVV) **(see illustration)**. **Note:** *1993 and 1994 models are equipped with a purge control solenoid that is controlled by the ECU. This solenoid switches vacuum to the purge control valve.*

3   Fuel vapors are transferred from the fuel tank and throttle body to a canister where they're stored when the engine isn't running. When the engine is running, the fuel vapors are purged from the canister by intake airflow and consumed in the normal combustion process. **Note:** *The ECU will set a code 89 if the purge control valve is defective or the circuit has shorted.*

4   The fuel tank is equipped with a pressure control valve. This valve opens and closes according to the pressure increase and decrease in the fuel tank.

Check

Refer to illustrations 7.11a, 7.11b and 7.12

5   Poor idle, stalling and poor driveability can be caused by an inoperative pressure relief valve, split or cracked hoses or hoses connected to the wrong fittings. Check the fuel filler cap for a damaged or deformed gasket.

6   Evidence of fuel loss or fuel odor can be caused by liquid fuel leaking from fuel lines, a cracked or damaged canister, an inoperative fuel tank control valve, disconnected, misrouted, kinked, deteriorated or damaged vapor or control hoses.

7   Inspect each hose attached to the canister for kinks, leaks and cracks along its entire length. Repair or replace as necessary.

8   Look for fuel leaking from the bottom of the canister. If fuel is leaking, replace the canister and check the hoses and hose routing.

9   Inspect the canister. If it's cracked or damaged, replace it.

10   Check for a clogged filter or a damaged pressure relief valve. Using low pressure compressed air, blow into the canister tank pipe. Air should flow freely from the other pipes. If a problem is found, replace the canister.

11   Check the operation of the thermal vacuum valve (TVV). With the engine cold and idling, check for ported vacuum to the temperature vacuum switch. Vacuum should be present **(see illustration)**. Now warm the engine to operating temperature (above 115-degrees F [43-degrees C]) and confirm that ported vacuum passes through the TVV **(see illustration)**. Replace the valve if the test results are incorrect.

12   Check the operation of the purge control valve. Apply vacuum to the purge control valve using a hand-held vacuum pump and confirm that the valve holds vacuum steadily **(see illustration)**. If the valve holds vacuum and the valve is opening, it is working properly.

Charcoal canister replacement

Refer to illustration 7.14

13   Clearly label, then detach the vacuum hoses from the canister.

14   Remove the mounting clamp bolts **(see illustration)**, lower the

7.12 Remove the front spoiler to gain access to the purge control valve (see Chapter 11). Apply vacuum to the valve and make sure the valve does not leak but remains steady once vacuum is applied

7.14 Remove the bolts (arrows) and lower the charcoal canister from the fenderwell

canister with the bracket, disconnect the hoses from the check valve and remove it from the vehicle.

15   Installation is the reverse of removal.

8   Crankcase ventilation system

General information

Refer to illustration 8.1

1   The crankcase ventilation system reduces hydrocarbon emissions by scavenging crankcase vapors. It does this by circulating fresh air from the air cleaner through the crankcase, where it mixes with blow-by gases and is then rerouted through a heating element to the intake manifold **(see illustration)**.

2   The main components of the crankcase ventilation system are the control orifice, a heating element and the vacuum hoses connecting these components with the engine.

3   Piston blow-by gasses are collected from the crankcase and the camshaft housing via the oil filler tube. These gasses are fed into the intake manifold at part throttle through the part throttle orifice and when the engine is at full throttle, the gasses are fed through the air intake elbow.

4   To prevent possible icing-up during cold weather operation, the control orifice and the hose to the intake system is electrically heated. The heater element is energized by a relay signal from the windshield washer jet temperature sensor.

Check

5   Remove the tubes and elbows that connect the crankcase ventilation system and inspect them for obstructions, oil deposits or clogging. Make sure the ventilation system is free of all obstructions to ensure complete recirculation of gasses from the crankcase back into the intake manifold. In the event of clogging, the pressure will increase causing blow-by and oil leaks through seals and gaskets.

6   Check the operation of the heating element. Check for battery voltage to the element while the engine is cold. If voltage is not available to the heating element, check the circuit from the windshield washer jet temperature sensor.

Replacement

Refer to illustration 8.7

7   Disconnect the electrical connector from the heating element **(see illustration)**.

8   Remove the clamps from the hoses and separate the heating ele-

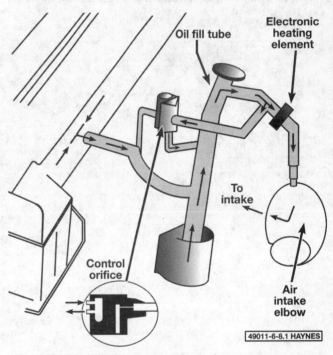

8.1 Schematic of the crankcase ventilation system

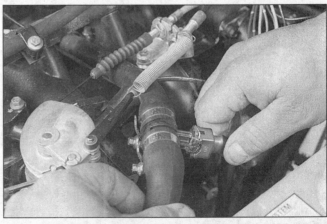

8.7 Disconnect the electrical connector from the electronic heating element

ment from the engine.

9   Remove the hoses from the intake manifold. These crankcase ventilation hoses are specially formed and must be replaced with special factory parts from Jaguar.

10   Installation is the reverse of removal.

9   Catalytic converter

Note: *Because of a federally mandated extended warranty which covers emissions-related components such as the catalytic converter, check with a dealer service department before replacing the converter at your own expense.*

General description

1   To reduce hydrocarbon, carbon monoxide and oxides of nitrogen emissions, all vehicles are equipped with a three-way catalyst system which oxidizes and reduces these chemicals, converting them into harmless nitrogen, carbon dioxide and water.

2   The catalytic converter is mounted in the exhaust system much like a muffler. **Note:** *The exhaust system configuration changes with later model updates. Older models (1988 and 1989) are equipped with a pre-catalytic converter near the exhaust manifold incorporating a single exhaust pipe to the muffler. Later models are equipped with dual exhaust pipes, dual catalytic converters and dual mufflers.*

Check

3   Periodically inspect the catalytic converter-to-exhaust pipe mating flanges and bolts. Make sure that there are no loose bolts and no leaks between the flanges.

4   Look for dents in or damage to the catalytic converter protector. If any part of the protector is damaged or dented enough to touch the converter, repair or replace it.

5   Inspect the heat insulator for damage. Make sure that there is adequate clearance between the heat insulator and the catalytic converter.

Replacement

6   To replace the catalytic converter, refer to Chapter 4. It is recommended that catalytic converters be replaced at a qualified muffler shop because of the numerous tack welds on the exhaust pipes.

Chapter 7
Automatic transmission

Contents

Specifications

Torque specifications

	Nm	Ft-lbs (unless otherwise indicated)
Driveplate-to-torque converter bolts	49 to 54	36 to 40
Oil cooler banjo bolt	32 to 36	24 to 26
Transmission-to-adapter bolts	49 to 54	36 to 40
Valve body bolts	8	70 to 71 in-lbs

1 General information

Refer to illustration 1.4

All models covered by this manual are equipped with a four-speed automatic transmission with a lock-up torque converter. 1988 and 1989 models are equipped with a ZF 4 HP 22. Under loads such as hills or passing situations, this unit is downshifted by a kickdown cable, which can be adjusted and replaced. 1990 and later models use a ZF 4 HP 24 E9 electronic transmission. This unit does not use a kickdown cable; it uses a kickdown switch (under the accelerator pedal) that signals the transmission computer to initiate a downshift. The kickdown switch must be serviced by a Jaguar dealer service department.

Because of the complexity of the clutch mechanisms and the hydraulic and electronic control systems, and because of the special tools and expertise needed to rebuild an automatic transmission, transmission servicing is usually beyond the scope of the home mechanic. The procedures in this Chapter are therefore limited to general diagnosis, routine maintenance, adjustments and transmission removal and installation.

Should the transmission require major repair work, take it to a dealer service department or a transmission repair shop. You can, however, save the cost of removing and installing the transmission by doing it yourself.

1.4 The transmission identification label is located on the left side of the transmission; always refer to this tag when replacing the transmission

If you have to replace the transmission with a new or rebuilt unit, make sure you purchase the right unit. The transmission identification plate is located on the left side of the housing, just behind the manual valve lever **(see illustration)**.

If the transmission warning light on a 1990 or later model comes on:

a) *Check the transmission oil level* (see Chapter 1).
b) *Check the kickdown cable* (see Section 3).
c) *Check the shift cable adjustment* (see Section 4).
d) *Check the state of tune of the engine* (see Chapter 1).

After performing the above, note whether the transmission warning light still comes on. If it does, take the vehicle to a dealer. Further diagnosis should be left to a Jaguar dealer service department or competent Jaguar independent garage.

2   Diagnosis - general

Note: *Automatic transmission malfunctions may be caused by five general conditions: poor engine performance, improper adjustments, hydraulic malfunctions, mechanical malfunctions or malfunctions in the computer or its signal network. Diagnosis of these problems should always begin with a check of the easily repaired items: fluid level and condition (see Chapter 1), kickdown cable adjustment and shift cable adjustment. Next, perform a road test to determine if the problem has been corrected or if more diagnosis is necessary. If the problem persists after the preliminary tests and corrections are completed, additional diagnosis should be done by a dealer service department or transmission repair shop. Refer to the Troubleshooting section at the front of this manual for information on symptoms of transmission problems.*

Preliminary checks

1   Drive the vehicle to warm the transmission to normal operating temperature.
2   Check the fluid level as described in Chapter 1:

a) *If the fluid level is unusually low, add enough fluid to bring the level within the designated area of the dipstick, then check for external leaks (see below).*
b) *If the fluid level is abnormally high, drain off the excess, then check the drained fluid for contamination by coolant. The presence of engine coolant in the automatic transmission fluid indicates that a failure has occurred in the internal radiator walls that separate the coolant from the transmission fluid (see Chapter 3).*
c) *If the fluid is foaming, drain it and refill the transmission, then check for coolant in the fluid or a high fluid level.*

3   Check the engine idle speed. **Note:** *If the engine is malfunctioning, do not proceed with the preliminary checks until it has been repaired and runs normally.*
4   Check the kickdown cable for freedom of movement. Adjust it if necessary (see Section 3). **Note:** *The kickdown cable may function properly when the engine is shut off and cold, but it may malfunction once the engine is hot. Check it cold and at normal engine operating temperature.*
5   Inspect the shift cable (see Section 4). Make sure that it's properly adjusted and that the cable operates smoothly.

Fluid leak diagnosis

6   Most fluid leaks are easy to locate visually. Repair usually consists of replacing a seal or gasket. If a leak is difficult to find, the following procedure may help.
7   Identify the fluid. Make sure it's transmission fluid and not engine oil or brake fluid (automatic transmission fluid is a deep red color).
8   Try to pinpoint the source of the leak. Drive the vehicle several miles, then park it over a large sheet of cardboard. After a minute or two, you should be able to locate the leak by determining the source of the fluid dripping onto the cardboard.
9   Make a careful visual inspection of the suspected component and the area immediately around it. Pay particular attention to gasket mating surfaces. A mirror is often helpful for finding leaks in areas that are hard to see.
10   If the leak still cannot be found, clean the suspected area thoroughly with a degreaser or solvent, then dry it.

11   Drive the vehicle for several miles at normal operating temperature and varying speeds. After driving the vehicle, visually inspect the suspected component again.
12   Once the leak has been located, the cause must be determined before it can be properly repaired. If a gasket is replaced but the sealing flange is bent, the new gasket will not stop the leak. The bent flange must be straightened.
13   Before attempting to repair a leak, check to make sure that the following conditions are corrected or they may cause another leak. **Note:** *Some of the following conditions cannot be fixed without highly specialized tools and expertise. Such problems must be referred to a transmission repair shop or a dealer service department.*

Gasket leaks

14   Check the pan periodically. Make sure the bolts are tight, no bolts are missing, the gasket is in good condition and the pan is flat (dents in the pan may indicate damage to the valve body inside).
15   If the pan gasket is leaking, the fluid level or the fluid pressure may be too high, the transmission breather (on top of the extension housing) may be plugged, the pan bolts may be too tight, the pan sealing flange may be warped, the sealing surface of the transmission housing may be damaged, the gasket may be damaged or the transmission casting may be cracked or porous. If sealant instead of gasket material has been used to form a seal between the pan and the transmission housing, it may be the wrong sealant.

Seal leaks

16   If a transmission seal is leaking, the fluid level or pressure may be too high, the transmission breather (on top of the extension housing) may be plugged, the seal bore may be damaged, the seal itself may be damaged or improperly installed, the surface of the shaft protruding through the seal may be damaged or a loose bearing may be causing excessive shaft movement.
17   Make sure the dipstick is a tight fit inside the filler tube. If the seal at the top of the dipstick is worn or damaged, replace the seal or the dipstick. If fluid continues to leak from the top of the dipstick tube, inspect the breather, which is a plastic cap secured by a clip to the top of the extension housing. This breather can be plugged by the noise-deadening foam installed in the transmission tunnel, causing transmission fluid to leak from the top of the dipstick tube.

Case leaks

18   If the case itself appears to be leaking, the casting is porous and will have to be repaired or replaced.
19   Make sure the oil cooler hose fittings are tight and in good condition.

Fluid comes out vent pipe or fill tube

20   If this condition occurs, the transmission is overfilled, there is coolant in the fluid, the case is porous, the dipstick is incorrect, the vent is plugged or the drain back holes are plugged.

3   Kickdown cable (1988 and 1989 models) - adjustment and replacement

Adjustment

Refer to illustrations 3.2, 3.3 and 3.4
Note: *The following procedure does not apply to 1990 and later models, which utilize a kickdown switch instead of a kickdown cable. The switch must be serviced by a Jaguar service department.*
1   Adjust the accelerator cable (see Chapter 4).
2   Open the throttle bellcrank to the kickdown (full-throttle) position (you should be able to feel the kickdown detent as the bellcrank is moved). Measure the distance from the cable housing to the cable plug **(see illustration)**. It should be 39 to 40 mm (1.54 to 1.58 inches). If the measurement is outside this range, replace the cable.
3   Return the bellcrank to the idle position and measure the gap between the cable plug and the cable housing **(see illustration)**. It

3.2 Open the throttle bellcrank to the kickdown (full-throttle) position and measure the distance from the cable housing to the cable plug

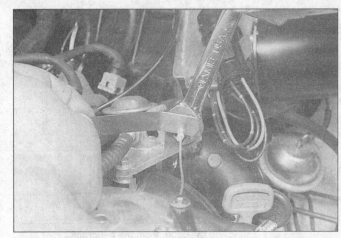

3.3 Return the bellcrank to the idle position and measure the gap between the cable plug and the cable housing

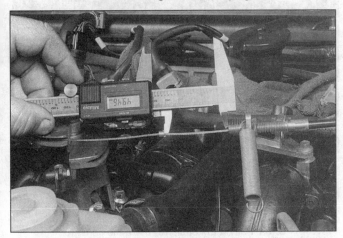

3.4 Depress the accelerator pedal, hold it to the floor and measure the distance between the plug and the cable housing

3.6a To disengage the kickdown cable from the throttle bellcrank, disconnect the return spring . . .

should be 0.76 ± 0.51 mm (0.030 ± 0.020 inch). If the measurement is outside this range, loosen the locknut and adjust the cable until this dimension is within the specified range.

4 Depress the accelerator pedal and hold it to the floor. Measure the distance between the plug and the cable housing **(see illustration)**. It should be at least 44 mm (1.74 inches). If the measured dimension is less than the specified dimension, recheck the throttle cable adjustment (see Chapter 4).

Replacement

Refer to illustrations 3.6a, 3.6b, 3.6c, 3.6d, 3.6e, 3.6f, 3.12, 3.13a, 3.13b, 3.14, 3.15, 3.16 and 3.18

5 Place the shift lever in the Neutral position.
6 Disengage the kickdown cable from the throttle bellcrank, loosen the cable locknuts and detach the cable from its bracket **(see illustrations)**.

3.6b . . . pry off the C-clip, remove the washer . . .

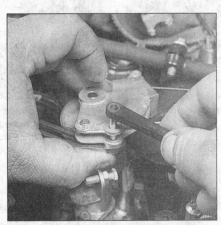

3.6c . . . lift off the return spring link . . .

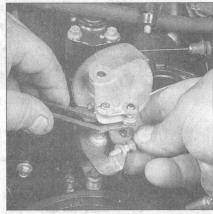

3.6d . . . pull out the pin, swing the cruise control link out of the way . . .

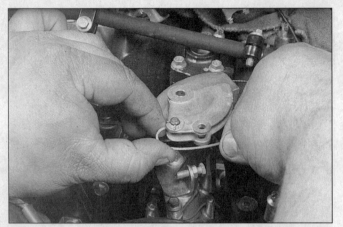

3.6e . . . disengage the cable from the bellcrank . . .

3.6f . . . loosen the locknuts and detach the cable from its bracket

3.12 To remove the valve body, remove these
T30 Torx bolts (arrows)

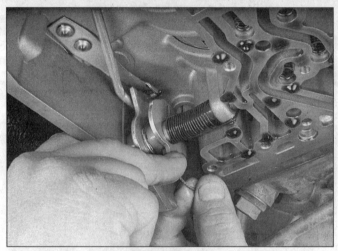

3.13a Pull on the cable to rotate the cam . . .

3.13b . . . and disengage the cable from the cam

3.14 To remove the cable from the transmission, use a small
socket to squeeze the nylon locking tangs together
while pulling up on the cable from above

7   Raise the vehicle and place it securely on jackstands.
8   Drain the transmission fluid (see Chapter 1).
9   Remove the transmission oil pan (see Chapter 1).
10   Pull down the upper end of the kickdown cable between the
engine and the firewall.
11   Remove the transmission filter (see Chapter 1).
12   Remove the valve body **(see illustration)**.
13   Rotate the cam and disengage the cable from the cam **(see
illustrations)**.

14   The cable housing is routed through the transmission case, and
locked into place by four nylon tangs. Pull the cable up until the plug
stops against these tangs, then squeeze the tangs together with a
small socket **(see illustration)** while pulling on the cable from above.
15   Remove the old cable assembly and install the new cable. Before
inserting the lower end of the new cable through the transmission,
make sure the O-ring **(see illustration)** is properly seated, lubricate the

3.15 Make sure that the O-ring on the new cable is properly seated (arrow), then lubricate it with clean automatic transmission fluid before inserting the cable into the transmission case

3.16 Pull down on the cable tangs until they snap into place (arrow); pull up on the cable from above and make sure it's locked in

3.18 When you install the valve body, make sure the manual lever pawl is properly engaged with the manual valve as shown

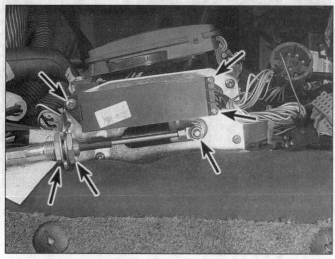

4.2 To detach the shift cable from the shift lever, remove the nut on the end of the cable (arrow); to detach the cable from the shift lever base, remove the two locknuts (arrows); don't loosen the retaining screws (arrows) for the neutral start/back-up light switch unless you plan to readjust or replace the switch

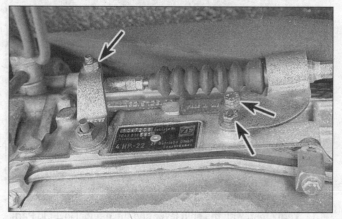

4.4 To detach the lower end of the shift cable from the transmission, remove the nut (arrow) which secures the cable end pin to the manual lever and remove the bolts (arrows) which attach the cable bracket to the transmission

4 Shift cable - replacement and adjustment

Replacement

Refer to illustrations 4.2, 4.4 and 4.7

Note: *The illustrations accompanying this procedure depict a 1988 or 1989 model, which uses a linear type Neutral start/back-up light switch. If you are replacing or adjusting the shift cable on a 1990 or later model, you'll see a rotary type Neutral start/back-up light switch at the manual lever shaft on the transmission. But even though it appears different at the transmission end of the cable, the cable replacement and adjustment procedures are identical.*

1   Remove the center console (see Chapter 11).
2   Detach the cable from the shift lever **(see illustration)**.
3   Raise the vehicle and place it securely on jackstands.
4   Remove the bolts securing the cable bracket to the transmission **(see illustration)**. Some early models may be equipped with a slightly different bracket than shown; on these models, the cable is attached to the bracket by a clamp and bolt, it's not necessary to remove the bracket - simply remove the bolt and clamp and detach the cable from the bracket.
5   On some early models, you'll find a cable bracket at the rear of the transmission; loosen the locknuts and disengage the cable from the bracket.
6   Disengage the shift cable from the manual lever **(see illustration 4.4)**.

O-ring with clean automatic transmission fluid.
16   Insert the cable through the transmission case and pull it down with a pair of pliers until the four locking tangs snap into place **(see illustration)**.
17   Rotate the cam and install the new cable end plug into the slot in the cam. Pull on the cable from above a couple of times to verify that the cable is properly engaged in its track in the cam and the locking tangs are fully seated.
18   Install the valve body, make sure the manual lever pawl is properly engaged with the manual control valve **(see illustration)** and tighten the valve body bolts to the torque listed in this Chapter's Specifications.
19   Install the oil pan and tighten the oil pan bolts to the torque listed in the Chapter 1 Specifications.
20   Route the cable up between the engine and the firewall.
21   Lower the vehicle.
22   Route the cable through its mounting bracket and connect the cable end to the throttle bellcrank **(see illustrations 3.6a through 3.6f)**.
23   Adjust the cable (see above) before tightening the locknuts.
24   Refill the transmission with the recommended fluid (see Chapter 1).

4.7 Pry the cable grommet out of the floor with a screwdriver

4.11 Loosen the cable adjuster locknut

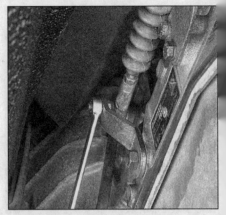

4.12 Remove the nut that secures the cable pin to the manual lever

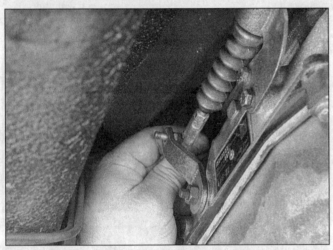

4.14 Verify that, with the shift lever and the manual lever in Park, the cable pin fits loosely through the hole in the manual lever as shown; if the pin does not align with the hole, pull out the pin and turn the adjuster one turn at a time, recheck the fit after each turn

5.3a On 1988 and 1989 models, disconnect the black electrical connector to the Neutral start/back-up light switch and verify that there's continuity between the white/pink and the black/pink wire terminals (on the switch side of the connector) with the shift lever in Park and Neutral and no continuity with the shift lever in Drive, 2 and 3

7   Pry the cable grommet out of the floorpan **(see illustration)** and remove the shift cable.

8   Installation is the reverse of removal. Be sure to adjust the cable (see below) before installing the Neutral start/back-up light switch, console and shift lever trim panel.

Adjustment

Refer to illustrations 4.11, 4.12 and 4.14

9   Place the shift lever in the Park position.

10   Raise the vehicle and place it securely on jackstands.

11   Loosen the cable adjuster locknut **(see illustration)**.

12   Remove the nut that secures the cable to the manual lever **(see illustration)**.

13   Place the manual lever in Park (the most forward detent position).

14   Adjust the cable so that the pin on the end of the cable fits into the manual lever without moving the lever **(see illustration)**. If the pin pushes or pulls on the lever, pull out the pin, rotate the adjuster one turn in or out as necessary, then insert the pin back through the lever and check it again.

15   When the pin on the end of the cable fits loosely into the manual lever as shown, install the cable-to-manual lever retaining nut and tighten it securely.

16   Tighten the adjuster locknut securely.

17   Lower the vehicle.

18   Adjust the Neutral start/back-up light switch (see Section 5).

5   Neutral start/back-up light switch - check and replacement

Check

Note: *Due to the manufacturers assembly line production changes, the wire colors used in the following checks may not match your vehicle. If this is the case, some experimentation may be necessary to find the correct wire terminals for testing.*

1   If the engine can be started with the shift lever in any position other than Park or Neutral, or if the back-up lights do not come on when the shift lever is placed in Reverse, check the neutral start/back-up light switch.

2   Remove the center console (see Chapter 11).

1988 and 1989 models

Refer to illustrations 5.3a and 5.3b

3   Place the shift lever in Park, disconnect the black electrical connector to the Neutral start/back-up light switch, then connect an ohmmeter between the terminals for the white/pink wire and the black/pink wire (on the *switch* side of the connector) and verify that there's continuity. Place the shift lever in Neutral and verify that there's still continuity between these same terminals **(see illustrations)**. Place the shift lever in Drive, 2 and 3, and verify there's no continuity. Place the shift lever in Reverse and verify that there's continuity between the terminal

5.3b On 1988 and 1989 models, place the shift lever in Reverse and verify that there's continuity between the terminal for the black wire and the terminal for the red wire and the gray/light green wire (again, on the *switch* side of the connector)

5.13b To remove a rotary type Neutral start/back-up light switch, disconnect the electrical connector (located in the console area inside the vehicle), snake the electrical lead through the grommet in the tunnel, and remove these nuts (arrows); the small rubber plug (arrow) must be removed to install the special switch adjustment tool

5.13a On 1990 and later models, remove these two bolts (arrows) and remove the protective cover for the Neutral start/back-up light switch

5.16 To adjust a rotary type Neutral start/back-up light switch on 1990 and later models, install this special tool (Jaguar tool no. JD161) as shown, then tighten the switch retaining nuts

for the black wire and the terminal for the red wire and the gray/light green wire (again, on the *switch* side of the connector).

4 If the switch fails the above tests, place the shift lever in Park, loosen the switch retaining screws **(see illustration 4.2)**, hook up the ohmmeter leads to the white/pink and black/pink wire terminals, move the switch until you get continuity, tighten the retaining screws, then recheck the Neutral and Reverse positions. If the switch can't be adjusted to produce continuity in Park, or if it still fails to produce continuity in Neutral or Reverse even after being adjusted, replace it (see below).

5 Install the center console (see Chapter 11).

1990 and later models

6 Place the shift lever in Park.

7 Disconnect the electrical connector from the Neutral start/back-up light switch, then connect an ohmmeter to the terminals for the white/purple wire and the red/white wire (1990 through 1992 models), or the terminals for the red/orange and the green/orange wires (1993 and later models), and verify that there's continuity. Place the shift lever in Neutral and verify that there's still continuity between the same terminals. Place the shift lever in Reverse and hook up the ohmmeter leads to the terminals for the gray/light green wire and the black wire and verify that there's continuity between these terminals.

8 If the switch fails the first of the above tests (Park), place the shift lever in Park, loosen the switch retaining screws, hook up the ohmmeter leads to the terminals for the Park position (white/purple wire and

red/white wire on 1990 through 1992 models, red/orange and green/orange wires on 1993 and later models), and adjust the switch until there's continuity. If the switch can't be adjusted to produce continuity in Park, or if it still fails to produce continuity in Neutral or Reverse even after being adjusted, replace it (see below).

9 Install the center console (see Chapter 11).

Replacement

Refer to illustrations 5.13a, 5.13b and 5.16

Note: *If you're replacing the switch on a 1990 or later model, you'll need a special switch adjustment tool (Jaguar tool no. JD161) to adjust the switch.*

10 Remove the center console (see Chapter 11).

11 On 1990 and later models, raise the vehicle and place it securely on jackstands.

12 Disconnect the electrical connector(s) from the switch (on 1990 and later models, the switch is located at the transmission and the electrical connector is routed through the top of the tunnel and into the console).

13 Remove the switch retaining nuts **(1988 and 1989 models, see illustration 4.2; 1990 and later models, see illustrations 5.13a and 5.13b)** and remove the switch.

14 Place the shift lever in Neutral, install the switch and install the switch retaining nuts, but don't tighten them yet.

15 On 1988 and 1989 models, hook up an ohmmeter to the Neutral terminals (see Step 3) and adjust the switch to produce continuity between these terminals with the shift lever in Neutral. Tighten the retaining nuts.

16 On 1990 and later models, remove the small rubber plug, install

6.5 Using a hooked seal removal tool or a large screwdriver, carefully pry the torque converter seal out of the transmission

6.16a Pry out the locking plate . . .

the special switch adjustment tool (JD161) as shown **(see illustration)**. This tool aligns the switch to produce continuity when the shift lever is in Neutral. If you don't have the special tool, you can use an ohmmeter to adjust the switch to produce continuity in Neutral (see Step 8), but you may have to experiment before determining which wires to use. Once the switch is adjusted, tighten the switch retaining nuts. Install the switch protective cover and tighten the two bolts securely.

17   On 1990 and later models, route the wire harness for the new switch through the grommet in the tunnel. Lower the vehicle.

18   Plug in the electrical connector(s).

19   Install the console (see Chapter 11).

20   Check the operation of the switch. Make sure the engine can be started in Park and Neutral, but not in any other gear, and that the back-up lights come on when the shift lever in placed in Reverse.

6   Oil seal - replacement

1   There are three seals in the automatic transmission - the torque converter seal, the manual valve seal and the transmission output shaft seal - that can cause automatic transmission fluid leaks. If the torque converter seal is leaking, you'll find automatic transmission fluid in the bottom of the bellhousing. If the manual valve seal leaks, you'll see automatic transmission fluid on the side of the transmission case and the pan. If the output shaft seal leaks, you'll find automatic transmission fluid on the extension housing and the front of the driveshaft.

2   You can replace all of these seals without disassembling the transmission, although replacing the torque converter seal requires removal of the transmission and the torque converter .

Torque converter seal

Refer to illustration 6.5

3   Remove the transmission and the torque converter (see Section 8).

4   Inspect the bushing in the torque converter hub. If it's worn, the new seal will soon leak. Try removing any sharp edges or burrs with fine emery cloth. If the hub is deeply scored, the torque converter must be replaced.

5   Using a hooked seal removal tool or screwdriver, pry the seal out of the transmission case **(see illustration)**. Make sure you don't gouge the surface of the seal bore.

6   Lubricate the lip of the new seal with automatic transmission fluid and carefully drive it into place with a socket or a section of pipe with an outside diameter slightly smaller than the outside diameter of the seal.

7   Install the torque converter, making sure it is completely engaged with the front pump (to do this, turn the converter as you push it into place - continue turning and pushing until you're sure it's fully seated). Install the transmission/converter assembly (see Section 8).

6.16b . . . immobilize the flange by inserting a bolt (arrow) through the flange and jamming it against a reinforcing rib as shown, then remove the flange nut

Manual valve seal

8   Raise the vehicle and place it securely on jackstands.

9   Remove the manual valve lever from the transmission. Do not disconnect the linkage from the lever or you'll have to readjust it.

10   Pry out the seal with a small hooked seal removal tool or a small screwdriver. Make sure you don't gouge the surface of the seal bore.

11   Lubricate the lip of the new seal with automatic transmission fluid and carefully drive it into place with a socket or a section of pipe with an outside diameter slightly smaller than the outside diameter of the seal.

12   Install the manual lever and tighten the nut to the torque listed in this Chapter's Specifications. If you didn't disconnect the linkage, it's unnecessary to readjust the linkage.

Output shaft seal

Refer to illustrations 6.16a and 6.16b

13   Raise the rear of the vehicle and support it securely on jackstands. Be sure to block the front wheels to keep the vehicle from rolling.

14   Remove the exhaust system (see Chapter 4).

15   Remove the driveshaft (see Chapter 8).

16   Pry out the lockplate **(see illustration)**, immobilize the flange with a bolt and remove the flange nut **(see illustration)**. Remove the flange from the output shaft. Use a puller, if necessary.

7.3 Support the transmission with a jack; place a wood block between the jack head and the transmission to protect the pan

7.5a With an assistant supporting the crossmember, remove these four transmission mount/crossmember retaining nuts (arrows) . . .

7.5b . . . then remove this retaining clip and clevis pin from the travel limiter strap

17   Using a seal removal tool or a small screwdriver, carefully pry out the old oil seal. Make sure you don't damage the seal bore when you pry out the seal.
18   Apply a light coat of oil to the lip of the new seal, clean off the end of the output shaft, slide the seal onto the shaft and carefully drive it into place using a short section of pipe with an outside diameter

slightly smaller than the outside diameter of the seal.
19   Install the flange. Coat the side of the nut that contacts the flange with sealant to prevent oil leaks. Tighten the flange nut to the torque listed in this Chapter's Specifications. Install a new lockplate by tapping it into place with a brass punch and hammer. Make sure the lockplate is fully seated.
20   The remainder of installation is the reverse of removal.

7   Transmission mount - check and replacement

Refer to illustrations 7.3, 7.5a, 7.5b, 7.6a, 7.6b, 7.6c, 7.6d, 7.6e, 7.6f, 7.6g, 7.6h and 7.6i

1   If you hear a rumbling sound coming from the tunnel when the vehicle is driven over rough roads, expansion joints, bumpy surfaces, etc., the rear transmission mount may be defective.
2   Raise the vehicle and support it securely on jackstands.
3   Place a transmission jack or floor jack under the transmission **(see illustration)**.
4   Remove the central exhaust pipe section (see Chapter 4).
5   With an assistant supporting the mount crossmember, remove the crossmember retaining nuts **(see illustration)** and lower the mount/crossmember assembly until you can see the travel limiter strap. To disconnect the strap, remove the retaining clip and clevis pin **(see illustration)**.
6   Disassemble the mount assembly as shown **(see illustrations)**.

7.6a To disassemble the transmission mount, remove this retaining screw (arrow) . . .

7.6b . . . place the mount/crossmember assembly in a bench vise, remove these two bolts (arrows) from one side . . .

7.6c . . . and this bolt (arrow) from the other side . . .

7.6d . . . place the assembly on a work bench and remove the upper spring . . .

7.6e . . . the retainer . . .

7.6f . . . the bump-stop . . .

7.6g . . . the upper insulator . . .

7.6h . . . the lower spring . . .

7.6i . . . and the lower insulator

7   Inspect the rubber bump-stop for cracks, tears and deformation. If it's damaged or worn, replace it.

8   Installation is otherwise the reverse of removal. Have your assistant hold the mount/crossmember assembly in position while you reattach the mount to the travel limiter strap with the clevis pin and retaining clip **(see illustration 7.5b)**. Then raise the mount/crossmember all the way up, install the crossmember retaining nuts and tighten them securely.

8   Automatic transmission - removal and installation

Refer to illustrations 8.3, 8.7, 8.14a, 8.14b, 8.14c, 8.14d, 8.15 and 8.17
Caution: *On 1994 models with engine numbers ranging from 9E-185496 to 9E-186799, four of the ten bolts that attach the transmission to the adapter plate were originally manufactured to substandard material specifications. These four bolts are black in color. Once these bolts are removed, discard them, DO NOT reuse these bolts. There is no danger of these bolts failing unless they are removed and reused.*

1   Disconnect the cable from the negative battery terminal. **Caution:** *If the radio in your vehicle is equipped with an anti-theft system, make sure you have the correct activation code before disconnecting the battery.*

2   On 1988 and 1989 models, if you're planning on installing the original transmission, disconnect the kickdown cable from the throttle linkage and from its mounting bracket (see Section 3). If you're planning on installing a new or rebuilt transmission, the cable should be disconnected from the *transmission* after the vehicle is lifted.

3   Remove the dipstick tube retaining bolt **(see illustration)**.

4   Raise the vehicle and support it securely on jackstands.

5   Drain the transmission fluid (see Chapter 1).

6   Place a drain pan underneath the dipstick tube, remove the tube, drain the oil in the tube and plug the hole.

7   Disconnect the oil cooler lines **(see illustration)**.

8   Remove the front exhaust pipe and hang the remainder of the exhaust system out of the way (see Chapter 4).

9   If you're *replacing* the transmission on a 1988 or 1989 model, disconnect the kickdown cable (see Section 3).

10   Disconnect the shift cable from the mounting bracket on the left side of the transmission and from the manual lever (see Section 4).

11   Support the engine from above with an engine hoist (see Chapter 2). **Caution:** *Do not allow the engine to remain unsupported while*

8.3 Remove the dipstick tube retaining bolt (arrow)

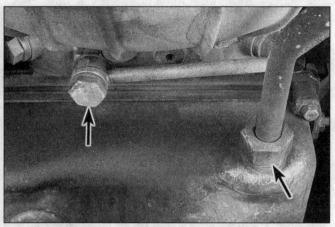

8.7 Disconnect the oil cooler line fittings (arrows)

8.14a Pry out the rubber torque converter access cover . . .

8.14b . . . and the plastic grille in the bellhousing . . .

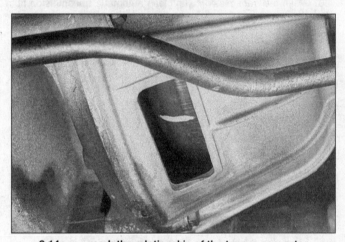

8.14c . . . mark the relationship of the torque converter
to the driveplate . . .

removing the transmission or damage to other components may occur.
12   Support the transmission with a transmission jack or a floor jack.
If you use a floor jack, place a wood block between the jack head and
the oil pan to protect the pan.
13   Remove the transmission mount (see Section 7).
14   Remove the torque converter access covers **(see illustrations)**,
mark the relationship of the torque converter to the driveplate and
remove the bolts that attach the torque converter to the driveplate **(see
illustrations)**.

15   On vehicles with a 4 HP 24 E9 transmission (1990 and later models), disconnect the control unit electrical connector from the left side
of the transmission, just above the pan **(see illustration)**.
16   Lower the engine and transmission. Make sure the engine doesn't
contact the steering gear. **Caution:** *Do NOT allow the torque converter
shaft to support the weight of the transmission or you will damage the
torque converter or transmission.*
17   Remove the bolts that attach the transmission bellhousing to the

8.14d . . . and remove the bolts that attach the torque converter
to the driveplate

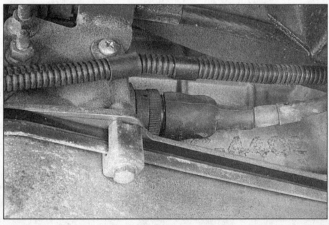

8.15 On vehicles with a 4 HP 24 E9 transmission (1990 and later
models), disconnect the control unit electrical connector from the
left side of the transmission, just above the pan

engine adapter plate **(see illustration)**, pull the transmission to the rear until it's free, then carefully lower the jack enough to make a last-minute check for anything that might still be connected to the transmission. As you lower the transmission, make sure the kickdown cable doesn't hang up on anything.

18   If you're replacing the transmission, remove the torque converter and install it on the new/rebuilt unit. To remove the torque converter from the transmission, install two long bolts halfway into the converter mounting holes and pull evenly on both bolts.

19   Installation is basically the reverse of removal, but note the following:

   a) *Tighten the transmission and torque converter bolts to the torque listed in this Chapter's Specifications.*

   b) *Before reattaching the cooler lines, flush them with clean automatic transmission fluid, to remove any friction lining particles that could clog the new or rebuilt transmission.*

   c) *Use a new gasket on the pan drain plug and a new O-ring on the dipstick/filler tube connection at the pan.*

20   Refill the transmission with clean automatic transmission fluid (see Chapter 1).

21   Adjust the kickdown cable and the shift cable (see Sections 3 and 4, respectively).

8.17 Transmission bellhousing bolts (arrows)

Chapter 8   Drivetrain

Contents

Specifications

Torque specifications

	Nm	Ft-lbs (unless otherwise indicated)
Driveshaft		
U-joint-to-flange (front or rear)	95 to 105	70 to 77
Flexible coupling-to-pinion flange	81	60
Center bearing assembly		
Crossmember-to-body bolts	22 to 28	16 to 20
Bearing-to-crossmember bolts	22 to 24	16 to 17
Driveaxles		
U-joint to output flange	78 to 95	58 to 70
Driveaxle nut	300 to 320	221 to 236
Differential		
Pinion turning torque	4 to 6	35 to 55 in-lbs
Output shaft housing bolts	51 to 58	38 to 42

2.3a To insure that the driveshaft is reinstalled in the same position, paint or scribe alignment marks across the transmission output flange and front U-joint flange

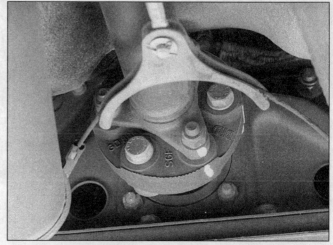

2.3b . . . and across the rear flexible coupling (shown), or U-joint, and the pinion flange

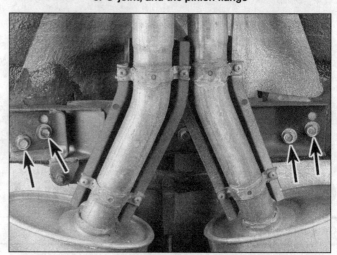

2.4 Remove the two bolts that attach the center bearing to the crossmember (one bolt is visible between the two exhaust pipes), then loosen the crossmember bolts (arrows) so you can lower it to clear the center bearing assembly when the driveshaft is removed

1   General information

Driveshaft

Power is transmitted from the transmission to the rear axle by a two-piece driveshaft joined ahead of the center bearing by a "slip joint," a sliding, splined coupling. The slip joint allows slight fore-and-aft movement of the driveshaft. The forward end of the driveshaft (and the rear end, on some early models) is attached to the extension housing output flange by a conventional universal joint. The rear end of the driveshaft is attached to the pinion flange of the differential by a flexible rubber coupling. This flex coupling, sometimes referred to as a "Jurid" coupling or a "flex-disc," isolates the differential from the sudden torque forces of the driveshaft. (If you have an early model with a U-joint at the rear end of the driveshaft, a flexible coupling can be retrofitted; see your Jaguar dealer for details.) The middle of the driveshaft is supported by the center bearing, which is rubber-mounted to isolate driveshaft vibrations. The center bearing crossmember is bolted to the vehicle body.

Differential assembly

The rear-mounted differential assembly includes the drive pinion, the ring gear, the differential and the output flanges. The drive pinion, which drives the ring gear, is also known as the differential input shaft. It's connected to the driveshaft via an input flange. The differential is bolted to the ring gear and drives the rear wheels through a pair of output flanges bolted to driveaxles with U-joints at either end. The differential allows the wheels to turn at different speeds when cornering (the outside wheel must travel farther - and therefore faster - than the inside wheel in the same period of time). The differential assembly is bolted to a large crossmember and to various suspension pieces. To replace it, you'll have to drop the entire rear axle/suspension assembly.

Major repair work on the differential assembly components (drive pinion, ring-and-pinion and differential) requires many special tools and a high degree of expertise, and therefore should not be attempted by the home mechanic. If major repairs become necessary, we recommend that they be performed by a dealer service department or other repair shop.

Driveaxles and universal joints

The driveaxles deliver power from the differential output flanges to the rear wheels. The driveaxles are equipped with U-joints at each end. The differential assembly, the driveaxles and the wheels are never in perfect alignment; U-joints allow the driveaxles to deliver power to the rear wheels while moving up and down with the rear suspension.

The inner U-joints are connected to flanges which are bolted to the differential output flanges. The outer U-joints are connected to stub shafts which engage the splines of the wheel hubs and are secured by an axle nut.

2   Driveshaft - removal and installation

Removal

Refer to illustrations 2.3a, 2.3b and 2.4

1   Raise the vehicle and support it securely on jackstands.
2   Remove the central section of the exhaust system (see Chapter 4).
3   Using paint, a punch or a scribe, make alignment marks across the transmission output flange and, and across the rear flexible coupling (or U-joint, on later models), to insure that the driveshaft is reinstalled in the same position **(see illustrations)**. **Note:** *If you're simply replacing a rear flexible coupling, it's not necessary to remove the driveshaft; all you have to do is unbolt it from the flexible coupling (see Section 3).*
4   Support the driveshaft at the center. Remove the two bolts that attach the center bearing to the crossmember, then remove the crossmember bolts **(see illustration)** and pull out the crossmember.
5   Remove the driveshaft assembly.

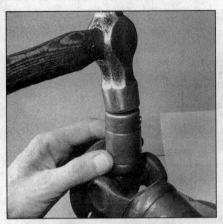
3.8a Tap the flange yoke down . . .

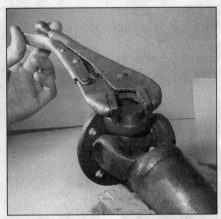
3.7B . . . and remove the bearing cup

3.12 Spider, bearings and snap-rings

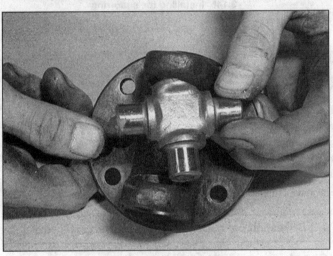
3.13a Place the spider in the yoke . . .

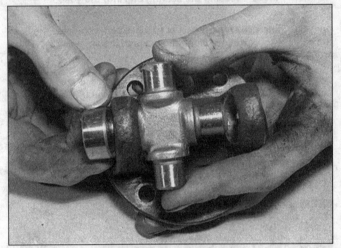
3.13b . . . and install a bearing cup

6   If you're replacing a U-joint or flexible coupling, refer to Section 3. If you're replacing the center bearing, refer to Section 4.
7   Installation is the reverse of removal. Be sure to tighten all fasteners to the torque listed in this Chapter's Specifications.

3   Driveshaft universal joint and flexible coupling - check and replacement

Check

Universal joint(s)
1   U-joint wear is characterized by vibration in the transmission, noise during acceleration or metallic squeaking and grating sounds as the bearings disintegrate.
2   It's easy to check the U-joint(s) for wear with the driveshaft installed. To check the rear U-joint, try to turn the driveshaft while immobilizing the differential input flange. To check the front U-joint, try to turn the driveshaft while holding the transmission output flange. Freeplay between the driveshaft and the front or rear flanges indicates excessive wear.
3   If the driveshaft is already removed, you can check the universal joints by holding the shaft in one hand and turning the yoke or flange with the other. If the axial movement is excessive, replace the driveshaft.

Flexible coupling
4   Although there's no maintenance interval for the flexible coupling, you should inspect it whenever you're working under the vehicle. The

coupling is made of rubber, so it's vulnerable to road grit, heat generated by the exhaust system, and the twisting torque of the driveshaft. Inspect the coupling for cracks, tears, missing pieces and distortion. If it's cracked or generally worn, replace it.

Replacement
U-joint
Refer to illustrations 3.8a, 3.8b, 3.12, 3.13a, 3.13b, 3.14a, 3.14b, 3.15a, 3.15b and 3.15c
5   Remove the driveshaft (see Section 2).
6   Remove the snap-rings from the bearing cups. Use a punch to free them if they're stuck.
7   Place the driveshaft in a vise with the yokes of the driveshaft (not the flange) resting on the open vise jaws (remember that the driveshaft is hollow and easily damaged by too much vise pressure).
8   Using a hammer and a socket which just fits over the bearing cups, gently tap the flange yoke down so that the uppermost bearing cup protrudes from the yoke **(see illustration)**. Remove the cup **(see illustration)**.
9   Rotate the driveshaft 180-degrees and repeat this operation on the opposite bearing.
10   The flange can now be removed from the driveshaft and the same procedure used to remove the spider from the shaft.
11   Clean the bearing seats in the flange and driveshaft yokes.
12   Remove the bearings from the new spider **(see illustration)** and make sure that the needle bearings are well greased. If they aren't, thoroughly lubricate them with chassis grease.
13   Place the spider in the flange yoke **(see illustration)** and install one bearing cup onto the yoke **(see illustration)**.

3.14a Pressing the bearing cup into the yoke

3.14b Installing the snap-ring

14   Using the vise and a socket of suitable diameter, press the bearing cup into the yoke **(see illustration)**. Install the snap-ring **(see illustration)**.
15   Repeat this procedure on the opposite side, then install the flange yoke and spider on the driveshaft yoke (remember to match up your alignment marks) and install the remaining bearing cups **(see illustrations)**.
16   Install the rest of the bearing retaining snap-rings.
17   Check the joint for full and free movement. If it feels too tight, rest it on the vise and gently tap it with a plastic mallet. This should center

the bearings and free the joint.
18   Install the driveshaft (see Section 2).

Flexible coupling

Refer to illustration 3.22
19   Raise the vehicle and place it securely on jackstands.
20   Make alignment marks between the driveshaft, the coupling and the pinion flange **(see illustration 2.3b)**.
21   Unbolt the driveshaft from the coupling.
22   Remove the nuts and bolts which hold the coupling to the flange **(see illustration)** and remove the coupling.
23   Installation is the reverse of removal. Be sure to match up the alignment marks on the driveshaft and the pinion flange.

---

4   Driveshaft center bearing - check and replacement

Check

1   The center bearing consists of a ball-bearing assembly encircled by a rubber mount. The bearing assembly is pressed onto the driveshaft and is secured by a snap-ring. The center bearing is protected by dust caps on either side, but water and dirt can still enter the bearing and ruin it. Driveshaft vibration can also lead to bearing failure. To inspect the center bearing properly, you'll need to remove the driveshaft (see Section 2). Conversely, whenever the driveshaft is removed for any reason, always use the opportunity to inspect the bearing. Rotate the bearing and see if it turns smoothly; if it's difficult to turn, or if it has a gritty feeling, replace it. Also inspect the rubber portion. If it's cracked or deteriorated, replace it.

3.15a Tap the first cup into the shaft yoke . . .

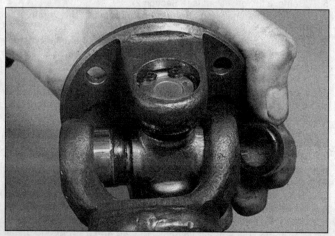

3.15b . . . install the other cup . . .

3.15c . . . and press it into place with the vise

3.22 After marking the alignment of the driveshaft, the flex coupling and the pinion flange, remove these three nuts (not visible) and bolts (arrows) and remove the coupling

Replacement

2   Remove the driveshaft assembly.
3   Take the driveshaft to an automotive machine shop to have the old bearing pressed off and a new bearing pressed on.

5   Pinion oil seal - replacement

Refer to illustration 5.3

1   Raise the rear of the vehicle and place it securely on jackstands.
2   Disconnect the driveshaft and flexible coupling or rear U-joint from the pinion flange (see Section 2).
3   Make matching marks on the pinion shaft, the flange nut and the flange **(see illustration)**.
4   Hold the input flange stationary and remove the flange nut.
5   Using a puller, remove the input flange.
6   Pry out the old seal with a seal removal tool or a screwdriver. Make sure you don't nick or gouge the seal bore.
7   Dip the new seal in differential lubricant and drive it into position with a seal driver. If you don't have a seal driver, a large socket or a section of pipe of the appropriate diameter will work.
8   Lightly lubricate the input shaft and press the input flange back on, but don't bottom it out. Install the flange nut and slowly tighten it until the marks line up **(see illustration 5.3)**.

5.3 Before removing the pinion nut, mark the relationship of the pinion flange, nut and shaft

9   Using an inch-pound torque wrench, measure the torque required to turn the pinion flange (turning torque) and compare your measurement to the turning torque in this Chapter's Specifications.
10   If the turning torque is less than the specified range, tighten the pinion flange nut a little bit at a time until the turning torque is within range.
11   If the turning torque is greater than the specified range, the pinion shaft sleeve probably needs to be replaced. Due to the special tools required and the critical nature of the job, replacement of the pinion shaft sleeve should be left to a dealer service department or other qualified repair shop.
12   If the specified torque is reached *before* the match marks line up, don't continue to turn the nut until they do. **Caution:** *Don't tighten the nut past the match marks and then back it off, as this could over-compress the pinion shaft sleeve.*

6   Driveaxle - removal and installation

Refer to illustrations 6.3a, 6.3b, 6.4 and 6.5

1   Set the parking brake firmly. Loosen the rear wheel lug nuts, raise the rear of the vehicle and support it securely on jackstands. Remove the wheel.
2   Remove the brake caliper and disc, disconnect the parking brake cable from the parking brake assembly and unbolt the ABS sensor (see Chapter 9).
3   Remove the driveaxle nut and washer **(see illustrations)**.

6.3a Install a couple of wheel lug nuts, insert a large prybar between them to hold the hub assembly, and break loose the driveaxle nut

6.3b After removing the driveaxle nut, remove this washer

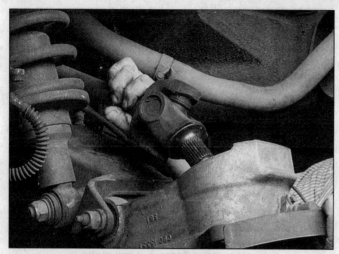

6.4　Swing the carrier assembly out and down and disengage the outer end of the driveaxle from the carrier (make sure you disconnect the parking brake cable and ABS sensor first, or they will be damaged)

4　Pull the carrier outward and detach the outer end of the driveaxle from the carrier **(see illustration)**. If the driveaxle is stuck in the hub splines, use a puller to push the driveaxle through the hub.
5　Remove the four nuts **(see illustration)** which attach the inner U-joint flange to the differential output shaft flange.
6　Remove the driveaxle assembly.
7　Installation is the reverse of removal. Be sure to tighten the inner U-joint flange nuts and the driveaxle nut to the torque listed in this Chapter's Specifications.

7　Driveaxle universal joints - check and replacement

1　Remove the driveaxle (see Section 6).
2　Replace the U-joints following the procedure described in Section 3.
3　Install the driveaxle (see Section 6).

8　Differential output shaft bearing and seal - replacement

Refer to illustration 8.4
1　Raise the rear of the vehicle and support it securely on jackstands.
2　Drain the differential lubricant (see Chapter 1).
3　Separate the driveaxle from the differential (see Section 6) and suspend it out of the way with a piece of wire.
4　Remove the output shaft housing bolts **(see illustration)** and remove the flange and housing assembly from the differential.
5　Take the flange and housing assembly to a Jaguar service department or an automotive machine shop to have the bearing and seal replaced.
6　Installation is the reverse of removal. Be sure to tighten the housing bolts to the torque listed in this Chapter's Specifications.

9　Differential - removal and installation

Removal

Refer to illustrations 9.5, 9.10, 9.12a, 9.12b and 9.14
Warning: *Do not attempt the following procedure without some help. The differential and rear suspension assembly is heavy. You will need an assistant to help you balance the assembly on the jack as it's lowered to the ground.*

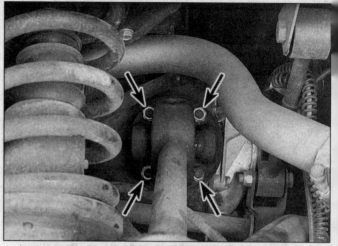

6.5　To detach the inner driveaxle U-joint from the differential output shaft flange, remove these four nuts (arrows)

1　Loosen the rear wheel lug nuts. Raise the rear of the vehicle and place it securely on jackstands. Remove the wheels.
2　Drain the differential lubricant (see Chapter 1).
3　Disconnect the driveshaft from the pinion flange (see Section 2). Support the end of the driveshaft with a piece of wire so the center bearing isn't damaged. Remove the pinion flange (see Section 5).
4　Remove the brake calipers and hang them out of the way (see Chapter 9). Remove the brake discs. Disconnect the parking brake cables from the parking brake shoes and snake the cables out of the crossmember. Unbolt and remove the ABS sensors. Remove all brackets and cut all cable ties which attach parking brake hoses or lines, ABS electrical harnesses and parking brake cables to the rear suspension. Hang all hoses, lines, harnesses and cables out of the way so that they won't be damaged when the rear suspension/differential assembly is lowered.
5　Unbolt the speed sensor **(see illustration)** and hang it out of the way (don't hang it by the electrical harness - use a piece of wire).
6　Disconnect the fuel lines (see Chapter 4) and tuck them out of the way. Make sure that the fuel pump, fuel filter and fuel return lines are all clear of the crossmember before proceeding.
7　Support the differential/crossmember assembly with a transmission jack or a floor jack equipped with a transmission holding fixture. Make sure the jack is positioned directly in the center of the crossmember/differential/suspension assembly, and secure the assembly to

8.4　To detach the output shaft housing from the differential, remove these bolts (arrows) (upper bolts not visible in this photo)

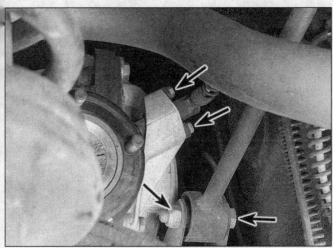

9.5 To detach the speed sensor from the differential, remove these two bolts (arrows), then hang the sensor out of the way with a piece of wire; to disconnect the tie bars from the differential, remove the nut (lower arrow) and bolt (left tie bar shown)

9.10 To detach the crossmember from the body, remove these bolts (arrows) from each mounting bracket (left bracket shown)

the jack with safety chains. Raise the jack just enough to take the weight of the crossmember mounting bolts.

8   Unbolt the lower ends of the shock absorbers from the control arms (see Chapter 10).

9   Disconnect the tie bars from the differential (see illustration 9.5).

10   Remove the crossmember mounting bracket bolts (see illustration).

11   Lower the crossmember/differential/rear suspension assembly and remove it from under the vehicle.

12   Disconnect the crossmember from the differential (see illustrations).

13   Disconnect the driveaxles from the differential (see Section 6).

14   Disconnect the rear control arms from the differential (see Chapter 10). Unbolt the front and rear control arm brackets from the differential (see illustration).

15   Installation is the reverse of removal. Be sure to tighten all critical fasteners to the torque listed in this Chapter's Specifications and the Chapter 9 and 10 Specifications.

Installation

16   Position the differential housing in place against its mounts and loosely install the bolts (don't tighten any of them until they are all installed), then tighten all of the fasteners securely.

17   The remainder of installation is the reverse of removal.

9.12a To detach the front of the differential from the crossmember, remove these four nuts (arrows) (two upper nuts not visible)

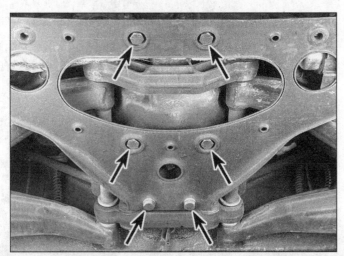

9.12b To detach the crossmember from the underside of the differential, remove these bolts (arrows) (assembly is shown still attached to vehicle)

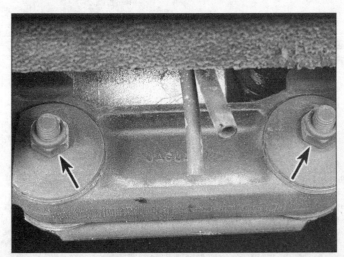

9.14 To detach the front and rear control arm mounting brackets from the differential, remove these nuts (arrows) and bolts (rear bracket shown)

Notes

Chapter 9   Brakes

Contents

Specifications

General

Brake fluid type	See Chapter 1

Disc brake system

Minimum brake pad thickness	See Chapter 1
Brake disc minimum permissible thickness	Cast into disc
Parallelism	0.013 mm (0.0005 inch) maximum
Runout	0.102 mm (0.004 inch) maximum

Torque specifications

	Nm	Ft-lbs (unless otherwise indicated)
Caliper bolts (front and rear)	31 to 40	23 to 29
Caliper bracket bolts		
Front bracket	102 to 128	75 to 94
Rear bracket	55 to 62	40 to 45
Master cylinder-to-brake booster nuts (1988 and 1989)	22 to 28	16 to 20
Power brake booster mounting nuts (1988 and 1989)	10	84 in-lbs
Hydraulic actuating unit-to-pedal box (1990 and later)	22 to 28	16 to 20
Wheel lug nuts	See Chapter 1	

1   General information

All models covered by this manual are equipped with hydraulically operated front and rear disc brake systems. Both front and rear brakes are self adjusting.

Hydraulic system

The hydraulic system consists of two separate circuits. The master cylinder has separate reservoirs for the two circuits, and, in the event of a leak or failure in one hydraulic circuit, the other circuit will remain operative. All models are equipped with an Anti-lock Braking System (ABS).

Power brake booster

A hydraulic brake booster system is used on all models covered by this manual. This system uses hydraulic pressure from an engine-driven pump on models equipped with a power hydraulic system, and an electric pump on models without the power hydraulic system.

Parking brake

The parking brake lever operates the rear brakes through cable actuation. It's activated by a lever mounted in the center console. The parking brake assembly uses a pair of brake shoes located inside the rear hub/brake disc.

Brake pad wear warning system

The brake pad wear warning system turns on a red light in the instrument cluster when the brake pads have worn down to the point at which they must be replaced. Do NOT ignore this reminder. If you don't replace the pads shortly after the brake pad wear warning light comes on, the brake discs will be damaged.

The wear sensors are attached to the brake pads. Once the pads wear down to the point at which they're flush with the sensor, the disc

3.5a   Before starting, wash down the caliper and disc with brake cleaner

3.5b   Attach a hose to the bleeder screw and put the other end in a catch bottle, then open the bleeder screw slightly and depress the piston into the caliper with a C-clamp; as the piston is depressed, the brake fluid will be expelled into the bottle (pumping dirty brake fluid back into the ABS system can damage the modulator). Tighten the bleeded screw when the piston has been bottomed

grinds away the side of the sensor facing the disc, the wire inside the sensor is broken, the circuit is opened and the red light on the instrument panel comes on.

Always check the sensor(s) when replacing the pads. If you change the pads before the warning light comes on, the sensor(s) may still be good; once the light has come on, replace the sensor.

Service

After completing any operation involving disassembly of any part of the brake system, always test drive the vehicle to check for proper braking performance before resuming normal driving. When testing the brakes, perform the tests on a clean, dry, flat surface. Conditions other than these can lead to inaccurate test results.

Test the brakes at various speeds with both light and heavy pedal pressure. The vehicle should stop evenly without pulling to one side or the other. Avoid locking the brakes, because this slides the tires and diminishes braking efficiency and control of the vehicle.

Tires, vehicle load and front-end alignment are factors which also affect braking performance.

2   Anti-lock Brake system (ABS) - general information

The Anti-lock Brake System is designed to maintain vehicle steerability, directional stability and optimum deceleration under severe braking conditions on most road surfaces. It does so by monitoring the rotational speed of each wheel and controlling the brake line pressure to each wheel during braking. This prevents the wheels from locking up.

The ABS system has three main components - the wheel speed sensors, the electronic control unit and the modulator (hydraulic control unit). The sensors - one at each wheel - send a variable voltage signal to the electronic control unit, which monitors these signals, compares them to its program and determines whether a wheel is about to lock up. When a wheel is about to lock up, the control unit signals the hydraulic unit to reduce hydraulic pressure (or not increase it further) at that wheel's brake caliper. Pressure modulation is handled by three electrically operated solenoid valves - one for each front wheel and one for the rear wheels - inside the modulator.

If a problem develops within the system, an "ABS" warning light will glow on the dashboard. Sometimes, a visual inspection of the ABS system can help you locate the problem. Carefully inspect the ABS wiring harness. Pay particularly close attention to the harness and connections near each wheel. Look for signs of chafing and other damage caused by incorrectly routed wires. If a wheel sensor harness is damaged, the sensor should be replaced (the harness and sensor are integral). **Warning:** *Do NOT try to repair an ABS wiring harness. The ABS system is sensitive to even the smallest changes in resistance. Repairing the harness could alter resistance values and cause the system to*

malfunction. If the ABS wiring harness is damaged in any way, it must be replaced. **Caution:** *Make sure the ignition is turned off before unplugging or reattaching any electrical connections.*

Diagnosis and repair

If a dashboard warning light comes on and stays on while the vehicle is in operation, the ABS system requires attention. Although special electronic ABS diagnostic testing tools are necessary to properly diagnose the system, you can perform a few preliminary checks before taking the vehicle to a dealer service department or other qualified repair shop.

a) Check the brake fluid level in the master cylinder reservoir.
b) Verify that all ABS system electrical connectors in the engine compartment are plugged in.
c) Check the fuses.
d) Follow the wiring harness to each front wheel and to the differential sensor and verify that all connections are secure and that the wiring is undamaged.

If the above preliminary checks do not rectify the problem, the vehicle should be diagnosed by a Jaguar service technician. Due to the complex nature of this system, all actual repair work must be done by a dealer service department or other qualified repair shop.

3   Disc brake pads - replacement

Refer to illustrations 3.5a through 3.5o
Warning: *Disc brake pads must be replaced on both front wheels or both rear wheels at the same time - never replace the pads on only one wheel. Also, the dust created by the brake system may contain asbestos, which is harmful to your health. Never blow it out with compressed air and don't inhale any of it. An approved filtering mask should be worn when working on the brakes. Do not, under any circumstances, use petroleum-based solvents to clean brake parts. Use brake system cleaner only!*
Note: *The following procedure applies to both the front and rear brake pads.*

1   Remove the cap from the brake fluid reservoir and siphon off about two-thirds of the fluid from the reservoir. Failing to do this could result in the reservoir overflowing when the caliper pistons are pressed into their bores.

2   Loosen the wheel lug nuts, raise the front of the vehicle and

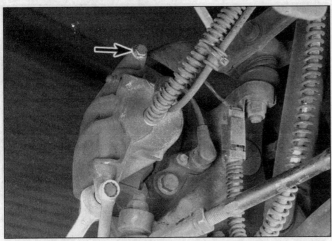

3.5c Remove the caliper mounting bolts (arrow indicates upper bolt); use a back-up wrench to hold the flats of the caliper guide pins while you back out the caliper bolts

3.5d Remove the caliper . . .

3.5e . . . and suspend it out of the way with a piece of wire

3.5f Remove the outer brake pad

support it securely on jackstands.

3   Remove the front wheels. Work on one brake assembly at a time, using the assembled brake for reference if necessary.

4   Inspect the brake disc carefully as outlined in Section 5. If machining is necessary, follow the information in that Section to

remove the disc, at which time the pads can be removed from the calipers as well.

5   Follow the accompanying photos, beginning with **illustration 3.5a**, for the pad removal procedure. Be sure to stay in order and read the caption under each illustration.

3.5g Remove the inner brake pad . . .

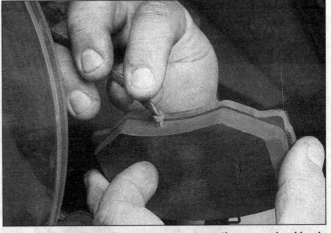

3.5h . . . and pull out the wear sensor, trace the sensor lead back to its connector, cut any cable ties attaching it to the suspension, unplug it and discard it

3.5i Remove the caliper guide pins and boots
(lower pin and boot shown) . . .

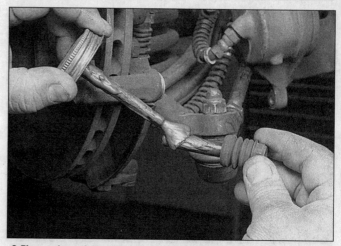

3.5j . . . clean them off with a clean rag, inspect the pin and boot
for damage, replace as necessary, then lubricate the pins with
silicone-based grease and reinstall them in the caliper bracket

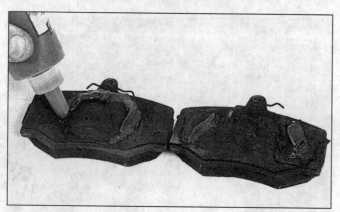

3.5k Apply anti-squeal compound to the new brake pads

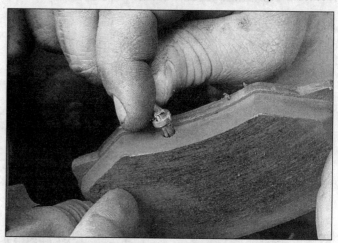

3.5l Insert the new wear sensor into the inner pad as shown . . .

6   Be sure to buy new pads with wear sensors. Some aftermarket
pads may not be equipped with wear sensors; installing pads without
wear sensors will cause the warning light on the dash to come on.
7   To install the new pads, reverse the removal procedure. When
reinstalling the caliper, be sure to tighten the mounting bolts to the
torque listed in this Chapter's Specifications.
8   After the job is completed, depress the brake pedal a few times to
bring the pads into contact with the discs. The pedal should be at nor-

mal height above the floorpan and firm. Check the brake fluid level and
add enough to top it up (see Chapter 1). Inspect carefully for leaks and
check the operation of the brakes before placing the vehicle into normal service.
9   Be sure to tighten the lug nuts to the torque listed in the Chapter 1
Specifications.

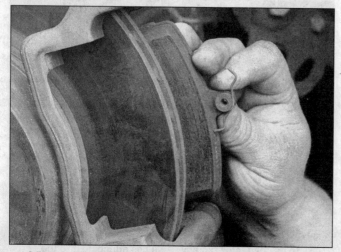

3.5m . . . then install the inner pad onto the caliper bracket

3.5n Install the outer pad

3.5o Install the caliper and the caliper mounting bolts, then tighten the bolts to the torque listed in this Chapter's Specifications

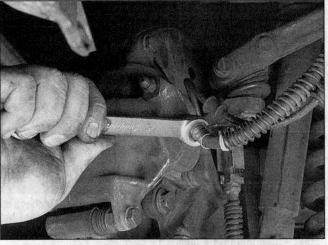

4.2 Use a flare-nut wrench to protect the brake hose fitting when unscrewing it from the caliper

4 Disc brake caliper - removal, overhaul and installation

Warning: *Dust created by the brake system may contain asbestos, which is harmful to your health. Never blow it out with compressed air and don't inhale any of it. An approved filtering mask should be worn when working on the brakes. Do not, under any circumstances, use petroleum-based solvents to clean brake parts. Use brake system cleaner only!*

Note 1: *The following procedure applies to both front and rear calipers.*

Note 2: *If an overhaul is indicated (usually because of fluid leakage), explore all options before beginning the job. New and factory rebuilt calipers are available on an exchange basis, which makes this job quite easy. If you decide to rebuild the calipers, make sure that a rebuild kit is available before proceeding. Always rebuild the calipers in pairs - never rebuild just one of them.*

Removal

Refer to illustration 4.2

1   Loosen the wheel lug nuts, raise the front or rear of the vehicle and place it securely on jackstands. Remove the wheel.

2   If you're just removing the caliper for access to other components, it isn't necessary to detach the brake line. If you're removing the caliper for overhaul, detach the hose from the metal line at the frame bracket (see Section 8), then disconnect the brake line from the caliper with a flare-nut wrench to protect the fitting **(see illustration)**. Plug the

metal line to keep contaminants out of the brake system and to prevent losing brake fluid.

3   Refer to **illustration 3.5c** and unbolt the front or rear caliper.

Overhaul

Refer to illustrations 4.5 and 4.7

4   Before you remove the piston, place a wood block between the piston and caliper to prevent damage as it is removed.

5   To remove the piston from the caliper, apply compressed air to the brake fluid hose connection on the caliper body **(see illustration)**. Use only enough pressure to ease the piston out of its bore. **Warning:** *Be careful not to place your fingers between the piston and the caliper as the piston may come out with some force. Be sure to wear eye protection when using compressed air.* Remove the dust boot.

6   Inspect the mating surfaces of the piston and caliper bore wall. If there is any scoring, rust, pitting or bright areas, replace the complete caliper unit with a new one.

7   If these components are in good condition, remove the piston seal from the caliper bore using a wooden or plastic tool **(see illustration)**. Metal tools may damage the cylinder bore.

8   Remove the caliper guide pins and the rubber dust boots from the caliper bracket.

9   Wash all the components in brake system cleaner.

10   Using the correct rebuild kit for your vehicle, reassemble the caliper as follows.

4.5 With the caliper padded to catch the piston, use compressed air to force the piston out of its bore - make sure your fingers are not between the piston and the caliper

4.7 Remove the piston seal from the caliper bore using a wooden or plastic tool (metal tools may damage the cylinder bore)

5.3 The brake pads on this vehicle were obviously neglected, as they wore down to the rivets and cut deep grooves into the disc - wear this severe means the disc must be replaced

5.4a To check disc runout, mount a dial indicator as shown and rotate the disc

5.4b Using a swirling motion, remove the glaze from the disc surface with sandpaper or emery cloth

11   Submerge the new rubber seal in clean brake fluid and install it in the lower groove in the caliper bore, making sure it isn't twisted.
12   Coat the piston with clean brake fluid and stretch the new dust boot over the bottom of the piston. Hold the piston over the caliper bore and insert the rubber flange of the dust boot into the upper groove in the bore. Start with the side farthest from you and work your way around toward the front until it is completely seated. Push the piston into the caliper bore until it is bottomed in the bore, then seat the top of the dust boot in the groove in the piston.
13   Lubricate the sliding surfaces of the guide pins with silicone-based grease (usually supplied in the kit), then install the new dust boots and pins into the caliper bracket.

Installation

14   Install the caliper by reversing the removal procedure (see Section 3).
15   If the brake hose was disconnected from the caliper, bleed the brake system (see Section 9).

---

5   Brake disc - inspection, removal and installation

Note: *The following procedure applies to both the front and rear brake discs.*

Inspection

Refer to illustrations 5.3, 5.4a, 5.4b, 5.5a and 5.5b
1   Loosen the wheel lug nuts, raise the vehicle and support it securely on jackstands. Remove the wheel and install three lug nuts to

hold the disc in place. If the rear brake disc is being worked on, release the parking brake.
2   Remove the brake caliper as outlined in Section 4. It is not necessary to disconnect the brake hose. After removing the caliper, suspend it out of the way with a piece of wire.
3   Visually inspect the disc surface for scoring or damage. Light scratches and shallow grooves are normal after use and may not always be detrimental to brake operation, but deep scoring - over 0.015 inch - requires disc removal and refinishing by an automotive machine shop. Be sure to check both sides of the disc **(see illustration)**. If pulsating has been noticed during application of the brakes, suspect disc runout.
4   To check disc runout, place a dial indicator at a point about 1/2-inch from the outer edge of the disc **(see illustration)**. Set the indicator to zero and turn the disc. The indicator reading should not exceed the specified allowable runout limit. If it does, the disc should be refinished by an automotive machine shop. **Note:** *It is recommended that the discs be resurfaced regardless of the dial indicator reading, as this will impart a smooth finish and ensure a perfectly flat surface, eliminating any brake pedal pulsation or other undesirable symptoms related to questionable discs. At the very least, if you elect not to have the discs resurfaced, remove the glazing from the surface with emery cloth or sandpaper using a swirling motion* **(see illustration)**.
5   It is absolutely critical that the disc not be machined to a thickness under the specified minimum allowable thickness. The disc thickness can be checked with a micrometer **(see illustration)**. Then compare your measurement to the minimum wear (or discard) thickness stamped into the hub of the disc after the disc is removed **(see illustration)**.

5.5a The disc thickness can be checked with a micrometer

5.5b Compare your measurement with the minimum thickness stamped into the disc

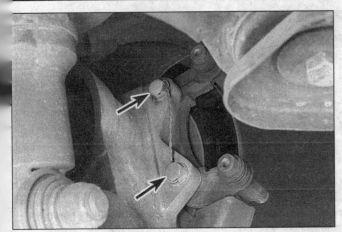

5.6a Before you can remove the caliper mounting bracket bolts (arrows) and the bracket, you'll have to cut the safety wire between them with a pair of diagonal cutters (rear bracket shown)

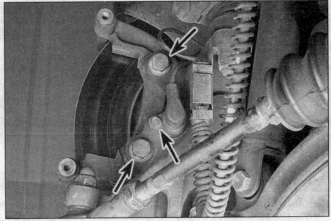

5.6b On front caliper brackets, remove the ABS wheel speed sensor bolt (center arrow) and pull out the sensor before removing the bracket bolts (upper and lower arrows) and bracket

Removal

Refer to illustrations 5.6a, 5.6b, 5.7a, 5.7b and 5.7c

6   Cut the safety wire from the caliper bracket mounting bolts **(see illustration)**. On front caliper brackets, remove the ABS wheel speed sensor **(see illustration)**, then remove the caliper bracket bolts and remove the bracket.

7   Remove the disc retaining screw **(see illustration)** and remove the disc from the hub. If the disc sticks, give it a few sharp raps with a hammer **(see illustration)**. If the disc is stuck to the hub, spray a generous amount of penetrant onto the area between the hub and the disc and allow the penetrant a few minutes to loosen the rust between the two components. If a rear disc still sticks, insert a thin, flat-bladed screwdriver or brake adjusting tool through the hub flange, rotate the star wheel on the parking brake adjusting screw and contract the parking brake shoes **(see illustration)**.

Installation

8   Place the disc on the hub and install the disc retaining screw. Tighten the screw securely.

9   Install the caliper mounting bracket, tightening the bolts to the torque listed in this Chapter's Specifications. Install new safety wire.

10   Install the brake pads and caliper (see Section 3). Tighten all fasteners to the torque listed in this Chapter's Specifications.

11   Install the wheel and lug nuts, then lower the vehicle to the ground. Tighten the lug nuts to the torque listed in the Chapter 1 Specifications. Depress the brake pedal a few times to bring the brake pads into contact with the disc.

12   Adjust the parking brake shoes, if necessary.

13   Check the operation of the brakes carefully before placing the vehicle into normal service.

6   Master cylinder - removal, overhaul and installation

Caution: *The following procedure applies to 1988 and 1989 models only. 1990 and later models do not use a conventional master cylinder, rather a complete hydraulic actuating unit incorporating a master cylinder, valve block and power booster is used. Do not attempt to separate the master cylinder section from the power booster section; if necessary, replace the complete assembly following the procedure described in Section 7.*
Note: *Although master cylinder parts and rebuild kits are available for most models, we recommend replacing the master cylinder with a new or remanufactured unit, if possible.*

Removal

Refer to illustrations 6.4, 6.5 and 6.6

1   The master cylinder is connected to the power brake booster, which is attached to the pedal box, in front of the firewall on the

5.7a Using an impact driver, if necessary, remove the disc retaining screw, then remove the disc from the hub

5.7b If the disc is stuck to the hub, give it a few sharp raps with a hammer; if that doesn't work, spray some penetrant onto the area between the hub and the disc, give the penetrant a few minutes to dissolve the rust between the two parts, then try again

5.7c If a rear disc still sticks to the hub, insert a thin, flat-bladed screwdriver or brake adjuster tool through the hub flange, rotate the star wheel on the parking brake adjusting screw and retract the parking brake shoes

6.4 Trace the electrical lead back from the reservoir cap and disconnect the low fluid level sensor

6.5 Loosen the hydraulic brake line fittings with a flare-nut wrench to protect the corners of the nuts

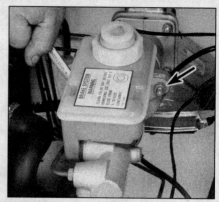

6.6 Remove the two master cylinder mounting nuts

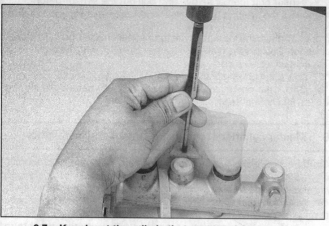

6.7a Knock out the roll pin that secures the reservoir to the master cylinder

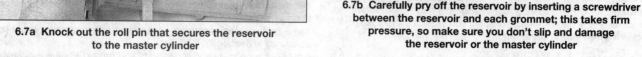
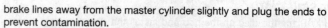

6.7b Carefully pry off the reservoir by inserting a screwdriver between the reservoir and each grommet; this takes firm pressure, so make sure you don't slip and damage the reservoir or the master cylinder

driver's side of the engine compartment.

2   Remove as much fluid as you can from the reservoir with a syringe.

3   Place rags under the line fittings and prepare caps or plastic bags to cover the ends of the lines once they are disconnected. **Caution: Brake fluid will damage paint. Cover all body parts and be careful not to spill fluid during this procedure.**

4   Disconnect the electrical connector for the low fluid level warning light **(see illustration)**.

5   Loosen the brake line fittings at the master cylinder **(see illustration)**. Use a flare-nut wrench to prevent rounding off the nuts. Pull the

brake lines away from the master cylinder slightly and plug the ends to prevent contamination.

6   Remove the nuts attaching the master cylinder to the power booster **(see illustration)**. Pull the master cylinder off the studs and lift it out of the engine compartment. Again, be careful not to spill fluid as this is done.

Overhaul

Refer to illustrations 6.7a through 6.7v

7   Follow the accompanying photo sequence, beginning with **illustration 6.7a**. Stay in order, don't skip steps, read each caption and study the photo carefully.

6.7c Remove the grommets

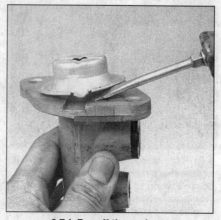

6.7d Pry off the end cap

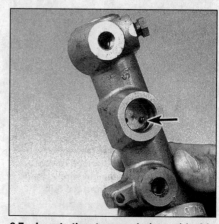

6.7e Locate the stopper pin (arrow) inside the forward grommet hole . . .

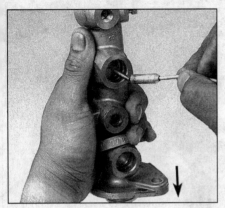

6.7f . . . insert a punch into the pocket of the primary piston, place the master cylinder and punch vertically as shown, push down on the master cylinder to depress the pistons and pull out the stopper pin with a magnet

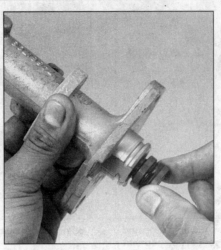

6.7g Remove the primary piston

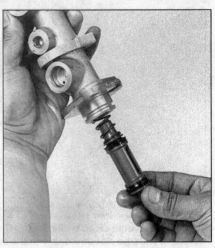

6.7h Remove the secondary piston

6.7i If the secondary piston is stuck, rap the master cylinder on a wood block to dislodge it

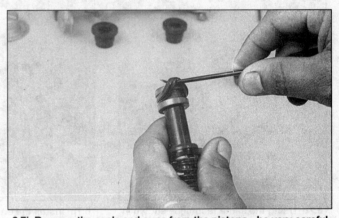

6.7j Remove the seals and cups from the pistons - be very careful not to scratch the piston surface - then wash the secondary piston with clean brake fluid and inspect it; if the secondary piston is damaged, you must replace the master cylinder with a new or rebuilt unit (a new primary piston is included with the rebuild kit)

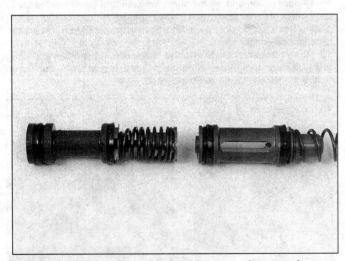

6.7k Install the new O-ring seals and cups as shown; make sure the cups on the primary piston (the one on the left) face forward as shown (toward the spring), and the cups on the secondary piston (the one on the right) face out, away from the piston (the one on the left faces toward the primary piston, the one on the right faces toward the spring)

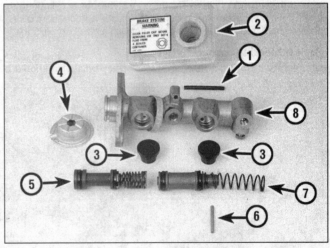

6.7l The master cylinder assembly

1	Roll pin	6	Secondary piston
2	Reservoir		stopper pin
3	Grommets	7	Secondary piston
4	End plate	8	Master cylinder body
5	Primary piston		

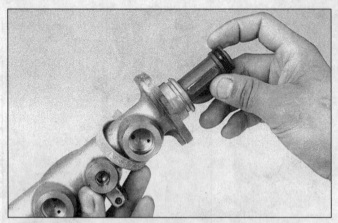

6.7m Apply some clean brake fluid to the secondary piston and install it with the slot oriented with the stopper pin hole, so that the stopper pin will go through the slot

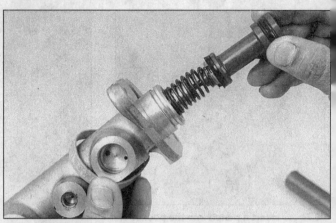

6.7n Apply a coat of clean brake fluid to the primary piston and install it into the bore

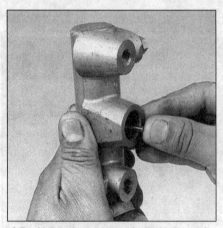

6.7o Using the same technique shown in illustration 6.7f, depress the pistons and install the stopper pin

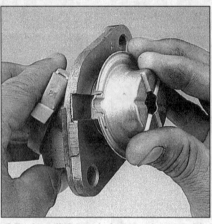

6.7p Install the end plate as shown, with the bend in the plate flange aligned with the groove in the master cylinder flange

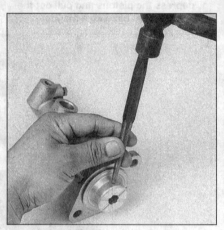

6.7q Using a hammer and punch, stake the end plate as shown (there's a dimple in the side of the plate for this purpose)

8   Once you have disassembled the master cylinder, clean everything thoroughly, blow the parts dry with compressed air and carefully inspect the secondary piston and the bore of the master cylinder with a bright light. If the secondary piston or the master cylinder bore is damaged or worn, replace the master cylinder with a new or rebuilt unit.

Bench bleeding procedure

9   Before installing a new or rebuilt master cylinder it should be bench bled. Because it will be necessary to apply pressure to the master cylinder piston and, at the same time, control flow from the brake line outlets, it is recommended that the master cylinder be mounted in a vise. Use caution not to clamp the vise too tightly, or the master cylinder body might crack.

10   Insert threaded plugs into the brake line outlet holes and snug them down so that there will be no air leakage past them, but not so tight that they cannot be easily loosened.

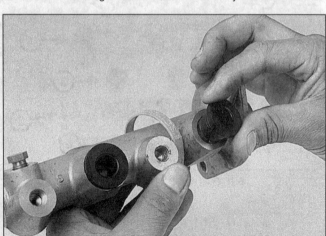

6.7r Install the grommets

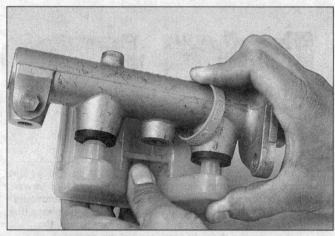

6.7s Align the reservoir pipes with the grommets as shown . . .

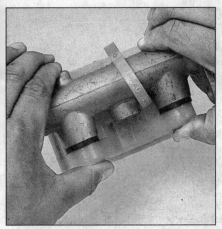

6.7t . . . and squeeze the reservoir and master cylinder together; make sure the reservoir is fully seated

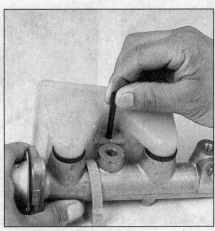

6.7u Install the reservoir roll pin . . .

6.7v . . . and tap it into place

11   Fill the reservoir with brake fluid of the recommended type (see *Recommended lubricants and fluids* in Chapter 1).

12   Remove one plug and push the piston assembly into the master cylinder bore to expel the air from the master cylinder. A large Phillips screwdriver can be used to push on the piston assembly.

13   To prevent air from being drawn back into the master cylinder, the plug must be replaced and tightened before releasing the pressure on the piston assembly.

14   Repeat the procedure until only brake fluid is expelled from the brake line outlet hole. When only brake fluid is expelled, repeat the procedure with the other outlet hole and plug. Be sure to keep the master cylinder reservoir filled with brake fluid to prevent the introduction of air into the system.

15   Since high pressure is not involved in the bench bleeding procedure, an alternative to the removal and replacement of the plugs with each stroke of the piston assembly is available. Before pushing in on the piston assembly, remove the plug as described in Step 12. Before releasing the piston, however, instead of replacing the plug, simply put your finger tightly over the hole to keep air from being drawn back into the master cylinder. Wait several seconds for brake fluid to be drawn from the reservoir into the piston bore, then depress the piston again, removing your finger as brake fluid is expelled. Be sure to put your finger back over the hole each time before releasing the piston, and when the bleeding procedure is complete for that outlet, replace the plug and snug it up before going on to the other port.

Installation

16   Install the master cylinder over the studs on the power brake

7.5 Use a flare-nut wrench to loosen the fittings, then pull the lines back from the power brake booster and plug them to prevent contamination

booster and tighten the mounting nuts only finger tight at this time.

17   Thread the brake line fittings into the master cylinder. Since the master cylinder is still a bit loose, it can be moved slightly to allow the fitting threads to start easily. Do not strip the threads as the fittings are tightened.

18   Tighten the brake fittings securely and the mounting nuts to the torque listed in this Chapter's Specifications.

19   Fill the master cylinder reservoir with fluid, then bleed the master cylinder and the brake system (see Section 9).

20   To bleed the master cylinder on the vehicle, have an assistant pump the brake pedal several times and then hold the pedal to the floor. Loosen the fitting nut to allow air and fluid to escape, then tighten the nut. Repeat this procedure on both fittings until the fluid is clear of air bubbles. Test the operation of the brake system carefully before placing the vehicle into service.

7   Power brake booster - general information, removal and installation

General information

1   A hydraulic brake booster system assists braking when the brake pedal is depressed. The booster unit, located between the brake pedal box and the master cylinder, is operated by hydraulic pressure generated by an engine-driven pump (on early models) or by an electric pump (on later models). When the engine is running, the pump supplies hydraulic pressure to an accumulator. The accumulator stores and regulates the pressure to the hydraulic brake booster. When you depress the brake pedal, the pressure in the booster helps actuate the master cylinder, reducing pedal effort.

2   The hydraulic brake booster isn't rebuildable; if it fails, it must be replaced. Basic operation can be checked (see Chapter 1, Section 15), but in-depth testing of the system requires special tools, so troubleshooting is beyond the scope of the home mechanic. If the system fails, take it to a dealer service department or other qualified repair shop for repairs. However, if the unit must be replaced, you can do it yourself as follows.

Removal and installation

Refer to illustrations 7.5, 7.6 and 7.7

3   With the engine off, discharge the hydraulic accumulator by depressing the brake pedal several times until it feels hard to depress.

4   Remove the master cylinder (see Section 6).

5   Clean the area around the return and supply tube nuts, then disconnect them with a flare-nut wrench **(see illustration)** and plug the lines to prevent contamination from entering the system. **Caution:** *Even a particle of dirt can damage the booster system, so be extremely*

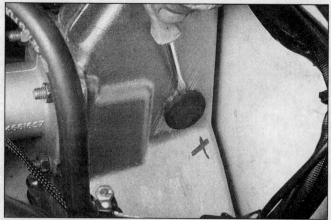

7.6 Pry off the two rubber caps from the pedal box

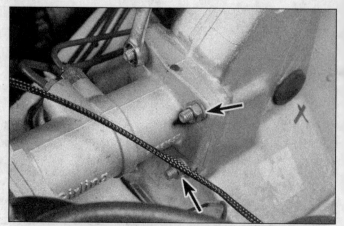

7.7 To detach the power brake booster from the pedal box, remove these four nuts (arrows) (lower right nut not visible in this photo)

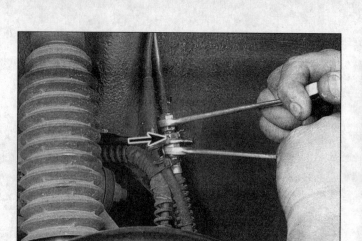

8.3a To remove a front flexible brake hose from a metal brake line, use a back-up wrench to hold the hose fitting just below the bracket (lower wrench), then break loose the nut on the metal line (upper wrench); to disconnect the flex hose from the bracket, remove the center nut (arrow) just above the bracket

8.3b The connection (arrow) for the rear hose and line is located right above the mounting bracket for the front corner of the differential crossmember; remove the hose as described in the previous illustration

careful to prevent dirt from entering the system while the lines are disconnected.

6   To disconnect the power brake booster pushrod from the brake pedal, remove the access plugs from both sides of the pedal box **(see illustration)**, remove the clevis pin retaining clip and drive out the clevis pin.

7   Remove the four mounting nuts and remove the brake booster **(see illustration)**.

8   Installation is the reverse of removal. Tighten the hydraulic line fittings securely.

9   On 1990 and later models, fill the fluid reservoir to the MAX mark, then turn the ignition key On. After the motor switches off, top-up the reservoir to the MAX mark.

10   When you're done, adjust the brake light switch (see Section 13).

8   Brake hoses and lines - inspection and replacement

Inspection

1   About every six months, with the vehicle raised and placed securely on jackstands, the flexible hoses which connect the steel brake lines with the front and rear brake assemblies should be inspected for cracks, chafing of the outer cover, leaks, blisters and other damage. These are important and vulnerable parts of the brake system and inspection should be complete. A light and mirror will

prove helpful for a thorough check. If a hose exhibits any of the above conditions, replace it with a new one.

Flexible hose replacement

Refer to illustrations 8.3a and 8.3b

2   Clean all dirt away from the ends of the hose.

3   To disconnect the hose at the frame end, use a backup wrench on the hex-shaped fitting on the end of the flexible hose and loosen the nut on the metal brake line **(see illustrations)**. If the nut is stuck, soak it with penetrating oil. After the hose is disconnected from the metal line, remove the nut right above the bracket and detach the hose from the bracket.

4   To detach the flexible hose from the caliper, simply unscrew it.

5   Installation is the reverse of the removal procedure. Make sure the brackets are in good condition and the locknuts are tightened securely.

6   Carefully check to make sure the suspension and steering components do not make contact with the hoses. Have an assistant push on the vehicle and also turn the steering wheel from lock-to-lock during inspection.

7   Bleed the brake system as described in Section 9.

Metal brake line replacement

8   When replacing brake lines, use the proper parts only. Do not use copper line for any brake system connections. Purchase steel brake lines from a dealer or an auto parts store.

9.9 When bleeding the brakes, a hose is connected to the bleed screw at the caliper or wheel cylinder and then submerged in brake fluid - air will be seen as bubbles in the tube and container (all air must be expelled before moving to the next brake)

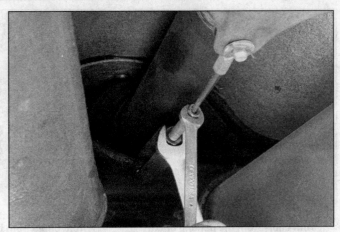

10.3 To adjust the parking brake cable, loosen the locknut, then turn the adjuster to remove any slack in the cable; be sure to tighten the locknut when the cable is properly adjusted

9   Unless you're using factory replacement brake lines, you may need a tubing bender to bend the lines to the proper shape.
10   First, remove the line you intend to replace, lay it on a clean workbench and measure it carefully. Obtain a new line of the same length and bend it to match the pattern of the old line. **Warning:** *Do not crimp or damage the line.* No bend should have a smaller radius than 9/16-inch. Make sure the protective coating on the new line is undamaged at the bends.
11   When installing the new line, make sure it's well supported by the brackets, the routing matches the original and there's plenty of clearance between moving or hot components.
12   After installation, check the master cylinder fluid level and add fluid as necessary. Bleed the brake system as outlined in Section 9 and test the brakes carefully before driving the vehicle. Be sure there are no leaks.

9   Brake hydraulic system - bleeding

Refer to illustration 9.9
Warning: *Wear eye protection when bleeding the brake system. If the fluid comes in contact with your eyes, immediately rinse them with water and seek medical attention.*
Note: *Bleeding the hydraulic system is necessary to remove any air which has entered the system during removal and installation of a hose, line, caliper or master cylinder.*
1   It will probably be necessary to bleed the system at all four brakes if air has entered the system due to low fluid level or if the brake lines have been disconnected at the master cylinder.
2   If a brake line was disconnected at only one wheel, then only that caliper or wheel cylinder must be bled.
3   If a brake line is disconnected at a fitting located between the master cylinder and any of the brakes, that part of the system served by the disconnected line must be bled.
4   Bleed the right rear, the left rear, the right front and the left front caliper, in that order, when the entire system is involved.
5   Discharge the pressure from the power brake booster and anti-lock brake system pressure (if equipped) by applying the brake about 30 times with the engine off.
6   Remove the master cylinder reservoir cover and fill the reservoir with brake fluid. Reinstall the cover. **Note:** *Check the fluid level often during the bleeding operation and add fluid as necessary to prevent the fluid level from falling low enough to allow air into the master cylinder.*
7   Have an assistant on hand, as well as a supply of new brake fluid, an empty clear plastic container, a length of 3/16-inch clear plastic or vinyl tubing to fit over the bleeder screws and a wrench to open and close the bleeder screws.

8   Beginning at the right rear wheel, loosen the bleeder screw slightly, then tighten it to a point where it is snug but can still be loosened quickly and easily.
9   Place one end of the tubing over the bleeder valve and submerge the other end in brake fluid in the container **(see illustration)**.
10   On 1988 and 1989 models, have your assistant pump the brakes a few times to build pressure in the system, then hold the pedal firmly depressed. While the pedal is depressed, open the bleeder screw just enough to allow fluid to flow from the caliper. Watch for air bubbles to exit the submerged end of the tube. When the fluid flow slows, close the screw and have your assistant release the pedal. Repeat the procedure until no air is observed leaving the tubing, tighten the bleeder screw. Proceed to the left rear wheel, the right front wheel and the left front wheel, in that order and perform the same procedure at each wheel. Be sure to check the fluid in the master cylinder reservoir frequently.
11   To bleed the rear brakes on 1990 and later models, have your assistant depress the brake pedal and hold it down. Open the bleeder screw and have your assistant turn the ignition key On. The pump motor should pump fluid out at a steady rate, when no air is observed leaving the tubing, tighten the bleeder screw. Have your assistant, slowly release the brake pedal and turn the ignition key Off. Proceed to the left rear wheel and perform the same procedure. Be sure to check the fluid in the master cylinder reservoir. **Caution:** *Do not allow the pump motor to run for longer than two minutes at a time. If further bleeding is required, allow the pump motor to cool for a minimum of ten minutes before proceeding.*
12   Bleed the front brakes on 1990 and later models, in the same manner as 1988 and 1989 models (see Step 10).
13   Never reuse old brake fluid. It contains contaminates and moisture which could damage the brake system.
14   Refill the master cylinder with fluid at the end of the operation.
15   Check the operation of the brakes. The pedal should feel solid when depressed, with no sponginess. If necessary, repeat the entire process. **Warning:** *Do not operate the vehicle if you are in doubt about the effectiveness of the brake system.*

10   Parking brake cable - adjustment

Refer to illustration 10.3
1   Slowly apply the parking brake and count the number of clicks at the lever. It should be fully applied within three to five clicks. If the lever is still not fully applied by the fifth click, adjust the parking brake cable as follows:
2   Raise the vehicle and place it securely on jackstands.
3   Loosen the locknut **(see illustration)** and tighten the cable adjuster until all slack has been removed. Tighten the locknut. Make sure the wheels turn freely with the parking brake lever released

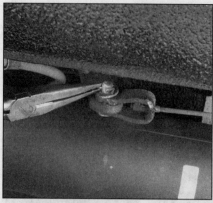

11.2 To disconnect the forward end of the front cable from the parking brake lever, remove this cotter pin, washer and clevis pin

11.3 To disconnect the rear end of the front cable from the adjuster lever, remove this cotter pin, washer and clevis pin (arrow)

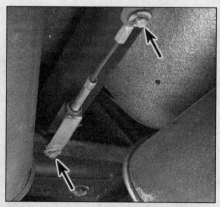

11.5 To disconnect the intermediate cable, remove the cotter pins, washers and clevis pins (arrows) from the adjuster lever and the yoke

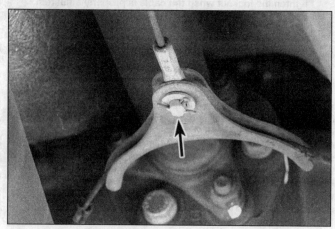

11.7 To disconnect the rear cables and yoke from the intermediate cable, remove this cotter pin, washer and clevis pin (arrow)

11.8 The rear parking brake cable-to-parking brake shoe connection is hidden behind the lower part of the brake backing plate, on the underside of the carrier (this view is looking straight up from underneath the carrier). To disconnect either rear parking brake cable, swing this clip (arrow) to the side and remove it - the rear cable is now disconnected

4   Lower the vehicle and recheck the parking brake lever. It should now be properly adjusted. If it's now fully applied within three to five clicks, raise the vehicle again and readjust the cable at the adjuster.

5   Make sure the parking brake holds the vehicle on an incline.

11 Parking brake cable(s) - replacement

1   Raise the vehicle and place it securely on jackstands.

Front cable

Refer to illustrations 11.2 and 11.3

2   Remove the cotter pin, washer and clevis pin from the forward end of the front cable **(see illustration)**. Disconnect the forward end of the front cable from the parking brake lever.

3   Follow the cable back to the adjuster lever and remove the cotter, washer and clevis pin **(see illustration)**. Remove the front cable.

4   Installation is the reverse of removal.

Intermediate cable

Refer to illustration 11.5

5   Remove the cotter pins, washers and clevis pin from both ends of the intermediate cable **(see illustration)**. Remove the cable.

6   Installation is the reverse of removal.

Rear cables

Refer to illustrations 11.7 and 11.8

7   Remove the cotter pin, washer and clevis pin from the intermedi-

ate cable-to-rear cable yoke **(see illustration)**.

8   Disconnect the rear end of each cable from the parking brake assembly **(see illustration)**., then pry the cable out of the carrier.

9   Installation is the reverse of removal.

All cables

10   Be sure to adjust the parking brake cable when you're done (see Section 10). The rear wheels should turn freely with the parking brake lever released.

11   Remove the jackstands and lower the vehicle. Apply the parking brake lever, make sure it's fully applied within three to five clicks and that it holds the vehicle on an incline. If it doesn't, readjust it (see Section 10).

12 Parking brake shoes - check and replacement

Warning: *Dust created by the brake system may contain asbestos, which is harmful to your health. Never blow it out with compressed air and don't inhale any of it. An approved filtering mask should be worn when working on the brakes. Do not, under any circumstances, use petroleum-based solvents to clean brake parts. Use brake system cleaner only!*

12.5a Wash down the parking brake assembly with
brake cleaner before disassembly

12.5b Back off the star wheel on the adjuster, then disengage the
adjuster mechanism from the parking brake shoes

12.5c Remove the front hold-down spring, washers and pin; note
that one washer goes below the spring and one above it

12.5d Remove the rear hold-down spring, washers and pin; put
the parts in a plastic bag so you don't lose them

Check

1   The parking brake system should be checked as a normal part of
driving. With the vehicle parked on a hill, apply the brake, place the
transmission in Neutral and check that the parking brake alone will
hold the vehicle (be sure to stay in the vehicle during this check). However, every 24 months (or whenever a fault is suspected), the assembly
itself should be visually inspected.
2   Loosen the wheel lug nuts, raise the rear of the vehicle and place
it securely on jackstands. Remove the rear wheels.
3   Remove the rear brake calipers and discs (see Sections 3, 4 and 5).
Support the caliper assemblies with a coat hanger or heavy wire and
do not disconnect the brake line from the caliper.
4   With the disc removed, the parking brake components are visible
and can be inspected for wear and damage. The linings should last the
life of the vehicle. However, they can wear down if the parking brake
system has been improperly adjusted. There is no minimum thickness
specification for the parking brake shoes, but as a rule of thumb, if the
shoe material is less 1/32-inch thick, you should replace them. Also
check the springs and adjuster mechanism and inspect the drum for
deep scratches and other damage.

Replacement

Refer to illustrations 12.5a through 12.5r

5   Loosen the wheel lug nuts, raise the rear of the vehicle and place
it securely on jackstands. Remove the rear wheels. Remove the brake

discs (see Section 5). Follow the accompanying photo sequence
beginning with **illustration 12.5a**. Work on only one side at a time, so
you can use the other side as a reference during reassembly.
6   Installation is the reverse of removal.

12.5e Push the shoes together and disengage the upper return
spring from the rear shoe . . .

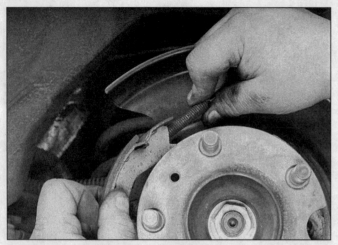

12.5f . . . and from the front shoe

12.5g Pull the shoes apart and remove them with the lower spring attached as shown, then disengage the lower return spring from both shoes

7   After installing the brake disc, adjust the parking brake shoes. Temporarily install two lug nuts, turn the adjuster **(see illustration 5.7c)** and expand the shoes until the disc locks, then back off the adjuster until you can spin the disc without the shoes dragging.

8   Adjust the parking brake cable (see Section 10).
9   Remove the jackstands and lower the vehicle. Tighten the lug nuts to the torque listed in the Chapter 1 Specifications.

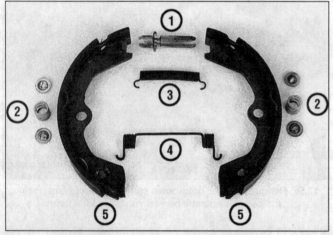

12.5h The parking brake shoe assembly

1	Adjuster	3	Upper return spring
2	Hold down springs and washers	4	Lower return spring
		5	Parking brake shoes

12.5i Lubricate the six friction points on the backing plate with high-temperature grease

12.5j Place the front shoe in position, insert the pin through the backing plate and the shoe . . .

12.5k . . . and install the hold-down spring and washers

12.5l Hook the lower return spring into its hole in the front shoe . . .

12.5m . . . hook the other end of the lower spring
into the rear shoe . . .

12.5n . . . stretch the spring over the top of the
parking brake lever box . . .

12.5o . . . place the rear shoe in position, insert the pin through
the backing plate and the shoe and install the
rear washers and hold-down spring

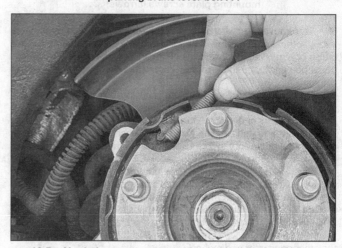

12.5p Hook the upper return spring into the front shoe . . .

13 Brake light switch - check and replacement

Refer to illustrations 13.6a, 13.6b, 13.7a, 13.7b and 13.8

1   The brake light switch activates the brake lights when the brake pedal is depressed. It's located at the top of the brake pedal, inside the pedal box.

2   If the brake lights don't come on when the brake pedal is depressed, check the fuses (the fuse for the left brake light is in the left fuse panel and the fuse for the right brake light is in the right panel).

3   If the fuses are okay, check the brake light bulbs (see Chapter 12).

4   If the fuses and bulbs are okay, either the switch isn't getting voltage (there's an open circuit between the voltage source and the switch), voltage isn't reaching the brake light bulbs (open circuit between the switch and the bulbs), or the switch is defective.

12.5q . . . and into the rear shoe

12.5r Pull the shoes apart and install the adjuster mechanism

13.6a To remove the brake light switch, remove the three mounting plate screws (arrows) . . .

13.6b . . . and carefully pry the switch plate away from the pedal box - be careful not to damage the gasket

5   To remove the switch, reach up under the dash and unplug the two electrical connectors - one for the brake lights and one for the cruise control system. Locate the two pairs of leads coming down the pedal box and trace them to their connectors on or near the steering column.

6   Remove the three switch-plate retaining bolts and remove the switch assembly **(see illustrations)**. Inspect the switch-plate rubber gasket for cracks or deterioration and replace it if it's damaged or worn.

7   Place the switch assembly on a workbench and connect an ohmmeter to the brake light switch terminals. With the switch plunger in its normal, extended position (brake pedal not applied), there should be no continuity (infinite resistance) **(see illustration)**; when the plunger is depressed (brake pedal applied), there should be continuity (zero resistance) **(see illustration)**. If the switch doesn't perform as described, replace it. If the switch performs in an opposite fashion, i.e. continuity when the plunger is free, no continuity when the plunger is depressed, you've tested the cruise control switch! Switch the ohmmeter leads to the other connector and recheck.

8   To remove the switch from the plate, remove the two small nuts on the back of the plate **(see illustration)**.

9   Install the switch assembly and the switch plate bolts but don't tighten the bolts yet.

10   Plug in the brake light and cruise control connectors.

11   The holes in the switch plate are slotted for adjustment. While an assistant presses the brake pedal, verify that the brake lights come on; with the pedal released, make sure the brake lights are off. If the lights don't come on when the pedal is depressed, or stay on when the pedal

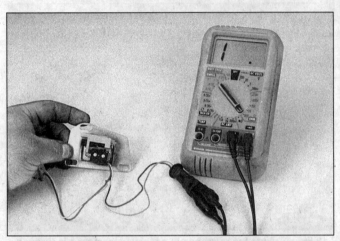

13.7a To check the brake light switch, connect the leads of an ohmmeter to the terminals of the brake light switch connector (red connector on this particular switch); with the switch plunger released, there should be no continuity (infinite resistance)

is released, adjust the switch by moving the plate until proper operation is achieved. Tighten the switch-plate bolts securely.

12   After tightening the switch-plate bolts, check the switch again to make sure it performs properly.

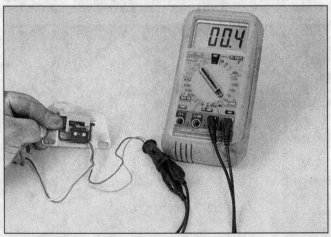

13.7b With the switch plunger depressed, there should be continuity (zero resistance)

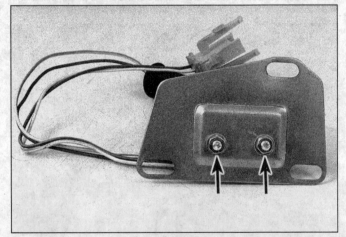

13.8 If you're replacing the switch, remove these two nuts (arrows) and transfer the retaining plate to the new switch

Chapter 10
Suspension and steering systems

Contents

Specifications

General

Power steering fluid type .... See Chapter 1

Torque specifications

	Nm	Ft-lbs
Front suspension		
Balljoints		
Retaining bolts	55 to 62	41 to 45
Ball stud nuts	47 to 68	35 to 50
Lower control arm		
Spring pan bolts	26 to 34	19 to 25
Pivot nuts/bolts	43 to 68	32 to 50
Shock absorber		
Lower nut	61 to 68	45 to 50
Upper nut	35 to 43	26 to 31
Stabilizer bar		
Bushing bracket bolts		
Upper	22 to 28	16 to 20
Lower	24 to 30	18 to 22
Link nuts	55 to 60	41 to 44
Upper control arm pivot nuts/bolts	61 to 75	45 to 55

Rear suspension

Carrier-to-control arm bolt/nut	70 to 80	51 to 59
Rear control arm-to-crossmember bolt/nut	85 to 105	62 to 77
Shock absorber/coil spring assembly		
Lower shock-to-control arm bolt/nut	160 to 200	118 to 147
Upper shock-to-body bolts...	22 to 28	16 to 20

Steering system

Steering wheel-to-steering shaft nut	35 to 45	26 to 33
Steering shaft-to-steering gear pinion shaft		
U-joint pinch bolt..	19 to 24	14 to 17
Steering gear mounting bracket bolts/nuts	26 to 29	19 to 21
Tie-rod end-to-steering knuckle nut...	61 to 68	45 to 50

1   General information

Refer to illustrations 1.1a, 1.1b and 1.2
Warning: *Whenever any of the suspension or steering fasteners are loosened or removed, they must be inspected and if necessary, replaced with new ones of the same part number or of original equipment quality and design. Torque specifications must be followed for proper reassembly and component retention. Never attempt to heat, straighten or weld any suspension or steering component. Instead, replace any bent or damaged part with a new one.*

The front suspension **(see illustrations)** consists of unequal-length upper and lower control arms, shock absorbers and coil springs. The upper ends of the shocks are attached to the body; the lower ends are attached to the lower control arms. The upper ends of the coil springs are seated against the suspension crossmember; the lower ends are seated against removable plates which are bolted to the lower control arms. The steering knuckles are attached to balljoints in the upper and lower control arms. A stabilizer bar is attached to the suspension crossmember with a pair of bushing brackets and to the lower control arms via a connecting link at each end.

The independent rear suspension **(see illustration)** uses control arms and integral shock absorber/coil spring units. The upper ends of the shocks are attached to the body; the lower ends are connected to the control arms.

The steering system consists of the steering wheel, a steering column, a universal joint on the lower end of the steering shaft, a rack-and-pinion power steering gear, a power steering pump and a pair of tie-rods which connects the steering gear to the steering knuckles.

1.1a Front suspension and steering systems

1	*Stabilizer bar*	*5*	*Steering knuckles*	*9*	*Steering gear*
2	*Stabilizer bushing brackets*	*6*	*Tie-rod ends*	*10*	*Suspension crossmember*
3	*Stabilizer links*	*7*	*Tie-rods*	*11*	*Lower control arm crossbrace*
4	*Lower control arms*	*8*	*Steering gear boots*		

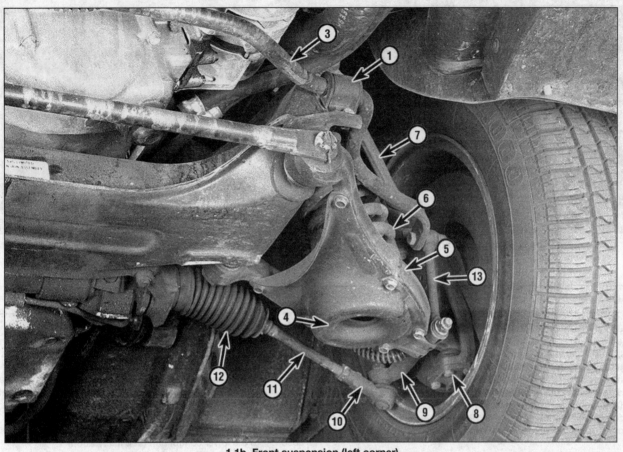

1.1b Front suspension (left corner)

1	Stabilizer bushing bracket	5	Lower control arm	9	Steering knuckle
2	Stabilizer link	6	Coil spring	10	Tie-rod end
3	Stabilizer bar	7	Upper control arm	11	Tie-rod
4	Coil spring pan	8	Lower balljoint	12	Steering gear boot

1.2 Rear suspension

1	Hub carrier	3	Crossmember mounting brackets	4	Crossmember
2	Control arms				

3.2 To detach the stabilizer bar from the suspension crossmember, remove these two bolts (arrows) from each bushing bracket

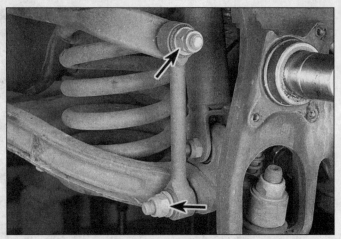

3.3 To disconnect the stabilizer bar from the link, remove the upper nut (arrow); to disconnect the link from the lower control arm, remove the lower nut (arrow)

2   Self-leveling rear suspension system

1988 through 1992 models were equipped with a system that provided hydraulic power for the rear suspension and for the power brakes. As the vehicle is loaded or unloaded, the rear suspension is automatically adjusted to maintain a constant ride height.

The system was discontinued on 1993 and later models, which are equipped with conventional shock absorber/coil spring units. A kit is available from your Jaguar dealer should you decide to retrofit the later, conventional shocks to a pre-1993 vehicle. Complete instructions for installing the kit are included in Section 10.

3   Stabilizer bar (front) - removal and installation

Refer to illustrations 3.2 and 3.3
1   Raise the front of the vehicle and support it securely on jackstands.
2   Remove the bolts from the stabilizer bar brackets that attach the stabilizer bar to the suspension crossmember **(see illustration)**.
3   Remove the nuts that attach the stabilizer to the links **(see illustration)**. If you're replacing the links themselves, or removing the control arm, remove the nuts attaching the links to the lower control arms.
4   Remove the stabilizer bar from the vehicle.
5   Installation is the reverse of the removal procedure. Be sure to tighten all fasteners to the torque listed in this Chapter's Specifications.

4   Shock absorber (front) - removal and installation

Refer to illustrations 4.2, 4.3 and 4.4
Note: *Always replace both left and right shocks at the same time to prevent handling peculiarities and abnormal ride quality.*
1   Loosen but do not remove the front wheel lug nuts. Raise the front of the vehicle and support it on jackstands. Remove the wheels.
2   Support the lower control arm with a floor jack **(see illustration)**. Place a block of wood between the jack head and the control arm to protect the arm and spring plate.
3   Remove the nut and bolt that attach the lower end of the shock absorber to the lower control arm **(see illustration)**.
4   Remove the nut that attaches the upper end of the shock to the body **(see illustration)**.
5   Remove the shock absorber.
6   Installation is the reverse of removal. Tighten the fasteners to the torque listed in this Chapter's Specifications.

5   Balljoints - check and replacement

Check
1   Raise the vehicle and support it securely on jackstands.
2   Visually inspect the rubber boot between the balljoints and the steering knuckle for cuts, tears or leaking grease. If you note any of

4.2 Support the lower control arm with a jack; put a block of wood between the jack head and the control arm to protect the arm and coil spring plate

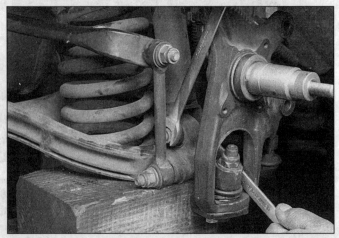

4.3 To disconnect the lower end of the shock absorber from the lower control arm, remove this nut and bolt

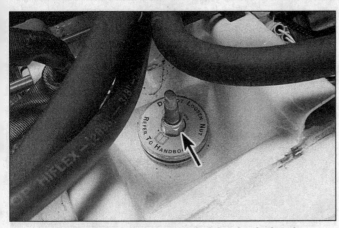

4.4 To disconnect the upper end of the shock absorber from the body, remove this nut (arrow)

5.7 To detach the upper balljoint from the steering knuckle, loosen the ballstud nut, install a small puller and break the ballstud loose from the knuckle

these conditions, replace the balljoint.

3   Place a large prybar between each control arm and the steering knuckle. If you can see or feel any movement during either check, a worn-out balljoint is indicated.

4   Have an assistant grasp the tire at the top and bottom and shake the top of the tire with an in-and-out motion. Touch the balljoint stud nut. If any looseness is felt, suspect a worn-out balljoint stud or a widened hole in the steering knuckle. If the latter problem exists, the steering knuckle should be replaced as well as the balljoint.

Replacement

5   Loosen the wheel lug nuts, raise the vehicle and support it securely on jackstands. Remove the wheel.

6   Support the lower control arm with a floor jack **(see illustration 4.2)**. Place a block of wood between the jack head and the control arm as shown to protect the arm and spring plate.

Upper balljoint

Refer to illustrations 5.7 and 5.8

7   Loosen - but don't remove - the ball stud nut, install a small puller **(see illustration)** and pop the ball stud loose from the steering knuckle.

8   Remove the two bolts that attach the balljoint to the upper arm **(see illustration)**. Count the number of shims installed and set them aside.

9   Installation is the reverse of removal. Don't forget to install the same number of shims. Tighten the bolts to the torque listed in this Chapter's Specifications.

10   Remove the jack from under the control arm, install the front wheel, lower the vehicle and tighten the wheel lug nuts to the torque listed in the Chapter 1 Specifications. Drive the vehicle to an alignment shop to have the wheel alignment checked, and if necessary, adjusted.

5.8 Remove the bolts and shims from the upper balljoint; be sure to put the shims back when installing the new balljoint

Lower balljoint

Refer to illustrations 5.11, 5.12 and 5.13

11   Loosen - but don't remove - the ball stud nut, then give the steering knuckle a few sharp raps with a hammer to pop the ball stud loose **(see illustration)**. Remove the ball stud nut.

12   Remove the four balljoint retaining bolts **(see illustration)**.

13   If the dust boot is damaged, pry it out **(see illustration)**.

14   Remove the balljoint.

5.11 Strike the steering knuckle in this area to pop the lower ball stud loose from the steering knuckle

5.12 To detach the lower balljoint from the lower control arm, remove these four bolts (arrows)

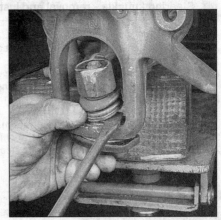

5.13 To detach the dust boot from the steering knuckle, pry the lower lip of the boot out of its groove in the knuckle

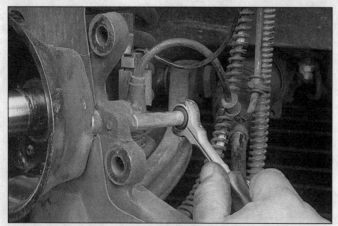

6.4 To detach the ABS sensor from the steering knuckle, remove this bolt

6.5 To detach the brake shield from the steering knuckle, remove these three screws (arrows)

7.4 If you're removing the right upper control arm on a vehicle equipped with the power hydraulic system, remove these three Torx screws (arrows) and move the accumulator assembly to the side a little to provide clearance for pulling out the pivot bolt

7.5 To detach the upper control arm from the suspension crossmember, remove the nut (at the rear) and pull the bolt out from the front; be sure to note the order in which the spacer washers are installed when you remove the nut, and put them back in the same order when the arm is installed

15   Installation is the reverse of removal. Tighten the balljoint bolts and the ball stud nut to the torque listed in this Chapter's Specifications.

16   Remove the jack from under the control arm, install the front wheel. Lower the vehicle and tighten the wheel lug nuts to the torque listed in the Chapter 1 Specifications.

6   Steering knuckle - removal and installation

Refer to illustrations 6.4 and 6.5

1   Loosen the wheel lug nuts, raise the front of the vehicle and place it securely on jackstands. Remove the wheel.

2   Remove the front brake caliper and mounting bracket (see Chapter 9). Do not disconnect the brake hose. Hang the caliper out of the way with a piece of wire.

3   Remove the brake disc (see Chapter 9).

4   Remove the ABS sensor **(see illustration)**.

5   Remove the brake shield **(see illustration)**.

6   Disconnect the tie-rod end from the steering knuckle (see Section 15).

7   Disconnect the upper and lower balljoints from the steering knuckle (see Section 5).

8   Remove the steering knuckle.

9   Installation is the reverse of removal. Tighten the balljoint nuts and the tie-rod end nuts to the torque listed in this Chapter's Specifications. Tighten the brake fasteners to the torque values listed in the Chapter 9 Specifications.

7   Upper control arm - removal and installation

Refer to illustrations 7.4 and 7.5

1   Loosen the wheel lug nuts, raise the vehicle and support it securely on jackstands. Remove the wheel.

2   Support the lower control arm with a floor jack **(see illustration 4.2)**.

3   Disconnect the upper balljoint from the steering knuckle (see Section 5).

4   If you're removing the right upper control arm on a vehicle equipped with the power hydraulic system, remove the three Torx screws which attach the accumulator **(see illustration)** and push the assembly aside just far enough to clear the pivot bolt.

5   Remove the upper control arm pivot bolt and nut **(see illustration)**. When removing the nut, note the number of washers used and the order in which they're installed. Put these parts in a plastic bag.

6   Remove the upper control arm. Inspect the bushings at either end of the arm and replace them if they're damaged or worn.

7   Installation is the reverse of removal. Be sure to install the washers in the same order in which they were removed. Raise the suspension with the floor jack to simulate normal ride height, then tighten the upper control arm pivot bolt and nut to the torque listed in this Chapter's Specifications.

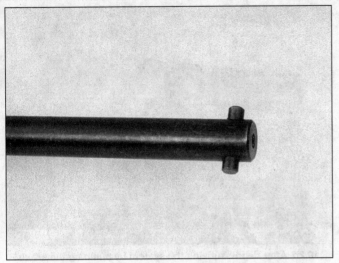

8.2a When installing the spring compressor tool (JD115), insert the upper end of the rod into the cross-shaped slot in the suspension crossmember, then rotate the rod 90-degrees so this pin on the upper end of the tool locks into the crossmember

8.2b This is how the spring compressor tool (JD115) looks when it's installed; note how the offset collet is oriented so that it's flush with the coil spring pan

8.3 To detach the coil spring pan from the lower control arm, compress the spring and remove these six bolts (arrows)

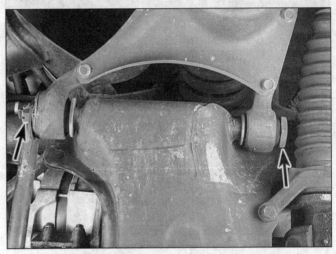

9.4 To detach the lower control arm from the suspension crossmember, remove this nut and bolt (arrows) (you'll have to unbolt the steering gear assembly and lower it far enough before you can pull out the pivot bolt)

8 Coil spring (front) - removal and installation

Refer to illustrations 8.2a, 8.2b and 8.3

Warning: *The coil springs cannot be removed without a special spring compressor tool (Jaguar tool no. JD115). Do not try to remove a coil spring without this special tool. If you do, you could be seriously injured.*

1   Loosen the wheel lug nuts, raise the vehicle and support it securely on jackstands. Remove the wheel.
2   Install the special spring compressor tool (JD115) as shown **(see illustrations)**.
3   Tighten the tool until the spacer is tight against the spring pan, then remove the spring pan bolts **(see illustration)**.
4   Slowly back off the wingnut on the special tool until all tension is relieved from the spring. Remove the tool, remove the pan, and remove the coil spring.
5   Installation is the reverse of removal. Place the coil spring in position with the spring pan below it, install the special tool and carefully tighten the wingnut until the spring is compressed enough to allow the pan to be positioned and bolted to the lower control arm. Be sure to tighten the pan bolts to the torque listed in this Chapter's Specifications.

9 Lower control arm - removal and installation

Refer to illustration 9.4

Warning: *The lower control arms cannot be removed without a special spring compressor tool (Jaguar tool no. JD115). Do not try to remove a lower control arm without this special tool. If you do, you could be seriously injured.*

1   Loosen the wheel lug nuts, raise the vehicle and support it securely on jackstands. Remove the wheel.
2   Remove the spring pan and the coil spring (see Section 8).
3   Detach the steering gear (see Section 17) and lower it far enough to provide clearance for the lower control arm pivot bolt.
4   Remove the pivot bolt and nut **(see illustration)**. Note any washers behind the nut and store them in a plastic bag.
5   Remove the lower control arm.
6   Installation is the reverse of removal. Be sure to install any washers removed. Raise the suspension with the floor jack to simulate normal ride height, then tighten the pivot bolt and nut to the torque listed in this Chapter's Specifications. Refer to Section 8 for coil spring installation.

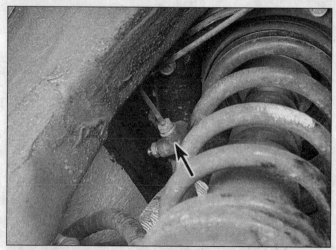

10.2a On a vehicle equipped with self-leveling rear suspension, the valve block (arrow) for the left rear shock is located just in front of the shock absorber

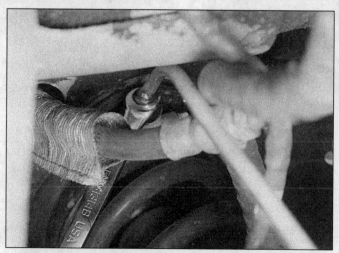

10.2b After depressurizing the system by pumping the brake pedal repeatedly until it feels hard, attach a bleeder hose to the bleeder screw on the left valve block, crack the bleeder and drain off any residual fluid into a catch bottle

10.3 To detach the lower end of the shock absorber/coil spring from the control arm, remove this nut and bolt, then pull out the bolt

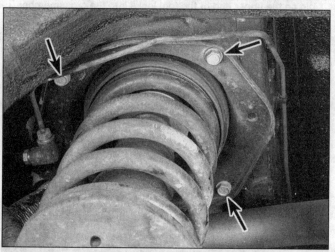

10.4 To detach the upper end of the shock absorber/coil spring assembly from the vehicle body, remove these bolts (arrows) (not all bolts visible in this photo)

10   Shock absorber/coil spring (rear) - removal and installation

Refer to illustrations 10.2a, 10.2b, 10.3, 10.4, 10.6a, 10.6b, 10.6c, 10.10a, 10.10b and 10.10c

Note 1: *Always replace both left and right shocks at the same time to prevent handling peculiarities and abnormal ride quality.*

Note 2: *If you're replacing the shock absorbers on an earlier vehicle with the self-leveling system, we strongly recommend (and so does Jaguar) that you replace the self-leveling units with conventional units (available at the dealer as a retrofit kit for older vehicles equipped with the self-leveling system).*

1   Loosen the rear wheel lug nuts. Raise the rear of the vehicle and support it securely on jackstands. Remove the rear wheels. Support the control arm with a floor jack. Place a block of wood on the jack head to serve as a cushion.

2   If you are removing/replacing the shocks on a vehicle equipped with the self-leveling rear suspension system, depressurize the system by pumping the brake pedal until it feels hard to push (this dissipates the pressure inside the accumulator), then locate the hydraulic line valve block just in front of the upper end of the left rear shock **(see illustration)**. Attach a plastic hose to the bleeder screw **(see illustra-**

tion), put the other end of the hose in a catch bottle, crack the bleeder and drain off as much fluid as possible. Disconnect the hydraulic line that connects the left shock to the valve block. Now locate the other valve block just in front of the right rear shock; disconnect the hydraulic line that connects the right shock to this valve block too.

3   Remove the lower shock absorber-to-control arm nut and bolt **(see illustration)**.

4   Remove the upper mounting bolts **(see illustration)** and remove the shock absorber/coil spring assembly.

5   The shock/coil spring assemblies must be disassembled, and the coil springs installed on the new shocks. Although the shock/coil spring assembly is similar in appearance to the a MacPherson strut/coil spring assembly, the spring on this unit is much stiffer. Therefore, DO NOT attempt to take apart this unit yourself with a strut spring compressor tool. Instead, take the unit to a Jaguar dealer service department or to a Jaguar specialist shop and have the springs installed on the new shocks by professionals.

6   If you are retrofitting conventional shocks - rather than installing the same or another pair of self-leveling shocks - unplug the electrical connector at the ride height sensor and fill the connector with silicone **(see illustration)** to prevent it from shorting out and causing electrical problems. Then disconnect and remove all hydraulic lines **(see illustrations)**.

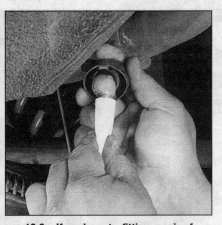

10.6a If you're retrofitting a pair of conventional shocks to a vehicle formerly equipped with a self-leveling system, unplug the electrical connector to the ride height sensor and fill the connector with silicone to prevent it from shorting out and causing electrical problems . . .

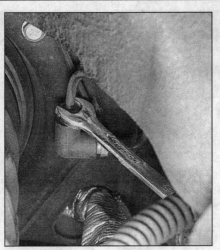

10.6b . . . then disconnect and remove both valve blocks . . .

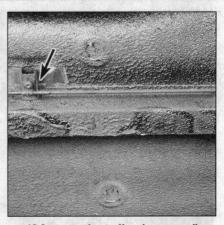

10.6c . . . and cut off and remove all associated plumbing, including the metal line going forward to the valve block in the engine compartment and the brackets which affix this line to the body (arrow) (you will remove the plumbing in the engine compartment after the vehicle is lowered)

10.10a After the vehicle has been lowered, disconnect the forward end of the hydraulic line from the valve block . . .

10.10b . . . install the plug included in the retrofit kit . . .

7   Installation is the reverse of removal. Be sure to tighten all fasteners to the torque values listed in this Chapter's Specifications.

8   Remove the jack supporting the control arm, install the rear wheels and lower the vehicle.

9   Tighten the rear wheel lug nuts to the torque listed in the Chapter 1 Specifications.

10   If you retrofitted conventional shocks to a vehicle formerly equipped with the self-leveling rear suspension system, disconnect the forward end of the hydraulic line from the valve block and install the plug included in the kit **(see illustrations)**. Then finish removing the forward section of hydraulic line and the brackets for the line **(see illustration)**.

11   If you installed another pair of self-leveling shocks, or removed and installed the same pair of self-leveling shocks, be sure to top up the power hydraulic system reservoir (see Chapter 1).

11 Hub carrier (rear) - removal and installation

Refer to illustrations 11.4 and 11.5

1   Loosen the wheel lug nuts, raise the rear of the vehicle and support it securely on jackstands. Remove the wheel.

2   Remove the rear caliper and brake pads, the caliper bracket, the brake disc, the parking brake cable and the parking brake shoe assembly (see Chapter 9).

3   Disconnect the outer end of the driveaxle from the hub carrier (see Chapter 8).

10.10c . . . then remove these bracket screws (arrows), the brackets and the forward section of hydraulic line

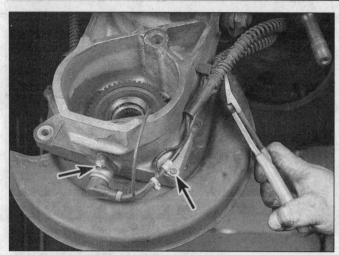

11.4 Before detaching the hub carrier from the rear control arm, be sure to remove the ABS sensor (left arrow), detach the ABS harness clip (right arrow) and cut off the cable tie securing the harness to the carrier

4   Remove the ABS sensor, the ABS harness clip and cut off the cable tie which secures the ABS harness to the carrier **(see illustration)**.
5   Remove the nut and bolt which attach the carrier to the control arm **(see illustration)**.
6   Remove the hub carrier assembly.
7   Installation is the reverse of removal. Be sure to tighten all fasteners to the torque values listed in this Chapter's Specifications.

12   Hub and bearing (rear) - replacement

If you want to replace the rear hub and bearing assembly (or the ABS trigger wheel), remove the hub carrier (see Section 11), then take the carrier to a Jaguar dealer service department or to an automotive machine shop. These parts require a hydraulic press and special fixtures to disassemble and reassemble.

13   Control arm (rear) - removal and installation

Refer to illustrations 13.6 and 13.7
1   Loosen the wheel lug nuts, raise the rear of the vehicle and support it securely on jackstands. Remove the wheel.
2   Remove the rear caliper and brake pads, the caliper bracket, the brake disc, the parking brake cable and the parking brake shoe assembly (see Chapter 9).
3   Disconnect the outer end of the driveaxle from the hub carrier (see Chapter 8).
4   Disconnect the lower end of the shock absorber/coil spring assembly from the control arm (see Section 10).
5   Remove the hub carrier (see Section 11).
6   Remove the control arm pivot bolt nut **(see illustration)**.
7   Support the differential/crossmember assembly with a floor jack. Place a block of wood between the jack head and the differential to protect the differential. Disconnect the lower end of the differential tie-bar **(see illustration)** and carefully lower the differential crossmember just enough to allow the control arm pivot bolt to be pulled out to the rear without hitting the trunk well.
8   Remove the control arm.
9   Inspect the control arm pivot bolt bushings. If they're cracked, dried out or torn, take the arm to an automotive machine shop and have them replaced.
10   Installation is the reverse of removal. Tighten all suspension fasteners to the torque listed in this Chapter's Specifications. Tighten all brake fasteners to the torque listed in the Chapter 9 Specifications.

11.5 To detach the hub carrier from the rear control arm, remove the carrier-to-control arm nut and bolt

13.6 Hold the pivot bolt and unscrew the nut

14   Steering wheel - removal and installation

Refer to illustrations 14.2, 14.3 and 14.4
Warning: *If the vehicle is equipped with an airbag, do not attempt this procedure. Have it performed by a dealer service department or other*

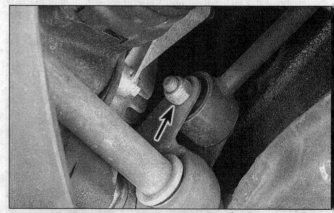

13.7 Support the differential/crossmember assembly with a jack, remove this nut (arrow) and bolt from the lower end of each tie-bar (right above the control arm pivot), lower the differential/crossmember assembly slightly and pull out the bolt to the rear

14.2 To remove the center pad from the steering wheel, simply pry it off

14.3 After removing the steering wheel nut, make a pair of alignment marks on the steering wheel and steering shaft to ensure proper reassembly

3   Remove the steering wheel nut and mark the relationship of the steering wheel hub to the shaft **(see illustration)**.
4   Slide the steering wheel off the steering shaft **(see illustration)**.
5   Installation is the reverse of removal. Be sure to align the match marks you made on the steering wheel and the shaft. Tighten the steering wheel nut to the torque listed in this Chapter's Specifications.

15   Tie-rod ends - removal and installation

Refer to illustrations 15.2 and 15.3
1   Loosen the wheel lug nuts, raise the front of the vehicle and support it securely on jackstands. Remove the front wheel.
2   Back off the jam nut that locks the tie-rod end to the tie-rod, then paint an alignment mark on the threads to ensure the new tie-rod end is installed in the same position **(see illustration)**.
3   Loosen the nut on the tie-rod ball stud, then install a small puller and pop the ball stud loose **(see illustration)**. Remove the nut and separate the ball stud from the steering knuckle. Unscrew the tie-rod end from the tie-rod.
4   Installation is the reverse of removal. Make sure you thread the tie-rod end all the way up to the mark on the threads, but no further. Tighten the ball stud nut to the torque listed in this Chapter's Specifications. Tighten the jam nut securely.
5   Have the toe-in checked and, if necessary, adjusted at a dealer service department or alignment shop.

14.4 To remove the steering wheel, simply pull it straight off

qualified repair shop.
1   Disconnect the negative battery cable. **Caution:** *If the radio in your vehicle is equipped with an anti-theft system, make sure you have the correct activation code before disconnecting the battery.*
2   Pry off the center pad **(see illustration)**.

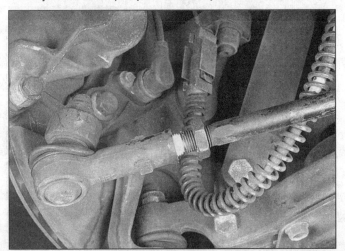

15.2 Back off this jam nut and mark the threads to ensure that the new tie-rod end is installed properly

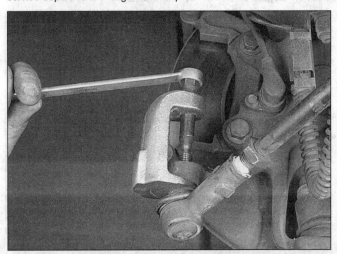

15.3 Loosen the ball stud nut, install a small puller and pop the ball stud loose from the steering knuckle

16.2 Cut off the boot clamps (arrows) and slide the
boot off the steering gear

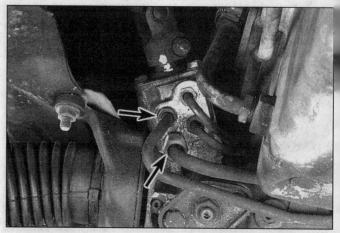

17.3 Mark the relationship of the steering shaft U-joint to the
steering gear pinion shaft, then unscrew the pressure and
return line fittings (arrows) - plug the lines to prevent
contamination from entering the system

16 Steering gear boots - replacement

Refer to illustration 16.2

1   Remove the tie-rod ends (see Section 15).
2   Cut the boot clamps at both ends of the old boots **(see illustration)** and slide off the boots.
3   While the boots are removed, inspect the seals in the end of the steering gear. If they're leaking, have them replaced by a dealer service department or other qualified repair shop, or replace the steering gear with a new or rebuilt unit (see Section 17).
4   Slide the new boots into place and install new boot clamps.
5   Install the tie-rod ends (see Section 15).

17 Steering gear - removal and installation

Refer to illustrations 17.3 and 17.6

Warning: *On models equipped with an airbag, do not apply excessive force or a sudden shock to the steering column shaft, or accidental deployment of the airbag could occur. Do not allow anyone inside the vehicle while performing this procedure.*

1   Using a large syringe or hand pump, empty the power steering fluid reservoir.
2   Loosen the wheel lug nuts, raise the vehicle and support it securely on jackstands. Remove the wheels.

3   Mark the relationship of the steering shaft U-joint to the steering gear pinion shaft **(see illustration)** to ensure proper alignment when they're reassembled. Remove the nut and bolt that clamp the U-joint to the pinion shaft.
4   Disconnect the power steering pressure and return lines from the steering gear. Place a container under the lines to catch spilled fluid. Plug the lines to prevent excessive fluid loss and contamination. Discard the sealing washers (new ones should be used when reassembling).
5   Disconnect the tie-rod ends from the steering knuckle arms (see Section 17).
6   Remove the nuts and bolts from the steering gear mounting brackets **(see illustration)**.
7   Remove the steering gear assembly, detaching the U-joint as you lower it. Take care not to damage the steering gear dust boots.
8   Installation is the reverse of removal. Make sure the marks you made on the U-joint and the pinion shaft are aligned before you tighten the U-joint clamp bolt and nut. Tighten the mounting bolts, the tie-rod end nuts and the U-joint shaft clamping bolts to the torque values listed in this Chapter's Specifications.
9   After lowering the vehicle, fill the reservoir with the recommended fluid (see Chapter 1).
10   Bleed the power steering system (see Section 19).
11   Have the front wheels aligned by a dealer service department or alignment shop after reassembly.

17.6 To detach the steering gear from the vehicle, remove these
nuts and bolts (arrows) from the mounting brackets
(right bracket shown, left bracket similar)

18.2 Before removing the pump and adapter, disconnect the power
steering fluid return hose from the upper pipe (arrow) and unscrew
and disconnect the pressure line from the back of the pump

18.3 To detach the pump adapter from the auxiliary shaft housing, remove these bolts

18.6a This driven coupling is the reason you can't remove the adapter from the pump at home; this procedure requires some special tools and the coupling must be installed on the shaft of the new or rebuilt pump at a very precise height - if you try to pry off the coupling, you will damage it

18 Power steering pump - removal and installation

Refer to illustrations 18.2, 18.3, 18.6a, 18.6b and 18.6c

1   Raise the vehicle and support it securely on jackstands. Remove the engine under-cover.
2   Loosen the hose clamp and disconnect the fluid return hose from the top of the pump **(see illustration)** and drain the power steering fluid from the reservoir into a clean container. Unscrew the pressure line fitting from the back of the pump. Plug the return hose and the pressure line to prevent fluid from leaking and to protect the power steering system from contamination.
3   Remove the bolts **(see illustration)** that attach the power steering pump adapter to the auxiliary shaft housing.
4   Remove the power steering pump and adapter.
5   Take the power steering pump and adapter to a Jaguar dealer service department and have the adapter removed from the old pump and installed on a new or rebuilt pump. (This procedure requires special tools, and the height of the driven coupling on the shaft must be set with a depth gauge.)
6   Installation is the reverse of removal. Study the accompanying photos carefully before reattaching the adapter to the auxiliary shaft housing **(see illustrations)**. Be sure to tighten the fasteners securely.
7   Top up the fluid level in the reservoir (see Chapter 1) and bleed the system (see Section 19).

19 Power steering system - bleeding

1   To bleed the power steering system, begin by checking the power steering fluid level and adding fluid if necessary (see Chapter 1).
2   Raise and support the front of the vehicle on jackstands.
3   Turn the steering wheel from lock-to-lock several times and recheck the fluid level.
4   Start the engine. Turn the steering wheel from lock-to-lock again (three or four times) and recheck the fluid level one more time.
5   Lower the front of the vehicle to the ground. Run the engine and again turn the wheels from lock-to-lock several more times. Position the wheels straight ahead and recheck the fluid level.

20 Wheels and tires - general information

Refer to illustration 20.1

1   All vehicles covered by this manual are equipped with metric-sized steel belted radial tires **(see illustration)**. Use of other size or

18.6b The coupling disc fits onto the driven coupling on the pump side . . .

18.6c . . . and on the drive coupling on the auxiliary shaft side; note that the two lugs on each drive coupling fit into their corresponding slots in the coupling disc, 180-degrees apart - all four of these lugs must be properly engaged or you won't be able to bolt the adapter to the auxiliary shaft housing

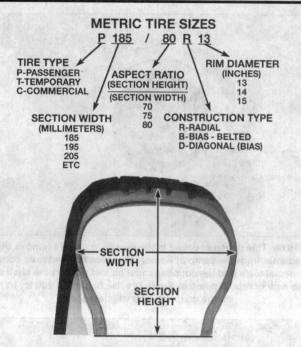

20.1 Metric tire size code

A = Section width   B = Section height

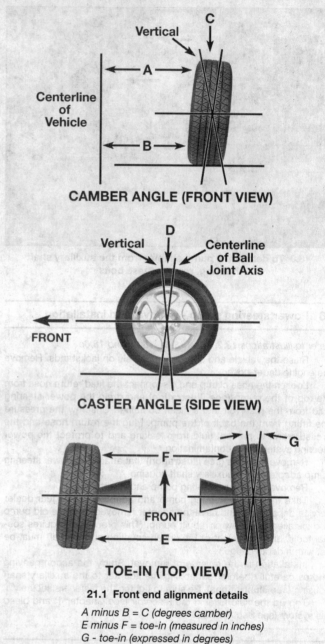

21.1 Front end alignment details

A minus B = C (degrees camber)
E minus F = toe-in (measured in inches)
G - toe-in (expressed in degrees)

type of tires may affect the ride and handling of the vehicle. Don't mix different types of tires, such as radials and bias belted, on the same vehicle as handling may be seriously affected. It's recommended that tires be replaced in pairs on the same axle, but if only one tire is being replaced, be sure it's the same size, structure and tread design as the other.

2   Because tire pressure has a substantial effect on handling and wear, the pressure on all tires should be checked at least once a month or before any extended trips (see Chapter 1).

3   Wheels must be replaced if they are bent, dented, leak air, have elongated bolt holes, are heavily rusted, out of vertical symmetry or if the lug nuts won't stay tight. Wheel repairs that use welding or peening are not recommended.

4   Tire and wheel balance is important in the overall handling, braking and performance of the vehicle. Unbalanced wheels can adversely affect handling and ride characteristics as well as tire life. Whenever a tire is installed on a wheel, the tire and wheel should be balanced by a shop with the proper equipment.

21   Wheel alignment - general information

Refer to illustration 21.1

A wheel alignment refers to the adjustments made to the wheels so they are in proper angular relationship to the suspension and the ground. Wheels that are out of proper alignment not only affect vehicle control, but also increase tire wear. The alignment angles normally measured are camber, caster and toe-in **(see illustration)**. Front-wheel toe-in and caster are adjustable; camber is not adjustable. None of these three angles are adjustable on the rear wheels. Even the non-adjustable angles should be checked to determine if any of the suspension components are bent.

Getting the proper wheel alignment is a very exacting process, one in which complicated and expensive machines are necessary to perform the job properly. Because of this, you should have a technician with the proper equipment perform these tasks. We will, however, use this space to give you a basic idea of what is involved with a wheel alignment so you can better understand the process and deal intelligently with the shop that does the work.

Toe-in is the turning in of the wheels. The purpose of a toe

specification is to ensure parallel rolling of the wheels. In a vehicle with zero toe-in, the distance between the front edges of the wheels will be the same as the distance between the rear edges of the wheels. The actual amount of toe-in is normally only a fraction of an inch. Toe-in is controlled by the tie-rod end position on the tie-rod. Incorrect toe-in will cause the tires to wear improperly by making them scrub against the road surface.

Camber is the tilting of the wheels from vertical when viewed from one end of the vehicle. When the wheels tilt out at the top, the camber is said to be positive (+). When the wheels tilt in at the top the camber is negative (-). The amount of tilt is measured in degrees from vertical and this measurement is called the camber angle. This angle affects the amount of tire tread which contacts the road and compensates for changes in the suspension geometry when the vehicle is cornering or traveling over an undulating surface.

Caster is the tilting of the front steering axis from the vertical. A tilt toward the rear is positive caster and a tilt toward the front is negative caster. Caster is adjusted by moving shims from one side of the upper control arm balljoint to the other.

Chapter 11 Body

Contents

1 General information

These models feature a "unibody" construction, using a floor pan with front and rear frame side rails which support the body components, front and rear suspension systems and other mechanical components. Certain components are particularly vulnerable to accident damage and can be unbolted and repaired or replaced. Among these parts are the body moldings, bumpers, front fenders, hood and trunk lids and all glass.

Only general body maintenance practices and body panel repair procedures within the scope of the do-it-yourselfer are included in this Chapter.

2 Body - maintenance

1   The condition of your vehicle's body is very important, because the resale value depends a great deal on it. It's much more difficult to repair a neglected or damaged body than it is to repair mechanical components. The hidden areas of the body, such as the wheel wells, the frame and the engine compartment, are equally important, although they don't require as frequent attention as the rest of the body.

2   Once a year, or every 12,000 miles, it's a good idea to have the underside of the body steam cleaned. All traces of dirt and oil will be removed and the area can then be inspected carefully for rust, damaged brake lines, frayed electrical wires, damaged cables and other problems. The front suspension components should be greased after completion of this job.

3   At the same time, clean the engine and the engine compartment with a steam cleaner or water soluble degreaser.

4   The wheel wells should be given close attention, since undercoating can peel away and stones and dirt thrown up by the tires can cause the paint to chip and flake, allowing rust to set in. If rust is found, clean down to the bare metal and apply an anti-rust paint.

5   The body should be washed about once a week. Wet the vehicle thoroughly to soften the dirt, then wash it down with a soft sponge and plenty of clean soapy water. If the surplus dirt is not washed off very carefully, it can wear down the paint.

6   Spots of tar or asphalt thrown up from the road should be removed with a cloth soaked in solvent.

7   Once every six months, wax the body and chrome trim. If a chrome cleaner is used to remove rust from any of the vehicle's plated parts, remember that the cleaner also removes part of the chrome, so use it sparingly.

3 Vinyl trim - maintenance

Don't clean vinyl trim with detergents, caustic soap or petroleum-based cleaners. Plain soap and water works just fine, with a soft brush to clean dirt that may be ingrained. Wash the vinyl as frequently as the rest of the vehicle.

After cleaning, application of a high quality rubber and vinyl protectant will help prevent oxidation and cracks. The protectant can also be applied to weather-stripping, vacuum lines and rubber hoses (which often fail as a result of chemical degradation) and to the tires.

4 Upholstery and carpets - maintenance

1   Every three months remove the carpets or mats and clean the interior of the vehicle (more frequently if necessary). Vacuum the upholstery and carpets to remove loose dirt and dust.

2   Leather upholstery requires special care. Stains should be removed with warm water and a very mild soap solution. Use a clean, damp cloth to remove the soap, then wipe again with a dry cloth. Never use alcohol, gasoline, nail polish remover or thinner to clean leather upholstery.

3   After cleaning, regularly treat leather upholstery with a leather wax. Never use car wax on leather upholstery.

4   In areas where the interior of the vehicle is subject to bright sunlight, cover leather seats with a sheet if the vehicle is to be left out for any length of time.

These photos illustrate a method of repairing simple dents. They are intended to supplement *Body repair - minor damage* in this Chapter and should not be used as the sole instructions for body repair on these vehicles.

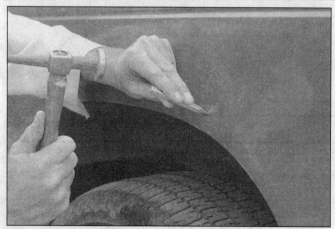

1   If you can't access the backside of the body panel to hammer out the dent, pull it out with a slide-hammer-type dent puller. In the deepest portion of the dent or along the crease line, drill or punch hole(s) at least one inch apart . . .

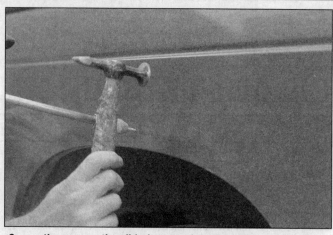

2   . . . then screw the slide-hammer into the hole and operate it. Tap with a hammer near the edge of the dent to help 'pop' the metal back to its original shape. When you're finished, the dent area should be close to its original contour and about 1/8-inch below the surface of the surrounding metal

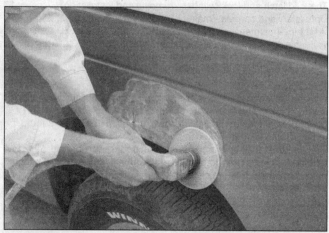

3   Using coarse-grit sandpaper, remove the paint down to the bare metal. Hand sanding works fine, but the disc sander shown here makes the job faster. Use finer (about 320-grit) sandpaper to feather-edge the paint at least one inch around the dent area

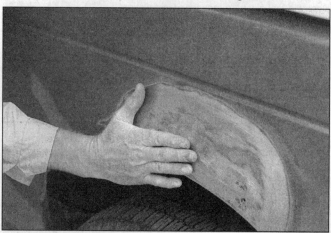

4   When the paint is removed, touch will probably be more helpful than sight for telling if the metal is straight. Hammer down the high spots or raise the low spots as necessary. Clean the repair area with wax/silicone remover

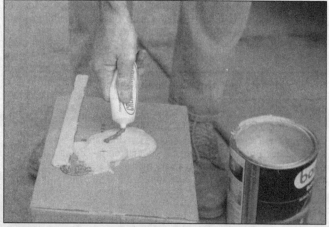

5   Following label instructions, mix up a batch of plastic filler and hardener. The ratio of filler to hardener is critical, and, if you mix it incorrectly, it will either not cure properly or cure too quickly (you won't have time to file and sand it into shape)

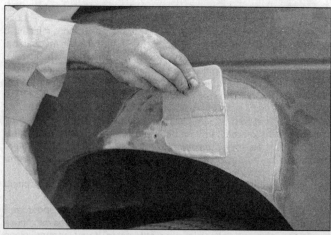

6   Working quickly so the filler doesn't harden, use a plastic applicator to press the body filler firmly into the metal, assuring it bonds completely. Work the filler until it matches the original contour and is slightly above the surrounding metal

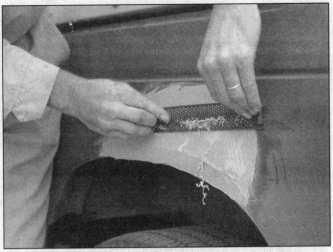

7   Let the filler harden until you can just dent it with your fingernail. Use a body file or Surform tool (shown here) to rough-shape the filler

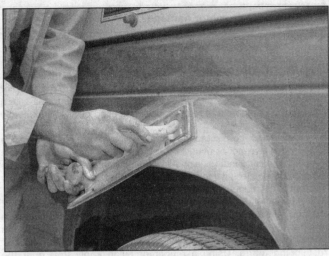

8   Use coarse-grit sandpaper and a sanding board or block to work the filler down until it's smooth and even. Work down to finer grits of sandpaper - always using a board or block - ending up with 360 or 400 grit

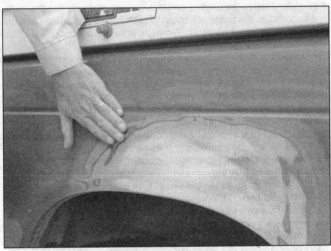

9   You shouldn't be able to feel any ridge at the transition from the filler to the bare metal or from the bare metal to the old paint. As soon as the repair is flat and uniform, remove the dust and mask off the adjacent panels or trim pieces

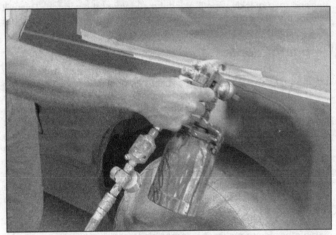

10   Apply several layers of primer to the area. Don't spray the primer on too heavy, so it sags or runs, and make sure each coat is dry before you spray on the next one. A professional-type spray gun is being used here, but aerosol spray primer is available inexpensively from auto parts stores

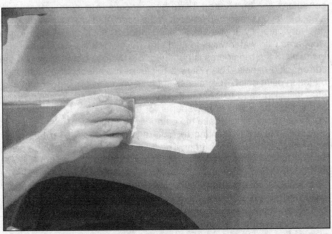

11   The primer will help reveal imperfections or scratches. Fill these with glazing compound. Follow the label instructions and sand it with 360 or 400-grit sandpaper until it's smooth. Repeat the glazing, sanding and respraying until the primer reveals a perfectly smooth surface

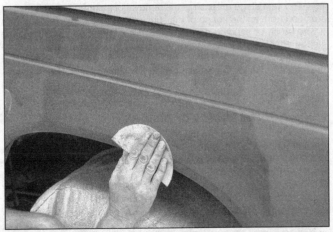

12   Finish sand the primer with very fine sandpaper (400 or 600-grit) to remove the primer overspray. Clean the area with water and allow it to dry. Use a tack rag to remove any dust, then apply the finish coat. Don't attempt to rub out or wax the repair area until the paint has dried completely (at least two weeks)

5   Body repair - minor damage

See photo sequence

Repair of minor scratches

1   If the scratch is superficial and does not penetrate to the metal of the body, repair is very simple. Lightly rub the scratched area with a fine rubbing compound to remove loose paint and built-up wax. Rinse the area with clean water.

2   Apply touch-up paint to the scratch, using a small brush. Continue to apply thin layers of paint until the surface of the paint in the scratch is level with the surrounding paint. Allow the new paint at least two weeks to harden, then blend it into the surrounding paint by rubbing with a very fine rubbing compound. Finally, apply a coat of wax to the scratch area.

3   If the scratch has penetrated the paint and exposed the metal of the body, causing the metal to rust, a different repair technique is required. Remove all loose rust from the bottom of the scratch with a pocket knife, then apply rust inhibiting paint to prevent the formation of rust in the future. Using a rubber or nylon applicator, coat the scratched area with glaze-type filler. If required, the filler can be mixed with thinner to provide a very thin paste, which is ideal for filling narrow scratches. Before the glaze filler in the scratch hardens, wrap a piece of smooth cotton cloth around the tip of a finger. Dip the cloth in thinner and then quickly wipe it along the surface of the scratch. This will ensure that the surface of the filler is slightly hollow. The scratch can now be painted over as described earlier in this section.

Repair of dents

4   When repairing dents, the first job is to pull the dent out until the affected area is as close as possible to its original shape. There is no point in trying to restore the original shape completely as the metal in the damaged area will have stretched on impact and cannot be restored to its original contours. It is better to bring the level of the dent up to a point which is about 1/8-inch below the level of the surrounding metal. In cases where the dent is very shallow, it is not worth trying to pull it out at all.

5   If the back side of the dent is accessible, it can be hammered out gently from behind using a soft-face hammer. While doing this, hold a block of wood firmly against the opposite side of the metal to absorb the hammer blows and prevent the metal from being stretched.

6   If the dent is in a section of the body which has double layers, or some other factor makes it inaccessible from behind, a different technique is required. Drill several small holes through the metal inside the damaged area, particularly in the deeper sections. Screw long, self-tapping screws into the holes just enough for them to get a good grip in the metal. Now the dent can be pulled out by pulling on the protruding heads of the screws with locking pliers.

7   The next stage of repair is the removal of paint from the damaged area and from an inch or so of the surrounding metal. This is done with a wire brush or sanding disk in a drill motor, although it can be done just as effectively by hand with sandpaper. To complete the preparation for filling, score the surface of the bare metal with a screwdriver or the tang of a file, or drill small holes in the affected area. This will provide a good grip for the filler material. To complete the repair, see the subsection on filling and painting later in this Section.

Repair of rust holes or gashes

8   Remove all paint from the affected area and from an inch or so of the surrounding metal using a sanding disk or wire brush mounted in a drill motor. If these are not available, a few sheets of sandpaper will do the job just as effectively.

9   With the paint removed, you will be able to determine the severity of the corrosion and decide whether to replace the whole panel, if possible, or repair the affected area. New body panels are not as expensive as most people think and it is often quicker to install a new panel than to repair large areas of rust.

10   Remove all trim pieces from the affected area except those which will act as a guide to the original shape of the damaged body, such as headlight shells, etc. Using metal snips or a hacksaw blade, remove all loose metal and any other metal that is badly affected by rust. Hammer the edges of the hole in to create a slight depression for the filler material.

11   Wire brush the affected area to remove the powdery rust from the surface of the metal. If the back of the rusted area is accessible, treat it with rust inhibiting paint.

12   Before filling is done, block the hole in some way. This can be done with sheet metal riveted or screwed into place, or by stuffing the hole with wire mesh.

13   Once the hole is blocked off, the affected area can be filled and painted. See the following subsection on filling and painting.

Filling and painting

14   Many types of body fillers are available, but generally speaking, body repair kits which contain filler paste and a tube of resin hardener are best for this type of repair work. A wide, flexible plastic or nylon applicator will be necessary for imparting a smooth and contoured finish to the surface of the filler material. Mix up a small amount of filler on a clean piece of wood or cardboard (use the hardener sparingly). Follow the manufacturer's instructions on the package, otherwise the filler will set incorrectly.

15   Using the applicator, apply the filler paste to the prepared area. Draw the applicator across the surface of the filler to achieve the desired contour and to level the filler surface. As soon as a contour that approximates the original one is achieved, stop working the paste. If you continue, the paste will begin to stick to the applicator. Continue to add thin layers of paste at 20-minute intervals until the level of the filler is just above the surrounding metal.

16   Once the filler has hardened, the excess can be removed with a body file. From then on, progressively finer grades of sandpaper should be used, starting with a 180-grit paper and finishing with 600-grit wet-or-dry paper. Always wrap the sandpaper around a flat rubber or wooden block, otherwise the surface of the filler will not be completely flat. During the sanding of the filler surface, the wet-or-dry paper should be periodically rinsed in water. This will ensure that a very smooth finish is produced in the final stage.

17   At this point, the repair area should be surrounded by a ring of bare metal, which in turn should be encircled by the finely feathered edge of good paint. Rinse the repair area with clean water until all of the dust produced by the sanding operation is gone.

18   Spray the entire area with a light coat of primer. This will reveal any imperfections in the surface of the filler. Repair the imperfections with fresh filler paste or glaze filler and once more smooth the surface with sandpaper. Repeat this spray-and-repair procedure until you are satisfied that the surface of the filler and the feathered edge of the paint are perfect. Rinse the area with clean water and allow it to dry completely.

19   The repair area is now ready for painting. Spray painting must be carried out in a warm, dry, windless and dust free atmosphere. These conditions can be created if you have access to a large indoor work area, but if you are forced to work in the open, you will have to pick the day very carefully. If you are working indoors, dousing the floor in the work area with water will help settle the dust which would otherwise be in the air. If the repair area is confined to one body panel, mask off the surrounding panels. This will help minimize the effects of a slight mismatch in paint color. Trim pieces such as chrome strips, door handles, etc., will also need to be masked off or removed. Use masking tape and several thickness of newspaper for the masking operations.

20   Before spraying, shake the paint can thoroughly, then spray a test area until the spray painting technique is mastered. Cover the repair area with a thick coat of primer. The thickness should be built up using several thin layers of primer rather than one thick one. Using 600-grit wet-or-dry sandpaper, rub down the surface of the primer until it is very smooth. While doing this, the work area should be thoroughly rinsed with water and the wet-or-dry sandpaper periodically rinsed as well. Allow the primer to dry before spraying additional coats.

21   Spray on the top coat, again building up the thickness by using several thin layers of paint. Begin spraying in the center of the repair area and then, using a circular motion, work out until the whole repair area and about two inches of the surrounding original paint is covered. Remove all masking material 10 to 15 minutes after spraying on the

9.2a Use a small screwdriver to pry the clip out of its locking groove, then detach the end of the strut from the mounting stud

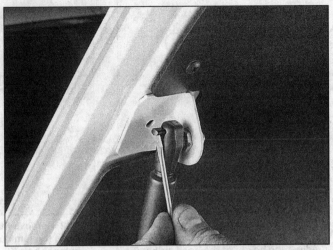

9.2b The trunk lid support strut requires prying out a locking pin to detach it from the locating stud

final coat of paint. Allow the new paint at least two weeks to harden, then use a very fine rubbing compound to blend the edges of the new paint into the existing paint. Finally, apply a coat of wax.

6 Body repair - major damage

1 Major damage must be repaired by an auto body shop specifically equipped to perform unibody repairs. These shops have the specialized equipment required to do the job properly.
2 If the damage is extensive, the body must be checked for proper alignment or the vehicle's handling characteristics may be adversely affected and other components may wear at an accelerated rate.
3 Due to the fact that most of the major body components (hood, front fenders, etc.) are separate and replaceable units, any seriously damaged components should be replaced rather than repaired. Sometimes the components can be found in a wrecking yard that specializes in used vehicle components, often at considerable savings over the cost of new parts.

7 Hinges and locks - maintenance

Once every 3000 miles, or every three months, the hinges and latch assemblies on the doors, hood and trunk should be given a few drops of light oil or lock lubricant. The door latch strikers should also be lubricated with a thin coat of grease to reduce wear and ensure free movement. Lubricate the door and trunk locks with spray-on graphite lubricant.

8 Windshield and fixed glass - replacement

Replacement of the windshield and fixed glass requires the use of special fast-setting adhesive/caulk materials and some specialized tools. It is recommended that these operations be left to a dealer or a shop specializing in glass work.

9 Hood and rear trunk lid support struts - removal and installation

Refer to illustrations 9.2a and 9.2b
1 Open the hood or rear trunk lid and support it securely.
2 Using a small screwdriver, detach the retaining clips at both ends of the support strut. Then pry or pull sharply to detach it from the vehicle (see illustrations).
3 Installation is the reverse of removal.

10.4 With the help of an assistant to hold the hood, remove the retaining bolts (arrows) from each hinge plate, then lift off the hood

10 Hood - removal, installation and adjustment

Note: *The hood is heavy and somewhat awkward to remove and install - at least two people should perform this procedure.*

Removal and installation
Refer to illustration 10.4
1 Use blankets or pads to cover the fenders and the area in front of the hood. This will protect the body and paint as the hood is lifted off.
2 Make marks or scribe a line around the hood hinge to ensure proper alignment during installation.
3 Disconnect any cables or wires that will interfere with removal.
4 Have an assistant support the hood. Remove the hinge-to-hood screws or bolts (see illustration).
5 Lift off the hood.
6 Installation is the reverse of removal.

Adjustment
Refer to illustrations 10.11 and 10.12
7 Before the hood can be adjusted properly, both hood striker assemblies which are located on the inside of the hood must first be loosened to allow correct alignment of the hood.
8 Fore-and-aft and side-to-side adjustment of the hood is done by moving the hood in relation to the hinge plates after loosening the bolts.

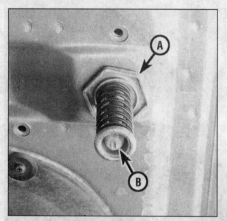

10.11 Adjust the position of the hood striker by loosening the locknut (A), then adjust the height of the hood striker (B) by turning it in or out with a screwdriver

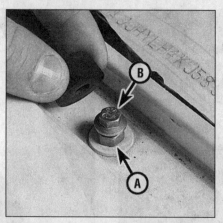

10.12 Remove the rubber bumper then loosen the jam nut (A) - adjust the hood bumper bolt (B) in or out so the hood is flush with the fenders in the closed position

11.1 Remove the cable retaining bolt(s) (arrow) then disengage the cable from the latch assembly

9   Scribe or trace a line around the entire hinge plate so you can judge the amount of movement.
10   Loosen the nuts or bolts and move the hood into correct alignment. Move it only a little at a time. Tighten the hinge bolts or nuts and carefully lower the hood to check the alignment.
11   After the hood is aligned properly with the cowl and front fenders, the height and position of the hood striker assembly should be adjusted to provide positive engagement with the latch assembly **(see illustration)**.
12   Adjust the hood bumpers on the fenders so the hood is flush with the fenders when closed **(see illustration)**.
13   The hood latch assembly, as well as the hinges, should be periodically lubricated with white lithium-base grease to prevent sticking and wear.

11   Hood release latch and cable - removal and installation

Latch

Refer to illustrations 11.1 and 11.2
1   Disconnect the hood release cables by removing the cable retaining bolts and disengaging the cable from the latch assembly **(see illustration)**.

2   Scribe a line around the latches to aid alignment when installing, then detach the retaining bolts from the inner fenderwell **(see illustration)** and remove the latch.
3   Installation is the reverse of removal.

Cable

Refer to illustration 11.6
4   Disconnect the hood release cable as described in (Section 11).
5   Detach all cable retaining clips located in the engine compartment.
6   Working in the passenger compartment, remove the drivers side kick panel surrounding the hood release lever. Pull the release lever forward and detach the release cables from the handle and bracket assembly **(see illustration)**.
7   Attach a piece of thin wire or string to the end of the cables to help aid the installation process.
8   Working in the engine compartment, pull the cables and grommet out of the firewall until you can see the wire or string. Ensure that the new cable has a grommet attached then remove the old cable from the wire or string and replace it with the new cable.
9   Working from passenger compartment pull the wire or string back through the firewall.
10   Installation is the reverse of removal. **Note:** *Push on the grommet with your fingers from the engine compartment to seat the grommet in the firewall.*

11.2 Hood latch retaining bolts (arrows) are located on both sides of the engine compartment

11.6 Remove the drivers side kick panel to access the hood release cables from the passenger compartment

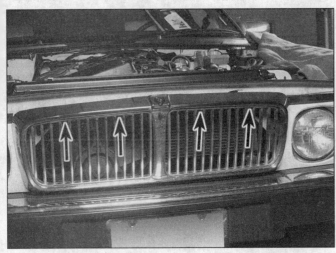

12.1 Removing one side at a time, remove the grille insert retaining screws (arrows) - tilt the top edge of the grille insert forward, then lift up and out to remove it from the vehicle

12.2 Working through the grille insert openings, remove the retaining screws from each edge of the grille frame

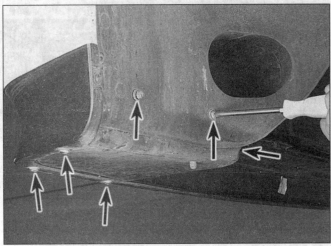

13.1 Working underneath the vehicle, remove the screws (arrows) securing the front spoiler lower cover

12 Radiator grille - removal and installation

Refer to illustrations 12.1 and 12.2

1   Using a Phillips screwdriver, detach the right and left hand grille inserts from the grille assembly **(see illustration)**. **Note:** *The grill can be removed without removing the inserts, but reaching the mounting screws from above is quite difficult.*
2   Working through the grille insert openings, remove the retaining screws securing both ends of the grille frame **(see illustration)**.
3   Pull the grille frame forward and remove it from the vehicle.
4   Installation is the reverse of removal.

13 Front spoiler - removal and installation

Refer to illustrations 13.1, 13.2, 13.3 and 13.4

1   Working on the left side of the vehicle, remove the front spoiler lower cover **(see illustration)**.
2   Remove the screws securing the front air dam panels in the left and right wheel openings **(see illustration)**, then detach the air dam panels from the vehicle. **Note:** *It will probably be necessary to turn the wheels to the right and left for access to the screws.*
3   Detach the retaining bolts securing the sides of the spoiler **(see illustration)**.

13.2 Working in the front wheel openings, remove the screws (arrows) securing the front air dam panels

13.3 The retaining bolts (arrows) securing the sides of the front spoiler are located behind the bumper

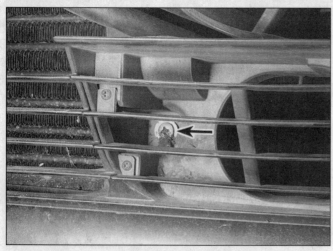

13.4 Working through the grille area of the spoiler, remove the screws (arrow) retaining the front of the spoiler

4   Working through the grille area of the spoiler, detach the retaining screws securing the front of the spoiler **(see illustration)**.
5   Pull the spoiler forward and detach it from the vehicle.
6   Installation is the reverse of removal.

14 Bumpers - removal and installation

Refer to illustrations 14.1a, 14.1b and 14.3
1   Detach the turn signal and side marker light assemblies from the bumper(s) **(see illustrations)**.
2   Disconnect all wire harness connectors attached to the bumper or light assemblies that would interfere with removal.
3   Remove two bumper retaining bolts located on the bottom side of the bumper **(see illustration)**. Pull the bumper assembly out and away from the vehicle to remove it.
4   Installation is the reverse of removal.

15 Front fender - removal and installation

Refer to illustrations 15.4, 15.7a, 15.7b, 15.7c, 15.7d and 15.7e
1   Loosen the front wheel lug nuts. Raise the vehicle, support it securely on jackstands and remove the front wheel.
2   Remove the front bumper assembly (see Section 14).
3   Remove the front spoiler (see Section 13).

14.1a Using a flat-bladed screwdriver, depress the retaining clips on each side of the side marker lamp assemblies, then gently pry forward to remove it . . .

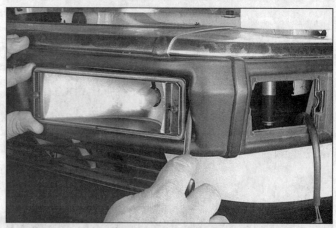

14.1b . . . then detach the turn signal assemblies from the bumper in the same manner

4   Detach the inner fender splash shield **(see illustration)**.
5   On 1988 and 1989 models, remove the coolant overflow reservoir located behind the splash shield (see Chapter 3).
6   On models with round headlights, remove the headlight bezel. On models with composite headlights (1992 Vanden Plas and all 1993 and later models), remove the headlight (see Chapter 12).

14.3 Remove the two retaining bolts from the bottom of the bumper, then remove the bumper from the vehicle

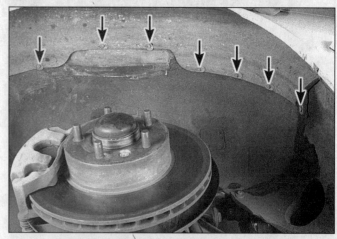

15.4 Remove the bolts (arrows) securing the inner fender splash shield

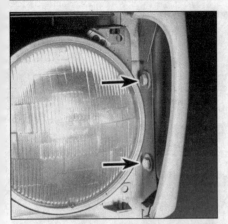

15.7a Detach the fender retaining bolts (arrows) at the front of the fender

15.7b Remove the fender-to-radiator support bolt (arrow)

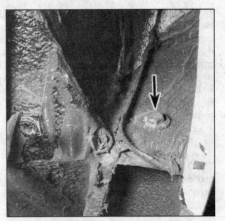

15.7c Working in the wheel opening, remove the fender-to-rocker panel bolt (arrow)

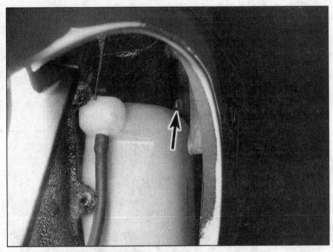

15.7d Remove the fender-to-door pillar bolt (arrow; lower bolt not visible)

7   Remove the fender mounting bolts and nuts **(see illustrations)**.

8   Detach the fender. It's a good idea to have an assistant support the fender while it's being moved away from the vehicle to prevent damage to the surrounding body panels.

9   Installation is the reverse of removal.

16 Trunk lid - removal, installation and adjustment

Note: *The trunk lid is heavy and somewhat awkward to remove and install - at least two people should perform this procedure.*

Removal and installation

Refer to illustration 16.4

1   Open the trunk lid and cover the edges of the trunk compartment with pads or cloths to protect the painted surfaces when the lid is removed.

2   Disconnect any cables or wire harness connectors attached to the trunk lid that would interfere with removal.

3   Make alignment marks around the hinge mounting bolts with a marking pen.

4   While an assistant supports the trunk lid, remove the lid-to-hinge bolts on both sides and lift it off **(see illustration)**.

5   Installation is the reverse of removal. **Note:** *When reinstalling the trunk lid, align the lid-to-hinge bolts with the marks made during removal.*

Adjustment

Refer to illustrations 16.9 and 16.10

6   Fore-and-aft and side-to-side adjustment of the trunk lid is done by moving the hood in relation to the hinge plate after loosening the bolts or nuts.

7   Scribe a line around the entire hinge plate as described earlier in this section so you can judge the amount of movement.

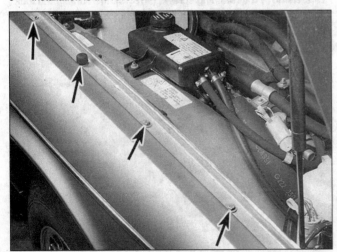

15.7e Detach the bolts along the top of the fender

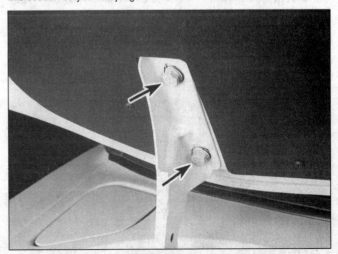

16.4 With the help of an assistant to hold the trunk lid, remove the retaining bolts and lift off the trunk lid

8   Loosen the bolts or nuts and move the trunk lid into correct alignment. Move it only a little at a time. Tighten the hinge bolts or nuts and
carefully lower the trunk lid to check the alignment.
9   If necessary after installation, the entire trunk lid striker assembly
can be adjusted up and down as well as from side to side on the trunk
lid so the lid closes securely and is flush with the rear quarter panels.
To do this, scribe a line around the trunk lid striker assembly to provide
a reference point. Then loosen the bolts and reposition the striker as
necessary **(see illustration)**. Following adjustment, retighten the
mounting bolts.
10   Adjust the bumpers on the trunk lid so the trunk lid is flush with
the rear fenders when closed **(see illustration)**.
11   The trunk lid latch assembly, as well as the hinges, should be
periodically lubricated with white lithium-base grease to prevent sticking and wear.

**17   Trunk lid latch and lock cylinder - removal and
        installation**

Trunk lid latch

Refer to illustration 17.2
1   Open the trunk and scribe a line around the trunk lid latch assembly for a reference point to help aid the installation procedure.
2   The trunk lid latch is retained by three Phillips-head screws **(see
illustration)**. For adjustment procedures, see Section 16.
3   Disengage the lock rod from the latch.
4   Disconnect all electrical connectors and remove the latch.
5   Installation is the reverse of removal.

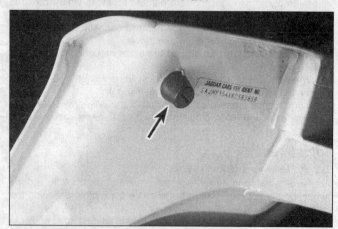

**16.10 Turn the bumpers in or out so the trunk lid is flush with the
rear fenders when in the closed position**

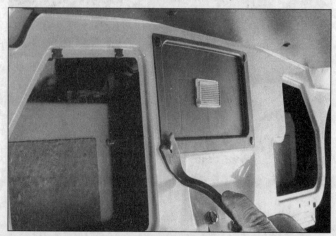

17.6 Detach the clips securing the trunk lamp finish panel

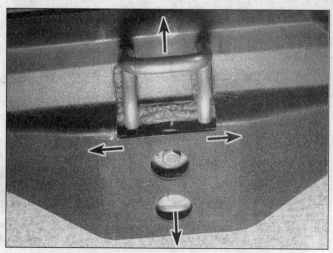

**16.9 Loosen the bolts and move the striker assembly as
necessary to adjust the trunk lid flush with the
quarter panels in closed position**

Trunk lock cylinder

Refer to illustrations 17.6 and 17.7
6   Remove the plastic clips securing the trunk light finish panel **(see
illustration)**.
7   Looking upward through the trunk lid access hole, remove the
lock rod and lock cylinder retaining bolts **(see illustration)**.

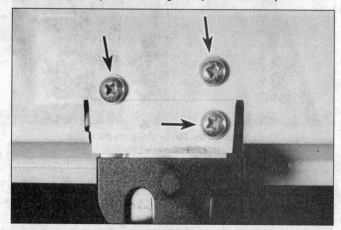

**17.2 Remove the retaining screws (arrows), then unclip the lock
rod and disconnect any electrical connections**

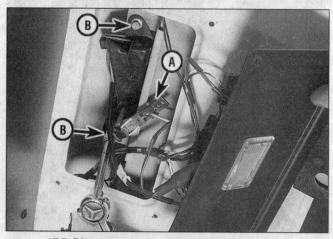

**17.7 Disengage the lock rod (A), then remove the
lock cylinder retaining bolts (B)**

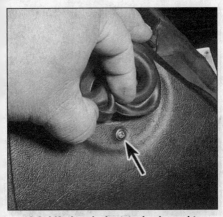

18.2 Lift the air duct-to-body seal to access the trim panel retaining screw (arrow)

18.3a Remove the trim cover . . .

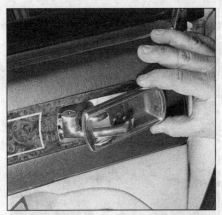

18.3b . . . then detach the inside handle retaining screw and bezel

18.4 Gently pry out the clips securing the wood finish panel

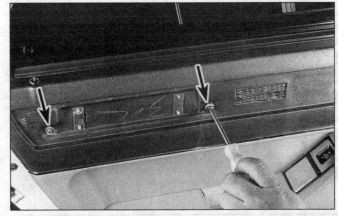

18.5 Detach the screws located behind the wood finish panel, then remove the upper portion of the door trim panel

8   Disconnect all electrical connections and remove the lock cylinder assembly.
9   Installation is the reverse of removal.

18 Door trim panel - removal and installation

Refer to illustrations 18.2, 18.3a, 18.3b, 18.4, 18.5, 18.6, 18.7a, 18.7b, 18.8a, 18.8b and 18.9

1   Disconnect the negative cable from the battery. **Caution:** *If the stereo in your vehicle is equipped with an anti-theft system, make sure you have the correct activation code before disconnecting the battery*

2   On front door trim panels, remove the retaining screw located under the air duct door seal **(see illustration)**.
3   Remove the inside handle trim bezel **(see illustrations)**.
4   Detach the wood finish panel **(see illustration)**.
5   Unscrew the inside lock knob, then remove the remaining screws securing the upper half of the door trim panel and detach it from the vehicle **(see illustration)**.
6   Detach the retaining screw from the top edge of the lower door trim panel **(see illustration)**.
7   Pry out the courtesy lamp lens, then detach the retaining screw from inside the lamp housing **(see illustrations)**.

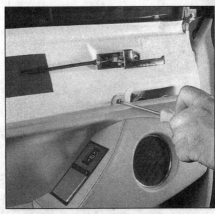

18.6 Detach the screws along the top edge of the lower trim panel

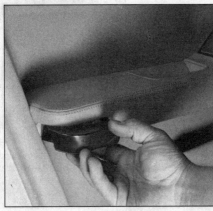

18.7a Pry out the courtesy lamp lens

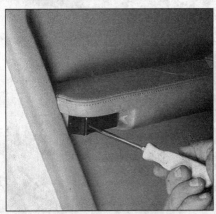

18.7b Remove the retaining screw from inside the lamp housing

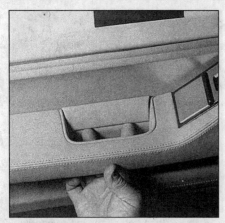 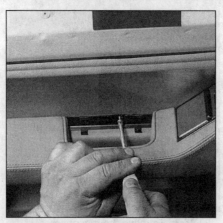 

18.8a Push up on the bottom to detach the armrest/pull handle trim cover

18.8b Remove the screws behind the armrest/pull handle trim cover

18.9 Disengage the retaining clips along the outer edge of the door trim panel

8   Remove the armrest trim cover, then detach the retaining screws from behind the cover **(see illustrations)**.
9   Insert a wide putty knife, a screwdriver or a special trim panel removal tool between the trim panel and the head of the retaining clips to disengage the retaining clips along the outer edges of the door panel **(see illustration)**. Pry only at the clip locations or the panel could be damaged.
10   Once all of the clips are disengaged, detach the trim panel, unplug any electrical connectors and remove the trim panel from the door by gently pulling it up and out.
11   For access to the inner door, peel back the watershield, taking care not to tear it. To install the trim panel, first press the watershield back into place. If necessary, add more sealant to hold it in place.
12   Installation is the reverse of removal.

19   Door - removal, installation and adjustment

Note: *The door is heavy and somewhat awkward to remove and install - at least two people should perform this procedure.*

Removal and installation
Refer to illustrations 19.7a and 19.7b
1   Raise the window completely in the door, then disconnect the negative cable from the battery. **Caution:** *If the stereo in your vehicle is equipped with an anti-theft system, make sure you have the correct*

activation code before disconnecting the battery.
2   Open the door all the way and support it on jacks or blocks covered with rags to prevent damaging the paint.
3   Remove the door trim panel and water deflector as described in Section 18.
4   Unplug all electrical connections, ground wires and harness retaining clips from the door. **Note:** *It is a good idea to label all connections to aid the reassembly process.*
5   From the door side, detach the rubber conduit between the body and the door, then carefully pull the wiring harness through the conduit hole and remove it from the door.
6   Mark around the door hinges with a pen or a scribe to facilitate realignment during reassembly.
7   On front doors, work through the door access hole to remove the hinge-to-door nuts. On rear doors the hinge-to-body bolts are more accessible and can be removed by simply opening the front door and removing the bolts **(see illustrations)**.
8   Have an assistant hold the door, remove the bolts or nuts and lift the door off.
9   Installation is the reverse of removal.

Adjustment
Refer to illustration 19.13
10   Having proper door to body alignment is a critical part of a well functioning door assembly. First check the door hinge pins for excessive play. **Note:** *If the door can be lifted (1/16-inch or more) without the car body moving, the hinges should be replaced.*

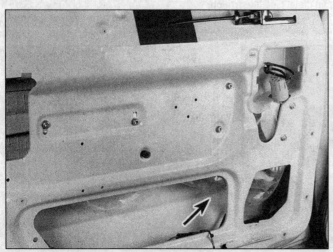 

19.7a Work through the door access hole (arrow) to remove the hinge-to-door retaining nuts from inside the door

19.7b Open the front door to access the rear door hinge-to-body bolts (arrows)

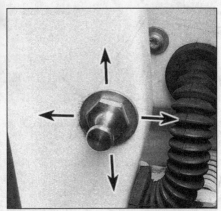

19.13 Adjust the door lock striker by loosening the hex nut and gently tapping the striker in the desired direction

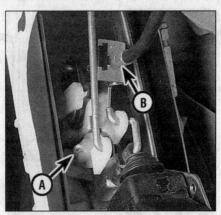

20.2 Detach the outside handle-to-latch rod (A), then remove the inside handle-to-latch cable (B)

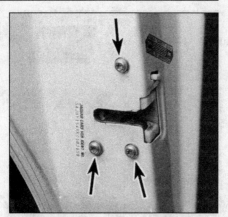

20.4 Remove the latch screws (arrows) from the end of the door, and pull the latch assembly through the access hole.

20.7 The outside handle retaining nuts (arrows) can be reached through the access hole in the door

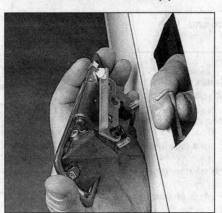

20.8 Detach the plastic clip securing the lock rod

20.13 After removing the cable from the latch assembly, detach the handle retaining bolts, then pull the handle and cable assembly free from the vehicle

11   Door-to-body alignment adjustments are made by loosening the hinge-to-body or hinge-to-door bolts and moving the door. Proper body alignment is achieved when the top of doors are parallel with the roof section, the front door is flush with the fender, the rear door is flush with the rear quarter panel and the bottom of the doors are aligned with the lower rocker panel. If these goals can't be reached by adjusting the hinge-to-body or hinge-to-door bolts, body alignment shims may have to be purchased and inserted behind the hinges to achieve correct alignment.

12   To adjust the door closed position, scribe a line or mark around the striker plate to provide a reference point. Check that the door latch is contacting the center of the latch striker. If not, adjust the up-and-down position first.

13   Finally, adjust the latch striker position, so the door skin is flush with the rear door (front) or rear quarter panel (rear) and provides positive engagement with the latch mechanism **(see illustration)**.

20   Door latch, lock cylinder and handles - removal and installation

Door latch

Refer to illustrations 20.2 and 20.4

1   Raise the window, then remove the door trim panel and watershield as described in Section 18.

2   Working through the large access hole, disengage the outside door handle-to-latch rod and the inside handle-to-latch cable **(see illustration)**.

3   All door locking rods are attached by plastic clips. The plastic clips can be removed by unsnapping the portion engaging the connecting rod and then by pulling the rod out of its locating hole.

4   Remove the screws securing the latch to the door **(see illustration)**, then remove the latch assembly from the door.

5   Installation is the reverse of removal.

Outside handle and door lock cylinder

Refer to illustrations 20.7 and 20.8

6   To remove the outside handle and lock cylinder assembly, raise the window then remove the door trim panel and watershield as described in Section 18.

7   Working through the access hole, detach the outside handle retaining nuts **(see illustration)**, then pull the handle away from the door.

8   Disengage the plastic clip that secures the outside handle-to-latch rod **(see illustration)**.

9   Remove the handle and lock cylinder assembly from the vehicle.

10   Installation is the reverse of removal.

Inside handle and cable

Refer to illustration 20.13

11   Remove the door trim panel as described in Section 18 and peel away the watershield.

12   Detach the inside handle-to-latch cable **(see illustration 20.2)**.

13   Remove the inside handle retaining bolts **(see illustration)**.

14   Pull the handle and cable assembly free and remove them from the door.

15   Installation is the reverse of removal.

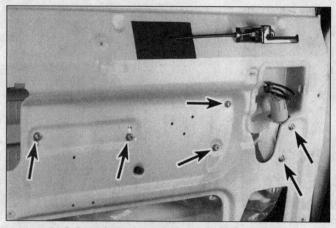

21.3 Detach the window regulator bolts (arrows)

21 Door window glass regulator - removal and installation

Refer to illustration 21.3

1   To remove the window regulator assembly, raise the window to its full upright position, then remove the door trim panel and watershield as described in Section 18.
2   Tape the window to the door glass frame to secure the window in the full upright position.
3   Remove the regulator and motor mounting bolts **(see illustration)**.
4   Disconnect the electrical connector from the window regulator motor.
5   Slide the equalizer arms out of the window glass channel and remove the regulator and motor assembly through the service hole in the door frame.
6   If the motor or regulator requires replacement, it is necessary to lock the sector gear to the regulator backplate. This can be done by fastening the sector gear to the backplate with a bolt inserted through one of the holes in the backplate and sector gear and secured with a

nut. If none of the holes line up, drill a hole through the backplate and sector gear. **Warning:** *The regulator arms are under pressure and can cause serious injury if the motor is removed without locking the sector gear.* The motor and regulator can now safely be separated.
7   Installation is the reverse of removal.

22 Door window glass - removal and installation

Refer to illustrations 22.4a, 22.4b and 22.5

1   Raise the window to its full upright position, then remove the door trim panel and watershield as described in Section 18.
2   Tape the window to the door glass frame to secure the window in the full upright position.
3   Detach the regulator assembly (see Section 21) and lower it to the bottom of the door.
4   Remove the window frame retaining bolts **(see illustrations)**.
5   Remove the window frame and glass assembly by pulling it up and out **(see illustration)**.
6   Installation is the reverse of removal.

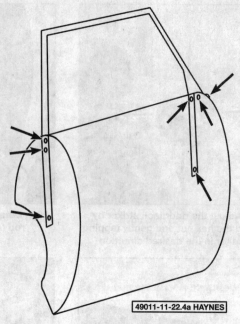

49011-11-22.4a HAYNES

22.4a Front door window frame screw locations

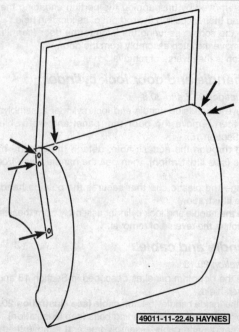

49011-11-22.4b HAYNES

22.4b Rear door window frame screw locations

22.5 After removing the window frame retaining screws, pull the window and frame assembly up and out to remove it

23.2 Remove the trim cover retaining screws

23.4 Disconnect the electrical connector, then detach the three mirror retaining screws and remove the mirror from the vehicle

24.2 Carefully pry out the gear selector trim bezel

23 Outside mirrors - removal and installation

Refer to illustrations 23.2 and 23.4
1   Raise the window to the fully closed position and remove the upper half of the door trim panel (see Section 18).
2   Detach the trim cover retaining screws (see illustration).
3   Disconnect the electrical connector from the mirror.
4   Remove the three mirror retaining screws and detach the mirror from the vehicle (see illustration).
5   Installation is the reverse of removal.

24 Center console - removal and installation

Floor console

Refer to illustrations 24.2, 24.3a, 24.3b, 24.4, 24.7, 24.8 and 24.9
1   Disconnect the negative battery cable. Caution: If the stereo in your vehicle is equipped with an anti-theft system, make sure you have the correct activation code before disconnecting the battery.
2   Pry out the gear selector trim bezel (see illustration).
3   Open the console compartment and remove the screws securing the ash tray. Pull the ash tray back towards the compartment to remove it (see illustrations).
4   Working through the ash tray opening, detach the plastic wingnuts securing the rear edge of the radio trim bezel (see illustration).

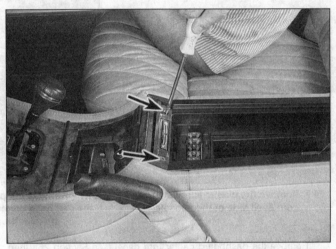

24.3a Open the console compartment to access the ash tray retaining screws (arrows)

5   Apply the parking brake, then move the gear selector towards the rear of the vehicle. Pull up on the rear half of the radio trim bezel while gently detaching the clips securing the front, then remove the bezel from the vehicle.
6   Remove the radio and heater control assembly (see Chapter 12).

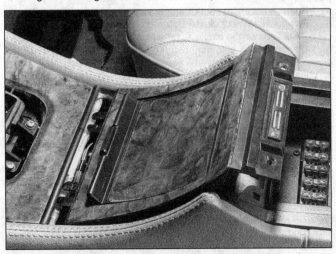

24.3b Pull the ash tray towards the rear of the vehicle to remove it - don't pull it straight up

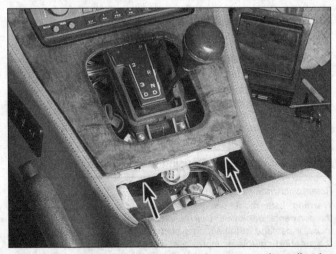

24.4 Working through the ash tray opening, remove the radio trim bezel wingnuts (arrows) located under the trim bezel

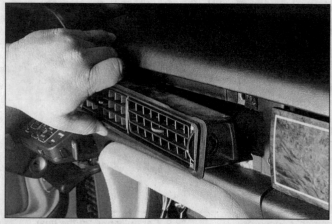

**24.7 After removing the center trim panel,
detach the air conditioning duct**

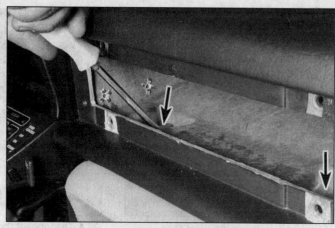

**24.8 Remove the retaining screws in the air
conditioning duct opening**

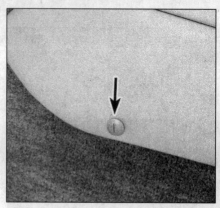

**24.9 Remove the plastic screws (arrow)
from each side of the console**

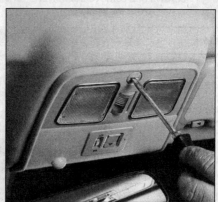

**24.13 Remove the plastic screw, then pull
the overhead console down and unplug
the electrical connectors**

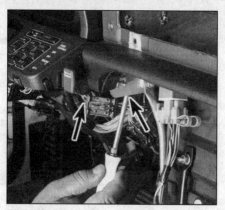

**25.4 Working in the knee bolster opening,
remove two retaining screws from each
end of the instrument cluster housing**

7   Remove the dashboard center trim panel (see Section 26), then remove the center air conditioning duct from the vehicle **(see illustration)**.

8   Remove the retaining screws located in the air conditioning duct opening **(see illustration)**.

9   Remove the plastic screws securing the lower front section of the console **(see illustration)**.

10   Unplug any electrical connectors that will interfere with the removal of the console.

11   Pull the console towards the rear of the vehicle, then lift the console up over the shift lever and remove it from the vehicle.

12   Installation is the reverse of removal.

Overhead console

Refer to illustration 24.13

13   Remove the plastic screw securing the overhead console, then carefully pull the console out of the headliner **(see illustration)**.

14   Disconnect the electrical connectors from the lights.

15   Installation is the reverse of removal.

25 Instrument cluster housing - removal and installation

Refer to illustrations 25.4 and 25.5

Warning: *Later model vehicles are equipped with airbags. To prevent the accidental deployment of the airbag, which could cause personal injury or damage to the airbag system, DO NOT work in the vicinity of the steering column or instrument panel. The manufacturer recommends that, on airbag equipped models, the following procedure should be left to a dealer service department or other repair shop*

because of the special tools and techniques required to disable the airbag system.

1   Disconnect the negative battery cable. **Caution:** *If the stereo in your vehicle is equipped with an anti-theft system, make sure you have the correct activation code before disconnecting the battery.*

2   Remove the drivers side knee bolster (see Section 26).

3   Place the steering wheel in the full rearward position. If the vehicle is equipped with a tilt column, place the steering wheel in the lowest position.

4   Remove the instrument cluster housing screws **(see illustration)**.

5   Pull the instrument cluster housing outward to access the electrical connections on the backside **(see illustration)**.

6   Disconnect all electrical connections from the backside of the cluster housing and remove the housing from the vehicle.

7   Installation is the reverse of removal.

26 Dashboard trim panels - removal and installation

Warning: *Later model vehicles are equipped with airbags. To prevent the accidental deployment of the airbag, which could cause personal injury or damage to the airbag system, DO NOT work in the vicinity of the steering column or instrument panel. The manufacturer recommends that, on airbag equipped models, the following procedure should be left to a dealer service department or other repair shop because of the special tools and techniques required to disable the airbag system.*

Caution: *If the stereo in your vehicle is equipped with an anti-theft system, make sure you have the correct activation code before disconnecting the battery.*

25.5 Pull outward on the instrument cluster housing and unplug the electrical connectors from the backside

26.2 Remove the retaining screws along the outer edge of the knee bolster, then remove it from the vehicle

conditioning components.

2   Detach the retaining screws along the edges of the knee bolster **(see illustration)**.

3   Pull outward on the lower edge of the knee bolster and detach it from the vehicle.

4   Installation is the reverse of removal.

Center trim panel

Refer to illustration 26.5

5   Carefully pull outward to detach the center trim panel from the instrument panel **(see illustration)**.

6   Installation is the reverse of removal.

Glove box

Refer to illustrations 26.8 and 26.11

7   Detach the passenger side knee bolster as described in Steps 2 and 3.

8   Remove the glove box door hinge bolts **(see illustration)**.

9   Open the glove box door, then detach it from the vehicle.

10   Detach the heater duct and the relay mounting panel from the bottom of the glove box.

11   Detach the remaining screws securing the upper edge of the glove box **(see illustration)**.

12   Disconnect the lamp from the glove box and remove the assembly from the vehicle.

13   Installation is the reverse of removal.

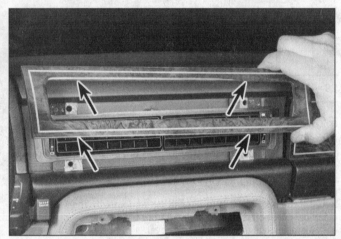

26.5 Grasp the center trim panel with both hands, then unsnap the retaining clips (arrows) from the dashboard assembly

Knee bolster

Refer to illustration 26.2

1   Knee bolsters are located on the lower half of the instrument panel on the driver and passenger sides of the vehicle. The removal of these covers will allow access to a variety of electrical, heating and air

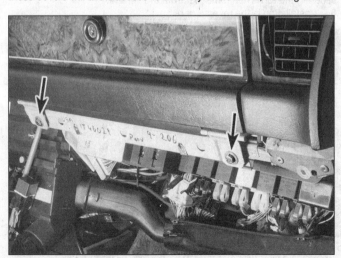

26.8 With the passenger side knee bolster removed, unscrew the glove box door hinge bolts

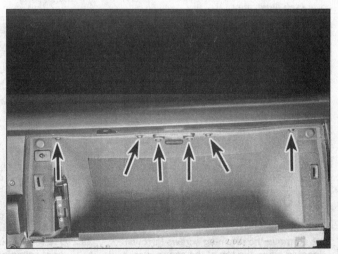

26.11 Remove the screws along the top edge (arrows), pull the glove box out and remove the lamp assembly

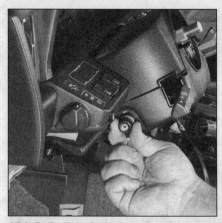

27.2 Pull off the knob from the instrument panel light rheostat

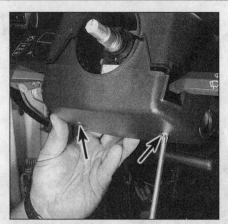

27.3 Remove the lower steering column cover screws

27.4 Remove the four screws securing the upper half of the steering column cover

27 Steering column cover - removal and installation

Refer to illustrations 27.2, 27.3 and 27.4

Warning: *Later model vehicles are equipped with airbags. To prevent the accidental deployment of the airbag, which could cause personal injury or damage to the airbag system, DO NOT work in the vicinity of the steering column or instrument panel. The manufacturer recommends that, on airbag equipped models, the following procedure should be left to a dealer service department or other repair shop because of the special tools and techniques required to disable the airbag system.*

1   Remove the steering wheel (see Chapter 10)
2   Remove the knob from the rheostat (dimmer) for the instrument panel lights **(see illustration)**.
3   Remove the lower steering column cover screws **(see illustration)**, then detach the lower cover.
4   Working through the lower cover opening, remove the four screws securing the upper half of the cover, then pull the cover forward and out to remove it **(see illustration)**.
5   Installation is the reverse of removal.

28 Cowl cover - removal and installation

Refer to illustration 28.2
1   Remove the windshield wiper arms (see Chapter 12).
2   Remove the retaining screws located along the top of the cowl cover **(see illustration)**.

3   Lift the cowl cover up slightly, then detach the electrical connectors and the spray nozzle hoses from the backside of the cowl cover.
4   Detach the cowl cover from the vehicle.
5   Installation is the reverse of removal.

29 Seats - removal and installation

Front seat

Refer to illustration 29.2
1   Position the seat all the way forward or all the way to the rear to access the front seat retaining bolts.
2   Detach any bolt trim covers and remove the retaining bolts **(see illustration)**.
3   Tilt the seat upward to access the underneath, then unplug any electrical connectors and lift the seat from the vehicle.
4   Installation is the reverse of removal.

Rear seat

Refer to illustration 29.5
5   Remove retaining screws at the lower edge of the seat cushion **(see illustration)**. Then lift up on the front edge and remove the cushion from the vehicle.
6   Detach the retaining bolts at the lower edge of the seat back.
7   Lift up on the lower edge of the seat back to release the clips securing the top. Then remove it from the vehicle.
8   Installation is the reverse of removal.

28.2 Remove the retaining screws (arrows) located along the top of the cowl cover

29.2 Use a Torx bit to remove the front seat retaining bolts (arrow)

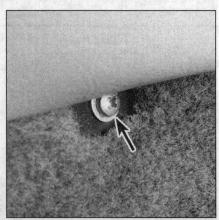

29.5 Detach the screws (arrow) along the lower edge of the seat cover

Chapter 12
Chassis electrical system

Contents

1 General information

The electrical system is a 12-volt, negative ground type. Power for the lights and all electrical accessories is supplied by a lead/acid-type battery which is charged by the alternator.

This Chapter covers repair and service procedures for the various electrical components not associated with the engine. Information on the battery, alternator, distributor and starter motor can be found in Chapter 5.

It should be noted that when portions of the electrical system are serviced, the cable should be disconnected from the negative battery terminal to prevent electrical shorts and/or fires. **Caution:** *If the stereo in your vehicle is equipped with an anti-theft system, make sure you have the correct activation code before disconnecting the battery.*

2 Electrical troubleshooting - general information

A typical electrical circuit consists of an electrical component, any switches, relays, motors, fuses, fusible links, inline fuses or circuit breakers related to that component and the wiring and electrical connectors that link the component to both the battery and the chassis. To help you pinpoint an electrical circuit problem, wiring diagrams are included at the end of this Chapter.

Before tackling any troublesome electrical circuit, first study the appropriate wiring diagrams to get a complete understanding of what makes up that individual circuit. Trouble spots, for instance, can often be narrowed down by noting if other components related to the circuit are operating properly. If several components or circuits fail at one time, chances are the problem is in a fuse or ground connection, because several circuits are often routed through the same fuse and ground connections.

Electrical problems usually stem from simple causes, such as loose or corroded connections, a blown fuse, a melted fusible link or a bad relay. Visually inspect the condition of all fuses, wires and connections in a problem circuit before troubleshooting it.

If testing instruments are going to be utilized, use the diagrams to plan ahead of time where you will make the necessary connections in order to accurately pinpoint the trouble spot.

The basic tools needed for electrical troubleshooting include a circuit tester or voltmeter (a 12-volt bulb with a set of test leads can also be used), a continuity tester, which includes a bulb, battery and set of test leads, and a jumper wire, preferably with a circuit breaker incorporated, which can be used to bypass electrical components. Before attempting to locate a problem with test instruments, use the wiring diagram(s) to decide where to make the connections.

Voltage checks

Voltage checks should be performed if a circuit is not functioning properly. Connect one lead of a circuit tester to either the negative battery terminal or a known good ground. Connect the other lead to a electrical connector in the circuit being tested, preferably nearest to the battery or fuse. If the bulb of the tester lights, voltage is present, which means that the part of the circuit between the electrical connector and the battery is problem free. Continue checking the rest of the circuit in the same fashion. When you reach a point at which no voltage is present, the problem lies between that point and the last test point with voltage. Most of the time the problem can be traced to a loose connection. **Note:** *Keep in mind that some circuits receive voltage only when the ignition key is in the Accessory or Run position.*

Finding a short

One method of finding shorts in a circuit is to remove the fuse and connect a test light or voltmeter in its place. There should be no voltage present in the circuit. Move the wiring harness from side to side while watching the test light. If the bulb goes on, there is a short to ground somewhere in that area, probably where the insulation has rubbed through. The same test can be performed on each component in the circuit, even a switch.

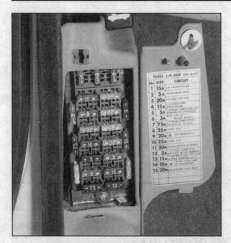

3.1a The left side fuse box is located in the driver's side kick panel, behind the fuse panel cover

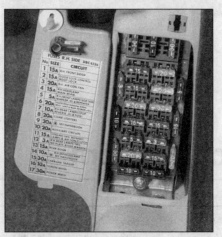

3.1b The right side fuse box is located in the passenger side kick panel, behind the fuse panel cover

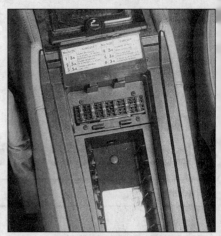

3.1c A third fuse box is located in the center console glove box

Ground check

Perform a ground test to check whether a component is properly grounded. Disconnect the battery and connect one lead of a self-powered test light, known as a continuity tester, to a known good ground. Connect the other lead to the wire or ground connection being tested. If the bulb goes on, the ground is good. If the bulb does not go on, the ground is not good.

Continuity check

A continuity check is done to determine if there are any breaks in a circuit - if it is passing electricity properly. With the circuit off (no power in the circuit), a self-powered continuity tester can be used to check the circuit. Connect the test leads to both ends of the circuit (or to the "power" end and a good ground), and if the test light comes on the circuit is passing current properly. If the light doesn't come on, there is a break somewhere in the circuit. The same procedure can be used to test a switch, by connecting the continuity tester to the power in and power out sides of the switch. With the switch turned On, the test light should come on.

Finding an open circuit

When diagnosing for possible open circuits, it is often difficult to locate them by sight because oxidation or terminal misalignment are hidden by the electrical connectors. Merely wiggling an electrical connector on a sensor or in the wiring harness may correct the open circuit condition. Remember this when an open circuit is indicated when troubleshooting a circuit. Intermittent problems may also be caused by oxidized or loose connections.

Electrical troubleshooting is simple if you keep in mind that all electrical circuits are basically electricity running from the battery, through the wires, switches, relays, fuses and fusible links to each electrical component (light bulb, motor, etc.) and to ground, from which it is passed back to the battery. Any electrical problem is an interruption in the flow of electricity to and from the battery.

3   Fuses - general information

Refer to illustrations 3.1a, 3.1b, 3.1c and 3.3

The electrical circuits of the vehicle are protected by a combination of fuses, circuit breakers and Inline fuses. The fuse blocks are located in the left and right side kick panels and in the center console glove box **(see illustrations)**.

Each of the fuses is designed to protect a specific circuit, and the various circuits are identified on the fuse panel cover.

Miniaturized fuses are employed in the fuse blocks. These com-

pact fuses, with blade terminal design, allow fingertip removal and replacement. If an electrical component fails, always check the fuse first. The best way to check the fuses is with a test light. Check for power at the exposed terminal tips of each fuse. If power is present on one side of the fuse but not the other, the fuse is blown. A blown fuse can also be confirmed by visually inspecting it **(see illustration)**.

Be sure to replace blown fuses with the correct type. Fuses of different ratings are physically interchangeable, but only fuses of the proper rating should be used. Replacing a fuse with one of a higher or lower value than specified is not recommended. Each electrical circuit needs a specific amount of protection. The amperage value of each fuse is molded into the fuse body.

If the replacement fuse immediately fails, don't replace it again until the cause of the problem is isolated and corrected. In most cases, this will be a short circuit in the wiring caused by a broken or deteriorated wire.

4   Inline fuses - general information

Some circuits are protected by inline fuses. Inline fuses are used in such circuits as the windshield wiper system, headlight power wash system, radio memory and the ABS main feed and pump circuits.

Inline fuses are located through out the vehicle depending on the year, make and model. Consult the wiring diagrams at the end of this Chapter for further information.

Inline fuses also have a blade terminal design, which allow fingertip removal and replacement. If an electrical component fails, always check the fuse first. A blown fuse is easily identified through the clear plastic body. Visually inspect the element for evidence of damage **(see illustration 3.3)**.

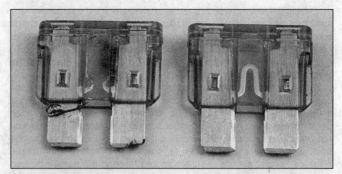

3.3 When a fuse blows, the element between the terminals burns - the fuse on the left is blown, the fuse on the right is good

Be sure to replace blown fuses with the correct type. Fuses of different ratings are physically interchangeable, but only fuses of the proper rating should be used. Replacing a fuse with one of a higher or lower value than specified is not recommended. Each electrical circuit needs a specific amount of protection. The amperage value of each fuse is molded into the fuse body.

If the replacement fuse immediately fails, don't replace it again until the cause of the problem is isolated and corrected. In most cases, this will be a short circuit in the wiring caused by a broken or deteriorated wire.

5   Circuit breakers - general information

Circuit breakers generally protect components such as power windows, power door locks and headlights. On some models the circuit breaker resets itself automatically, so an electrical overload in the circuit will cause it to fail momentarily, then come back on. If the circuit

doesn't come back on, check it immediately. Once the condition is corrected, the circuit breaker will resume its normal function. Some circuit breakers have a button on top and must be reset manually.

To test a circuit breaker , simply use an ohmmeter to check continuity between the terminals. A reading of zero to 1.0 ohms indicates a good circuit breaker. An open circuit reading on the meter indicates a bad circuit breaker.

6   Relays - general information and testing

General information
Refer to illustrations 6.1a, 6.1b and 6.1c

1   Several electrical accessories in the vehicle, such as the fuel injection system, power windows, power door locks, power seats, cruise control and air conditioning use relays to transmit the electrical signal to the component. Relays use a low-current circuit (the control

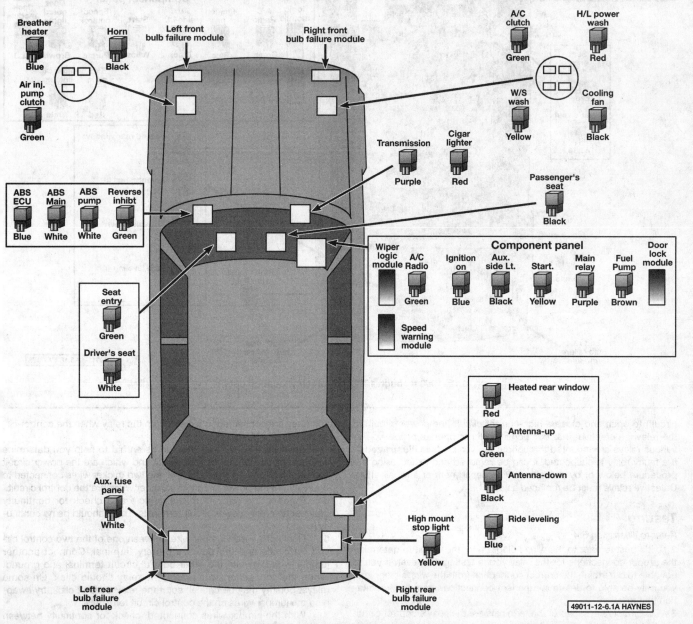

6.1a 1988 and 1989 model relay location details

49011-12-6.1A HAYNES

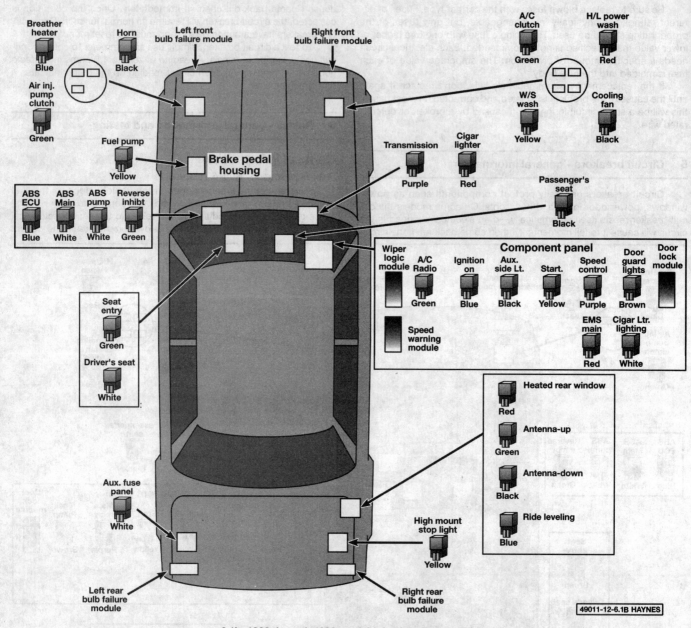

6.1b 1990 through 1992 model relay location details

circuit) to open and close a high-current circuit (the power circuit). If the relay is defective, that component will not operate properly. The various relays are mounted throughout the vehicle **(see illustrations)**. If a faulty relay is suspected, it can be removed and tested using the procedure below or by a dealer service department or a repair shop. Defective relays must be replaced as a unit.

Testing

Refer to illustration 6.4

2   It's best to refer to the wiring diagram for the circuit to determine the proper connections for the relay you're testing. However, if you're not able to determine the correct connection from the wiring diagrams, you may be able to determine the test connections from the information that follows.

3   On most relays, two of the terminals are the relay's control circuit (they connect to the relay coil which, when energized, closes the large contacts to complete the circuit). The other terminals are the power cir-

cuit (they are connected together within the relay when the control-circuit coil is energized).

4   Relays are sometimes marked as an aid to help you determine which terminals are the control circuit and which are the power circuit **(see illustration)**. As a general rule, the two thicker wires connected to the relay are the power circuit; the thinner wires are the control circuit.

5   Remove the relay from the vehicle and check for continuity between the relay power circuit terminals. There should be no continuity.

6   Connect a fused jumper wire between one of the two control circuit terminals and the positive battery terminal. Connect another jumper wire between the other control circuit terminal and ground. When the connections are made, the relay should click. On some relays, polarity may be critical, so, if the relay doesn't click, try swapping the jumper wires on the control circuit terminals.

7   With the jumper wires connected, check for continuity between the power circuit terminals. Now, there should be continuity.

8   If the relay fails any of the above tests, replace it.

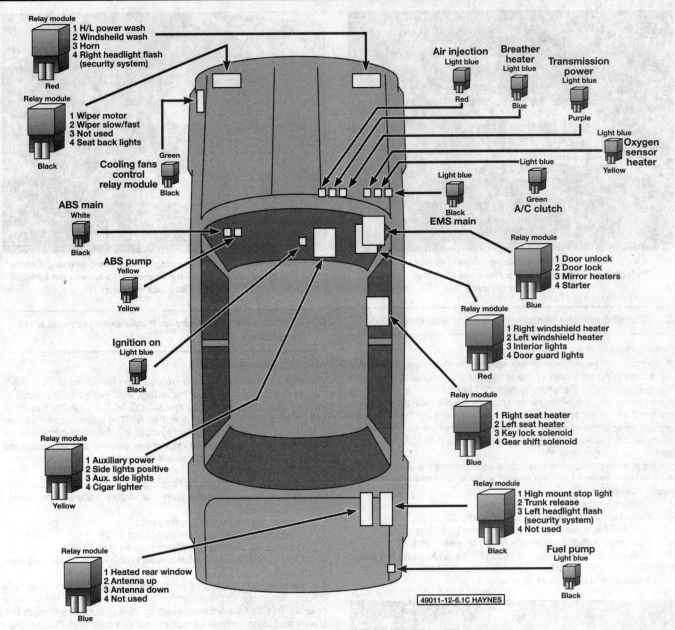

Relay module
1 H/L power wash
2 Windsheild wash
3 Horn
4 Right headlight flash
(security system)
Red

Relay module
1 Wiper motor
2 Wiper slow/fast
3 Not used
4 Seat back lights
Black

Cooling fans control relay module
Green
Black

ABS main
White
Black

ABS pump
Yellow
Yellow

Ignition on
Light blue
Black

Relay module
1 Auxiliary power
2 Side lights positive
3 Aux. side lights
4 Cigar lighter
Yellow

Relay module
1 Heated rear window
2 Antenna up
3 Antenna down
4 Not used
Blue

Air injection
Light blue
Red

Breather heater
Light blue
Blue

Transmission power
Light blue
Purple

Light blue
Oxygen sensor heater
Yellow

Light blue

Light blue
Black
EMS main

Green
A/C clutch

Relay module
1 Door unlock
2 Door lock
3 Mirror heaters
4 Starter
Blue

Relay module
1 Right windshield heater
2 Left windshield heater
3 Interior lights
4 Door guard lights
Red

Relay module
1 Right seat heater
2 Left seat heater
3 Key lock solenoid
4 Gear shift solenoid
Blue

Relay module
1 High mount stop light
2 Trunk release
3 Left headlight flash
(security system)
4 Not used
Black

Fuel pump
Light blue
Black

49011-12-6.1C HAYNES

6.1c 1993 and 1994 model relay location details

6.4 Most relays are marked on the outside to easily identify the control circuit and power circuits

7 Turn signal/hazard flasher - general information

Warning: *Later model vehicles are equipped with airbags. To prevent the accidental deployment of the airbag, which could cause personal injury or damage to the airbag system, DO NOT work in the vicinity of the steering column or instrument panel. The manufacturer recommends that, on airbag equipped models, the following procedure be performed at a dealer service department or other properly equipped repair facility because of the special tools and techniques required to disable the airbag system.*

The turn signal and hazard flasher systems are governed by the central processing unit. The central processing unit requires special testers and diagnostic procedures which are beyond the scope of this manual.

If the turn signal/hazard flasher system fails and the indicator bulbs are in working condition take the vehicle to a dealer service department or an automotive electrical specialist for further diagnosis and repair.

8.4 Remove the switch retaining screws, disconnect the electrical connectors and pull outward to remove the switches (arrows)

9.4 Remove the switch mounting plate screws (arrows). Lower the mounting plate and switch assembly to access the ignition switch/key lock cylinder

8   Steering column switches - removal and installation

Refer to illustration 8.4

Warning: *Later model vehicles are equipped with airbags. To prevent the accidental deployment of the airbag, which could cause personal injury or damage to the airbag system, DO NOT work in the vicinity of the steering column or instrument panel. The manufacturer recommends that, on airbag equipped models, the following procedure be performed at a dealer service department or other properly equipped repair facility because of the special tools and techniques required to disable the airbag system.*

Caution: *If the stereo in your vehicle is equipped with an anti-theft system, make sure you have the correct activation code before disconnecting the battery.*

1   Disconnect the negative battery cable.
2   Remove the steering wheel (see Chapter 10).
3   Remove the lower steering column cover (see Chapter 11).
4   Remove the switch retaining screw(s) **(see illustration)**.
5   Disconnect the electrical connectors from underneath the steering column and remove the switch or switches from the vehicle.
6   Installation is the reverse of removal.

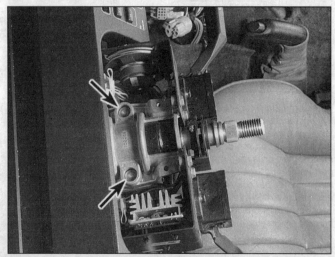

9.5 To remove the ignition switch/lock cylinder assembly, drill out the center of the two retaining bolts (arrows) and remove them with a screw extractor

9   Ignition switch and key lock cylinder - removal and installation

Refer to illustrations 9.4 and 9.5

Warning: *Later model vehicles are equipped with airbags. To prevent the accidental deployment of the airbag, which could cause personal injury or damage to the airbag system, DO NOT work in the vicinity of the steering column or instrument panel. The manufacturer recommends that, on airbag equipped models, the following procedure be performed at a dealer service department or other properly equipped repair facility because of the special tools and techniques required to disable the airbag system.*

Caution: *If the stereo in your vehicle is equipped with an anti-theft system, make sure you have the correct activation code before disconnecting the battery.*

1   Disconnect the negative battery cable.
2   Remove the steering wheel (see Chapter 10).
3   Remove the steering column trim covers (see Chapter 11).
4   Remove the steering column switch mounting plate screws **(see illustration)**.
5   Remove the shear-head bolts retaining the ignition switch/lock cylinder assembly and separate the bracket halves from the steering column. This can be accomplished by drilling out the center of the screws and using a screw extractor to remove them **(see illustration)**.
6   Place the new switch assembly in position, install the new shear-head bolts and tighten them until the heads snap off.
7   The remainder of the installation is the reverse of removal.

10   Instrument panel switches - removal and installation

Refer to illustrations 10.1, 10.2 and 10.3

Warning: *Later model vehicles are equipped with airbags. To prevent the accidental deployment of the airbag, which could cause personal injury or damage to the airbag system, DO NOT work in the vicinity of the steering column or instrument panel. The manufacturer recommends that, on airbag equipped models, the following procedure be performed at a dealer service department or other properly equipped repair facility because of the special tools and techniques required to disable the airbag system.*

Caution: *If the stereo in your vehicle is equipped with an anti-theft system, make sure you have the correct activation code before disconnecting the battery.*

1   Remove the lower trim cover(s) **(see illustration)**.
2   To remove the vehicle condition monitor (VCM) switch assembly,

10.1 Remove the lower trim cover(s) from the instrument panel switch assembly

10.2 Depress the retaining clip on the front, lower the switch assembly from the instrument panel and disconnect the electrical connectors

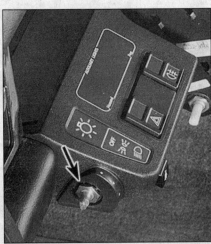

10.3 Detach the headlight switch knob, then remove the hex nut securing the switch to the instrument panel (arrow)

simply depress the switch retaining clip and lower the switch assembly from the instrument panel **(see illustration)**.

3   To remove the headlight switch assembly, detach the switch knob and remove the hex nut securing the switch to the instrument panel **(see illustration)**. Depress the retaining clip securing the switch, disconnect the electrical connectors and remove the switch assembly from the instrument panel.

4   Installation is the reverse of removal.

11 Fuel, oil and temperature gauges - check

Warning: *Later model vehicles are equipped with airbags. To prevent the accidental deployment of the airbag, which could cause personal injury or damage to the airbag system, DO NOT work in the vicinity of the steering column or instrument panel. The manufacturer recommends that, on airbag equipped models, the following procedure be performed at a dealer service department or other properly equipped repair facility because of the special tools and techniques required to disable the airbag system.*

1   All tests below require the ignition switch to be turned to ON position when testing.

2   Check the fuse if the gauge pointer does not move from the empty, low or cold positions. If the fuse is OK, locate the particular sending unit for the circuit you're working on (see Chapter 4 for fuel sending unit location, Chapter 2 for oil sending unit location or Chapter 3 for temperature sending unit location). Connect the sending unit connector to ground If the pointer goes to the full, high or hot position replace the sending unit. If the pointer stays in same position use a jumper wire to ground the terminal on the back of the gauge. If the pointer moves with the back of the gauge grounded the problem lies in the wire between the gauge and the sending unit. If the pointer does not moves with the back of the gauge grounded check for voltage at the other terminal of the gauge. If voltage is present replace the gauge.

12 Instrument cluster - removal and installation

Refer to illustration 12.3

Warning: *Later model vehicles are equipped with airbags. To prevent the accidental deployment of the airbag, which could cause personal injury or damage to the airbag system, DO NOT work in the vicinity of the steering column or instrument panel. The manufacturer recommends that, on airbag equipped models, the following procedure be performed at a dealer service department or other properly equipped*

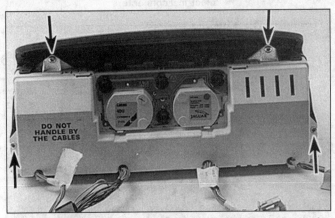

12.3 Remove the instrument cluster retaining screws (arrows) then separate the instrument cluster from the cluster housing

repair facility because of the special tools and techniques required to disable the airbag system.

Caution: *If the stereo in your vehicle is equipped with an anti-theft system, make sure you have the correct activation code before disconnecting the battery.*

1   Disconnect the negative battery cable.

2   Remove the instrument cluster housing (see Chapter 11).

3   Remove the instrument cluster mounting screws **(see illustration)**. Separate the instrument cluster from the cluster housing.

4   Installation is the reverse of removal.

13 Radio and speakers - removal and installation

Warning: *Later model vehicles are equipped with airbags. To prevent the accidental deployment of the airbag, which could cause personal injury or damage to the airbag system, DO NOT work in the vicinity of the steering column or instrument panel. The manufacturer recommends that, on airbag equipped models, the following procedure be performed at a dealer service department or other properly equipped repair facility because of the special tools and techniques required to disable the airbag system.*

Caution: *If the stereo in your vehicle is equipped with an anti-theft system, make sure you have the correct activation code before disconnecting the battery.*

1   Disconnect the negative battery cable.

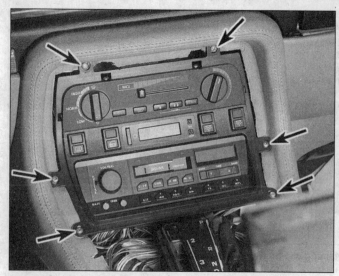

13.3 Remove the retaining screws (arrows) and pull the radio/control panel out enough to disconnect the electrical connectors

13.6 Remove the nuts from the retaining studs (arrows) to remove the speaker

Radio

Refer to illustration 13.3
2   Remove the radio trim bezel (see Chapter 11).
3   Remove the retaining screws **(see illustration)**, pull the radio/control panel outward to access the backside and disconnect the electrical connectors and antenna lead. Detach the retaining clips and separate the radio from the control panel.
4   Installation is the reverse of removal.

Speakers

Refer to illustration 13.6
5   Remove the door trim panel (see Chapter 11).
6   Remove the nuts from the speaker mounting studs **(see illustration)**. Disconnect the electrical connector and remove the speaker from the vehicle.
7   Installation is the reverse of removal.

14   Power antenna - removal and installation

Antenna motor assembly

Refer to illustrations 14.1 and 14.3
1   Remove the antenna mast retaining nut **(see illustration)**.
2   Working in the trunk, pry out the plastic clips securing the right side trunk finishing panels to allow access to the antenna motor assembly.
3   Detach the motor assembly retaining bolts **(see illustration)**. Disconnect the electrical connector and ground strap then remove the antenna motor assembly from the vehicle.
4   Installation is the reverse of removal.

Antenna mast

Refer to illustration 14.6
5   Remove the antenna mast retaining nut **(see illustration 14.1)**.
6   With an assistant controlling the ignition switch, turn the ignition key and the radio to the ON position. Guide the antenna mast out of the body as the cable unwinds from the motor assembly **(see illustration)**. Note the direction the "teeth" on the antenna cable are facing for installation purposes.
7   To install the antenna mast, insert the antenna cable into the motor assembly with the cable teeth facing the direction as noted above. Have your assistant turn the ignition key and the radio to the ON position. Guide the cable and antenna mast through the opening as the cable winds back into the motor assembly.
8   Install the antenna mast retaining nut.

14.3 Remove the retaining bolts (arrows), pull the antenna assembly out and disconnect the electrical connectors and antenna lead

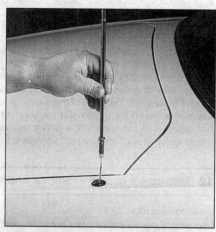

14.6 With the ignition key and the radio in the ON position, guide the antenna mast out of the motor assembly - Note the direction of the "teeth" on the antenna cable

14.1 The antenna mast retaining nut can be removed with an open end wrench

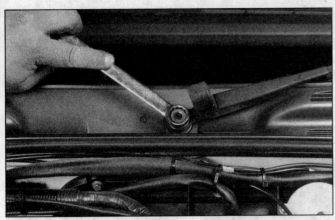

15.1 Lift up the wiper arm nut cover, remove the nut and pull the wiper arm straight off the shaft

15 Windshield wiper motor - removal and installation

Refer to illustrations 15.1, 15.3 and 15.4

1   Pull the wiper arm nut cover back to access the wiper arm nuts. Remove the nuts and pull the wiper arm straight off the shaft **(see illustration)**.
2   Remove the screws and detach the cowl cover (see Chapter 11).
3   Remove the drive spindle nut **(see illustration)**.
4   Remove the retaining bolts located along the top edge of the wiper motor housing and detach three retaining clips along the bottom edge of the wiper motor housing **(see illustration)**.
5   Disconnect the electrical connector and remove the motor assembly from the vehicle.
6   Installation is the reverse of removal.

16 Rear window defogger - check and repair

1   The rear window defogger consists of a number of horizontal elements baked onto the glass surface.
2   Small breaks in the element can be repaired without removing the rear window.

Check

Refer to illustrations 16.4, 16.5 and 16.7

3   Turn the ignition switch and defogger system switches to the ON position.

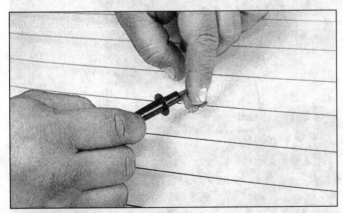

16.4 When measuring the voltage at the rear window defogger grid, wrap a piece of aluminum foil around the negative probe of the voltmeter and press the foil against the element with your finger

15.3 Use a wrench or socket to remove the drive spindle retaining nut

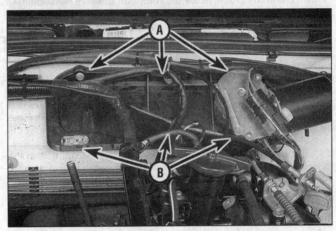

15.4 Remove the bolts (A) along the top edge of the housing and detach the clips (B) along the bottom edge

4   When measuring voltage during the next two tests, wrap a piece of aluminum foil around the tip of the voltmeter negative probe and press the foil against the heating element with your finger **(see illustration)**. Place the voltmeter positive lead against the defogger positive terminal.
5   Check the voltage at the center of each heating element **(see illustration)**.

16.5 To determine if a heating element has broken, check the voltage at the center of each element. If the voltage is 6-volts, the element is unbroken; if the voltage is 12-volts, the element is broken between the center and the positive end. If there is no voltage, the element is broken between the center and ground

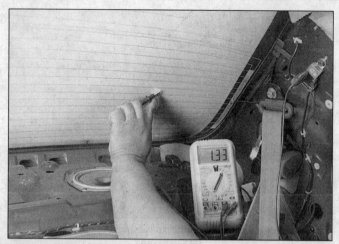

16.7 To find the break, place the voltmeter positive lead against the defogger positive terminal, place the voltmeter negative lead with the foil strip against the heating element at the positive terminal end and slide it toward the negative terminal end - the point at which the voltmeter reading changes abruptly is the point at which the element is broken

6   If the voltage is 6-volts, the element is okay (there is no break). If the voltage is 12-volts, the element is broken between the center of the element and the positive end. If the voltage is 0-volts the element is broken between the center of the element and ground.

7   To find the break, place the voltmeter positive lead against the defogger positive terminal. Place the voltmeter negative lead with the foil strip against the heating element at the positive terminal end and slide it toward the negative terminal end. The point at which the voltmeter deflects from zero to several volts is the point at which the heating element is broken **(see illustration)**.

Repair
Refer to illustration 16.13

8   Repair the break in the element using a repair kit specifically recommended for this purpose, such as Dupont paste No. 4817 (or equivalent). Included in this kit is plastic conductive epoxy.

9   Prior to repairing a break, turn off the system and allow it to cool off for a few minutes.

10   Lightly buff the element area with fine steel wool, then clean it thoroughly with rubbing alcohol.

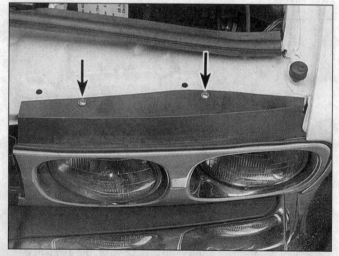

17.2 Remove the screws (arrows) and detach the headlight bezel trim cover

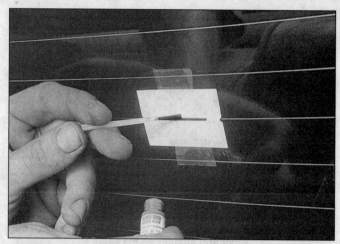

16.13 To use a defogger repair kit, apply masking tape to the inside of the window at the damaged area, then brush on the special conductive coating

11   Use masking tape to mask off the area being repaired.

12   Thoroughly mix the epoxy, following the instructions provided with the repair kit.

13   Apply the epoxy material to the slit in the masking tape, overlapping the undamaged area about 3/4-inch on either end **(see illustration)**.

14   Allow the repair to cure for 24 hours before removing the tape and using the system.

17   Headlights - replacement

Warning: *Later models are equipped with halogen gas-filled headlight bulbs which are under pressure and may shatter if the surface is damaged or the bulb is dropped. Wear eye protection and handle the bulbs carefully, grasping only the base whenever possible. Do not touch the surface of the bulb with your fingers because the oil from your skin could cause it to overheat and fail prematurely. If you do touch the bulb surface, clean it with rubbing alcohol.*

Sealed beam type bulbs
Refer to illustrations 17.2, 17.3a, 17.3b and 17.4

1   Remove the radiator grille (see Chapter 11).

17.3a Remove the two retaining screws at the top edge and the one in the grille opening (arrows)

17.3b The outside lower corner retaining screw can be accessed from under the bumper

17.4 Loosen the retaining ring screws (arrows) a few turns - rotate the retaining ring counterclockwise to remove it

2   Detach the headlight bezel trim cover (see illustration).
3   Remove the headlight bezel (see illustrations).
4   Remove the screws which secure the retaining ring and withdraw the ring. Support the light as this is done (see illustration).
5   Pull the headlight out slightly and disconnect the electrical connector from the rear of the light, then remove the light from the vehicle.
6   To install, position the new unit close enough to connect the electrical connector. Make sure that the numbers molded into the lens are at the top.
7   Install and tighten the retaining ring. Test the headlight operation.
8   The remainder of the installation is the reverse of removal.

Halogen gas filled bulbs

Refer to illustration 17.9
9   Disconnect the electrical connector from the bulb assembly. Rotate the headlight bulb connector 1/4-turn counterclockwise (viewed from the rear) (see illustration).
10   Withdraw the bulb assembly from the headlight housing.
11   Without touching the glass with your bare fingers (see Warning above), insert the new bulb assembly into the headlight housing and rotate the bulb socket 1/4-turn clockwise to install it.
12   Plug in the electrical connector and test headlight operation.

18   Headlights - adjustment

Refer to illustrations 18.2 and 18.6
Note: *It is important that the headlights are aimed correctly. If adjusted incorrectly they could blind the driver of an oncoming vehicle and cause a serious accident or seriously reduce your ability to see the road. The headlights should be checked for proper aim every 12 months and any time a new headlight is installed or front end body work is performed.*
1   Adjustment should be made with the vehicle sitting level, the gas tank half-full and no unusually heavy load in the vehicle.
2   Early models with sealed beam headlights have four adjusting knobs protruding through the backside of the radiator support. The vertical (up and down) adjustment knobs are located above the headlight and the horizontal (left to right) adjusting knobs are located below the headlight (see illustration).
3   On later models with halogen bulbs, adjustments are made in the same manner as described in the previous step, except there are only two adjusting knobs which tilt the headlight housing to the desired angle.
4   If the headlight housing has been replaced or the vehicle has suf-

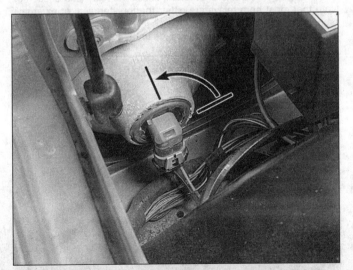

17.9 Disconnect the electrical connector and rotate the bulb assembly 1/4-turn counterclockwise

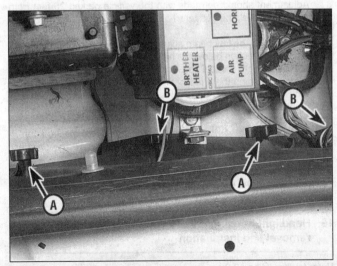

18.2 The headlight horizontal adjustment knob (A) is located at the top of the headlight and the vertical adjustment knob (B) is below the headlight

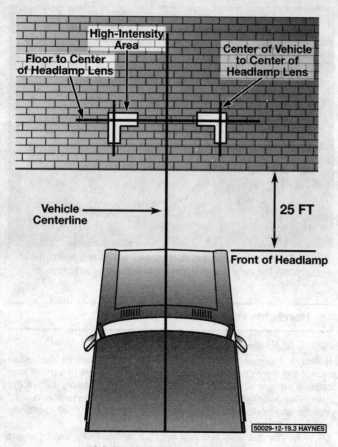

18.6 Headlight adjustment details

19.2 Remove the headlight housing retaining nuts (arrows) from the backside of the radiator support

fered front end damage refer to following procedure.

5   This method requires a blank wall, masking tape and a level floor.

6   Position masking tape vertically on the wall in reference to the vehicle centerline and the centerlines of both headlights **(see illustration)**.

7   Position a horizontal tape line in reference to the centerline of all the headlights. **Note:** *It may be easier to position the tape on the wall with the vehicle parked only a few inches away.*

8   Adjustment should be made with the vehicle parked 25 feet from the wall, sitting level, the gas tank half-full and no unusually heavy load in the vehicle.

9   Starting with the low beam adjustment, position the high intensity zone so it is two inches below the horizontal line and two inches to the right of the headlight vertical line. Adjustments are made by turning the knobs located behind the headlight housings **(see illustration 18.2)**.

10   With the high beams on, the high intensity zone should be vertically centered with the exact center just below the horizontal line. **Note:** *It may not be possible to position the headlight aim exactly for both high and low beams. If a compromise must be made, keep in mind that the low beams are the most used and have the greatest effect on safety.*

11   Have the headlights adjusted by a dealer service department or service station at the earliest opportunity.

19   Headlight housing (1992 through 1994 models) - removal and installation

Refer to illustration 19.2

Warning: *These vehicles are equipped with halogen gas-filled headlight bulbs which are under pressure and may shatter if the surface is*

damaged or the bulb is dropped. Wear eye protection and handle the bulbs carefully, grasping only the base whenever possible. Do not touch the surface of the bulb with your fingers because the oil from your skin could cause it to overheat and fail prematurely. If you do touch the bulb surface, clean it with rubbing alcohol.

1   Remove the headlight bulb (see Section 17).

2   Remove the retaining nuts, detach the housing and withdraw it from the vehicle **(see illustration)**.

3   Installation is the reverse of removal.

20   Horn - check and replacement

Check

Refer to illustration 20.3

Note: *Check the fuses before beginning electrical diagnosis.*

1   Disconnect the electrical connector from the horn.

2   To test the horn, connect battery voltage to the two terminals with a pair of jumper wires. If the horn doesn't sound, replace it.

3   If the horn does sound, check for voltage at the terminal when the horn button is depressed **(see illustration)**. If there's voltage at the terminal, check for a bad ground at the horn.

4   If there's no voltage at the horn, check the relay (see Section 6). Note that most horn relays are either the four-terminal or externally grounded three-terminal type.

5   If the relay is OK, check for voltage to the relay power and control

20.3 Check for power at the horn terminal with the horn button depressed

20.9 Disconnect the electrical connector, remove the retaining nuts (arrows) - then detach the horn(s)

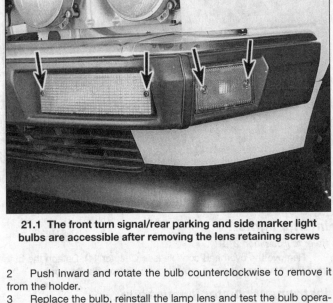

21.1 The front turn signal/rear parking and side marker light bulbs are accessible after removing the lens retaining screws

circuits. If either of the circuits are not receiving voltage, inspect the wiring between the relay and the fuse panel.

6　If both relay circuits are receiving voltage, depress the horn button and check the circuit from the relay to the horn button for continuity to ground. If there's no continuity, check the circuit for an open. If the circuit is good, replace the horn button.

7　If there's continuity to ground through the horn button, check for an open or short in the circuit from the relay to the horn.

Replacement

Refer to illustration 20.9

8　Remove the radiator grille inserts (see Chapter 11).

9　Disconnect the electrical connector and remove the retaining nuts securing the horn brackets **(see illustration)**.

10　Installation is the reverse of removal.

21 Bulb replacement

Front turn signal/rear parking and side marker lights

Refer to illustration 21.1

1　Remove the lens retaining screws and the lens **(see illustration)**.

2　Push inward and rotate the bulb counterclockwise to remove it from the holder.

3　Replace the bulb, reinstall the lamp lens and test the bulb operation.

Rear turn signal, brake, tail and back-up lights

Refer to illustrations 21.4 and 21.5

4　Open the trunk and remove the plastic knobs securing the tail light housing trim cover **(see illustration)**.

5　Remove two more plastic knobs and detach the tail light bulb cluster from the rear tail light housing. The defective bulb can then be pulled out of the socket and replaced **(see illustration)**.

License plate light

Refer to illustration 21.6

6　Remove the lens retaining screws **(see illustration)**.

7　Detach the lens and replace the defective bulb.

High-mounted brake light

8　The brake light cover is retained by screws. Remove the cover and replace the bulb.

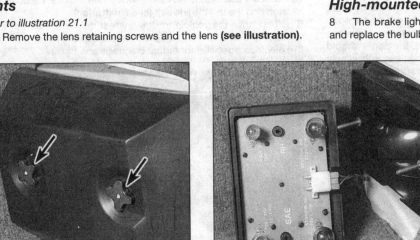

21.4 The rear turn signal, brake, tail and back-up light bulbs are accessible from the trunk compartment after removing the plastic knobs (arrows) securing the bulb housing covers

21.5 Remove the bulb cluster from the tail light housing - the bulb is removed by pushing in and turning the bulb counterclockwise

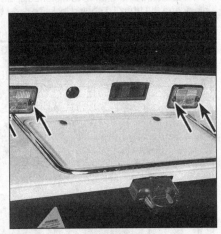

21.6 Remove the lens retaining screws (arrows) and the lens to access the license plate light bulbs

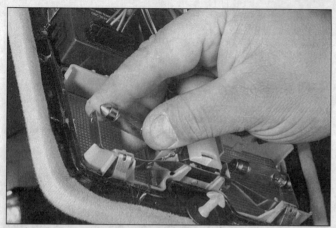

21.9 The interior dome light bulbs can be accessed after lowering the overhead console

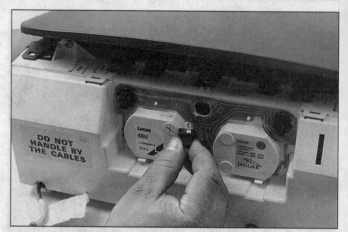

21.10 To remove an instrument cluster bulb, depress the bulb holder and rotate it counterclockwise

Interior lights

Refer to illustration 21.9

9   Remove the overhead console (see Chapter 11). Detach the bulb from the retaining clips and replace the bulb **(see illustration)**.

Instrument cluster illumination

Refer to illustration 21.10

10   To gain access to the instrument cluster illumination lights, the instrument cluster housing will have to be removed (see Chapter 11). The bulbs can then be removed and replaced from the rear of the cluster **(see illustration)**.

22   Inertia switch - description and check

Refer to illustration 22.2

1   The inertia switch is a safety mechanism which governs various electrical circuits such as the power door lock, power window and ignition circuits. In the event of a crash the inertia switch will automatically unlock the doors, shut off power to all ignition circuits and lock the trunk lid and the fuel filler cap.

2   To test the inertia switch, turn the ignition key to the ON position, then lock the driver and passenger side doors and unlock the trunk lid. Then simply pull upward on the trip/reset button located on top of the inertia switch. All ignition circuits should shut off, the doors should unlock and the trunk lid should lock. To reset the inertia switch, simply push downward on the trip/reset button **(see illustration)**.

23   Cruise control system - description and check

Refer to illustration 23.5

1   The cruise control system maintains vehicle speed with an independently operated vacuum motor located on the left side inner fender panel of the engine compartment. When the cruise control switch is turned on, a vacuum actuator (connected the throttle linkage) is activated by vacuum from the vacuum motor. The system consists of the vacuum motor, vacuum actuator, brake switch, control switches, a relay and associated vacuum hoses. Some features of the system require special testers and diagnostic procedures which are beyond the scope of this manual. Listed below are some general procedures that may be used to locate common problems.

2   Locate and check the fuse (see Section 3).

3   Have an assistant operate the brake lights while you check their operation (voltage from the brake light switch deactivates the cruise control).

4   If the brake lights don't come on or don't shut off, correct the problem and retest the cruise control.

5   Visually inspect the vacuum hose connected to the vacuum motor and vacuum actuator. Check the freeplay between the vacuum actuator stop and the throttle link slot **(see illustration)**.

6   Test drive the vehicle to determine if the cruise control is now working. If it isn't, take it to a dealer service department or an automotive electrical specialist for further diagnosis and repair.

22.2 The inertia switch is located behind the drivers side kick panel - pull upward on the button to trip the switch - push downward on the button to reset the switch

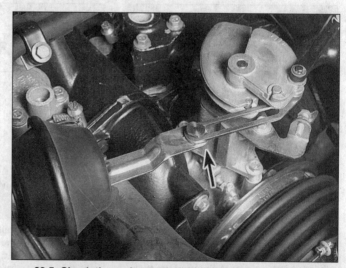

23.5 Check the cruise control throttle linkage for binding

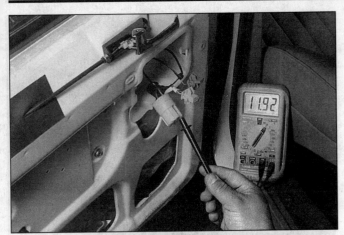

24.12 If no voltage is present at the motor with the switch depressed, check for voltage at the switch

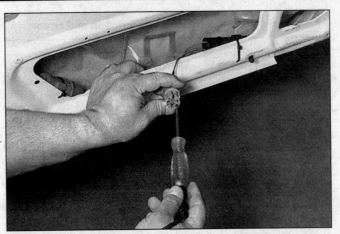

25.6 Check for voltage at the lock solenoid while the lock switch is operated

24 Power window system - description and check

Refer to illustration 24.12

1   The power window system operates electric motors, mounted in the doors, which lower and raise the windows. The system consists of the control switches, relays, the motors, regulators, glass mechanisms and associated wiring.

2   The power windows can be lowered and raised from the master control switch by the driver or by remote switches located at the individual windows. Each window has a separate motor which is reversible. The position of the control switch determines the polarity and therefore the direction of operation.

3   The circuit is protected by a fuse. Each motor is also equipped with an internal circuit breaker, this prevents one stuck window from disabling the whole system.

4   The power window system will only operate when the ignition switch is ON. In addition, many models have a window lockout switch at the master control switch which, when activated, disables the switches at the rear windows and, sometimes, the switch at the passenger's window also. Always check these items before troubleshooting a window problem.

5   These procedures are general in nature, so if you can't find the problem using them, take the vehicle to a dealer service department or other properly equipped repair facility.

6   If the power windows won't operate, always check the fuse first.

7   If only the rear windows are inoperative, or if the windows only operate from the master control switch, check the rear window lockout switch for continuity in the unlocked position. Replace it if it doesn't have continuity.

8   Check the wiring between the switches and fuse panel for continuity. Repair the wiring, if necessary.

9   If only one window is inoperative from the master control switch, try the other control switch at the window. **Note:** *This doesn't apply to the left door window.*

10   If the same window works from one switch, but not the other, check the switch for continuity.

11   If the switch tests OK, check for a short or open in the circuit between the affected switch and the window motor.

12   If one window is inoperative from both switches, remove the trim panel from the affected door and check for voltage at the switch and at the motor while the switch is operated **(see illustration)**.

13   If voltage is reaching the motor, disconnect the glass from the regulator (see Chapter 11). Move the window up and down by hand while checking for binding and damage. Also check for binding and damage to the regulator. If the regulator is not damaged and the window moves up and down smoothly, replace the motor. If there's binding or damage, lubricate, repair or replace parts, as necessary.

14   If voltage isn't reaching the motor, check the wiring in the circuit

for continuity between the switches and motors. You'll need to consult the wiring diagram for the vehicle. If the circuit is equipped with a relay, check that the relay is grounded properly and receiving voltage.

15   Test the windows after you are done to confirm proper repairs.

25 Power door lock system - description and check

Refer to illustration 25.6

The power door lock system operates the door lock actuators mounted in each door. The system consists of the switches, relays, actuators, a control unit and associated wiring. Diagnosis can usually be limited to simple checks of the wiring connections and actuators for minor faults which can be easily repaired. Since this system uses an electronic control unit, in-depth diagnosis should be left to a dealership service department.

Power door lock systems are operated by bi-directional solenoids located in the doors. The lock switches have two operating positions; Lock and Unlock. When activated, the switch sends a signal to the door lock control unit to lock or unlock the doors. Depending on which way the switch is activated, the control unit reverses polarity to the solenoids, allowing the two sides of the circuit to be used alternately as the feed (positive) and ground side.

Some vehicles may have an anti-theft system incorporated into the power locks. If you are unable to locate the trouble using the following general Steps, consult a dealer service department or other properly equipped repair facility.

1   Always check the circuit protection first. Some vehicles use a combination of circuit breakers and fuses.

2   Operate the door lock switches in both directions (Lock and Unlock) with the engine off. Listen for the click of the solenoids operating.

3   Test the switches for continuity. Replace the switch if there's not continuity in both switch positions.

4   Check the wiring between the switches, control unit and solenoids for continuity. Repair the wiring if there's no continuity.

5   Check for a bad ground at the switches or the control unit.

6   If all but one lock solenoid operates, remove the trim panel from the affected door (see Chapter 11) and check for voltage at the solenoid while the lock switch is operated **(see illustration)**. One of the wires should have voltage in the Lock position; the other should have voltage in the Unlock position.

7   If the inoperative solenoid is receiving voltage, replace the solenoid.

8   If the inoperative solenoid isn't receiving voltage, check for an open or short in the wire between the lock solenoid and the control unit. **Note:** *It's common for wires to break in the portion of the harness between the body and door (opening and closing the door fatigues and eventually breaks the wires).*

26 Electric side view mirrors - description and check

1   Most electric rear view mirrors use two motors to move the glass; one for up-and-down adjustments and one for left-right adjustments.

2   The control switch has a selector portion which sends voltage to the left or right side mirror. With the ignition ON but the engine OFF, roll down the windows and operate the mirror control switch through all functions (left-right and up-down) for both the left and right side mirrors.

3   Listen carefully for the sound of the electric motors running in the mirrors.

4   If the motors can be heard but the mirror glass doesn't move, there's probably a problem with the drive mechanism inside the mirror. Remove and disassemble the mirror to locate the problem.

5   If the mirrors don't operate and no sound comes from the mirrors, check the fuse (see Chapter 1).

6   If the fuse is OK, remove the mirror control switch from its mounting without disconnecting the wires attached to it. Turn the ignition ON and check for voltage at the switch. There should be voltage at one terminal. If there's no voltage at the switch, check for an open or short in the circuit between the fuse panel and the switch.

7   If there's voltage at the switch, disconnect it. Check the switch for continuity in all its operating positions. If the switch does not have continuity, replace it.

8   Re-connect the switch. Locate the wire going from the switch to ground. Leaving the switch connected, connect a jumper wire between this wire and ground. If the mirror works normally with this wire in place, repair the faulty ground connection.

9   If the mirror still doesn't work, remove the mirror and check the wires at the mirror for voltage. Check with ignition ON and the mirror selector switch on the appropriate side. Operate the mirror switch in all its positions. There should be voltage at one of the switch-to-mirror wires in each switch position (except the neutral "off" position).

10   If there's not voltage in each switch position, check the circuit between the mirror and control switch for opens and shorts.

11   If there's voltage, remove the mirror and test it off the vehicle with jumper wires. Replace the mirror if it fails this test.

27 Electric sunroof - description and check

Refer to illustration 27.9

1   The electric sunroof is powered by a single motor located in the roof behind the overhead console. The power circuit is protected by a fuse.

2   The control switches (tilt and slide) send a ground signal to the sunroof motor when the switches are pressed. Power is supplied to the motor from the relay. With the ignition ON but the engine OFF, operate the sunroof control switch through the tilt and slide functions.

3   Listen carefully for the sound of the sunroof motor running in the roof.

4   If the motors can be heard but the sunroof glass doesn't move, there's probably a problem with the drive mechanism or drive cables.

5   If the sunroof does not operate and no sound comes from the motor, check the fuse (see Chapter 1).

6   If the fuse is OK, remove the control switches (see Chapter 11). Disconnect the wires attached to it. Turn the ignition ON and check for voltage at the switch. If there's no voltage at the switch, check for power and ground at the motor. If power and ground exist at the motor and there's still no voltage at the switch replace the motor. If there's no voltage at the motor, check the relay or an open or short in the wiring between the relay and the motor.

7   If there's voltage at the switch, disconnect it. Check the switch for continuity in all its operating positions. If the switch does not have continuity, replace it.

8   If the switch has continuity re-connect the switch. Locate the wire going from the switch to ground. Leaving the switch connected, con-

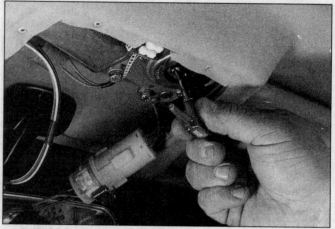

27.9 To close the sunroof manually, insert the T-handle wrench in the motor shaft and rotate it clockwise

nect a jumper wire between this wire and ground. If the motor works normally with this wire in place, repair the faulty ground connection.

9   The sunroof can be closed manually by inserting the T-handle wrench which is located inside the overhead console. Insert the wrench into the motor drive shaft and rotate the shaft clockwise **(see illustration)**.

28 Airbag system - general information

Warning: *Failure to follow these precautions could result in accidental deployment of the airbag and personal injury.*

Later models are equipped with a Supplemental Restraint System (SRS), more commonly known as an airbag. This system is designed to protect the driver, and on 1994 models, the passenger from serious injury in the event of a head-on or frontal collision. It consists of an airbag module in the center of the steering wheel and a passenger airbag module on the right side of the dash above the glove box on 1994 models.

The airbag modules contain an inflator and a sensor assembly which activates from impact energy that is transmitted through the body and steering column upon impact or collision.

DO NOT try to disassemble or remove any component in the vicinity of the steering column or instrument panel on models equipped with airbags. Serious personal injury or damage may result. The manufacturer recommends that, on airbag equipped models, service which requires removal of any component in the vicinity of the instrument panel or steering column should be left to a dealer service department or other properly equipped repair facility because of the special tools and techniques required to disable the airbag system.

29 Wiring diagrams - general information

Since it isn't possible to include a complete wiring diagram for every year covered by this manual, the following diagrams are those that are typical and most commonly needed.

Prior to troubleshooting any circuits, check the fuse and circuit breakers (if equipped) to make sure they are in good condition. Make sure the battery is properly charged and has clean, tight cable connections (see Chapter 1).

When checking the wiring system, make sure that all electrical connectors are clean, with no broken or loose pins. When unplugging an electrical connector, do not pull on the wires, only on the connector housings themselves.

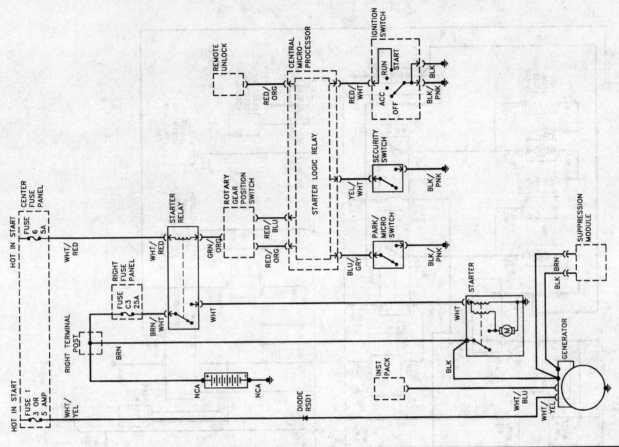

Typical 1993 and 1994 starting and charging system

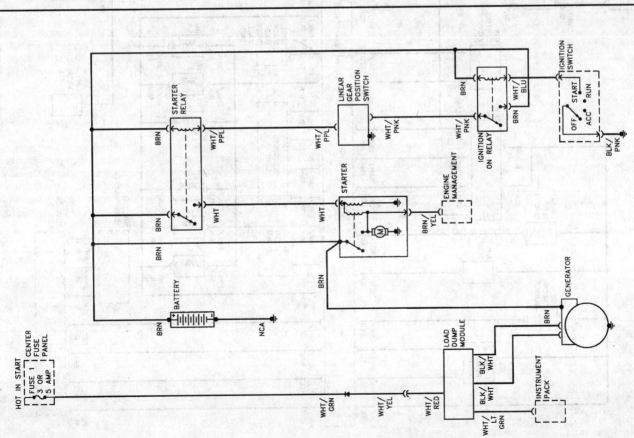

Typical 1988 thru 1992 starting and charging system

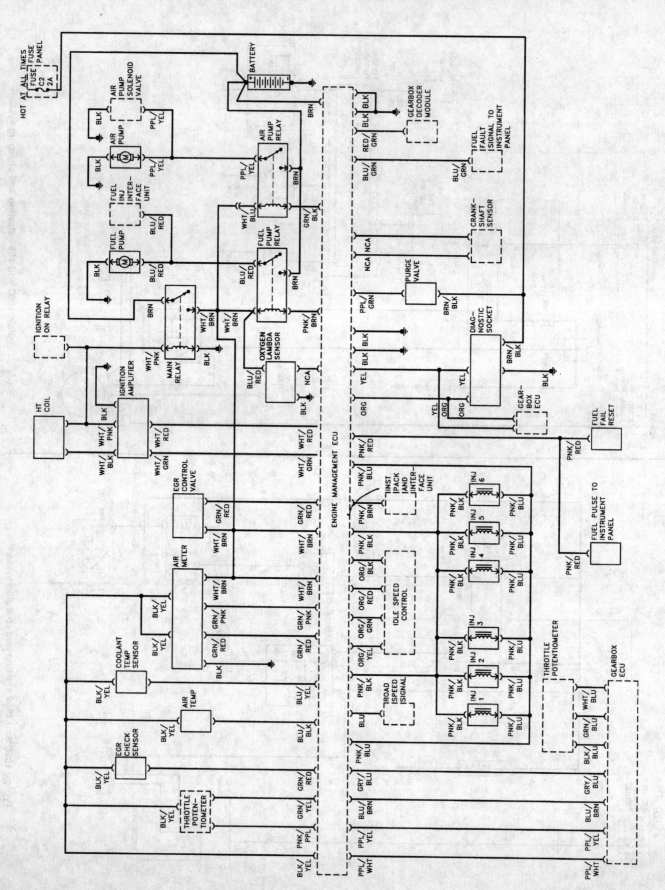

Typical 1988 thru 1992 engine management system

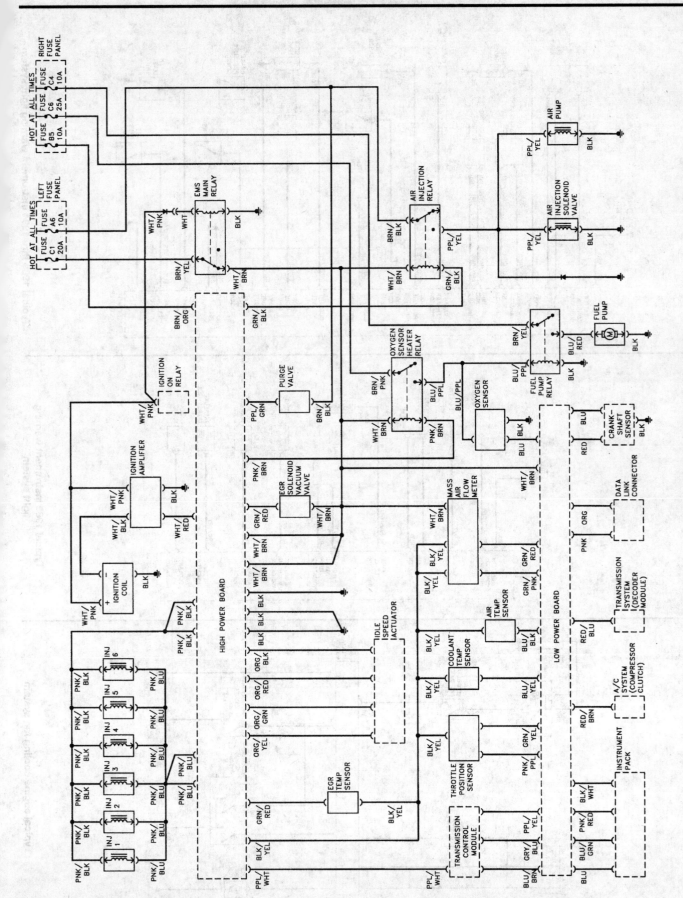

Typical 1993 and 1994 engine management system

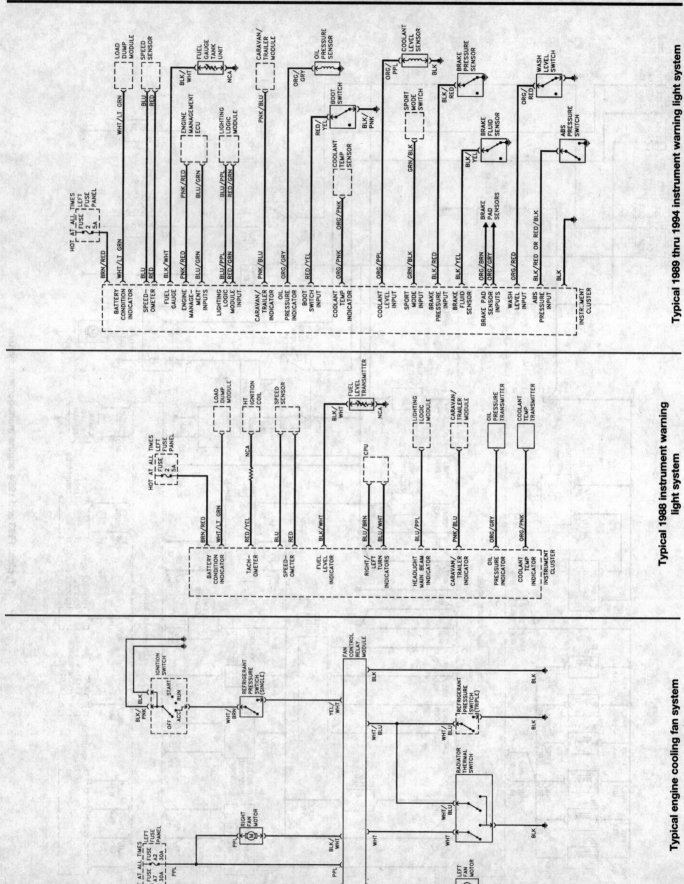

Typical 1989 thru 1994 instrument warning light system

Typical 1988 instrument warning light system

Typical engine cooling fan system

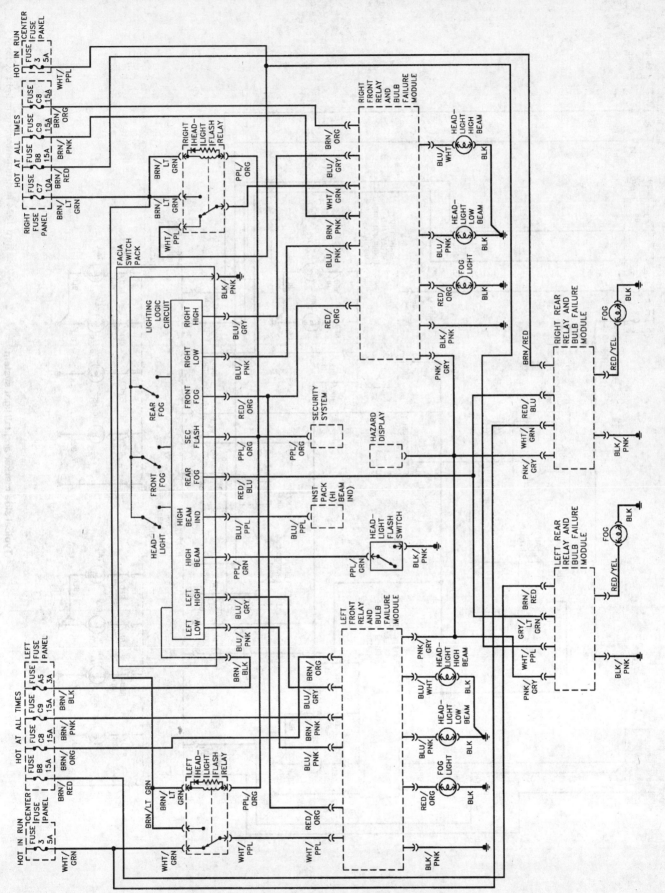

Typical headlight system

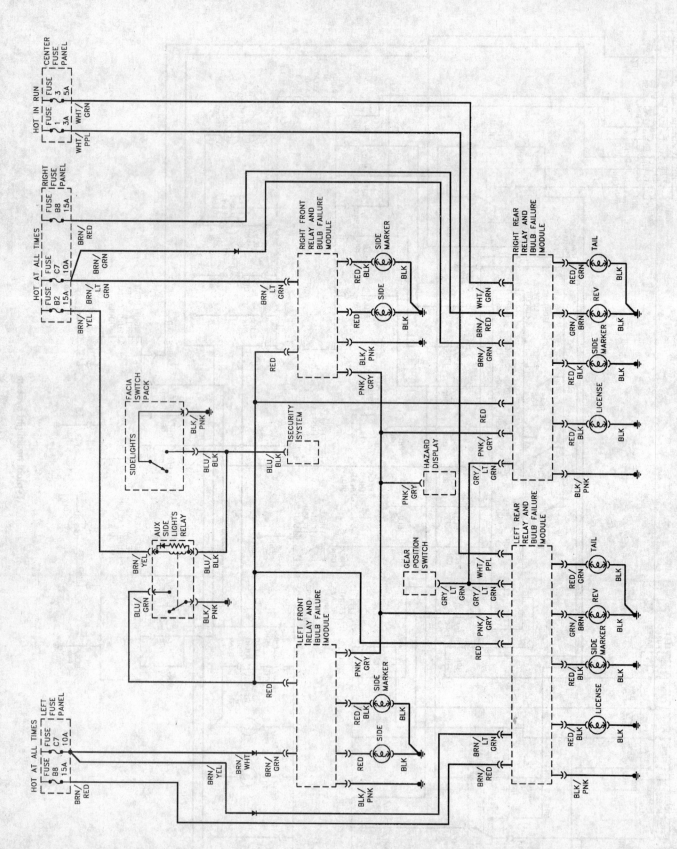

Typical side marker and tail light system

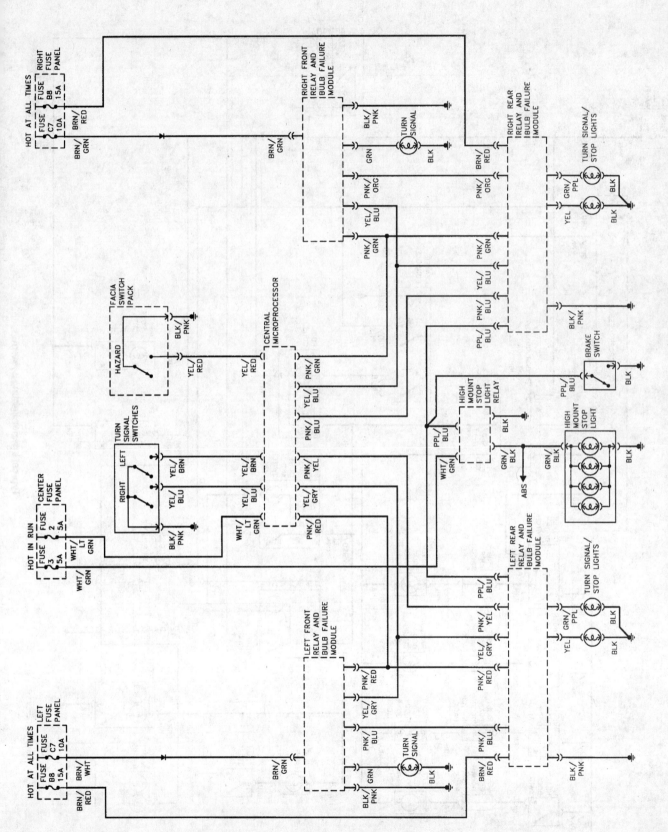

Typical hazard/turn signal and stop light system

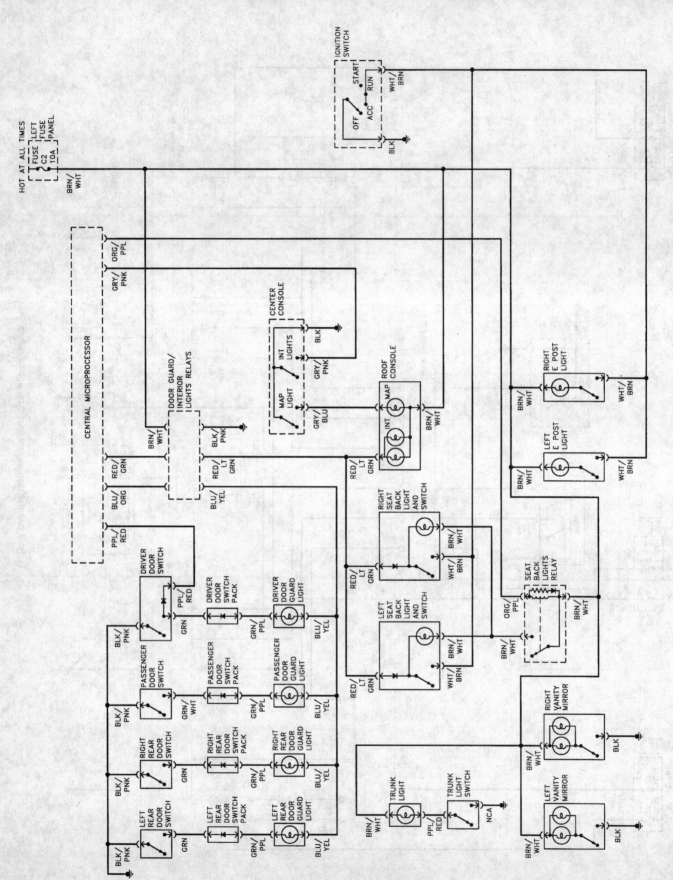

Typical interior lighting system

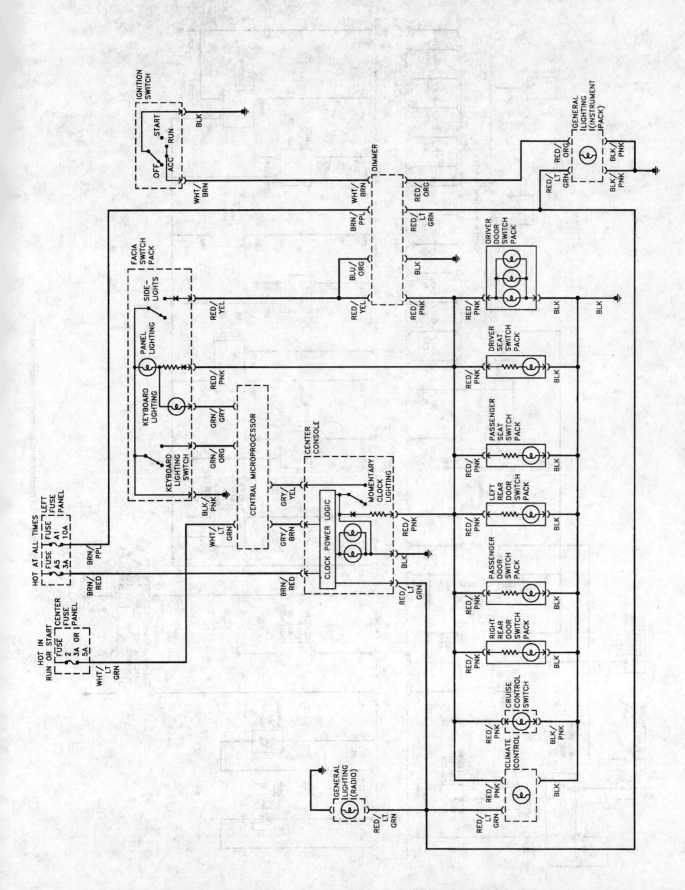

Typical instrument cluster lighting system

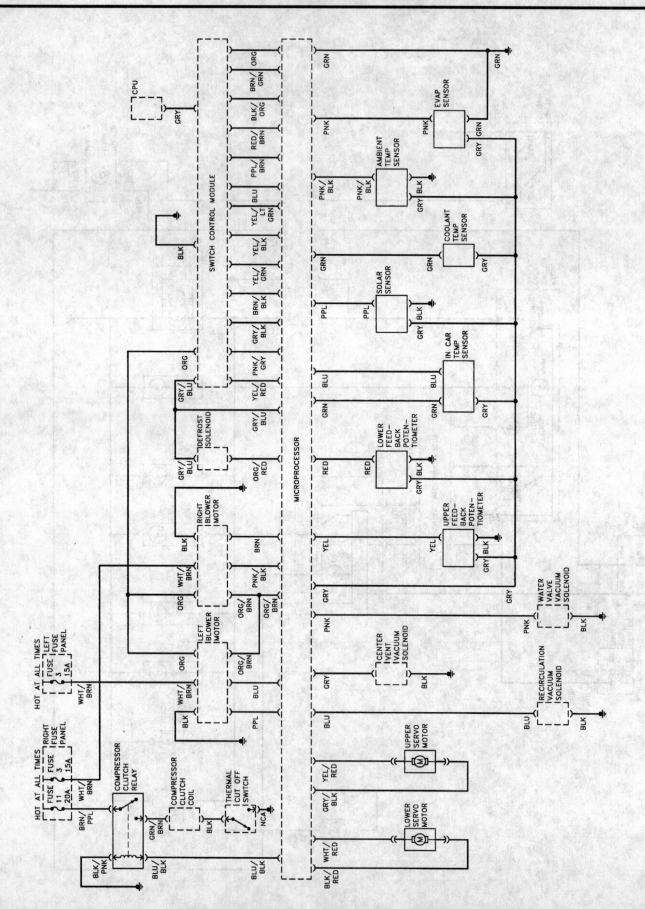

Typical 1988 heater and air conditioning system

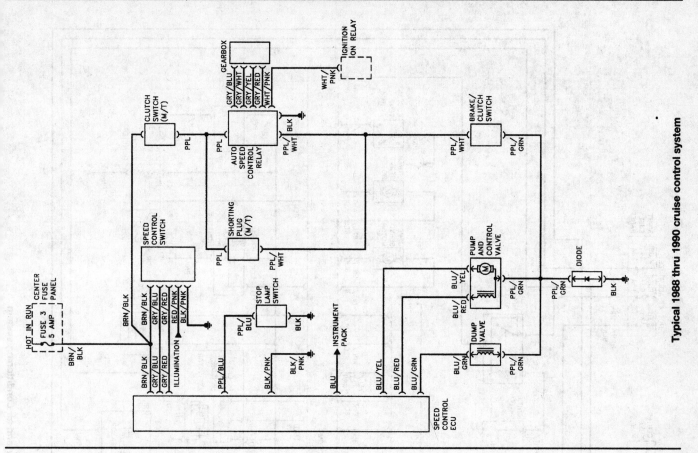

Typical 1988 thru 1990 cruise control system

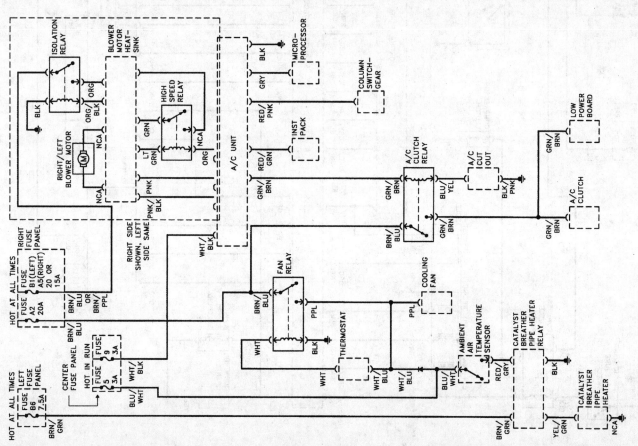

Typical 1989 thru 1992 heater and air conditioning system

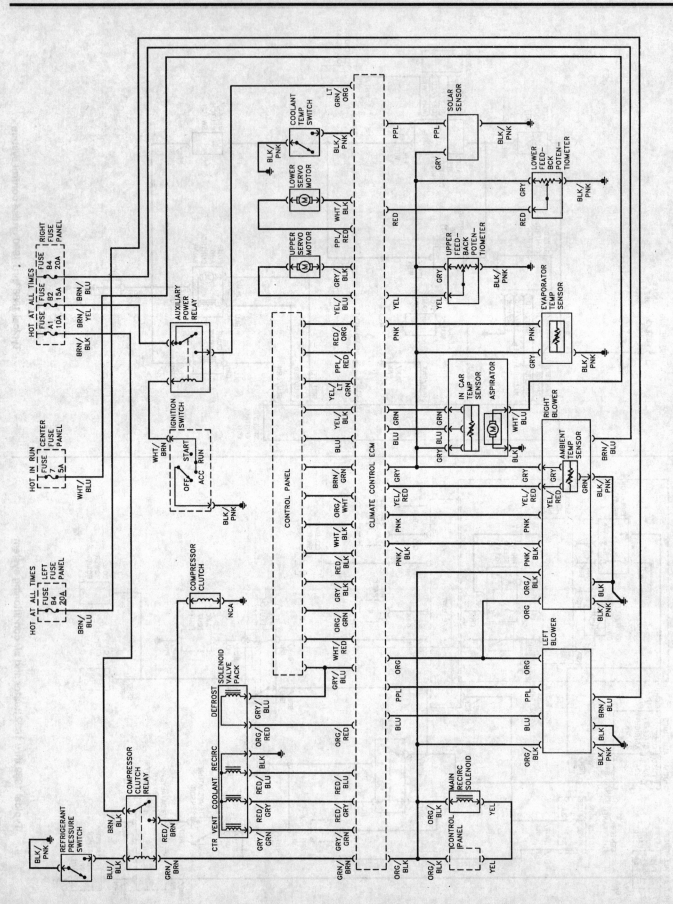

Typical 1993 and 1994 heater and air conditioning system

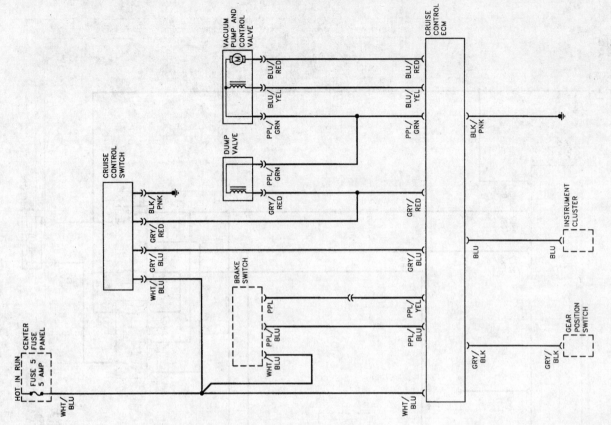

Typical 1993 and 1994 cruise control system

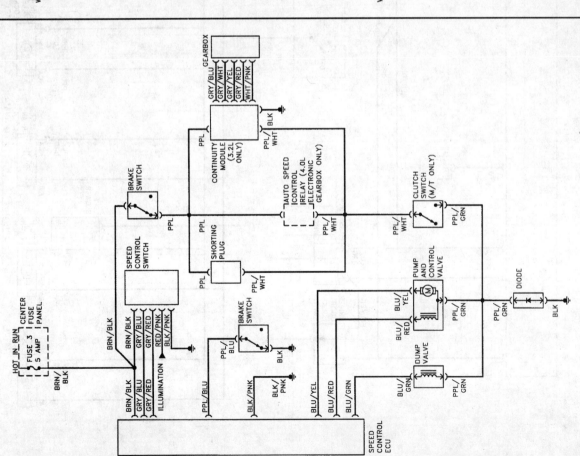

Typical 1991 and 1992 cruise control system

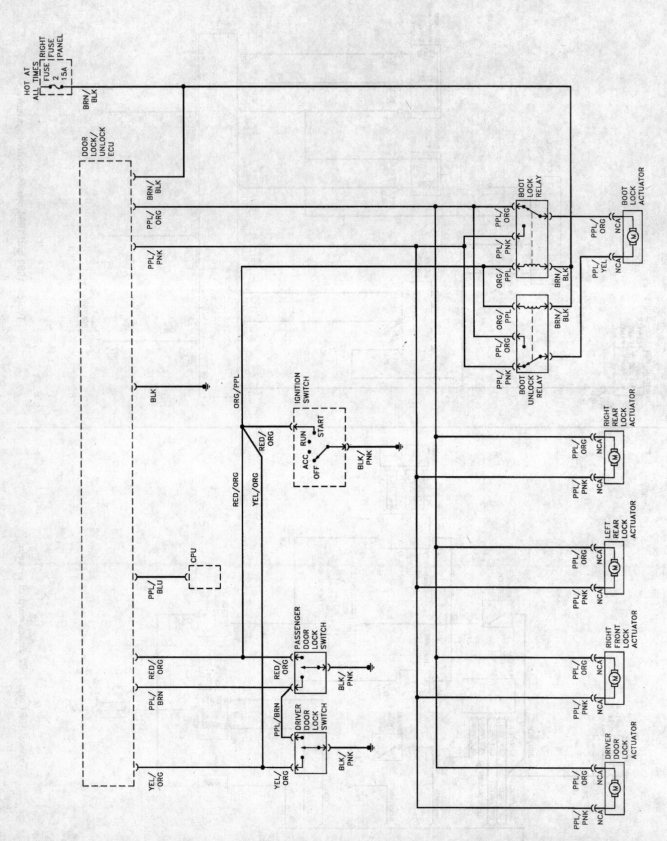

Typical 1988 power door lock system

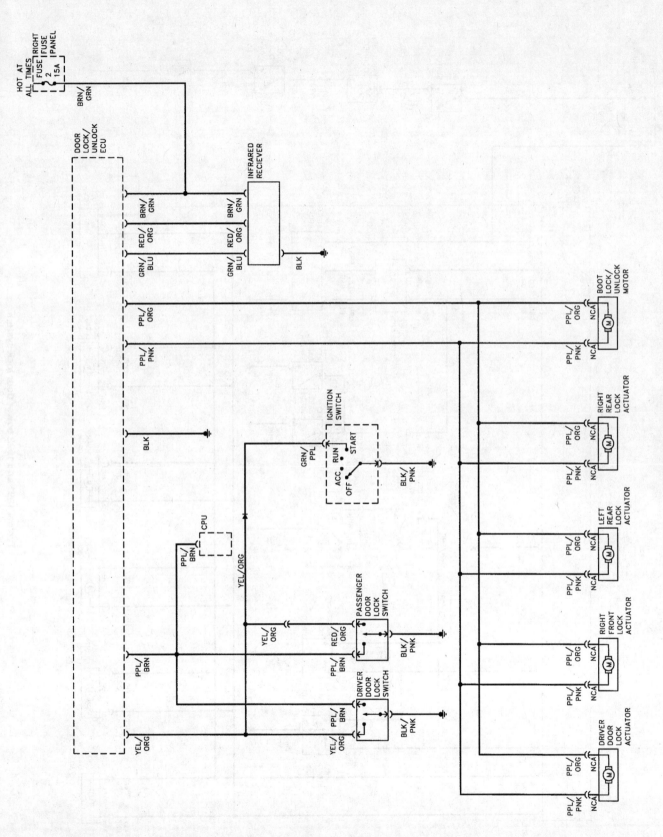

Typical 1989 and 1990 power door lock system

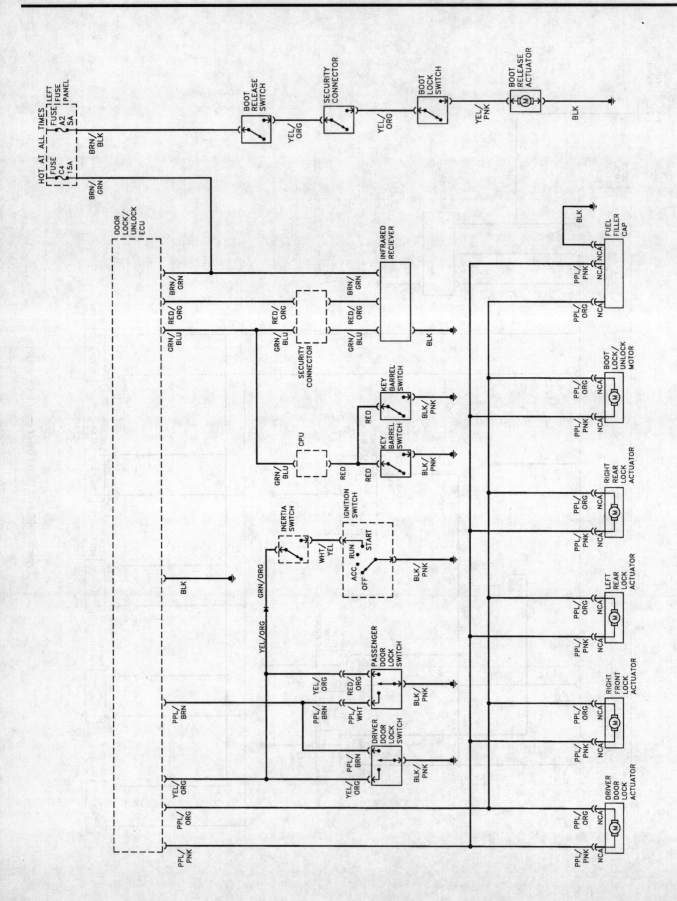

Typical 1991 and 1992 power door lock system

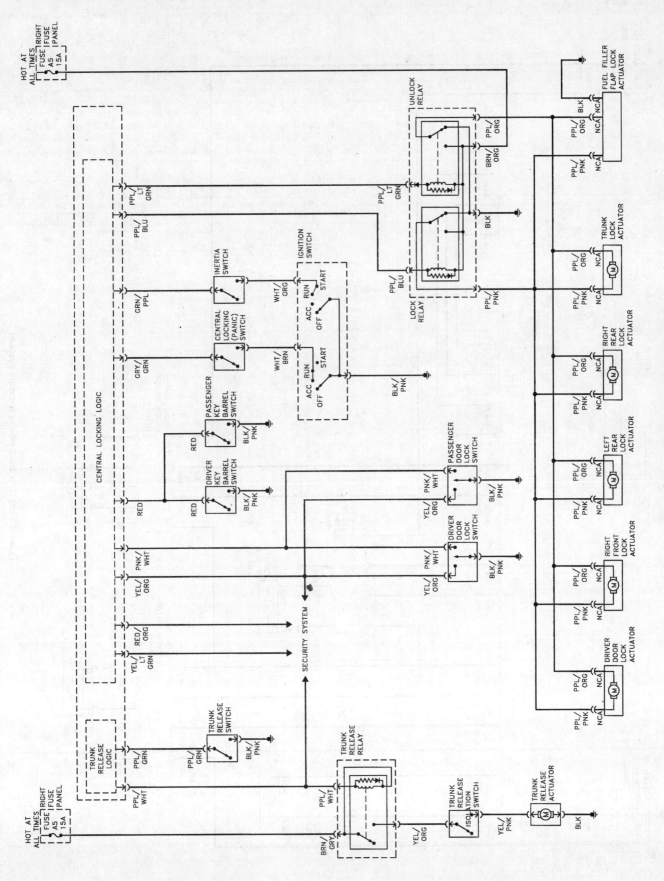

Typical 1993 and 1994 power door lock system

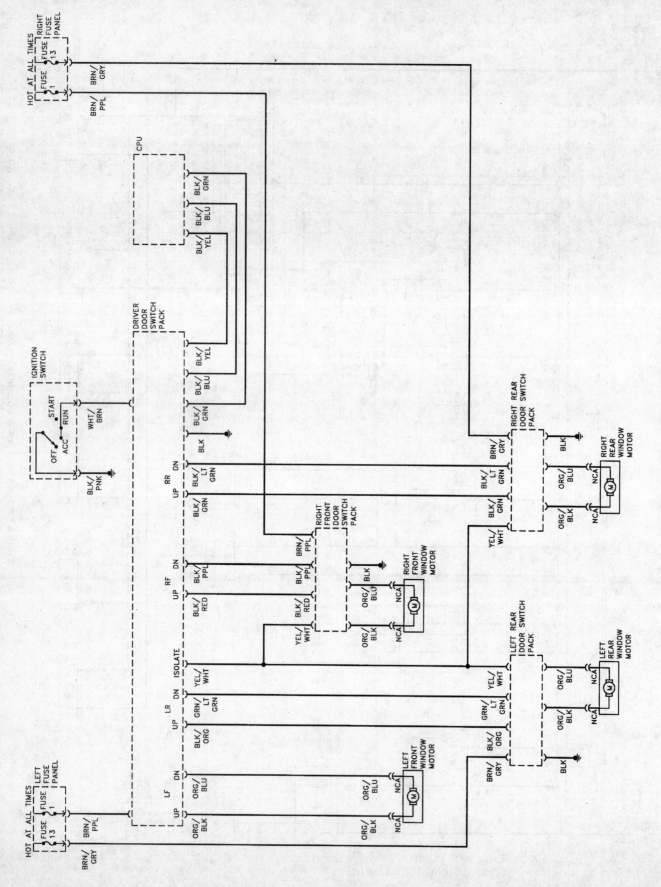

Typical 1988 thru 1992 power window system

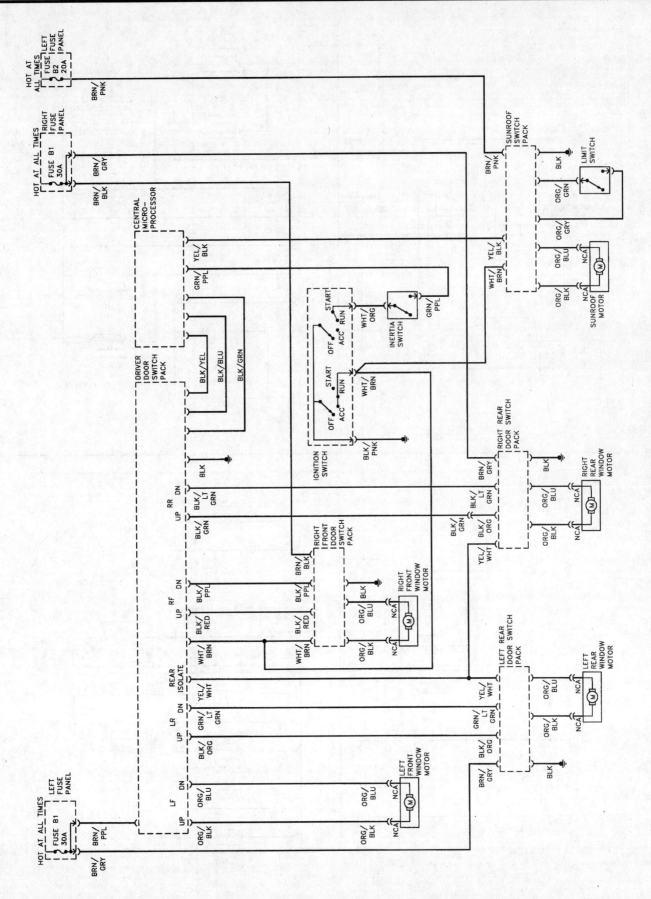

Typical 1993 and 1994 power window system

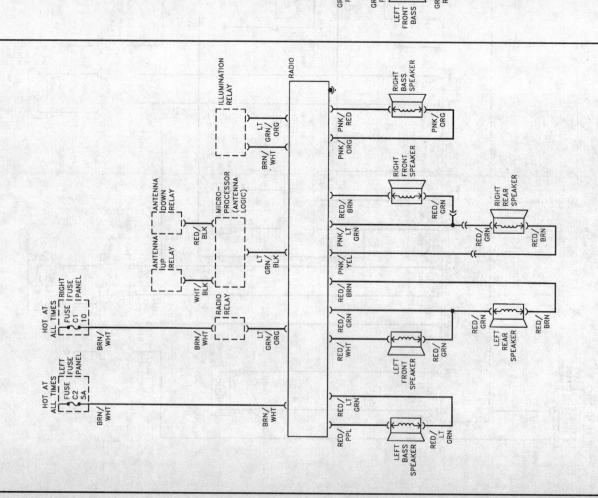

Typical 1993 and 1994 audio system

Typical 1988 thru 1992 audio system

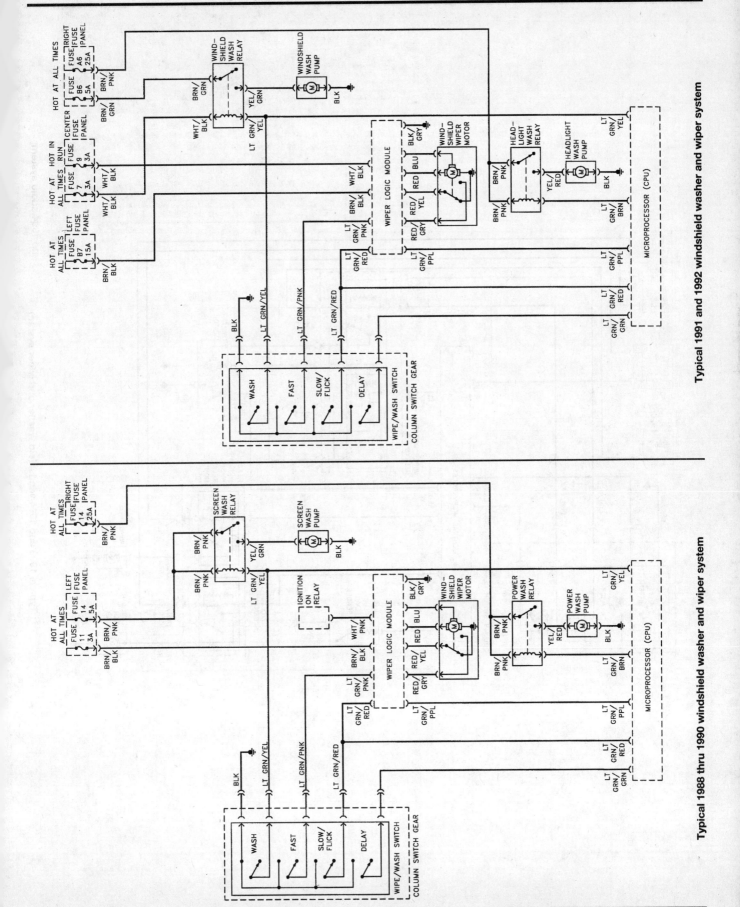

Typical 1991 and 1992 windshield washer and wiper system

Typical 1988 thru 1990 windshield washer and wiper system

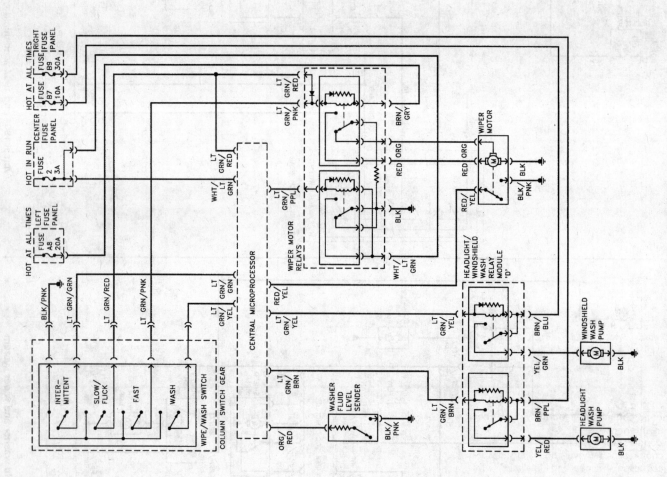

Typical 1993 and 1994 windshield washer and wiper system

Index

Notes

Haynes Automotive Manuals

NOTE: If you do not see a listing for your vehicle, consult your local Haynes dealer for the latest product information.

ACURA
12020 **Integra** '86 thru '89 & **Legend** '86 thru '90
12021 **Integra** '90 thru '93 & **Legend** '91 thru '95
Integra '94 thru '00 - see HONDA Civic (42025)
MDX '01 thru '07 - see HONDA Pilot (42037)
12050 **Acura TL** all models '99 '08

AMC
Jeep CJ - see JEEP (50020)
14020 **Mid-size models** '70 thru '83
14025 **(Renault) Alliance & Encore** '83 thru '87

AUDI
15020 **4000** all models '80 thru '87
15025 **5000** all models '77 thru '83
15026 **5000** all models '84 thru '88
Audi A4 '96 thru '01 - see VW Passat (96023)
15030 **Audi A4** '02 thru '08

AUSTIN-HEALEY
Sprite - see MG Midget (66015)

BMW
18020 **3/5 Series** '82 thru '92
18021 **3-Series** incl. Z3 models '92 thru '98
18022 **3-Series** incl. Z4 models '99 thru '05
18023 **3-Series** '06 thru '10
18025 **320i** all 4 cyl models '75 thru '83
18050 **1500 thru 2002** except Turbo '59 thru '77

BUICK
19010 **Buick Century** '97 thru '05
Century (front-wheel drive) - see GM (38005)
19020 **Buick, Oldsmobile & Pontiac Full-size (Front-wheel drive)** '85 thru '05
Buick Electra, LeSabre and Park Avenue; **Oldsmobile** Delta 88 Royale, Ninety Eight and Regency; **Pontiac** Bonneville
19025 **Buick, Oldsmobile & Pontiac Full-size (Rear wheel drive)** '70 thru '90
Buick Estate, Electra, LeSabre, Limited, **Oldsmobile** Custom Cruiser, Delta 88, Ninety-eight, **Pontiac** Bonneville, Catalina, Grandville, Parisienne
19030 **Mid-size Regal & Century** all rear-drive models with V6, V8 and Turbo '74 thru '87
Regal - see GENERAL MOTORS (38010)
Riviera - see GENERAL MOTORS (38030)
Roadmaster - see CHEVROLET (24046)
Skyhawk - see GENERAL MOTORS (38015)
Skylark - see GM (38020, 38025)
Somerset - see GENERAL MOTORS (38025)

CADILLAC
21015 **CTS & CTS-V** '03 thru '12
21030 **Cadillac Rear Wheel Drive** '70 thru '93
Cimarron - see GENERAL MOTORS (38015)
DeVille - see GM (38031 & 38032)
Eldorado - see GM (38030 & 38031)
Fleetwood - see GM (38031)
Seville - see GM (38030, 38031 & 38032)

CHEVROLET
10305 **Chevrolet Engine Overhaul Manual**
24010 **Astro & GMC Safari Mini-vans** '85 thru '05
24015 **Camaro V8** all models '70 thru '81
24016 **Camaro** all models '82 thru '92
24017 **Camaro & Firebird** '93 thru '02
Cavalier - see GENERAL MOTORS (38016)
Celebrity - see GENERAL MOTORS (38005)
24020 **Chevelle, Malibu & El Camino** '69 thru '87
24024 **Chevette & Pontiac T1000** '76 thru '87
Citation - see GENERAL MOTORS (38020)
24027 **Colorado & GMC Canyon** '04 thru '10
24032 **Corsica/Beretta** all models '87 thru '96
24040 **Corvette** all V8 models '68 thru '82
24041 **Corvette** all models '84 thru '96
24045 **Full-size Sedans** Caprice, Impala, Biscayne, Bel Air & Wagons '69 thru '90
24046 **Impala SS & Caprice and Buick Roadmaster** '91 thru '96
Impala '00 thru '05 - see LUMINA (24048)
24047 **Impala & Monte Carlo** all models '06 thru '11
Lumina '90 thru '94 - see GM (38010)
24048 **Lumina & Monte Carlo** '95 thru '05
Lumina APV - see GM (38035)
24050 **Luv Pick-up** all 2WD & 4WD '72 thru '82
Malibu '97 thru '00 - see GM (38026)
24055 **Monte Carlo** all models '70 thru '88
Monte Carlo '95 thru '01 - see LUMINA (24048)
24059 **Nova** all V8 models '69 thru '79
24060 **Nova and Geo Prizm** '85 thru '92
24064 **Pick-ups** '67 thru '87 - Chevrolet & GMC
24065 **Pick-ups** '88 thru '98 - Chevrolet & GMC

24066 **Pick-ups** '99 thru '06 - Chevrolet & GMC
24067 **Chevrolet Silverado & GMC Sierra** '07 thru '12
24070 **S-10 & S-15 Pick-ups** '82 thru '93, **Blazer & Jimmy** '83 thru '94,
24071 **S-10 & Sonoma Pick-ups** '94 thru '04, including **Blazer, Jimmy & Hombre**
24072 **Chevrolet TrailBlazer, GMC Envoy & Oldsmobile Bravada** '02 thru '09
24075 **Sprint** '85 thru '88 & **Geo Metro** '89 thru '01
24080 **Vans - Chevrolet & GMC** '68 thru '96
24081 **Chevrolet Express & GMC Savana** Full-size Vans '96 thru '10

CHRYSLER
10310 **Chrysler Engine Overhaul Manual**
25015 **Chrysler Cirrus, Dodge Stratus, Plymouth Breeze** '95 thru '00
25020 **Full-size Front-Wheel Drive** '88 thru '93
K-Cars - see DODGE Aries (30008)
Laser - see DODGE Daytona (30030)
25025 **Chrysler LHS, Concorde, New Yorker, Dodge** Intrepid, **Eagle** Vision, '93 thru '97
25026 **Chrysler LHS, Concorde, 300M, Dodge** Intrepid, '98 thru '04
25027 **Chrysler 300, Dodge Charger & Magnum** '05 thru '09
25030 **Chrysler & Plymouth Mid-size** front wheel drive '82 thru '95
Rear-wheel Drive - see Dodge (30050)
25035 **PT Cruiser** all models '01 thru '10
25040 **Chrysler** Sebring '95 thru '06, **Dodge** Stratus '01 thru '06, **Dodge** Avenger '95 thru '00

DATSUN
28005 **200SX** all models '80 thru '83
28007 **B-210** all models '73 thru '78
28009 **210** all models '79 thru '82
28012 **240Z, 260Z & 280Z** Coupe '70 thru '78
28014 **280ZX** Coupe & 2+2 '79 thru '83
300ZX - see NISSAN (72010)
28018 **510 & PL521 Pick-up** '68 thru '73
28020 **510** all models '78 thru '81
28022 **620 Series Pick-up** all models '73 thru '79
720 Series Pick-up - see NISSAN (72030)
28025 **810/Maxima** all gasoline models '77 thru '84

DODGE
400 & 600 - see CHRYSLER (25030)
30008 **Aries & Plymouth Reliant** '81 thru '89
30010 **Caravan & Plymouth Voyager** '84 thru '95
30011 **Caravan & Plymouth Voyager** '96 thru '02
30012 **Challenger/Plymouth Saporro** '78 thru '83
30013 **Caravan, Chrysler Voyager, Town & Country** '03 thru '07
30016 **Colt & Plymouth Champ** '78 thru '87
30020 **Dakota Pick-ups** all models '87 thru '96
30021 **Durango** '98 & '99, **Dakota** '97 thru '99
30022 **Durango** '00 thru '03 **Dakota** '00 thru '04
30023 **Durango** '04 thru '09, **Dakota** '05 thru '11
30025 **Dart, Demon, Plymouth Barracuda, Duster & Valiant** 6 cyl models '67 thru '76
30030 **Daytona & Chrysler Laser** '84 thru '89
Intrepid - see CHRYSLER (25025, 25026)
30034 **Neon** all models '95 thru '99
30035 **Omni & Plymouth Horizon** '78 thru '90
30036 **Dodge and Plymouth Neon** '00 thru '05
30040 **Pick-ups** all full-size models '74 thru '93
30041 **Pick-ups** all full-size models '94 thru '01
30042 **Pick-ups** full-size models '02 thru '08
30045 **Ram 50/D50 Pick-ups & Raider and Plymouth Arrow Pick-ups** '79 thru '93
30050 **Dodge/Plymouth/Chrysler RWD** '71 thru '89
30055 **Shadow & Plymouth Sundance** '87 thru '94
30060 **Spirit & Plymouth Acclaim** '89 thru '95
30065 **Vans - Dodge & Plymouth** '71 thru '03

EAGLE
Talon - see MITSUBISHI (68030, 68031)
Vision - see CHRYSLER (25025)

FIAT
34010 **124 Sport Coupe & Spider** '68 thru '78
34025 **X1/9** all models '74 thru '80

FORD
10320 **Ford Engine Overhaul Manual**
10355 **Ford Automatic Transmission Overhaul**
11500 **Mustang** '64-1/2 thru '70 Restoration Guide
36004 **Aerostar Mini-vans** all models '86 thru '97
36006 **Contour & Mercury Mystique** '95 thru '00
36008 **Courier Pick-up** all models '72 thru '82
36012 **Crown Victoria & Mercury Grand Marquis** '88 thru '10
36016 **Escort/Mercury Lynx** all models '81 thru '90
36020 **Escort/Mercury Tracer** '91 thru '02

36022 **Escape & Mazda Tribute** '01 thru '11
36024 **Explorer & Mazda Navajo** '91 thru '01
36025 **Explorer/Mercury Mountaineer** '02 thru '10
36028 **Fairmont & Mercury Zephyr** '78 thru '83
36030 **Festiva & Aspire** '88 thru '97
36032 **Fiesta** all models '77 thru '80
36034 **Focus** all models '00 thru '11
36036 **Ford & Mercury Full-size** '75 thru '87
36044 **Ford & Mercury Mid-size** '75 thru '86
36045 **Fusion & Mercury Milan** '06 thru '10
36048 **Mustang V8** all models '64-1/2 thru '73
36049 **Mustang II** 4 cyl, V6 & V8 models '74 thru '78
36050 **Mustang & Mercury Capri** '79 thru '93
36051 **Mustang** all models '94 thru '04
36052 **Mustang** '05 thru '10
36054 **Pick-ups & Bronco** '73 thru '79
36058 **Pick-ups & Bronco** '80 thru '96
36059 **F-150 & Expedition** '97 thru '09, **F-250** '97 thru '99 & **Lincoln Navigator** '98 thru '09
36060 **Super Duty Pick-ups, Excursion** '99 thru '10
36061 **F-150** full-size '04 thru '10
36062 **Pinto & Mercury Bobcat** '75 thru '80
36066 **Probe** all models '89 thru '92
Probe '93 thru '97 - see MAZDA 626 (61042)
36070 **Ranger/Bronco II** gasoline models '83 thru '92
36071 **Ranger** '93 thru '10 & **Mazda Pick-ups** '94 thru '09
36074 **Taurus & Mercury Sable** '86 thru '95
36075 **Taurus & Mercury Sable** '96 thru '05
36078 **Tempo & Mercury Topaz** '84 thru '94
36082 **Thunderbird/Mercury Cougar** '83 thru '88
36086 **Thunderbird/Mercury Cougar** '89 thru '97
36090 **Vans** all V8 Econoline models '69 thru '91
36094 **Vans** full size '92 thru '10
36097 **Windstar Mini-van** '95 thru '07

GENERAL MOTORS
10360 **GM Automatic Transmission Overhaul**
38005 **Buick Century, Chevrolet Celebrity, Oldsmobile Cutlass Ciera & Pontiac 6000** all models '82 '96
38010 **Buick Regal, Chevrolet Lumina, Oldsmobile Cutlass Supreme & Pontiac Grand Prix (FWD)** '88 thru '07
38015 **Buick Skyhawk, Cadillac Cimarron, Chevrolet Cavalier, Oldsmobile Firenza & Pontiac J-2000 & Sunbird** '82 thru '94
38016 **Chevrolet Cavalier & Pontiac Sunfire** '95 thru '05
38017 **Chevrolet Cobalt & Pontiac G5** '05 thru '11
38020 **Buick Skylark, Chevrolet Citation, Olds Omega, Pontiac Phoenix** '80 thru '85
38025 **Buick Skylark & Somerset, Oldsmobile Achieva & Calais and Pontiac Grand Am** all models '85 thru '98
38026 **Chevrolet Malibu, Olds Alero & Cutlass, Pontiac Grand Am** '97 thru '03
38027 **Chevrolet Malibu** '04 thru '10
38030 **Cadillac Eldorado, Seville, Oldsmobile Toronado, Buick Riviera** '71 thru '85
38031 **Cadillac Eldorado & Seville, DeVille, Fleetwood & Olds Toronado, Buick Riviera** '86 thru '93
38032 **Cadillac DeVille** '94 thru '05 & **Seville** '92 thru '04 **Cadillac DTS** '06 thru '10
38035 **Chevrolet Lumina APV, Olds Silhouette & Pontiac Trans Sport** all models '90 thru '96
38036 **Chevrolet Venture, Olds Silhouette, Pontiac Trans Sport & Montana** '97 thru '05
General Motors Full-size Rear-wheel Drive - see BUICK (19025)
38040 **Chevrolet Equinox** '05 thru '09 **Pontiac Torrent** '06 thru '09
38070 **Chevrolet HHR** '06 thru '11

GEO
Metro - see CHEVROLET Sprint (24075)
Prizm - '85 thru '92 see CHEVY (24060), '93 thru '02 see TOYOTA Corolla (92036)
40030 **Storm** all models '90 thru '93
Tracker - see SUZUKI Samurai (90010)

GMC
Vans & Pick-ups - see CHEVROLET

HONDA
42010 **Accord CVCC** all models '76 thru '83
42011 **Accord** all models '84 thru '89
42012 **Accord** all models '90 thru '93
42013 **Accord** all models '94 thru '97
42014 **Accord** all models '98 thru '02
42015 **Accord** '03 thru '07
42020 **Civic 1200** all models '73 thru '79
42021 **Civic 1300 & 1500 CVCC** '80 thru '83
42022 **Civic 1500 CVCC** all models '75 thru '79

(Continued on other side)

Haynes North America, Inc., 861 Lawrence Drive, Newbury Park, CA 91320-1514 • (805) 498-6703 • http://www.haynes.com

Haynes Automotive Manuals (continued)

NOTE: If you do not see a listing for your vehicle, consult your local Haynes dealer for the latest product information.

42023 **Civic** all models '84 thru '91
42024 **Civic & del Sol** '92 thru '95
42025 **Civic** '96 thru '00, **CR-V** '97 thru '01, **Acura Integra** '94 thru '00
42026 **Civic** '01 thru '10, **CR-V** '02 thru '09
42035 **Odyssey** all models '99 thru '10
     Passport - see ISUZU Rodeo (47017)
42037 **Honda Pilot** '03 thru '07, **Acura MDX** '01 thru '07
42040 **Prelude CVCC** all models '79 thru '89

HYUNDAI
43010 **Elantra** all models '96 thru '10
43015 **Excel & Accent** all models '86 thru '09
43050 **Santa Fe** all models '01 thru '06
43055 **Sonata** all models '99 thru '08

INFINITI
     G35 '03 thru '08 - see NISSAN 350Z (72011)

ISUZU
     Hombre - see CHEVROLET S-10 (24071)
47017 **Rodeo, Amigo & Honda Passport** '89 thru '02
47020 **Trooper & Pick-up** '81 thru '93

JAGUAR
49010 **XJ6** all 6 cyl models '68 thru '86
49011 **XJ6** all models '88 thru '94
49015 **XJ12 & XJS** all 12 cyl models '72 thru '85

JEEP
50010 **Cherokee, Comanche & Wagoneer Limited** all models '84 thru '01
50020 **CJ** all models '49 thru '86
50025 **Grand Cherokee** all models '93 thru '04
50026 **Grand Cherokee** '05 thru '09
50029 **Grand Wagoneer & Pick-up** '72 thru '91 Grand Wagoneer '84 thru '91, Cherokee & Wagoneer '72 thru '83, Pick-up '72 thru '88
50030 **Wrangler** all models '87 thru '11
50035 **Liberty** '02 thru '07

KIA
54050 **Optima** '01 thru '10
54070 **Sephia** '94 thru '01, **Spectra** '00 thru '09, **Sportage** '05 thru '10

LEXUS
     ES 300/330 - see TOYOTA Camry (92007) (92008)
     RX 330 - see TOYOTA Highlander (92095)

LINCOLN
     Navigator - see FORD Pick-up (36059)
59010 **Rear-Wheel Drive** all models '70 thru '10

MAZDA
61010 **GLC Hatchback** (rear-wheel drive) '77 thru '83
61011 **GLC** (front-wheel drive) '81 thru '85
61012 **Mazda3** '04 thru '11
61015 **323 & Protogé** '90 thru '03
61016 **MX-5 Miata** '90 thru '09
61020 **MPV** all models '89 thru '98
     Navajo - see Ford Explorer (36024)
61030 **Pick-ups** '72 thru '93
     Pick-ups '94 thru '00 - see Ford Ranger (36071)
61035 **RX-7** all models '79 thru '85
61036 **RX-7** all models '86 thru '91
61040 **626** (rear-wheel drive) all models '79 thru '82
61041 **626/MX-6** (front-wheel drive) '83 thru '92
61042 **626, MX-6/Ford Probe** '93 thru '02
61043 **Mazda6** '03 thru '11

MERCEDES-BENZ
63012 **123 Series Diesel** '76 thru '85
63015 **190 Series** four-cyl gas models, '84 thru '88
63020 **230/250/280** 6 cyl sohc models '68 thru '72
63025 **280 123 Series** gasoline models '77 thru '81
63030 **350 & 450** all models '71 thru '80
63040 **C-Class**: C230/C240/C280/C320/C350 '01 thru '07

MERCURY
64200 **Villager & Nissan Quest** '93 thru '01
     All other titles, see FORD Listing.

MG
66010 **MGB** Roadster & GT Coupe '62 thru '80
66015 **MG Midget, Austin Healey Sprite** '58 thru '80

MINI
67020 **Mini** '02 thru '11

MITSUBISHI
68020 **Cordia, Tredia, Galant, Precis & Mirage** '83 thru '93
68030 **Eclipse, Eagle Talon & Ply. Laser** '90 thru '94
68031 **Eclipse** '95 thru '05, **Eagle Talon** '95 thru '98
68035 **Galant** '94 thru '10
68040 **Pick-up** '83 thru '96 & **Montero** '83 thru '93

NISSAN
72010 **300ZX** all models including Turbo '84 '89
72011 **350Z & Infiniti G35** all models '03 thru '08
72015 **Altima** all models '93 thru '06
72016 **Altima** '07 thru '10
72020 **Maxima** all models '85 thru '92
72021 **Maxima** all models '93 thru '04
72025 **Murano** '03 thru '10
72030 **Pick-ups** '80 thru '97 **Pathfinder** '87 thru '95
72031 **Frontier Pick-up, Xterra, Pathfinder** '96 thru '04
72032 **Frontier & Xterra** '05 thru '14
72040 **Pulsar** all models '83 thru '86
     Quest - see MERCURY Villager (64200)
72050 **Sentra** all models '82 thru '94
72051 **Sentra & 200SX** all models '95 thru '06
72060 **Stanza** all models '82 thru '90
72070 **Titan pick-ups** '04 thru '10 **Armada** '05 thru '10

OLDSMOBILE
73015 **Cutlass** V6 & V8 gas models '74 thru '88
     For other OLDSMOBILE titles, see BUICK, CHEVROLET or GENERAL MOTORS listing.

PLYMOUTH
     For PLYMOUTH titles, see DODGE listing.

PONTIAC
79008 **Fiero** all models '84 thru '88
79018 **Firebird** V8 models except Turbo '70 thru '81
79019 **Firebird** all models '82 thru '92
79025 **G6** all models '05 thru '09
79040 **Mid-size Rear-wheel Drive** '70 thru '87
     Vibe '03 thru '11 - see TOYOTA Matrix (92060)
     For other PONTIAC titles, see BUICK, CHEVROLET or GENERAL MOTORS listing.

PORSCHE
80020 **911** except Turbo & Carrera 4 '65 thru '89
80025 **914** all 4 cyl models '69 thru '76
80030 **924** all models including Turbo '76 thru '82
80035 **944** all models including Turbo '83 thru '89

RENAULT
     Alliance & Encore - see AMC (14020)

SAAB
84010 **900** all models including Turbo '79 thru '88

SATURN
87010 **Saturn** all S-series models '91 thru '02
87011 **Saturn Ion** '03 thru '07
87020 **Saturn** all L-series models '00 thru '04
87040 **Saturn VUE** '02 thru '07

SUBARU
89002 **1100, 1300, 1400 & 1600** '71 thru '79
89003 **1600 & 1800** 2WD & 4WD '80 thru '94
89100 **Legacy** all models '90 thru '99
89101 **Legacy & Forester** '00 thru '09

SUZUKI
90010 **Samurai/Sidekick & Geo Tracker** '86 thru '01

TOYOTA
92005 **Camry** all models '83 thru '91
92006 **Camry** all models '92 thru '96
92007 **Camry, Avalon, Solara, Lexus ES 300** '97 thru '01
92008 **Toyota Camry, Avalon and Solara and Lexus ES 300/330** all models '02 thru '06
92009 **Camry** '07 thru '11
92015 **Celica Rear Wheel Drive** '71 thru '85
92020 **Celica Front Wheel Drive** '86 thru '99
92025 **Celica Supra** all models '79 thru '92
92030 **Corolla** '75 thru '79
92032 **Corolla** all rear wheel drive models '80 thru '87
92035 **Corolla** all front wheel drive models '84 thru '92
92036 **Corolla & Geo Prizm** '93 thru '02
92037 **Corolla** models '03 thru '11
92040 **Corolla Tercel** all models '80 thru '82
92045 **Corona** all models '74 thru '82
92050 **Cressida** all models '78 thru '82
92055 **Land Cruiser FJ40, 43, 45, 55** '68 thru '82
92056 **Land Cruiser FJ60, 62, 80, FZJ80** '80 thru '96
92060 **Matrix & Pontiac Vibe** '03 thru '11
92065 **MR2** all models '85 thru '87
92070 **Pick-up** all models '69 thru '78
92075 **Pick-up** all models '79 thru '95
92076 **Tacoma, 4Runner, & T100** '93 thru '04
92077 **Tacoma** '05 thru '09
92078 **Tundra** '00 thru '06 & **Sequoia** '01 thru '07
92079 **4Runner** all models '03 thru '09
92080 **Previa** all models '91 thru '95
92081 **Prius** all models '01 thru '08
92082 **RAV4** all models '96 thru '10
92085 **Tercel** all models '87 thru '94
92090 **Sienna** all models '98 thru '09
92095 **Highlander & Lexus RX-330** '99 thru '07

TRIUMPH
94007 **Spitfire** all models '62 thru '81
94010 **TR7** all models '75 thru '81

VW
96008 **Beetle & Karmann Ghia** '54 thru '79
96009 **New Beetle** '98 thru '11
96016 **Rabbit, Jetta, Scirocco & Pick-up** gas models '75 thru '92 & Convertible '80 thru '92
96017 **Golf, GTI & Jetta** '93 thru '98, **Cabrio** '95 thru '02
96018 **Golf, GTI, Jetta** '99 thru '05
96019 **Jetta, Rabbit, GTI & Golf** '05 thru '11
96020 **Rabbit, Jetta & Pick-up** diesel '77 thru '84
96023 **Passat** '98 thru '05, **Audi A4** '96 thru '01
96030 **Transporter 1600** all models '68 thru '79
96035 **Transporter 1700, 1800 & 2000** '72 thru '79
96040 **Type 3 1500 & 1600** all models '63 thru '73
96045 **Vanagon** all air-cooled models '80 thru '83

VOLVO
97010 **120, 130 Series & 1800 Sports** '61 thru '73
97015 **140 Series** all models '66 thru '74
97020 **240 Series** all models '76 thru '93
97040 **740 & 760 Series** all models '82 thru '88
97050 **850 Series** all models '93 thru '97

TECHBOOK MANUALS
10205 **Automotive Computer Codes**
10206 **OBD-II & Electronic Engine Management**
10210 **Automotive Emissions Control Manual**
10215 **Fuel Injection Manual** '78 thru '85
10220 **Fuel Injection Manual** '86 thru '99
10225 **Holley Carburetor Manual**
10230 **Rochester Carburetor Manual**
10240 **Weber/Zenith/Stromberg/SU Carburetors**
10305 **Chevrolet Engine Overhaul Manual**
10310 **Chrysler Engine Overhaul Manual**
10320 **Ford Engine Overhaul Manual**
10330 **GM and Ford Diesel Engine Repair Manual**
10333 **Engine Performance Manual**
10340 **Small Engine Repair Manual,** 5 HP & Less
10341 **Small Engine Repair Manual,** 5.5 - 20 HP
10345 **Suspension, Steering & Driveline Manual**
10355 **Ford Automatic Transmission Overhaul**
10360 **GM Automatic Transmission Overhaul**
10405 **Automotive Body Repair & Painting**
10410 **Automotive Brake Manual**
10411 **Automotive Anti-lock Brake (ABS) Systems**
10415 **Automotive Detailing Manual**
10420 **Automotive Electrical Manual**
10425 **Automotive Heating & Air Conditioning**
10430 **Automotive Reference Manual & Dictionary**
10435 **Automotive Tools Manual**
10440 **Used Car Buying Guide**
10445 **Welding Manual**
10450 **ATV Basics**
10452 **Scooters 50cc to 250cc**

SPANISH MANUALS
98903 **Reparación de Carrocería & Pintura**
98904 **Manual de Carburador Modelos Holley & Rochester**
98905 **Códigos Automotrices de la Computadora**
98906 **OBD-II & Sistemas de Control Electrónico del Motor**
98910 **Frenos Automotriz**
98913 **Electricidad Automotriz**
98915 **Inyección de Combustible** '86 al '99
99040 **Chevrolet & GMC Camionetas** '67 al '87
99041 **Chevrolet & GMC Camionetas** '88 al '98
99042 **Chevrolet & GMC Camionetas Cerradas** '68 al '95
99043 **Chevrolet/GMC Camionetas** '94 al '04
99048 **Chevrolet/GMC Camionetas** '99 al '06
99055 **Dodge Caravan & Plymouth Voyager** '84 al '95
99075 **Ford Camionetas y Bronco** '80 al '94
99076 **Ford F-150** '97 al '09
99077 **Ford Camionetas Cerradas** '69 al '91
99088 **Ford Modelos de Tamaño Mediano** '75 al '86
99089 **Ford Camionetas Ranger** '93 al '10
99091 **Ford Taurus & Mercury Sable** '86 al '95
99095 **GM Modelos de Tamaño Grande** '70 al '90
99100 **GM Modelos de Tamaño Mediano** '70 al '88
99106 **Jeep Cherokee, Wagoneer & Comanche** '84 al '00
99110 **Nissan Camioneta** '80 al '96, **Pathfinder** '87 al '95
99118 **Nissan Sentra** '82 al '94
99125 **Toyota Camionetas y 4Runner** '79 al '95

Over 100 Haynes motorcycle manuals also available

7-12

Haynes North America, Inc., 861 Lawrence Drive, Newbury Park, CA 91320-1514 • (805) 498-6703 • http://www.haynes.com